STRANGERS IN THEIR MIDST

The Free Black Population of Amherst County Virginia

— Revised Edition —

Sherrie S. McLeRoy
and
William R. McLeRoy

HERITAGE BOOKS
2007

HERITAGE BOOKS
AN IMPRINT OF HERITAGE BOOKS, INC.

Books, CDs, and more—Worldwide

For our listing of thousands of titles see our website
at
www.HeritageBooks.com

Published 2007 by
HERITAGE BOOKS, INC.
Publishing Division
65 East Main Street
Westminster, Maryland 21157-5026

Other books by the authors:

More Passages: A New History of Amherst County, Virginia

Strangers in Their Midst: The Free Black Population of Amherst County, Virginia

International Standard Book Number: 978-0-7884-4373-2

TABLE OF CONTENTS

LIST OF ILLUSTRATIONS

PREFACE

The people of the antebellum United States are often seen in simple, concrete terms: Northerner and Southerner, white and black, master and slave. But there was another segment of that population as well, one which spilled over geographical, legal, and even racial barriers: the free coloreds.

A white society generically termed them "free coloreds:" non-white, non-Asian free persons. Many of them were freeborn and had never known slavery, yet they were bound by laws that tried to restrict them to a position of near-slavery. Especially in the South, they were a third class in a two-class society. Rev. James Freeman Clarke, in his 1859 book, *Present Condition of the Free Colored People of the United States*, wrote: "They stand among us, yet not of us. We know less of them than we know of the people of France and Italy."

Their story was long hidden in the shadows because of the dearth of extant and available primary sources. The first edition of *Strangers in Their Midst* was an attempt to illuminate one of those shadowy corners by examining in detail a typical rural population of free coloreds, that of Amherst County in the Blue Ridge Mountains of Virginia. It began in 1977 with the accidental discovery, by one of the authors, of the "Amherst County Register of Free Blacks, 1822 – 1864." Probably copied from an older, and now lost, ledger book, the Register had been recorded in a leather-bound volume labeled on the spine only as an "Index to Deeds, 1845-1850, Invested and Reversed." Because of this, it had escaped discovery over the years. Within its pages was a wealth of physical, genealogical, and occupational information on nearly 400 free persons of color who lived in Amherst County prior to and during the Civil War.

In the years following our discovery, we found material on an additional 800 persons, material drawn from an intensive search of census listings, tax records, deeds, wills, marriages, and land plats, covering the years 1761 to 1865. These are all governmental records—either federal, state, or county; we did not seek out descendants and obtain family lore, feeling that that was beyond the scope of this study.

When *Strangers* first debuted, there were very few published registers; now dozens are available. Our book went through several printings to meet the demand for it but finally went "out of print" several years ago. However, because interest in this subject has only continued to grow, Heritage Books decided to republish it. That has given the authors the opportunity to include much new material that has been researched, found, or published since 1993. This second edition contains well over 350 new names, and more than a hundred from the previous book have been expanded with new information. We have added an entire chapter on the Indian population of the county and substantially expanded the one dealing with the history of slaves and free colored persons in Virginia and, to a very limited extent, the United States. We have included a new glossary of terms and names from the text, and endnotes have been expanded to provide more background for the interested reader/researcher. We deeply appreciate the help of the staff at the Library of Virginia in compiling this new research.

Following the historical narrative is a verbatim transcript of the Amherst County Register; misspellings and capitalizations have been preserved as they were recorded, and the entries are presented in the original chronological order. The last section is alphabetical by name and lists information on all known free coloreds in the county during the study period, 1761 to 1865.

Lastly, a word about the terms that will be used. "Free blacks," "free colored," "free person of color," "free negro," and "free issue" are all historical terms that appear in the legal documents upon which this study is based. They are used here for that reason and are not intended to convey a sense of racial bias.

Sherrie S. McLeRoy
William R. McLeRoy
May 2007

Chapter 1

SLAVES AND "FREE COLOREDS" IN VIRGINIA HISTORY

There were "free persons of color" in colonial America even before European colonization began, descendants of escaped Negro servants/slaves brought by Spanish and French explorers in the 16th century.[1] The first "Negars" to be well-documented, however, were those who arrived in August 1619 when, as John Rolfe wrote, "a dutch man of warre," the *White Lion*, arrived at Point Comfort, Virginia (modern Hampton), with twenty Angolans seized in a raid on a Portuguese slave ship.[2] Sir George Yeardley, governor of the twelve-year-old colony, traded food and water for them to outfit the *White Lion* on its return voyage.

Though they had been captured in their homeland to serve as slaves, the twenty were treated in Virginia as indentured servants [see glossary, page 82], since the legal concept of slavery did not then exist in the colony. Working for a set period of years alongside white indentures from England—the first group of whom also arrived in 1619—these African captives and the blacks who followed over the next few decades eventually received their freedom, just as did whites.[3] And though most did not have the advantage of written contracts of indenture, they did possess some legal rights, including a court in which to settle disputes with their masters.

The black population of Virginia at first grew slowly as they arrived primarily in small numbers on irregular Dutch traders or privateers. Unofficial census lists from the 1620s show a mere few dozen, and only several hundred by 1648. This was the tiny beginning of a population that would become, by the end of the eighteenth century, the largest in the country.

But their social and legal status changed much quicker.

FIRST RESTRICTIONS IN VIRGINIA

In the first few decades of English settlement, whites and blacks alike worked side by side in the fields of "golden weed"—

the tobacco that John Rolfe was building into Virginia's first cash crop—since labor to build a new civilization on the colony's untouched land was in short supply and all hands had to work.[4] Indentured servants, whatever their color, also lived together and socialized, and interracial marriages were not unknown (females being in short supply, too). But in the late 1630s, with more settlers arriving to expand the labor force, colonial leaders began to separate the races, first in the fields and, eventually, within the law.

The first statute (1639) forbade Negroes to have or use firearms, except on the western frontier and in the event of Indian attacks. A second, in 1640, addressed the issue of runaways and implied lifetime service for blacks; that year had brought a flood of runaways, both black and white, with which the governing authorities had to deal. By autumn, in fact, escapes were so frequent that county sheriffs were authorized to immediately pursue runaways without waiting for official permission.

The case which led to the statute of 1640 involved two white indentured servants (one Dutch, the other a Scot) and a Negro indenture named John Punch. Recaptured in Maryland and returned to Jamestown—the first "interstate" extradition in America—the three were each sentenced to receive 30 lashes. The two Europeans also had to serve their master an additional year, then the colony for three more years. But John Punch was ordered "to serve his said master or his assigns for the time of his natural Life . . .." Punch had just been made a slave for life, the first to be so documented in Virginia. A second case that same summer drove home the growing racial distinctions. One Negro and six white servants ran away together but were captured. Only the ringleader and the Negro were ordered to be whipped, branded with an "R", and shackled for one year.

In 1642, the House of Burgesses limited the length of the term which *white* indentured servants had to work in an effort to encourage immigration, but it did not address term lengths for Negroes. [Paradoxically, the courts would uphold the right of free coloreds to own slaves themselves in 1654.] Increasingly during this decade, Negroes came to be viewed as different and inferior. After all, were they not also being enslaved throughout other parts of the European-controlled world?

In 1661, the House of Burgesses took a major step toward the official recognition of slavery in Virginia by declaring that, since blacks served their indenture for life anyway, years could not be added to their terms of service. This move culminated late the following year when legislation provided that children would inherit the status of their mother—not their father, as was customary in England—an act slyly couched in terms of legally defining a mulatto: "Whereas some doubts have arisen whether a child got by an Englishman upon a negro should be free or slave, be it therefore enacted . . . that all children born in this country shall be bound or free according to the condition of the mother." In 1667, the House further consolidated this distinction by formally reversing the old common law that held Christians could not be enslaved and prohibiting baptism as a means of achieving freedom.

As early as 1670, Negroes were classified with Indians. Even though such persons might be free and Christian themselves, the law now forbade them to purchase another Christian or an European/American as a slave, or to keep white servants. They were not barred, however, from buying "any of their owne [sic] nation," an adroit turn of phrase that indicates the Virginia Burgesses did not really consider them on equal footing with "civilized" people. This statute was amended some thirty years later to add that, if any Negro did purchase a white Christian servant, the servant would automatically become free.

In the same year, the Burgesses also ruled that blacks brought to Virginia by ship after that date would automatically become slaves; in 1682, they revised the law to include those who came by land, too, and all "except Turks and Moors, [who are] in amity with her [sic] majesty" [Charles II] and whose native religion was not Christianity.

In 1672, Virginia passed the first fugitive slave act in the colonies "forasmuch as it hath beene manifested to this grand assembly that many negroes have lately beene, and now are out in rebellion in sundry parts of this country;" the law applied to any Negro, mulatto, or Indian slave, also euphemistically described as "a servant for life."

Nathaniel Bacon's Rebellion of 1676 led to even more strictures, as an emerging plantation economy began to transform

Tidewater Virginia. Bacon, a Surry planter and recent immigrant, led a rag-tag army of angry small landowners, servants, slaves, and even some Indians he bullied into helping, against the governor. Their grievances were complicated, and mostly financial, but their avowed complaint was that they felt Gov. William Berkeley was not doing enough to protect them from Indian attacks. Idealistically, they also hoped to create a society that would place them on more even footing, both social and political, with the new planter class. The uprising collapsed, as did the rebels' hopes, and wealthy planters moved to shore up their own growing political control and prevent any further disturbances. Their solution was to limit the number of future white indentures, replace them with black slaves, and severely restrain the latter.

1691 brought the first anti-miscegenation law, which prohibited interracial marriage (black/white or Indian/white) on pain of banishment. A new transportation law also restricted manumission of slaves by requiring that those set free had to be transported "out of the country" [Virginia], at the owner's expense, within six months. This "Act for Suppressing Outlying Slaves" was in response to the slaves who "unlawfully absent themselves . . . and lie hid and lurk in obscure places killing hoggs [sic] and committing other injuries to the inhabitants of this dominion."[5]

INDIAN SERVITUDE

Although American slavery is usually considered in terms of blacks, it was also customary in the early decades of all royal colonies to enslave Indians as well. Indeed, South Carolina made a business of capturing and selling natives (perhaps as many as 50,000 altogether in the late 17th and early 18th centuries), and sometimes decimated entire villages.

In 1785, Thomas Jefferson blamed the origins of this "inhuman practice" on the Spanish who, beginning with Christopher Columbus in 1494, had enslaved South American Indians, then moved on to those of North America when so many died. Virginia, as did other English colonies, considered natives captured in military actions, such as the uprisings of 1622 and 1644, to be legitimate slaves.[6] At least as early as the 1640s, then, Indian slaves appear in the colony's records, their value "praysed" [appraised] in pounds of tobacco, their years of servitude determined by the courts.

Initially, Virginians treated the natives more like Englishmen than Negroes, but the official attitude toward them wavered regularly from condescension to fear and distrust. In 1655, for example, the colonial government made a stab at "civilizing" Virginia's tribes. Indian children brought in "as gages [pledges] of their [the Indians'] good intentions to us and amity with us" would be raised by the English, not as slaves, but "to bring them up in Christianity, civillity [sic] and the knowledge of necessary trades . . .." This was most likely a covert bid to begin controlling tribal lands and separating the Indians from the blacks, whom the English feared would conspire together against them. Yet in 1661, the same Burgesses declared no Indian servant could be made to serve longer than an Englishman; they also freed a Powhatan Indian from slavery because he spoke perfect English and desired baptism.

Bacon's 1676 Rebellion changed that attitude. Many Indians were killed and villages destroyed, regardless of whether or not they were peaceable. Those who had fought with Bacon and been captured were declared slaves for life. The Middle Plantation Treaty that followed the uprising required "the respective Indian Kings and Queens" to "acknowledge to have their immediate dependency on, and own all Subjection to the Great King of England." If they did so, they could keep their lands and their freedom. Within a few years, however, Indians sold as slaves by other Indians were legally slaves under English law, too, and increasingly, Virginia's natives were classed with Negroes in the eyes of the law.

By the end of the 17th century, Virginia's native tribes had lost control of their lands, been decimated by disease, and been driven out of their ancestral homelands by colonists moving ever westward. In the early 1700s, hundreds more were sold and shipped to the West Indies and northern English colonies. The latter soon responded with a firm "no thanks": between 1712 and 1715, Connecticut, Massachusetts, New Hampshire, Pennsylvania, and Rhode Island prohibited the import of Indian slaves because they were "malicious, surly, and very ungovernable."[7]

CODIFYING THE LAW

In the fall of 1705, Virginia organized all its existing slave regulations—some contradictory and others in effect for many years—into one code, the culmination of the change from *servant* to *slave*. This legislation, "An Act declaring the Negro, Mulatto, and Indian slaves within this dominion, to be real estate and not chattels," contained 34 chapters dealing with both indentured servants and slaves which legalized decades of custom and social practice. It provided that:

- All non-Christians brought into Virginia as servants were slaves.
- No slave, even a Christian, and no "Jews, Moors, Mahometans, or other infidels," could own a servant—Christian or otherwise—"except of their own complexion, or such as are declared slaves by this act."
- All slaves currently in the colony were deemed real estate and could, therefore, be inherited. [In 1748, this was changed to make them part of the personal estate of the owner.] It also meant families could be broken up and sold.
- If a master killed a slave in the course of administering punishment, he was "free of all punishment" himself.
- A slave could not be a witness in a court case and could not call other slaves as witnesses.
- To prevent "that abominable mixture and spurious issue," any free white free person marrying a Negro or mulatto (bond or free) would be imprisoned and fined.
- No slave could leave his master's plantation for more than four hours without written permission.
- No one could conduct transactions involving money with a slave without permission of the master.
- If a freed slave did not leave Virginia, he could be re-enslaved.
- The child of an Indian and Negro would "be deemed, accounted, held and taken to be a mullato [sic]."
- A slave could not own property or be a party to a contract, thus slave marriages were not legally valid.[8]

By comparison, masters were required to provide "wholesome and competent diet, clothing, and lodging" and could not administer "immoderate correction." A Christian white servant could not be whipped while naked, but any others could be. And the Act did not prohibit free coloreds from voting. This slave code, which became a model for other colonies, was a legislative response to the rapid rise of the Negro population in Virginia, from a few dozen in 1619 to over 16,000 by 1700.

And it was by no means the last response. In 1723, with the colony's black population doubled, and because "the laws now in force . . . are found insufficient to restrain their tumultuous and unlawful meetings, or to punish the secret plots and conspiracies carried on amongst them," the House of Burgesses ruled that no Negro or Indian slave could be freed at all except for "some meritorious services," and then only at the discretion of the royal governor.[9] The act reiterated that "Negros [sic], Mulatos [sic], or Indians, bond or free" were not Christian. A 1732 law put the point even more bluntly: free blacks could not testify against whites because "they are people of such base and corrupt natures."

PRELUDE TO REVOLUTION

This environment of constraint remained fairly constant until the American Revolution. In the decades leading up to that conflict, the number of slaves in the American colonies grew rapidly. It is estimated that by 1770, more than 250,000 slaves had been imported into North America, and every colony had recognized slavery as lawful; it was the presumed legal status of every Negro.[10] Typical was a South Carolina law of 1740: every Negro, Indian, mulatto, and mestizo would automatically be considered a slave unless proven otherwise.

This presumed status of slavery placed free persons of color, whose numbers were also increasing steadily, in a precarious position; the burden of proof of their freedom was on them. The royal governor of Virginia put the matter in no uncertain terms in 1723. The laws of the colony, he wrote, were meant to fix "a perpetual Brand upon Free-Negros [sic] & Mulattos by excluding them from the great Priviledge [sic] of a Freeman." Only then, he continued, could they be made to understand that "a distinction ought to be made between their offspring and the Descendants of an Englishman, with whom they never were to be Accounted Equal."[11]

Several colonies, such as Maryland (1752-1772), completely prohibited manumission. And the harsh controls being placed on manumission meant that most Virginia free blacks of the early 18th century were likely descendants of their free 17th century forebears, rather than of emancipated slaves.

While they did enjoy certain property rights, most American free coloreds were forbidden suffrage and in only one colony, Delaware, could they testify against whites. Marriage between Negroes and whites was also generally prohibited. They could not hold an office ("ecclesiastical, civil, or military"), join the militia, entertain slaves in their homes without the master's permission, congregate in large groups, or own firearms (and sometimes even dogs). Many colonies required freedmen to carry their "free papers" at all times. New York, reeling from a slave revolt in 1712, prohibited free blacks from owning real estate. There, and in other New England colonies, masters had to post heavy bonds to vouch for the future good conduct of freed slaves. A 1724 Virginia law for "the better government of Negroes, Mulattoes, and Indians" stripped them of the right to have "any vote at the election of burgesses, or any other election whatsoever."

Inevitably, the numbers of slave runaways grew as both the slave population and the severity of the laws also increased. In Virginia, many fled into swamps such as the Great Dismal or to the western mountains of the Blue Ridge—the "Great Mountains" or the "Blue Ledge"—where they formed "maroon" (fugitive) colonies; a large one near Lexington, for example, was later destroyed by state troops.

Meanwhile, Tidewater planters in search of fresh tobacco fields also moved into the mountains and took their slaves with them, displacing both runaways and Indians.[12] [By mid-century, most of these slaves were American born, not imported from Africa, and knew the domestic language and culture well.] The Piedmont (which includes Amherst County, the focus of this study) quickly displaced the older coastal region as the center of Virginia's slave population. By 1750, 40,000 slaves—one-third of the total—were held there, and that number nearly tripled by 1800.[13]

INDEPENDENCE FOR ALL?

Even as the number of blacks, free and slave, was growing, so was the colonial sentiment for independence from England. a And that led to a significant—though temporary—shift in the treatment of both slaves and freedmen of color.

Antislavery sentiment did not begin to manifest itself in colonial and then state legislation until the 1770s and 1780s. Vermont was the first colony to ban slavery outright in 1777. New York debated it endlessly but didn't pass even a partial bill until 1799; Pennsylvania had the Gradual Abolition Act of 1780, which still kept children in service until 21; and Delaware in 1787 actually repealed its law banning the import and export of slaves. Several colonies, including Virginia, tried repeatedly to veto importation but were overridden by the British Crown, which still had a substantial slave trade business. [As late as 1793, Great Britain and the United States still controlled most of the world slave trade.] As a commonwealth, not a colony, Virginia was finally able in 1778 to pass "An Act to prevent the further importation of Slaves."

Many American intellectuals worried how generations of bondage would leave slaves prepared for a life of freedom, and if they could compete intellectually with whites. Both Thomas Jefferson and James Madison, for example, believed that violence between the races would be inevitable, and that blacks would have to be moved to another territory, away from whites. Madison recommended Africa, fearing that Indians would kill them if moved to the western frontier. Jefferson suggested the West Indies.[14] Failing that solution, however, he tried unsuccessfully to ease Virginia's emancipation laws in 1769, recommended freedmen's removal to Africa in the Fairfax Resolves of 1774,[15] and endorsed a bill banning slavery during Virginia's 1776 Convention (the same gathering which passed the Declaration of Rights and instructed its delegates to the Continental Congress to make the first formal motion for American independence). Even John Adams feared racial warfare if the slaves were freed and worried that they could not handle it. "Emancipation had to come slowly & carefully," he wrote. "If congress suddenly freed them, 99% would ask their masters to care for them again."[16]

Open warfare with Britain inspired new thinking on the subject. American colonists were fighting for property and rights, but equally for an ideal that Jefferson summarized as "life, liberty, and the pursuit of happiness." If they were willing to die to secure that for themselves, went the now-popular feeling, how, then, could they deny it to others? Indeed, Jefferson's original draft of the Declaration of Independence sharply—and perhaps self-righteously—criticized King George and his country for promoting the slave trade, "an execrable Commerce" and "assemblage of Horrors." Moreover, the King was encouraging slave uprisings, "exciting those very people to rise in Arms among us and purchase their Liberty of which he has deprived them, by murdering the people upon whom he also obtruded them." The English King, wrote Jefferson, had caused "a distant people, who never offended him" to be captured and carried off.[17]

But there were also practical reasons for these generous and high-minded sentiments regarding freedom. Thousands of male slaves—about 800 in Virginia alone—would escape over the course of the war to fight with the British in exchange for the promise of freedom afterward (though many units refused to fight beside them), and Americans needed to stop the hemorrhage in the labor force by offering the same terms. And as the war dragged on, blacks were needed to supplement both fighting forces and the laborers who kept them moving. Virginia reversed its ban on "coloreds" in the military (May 1777), allowing slaves to substitute for their masters, and those who could prove their freedom to enlist; in 1783, the state formally freed those slaves who had served.[18] The Continental Army, from which George Washington had banned both slaves and colored freedmen in 1775, eventually followed suit, though South Carolina and Georgia objected vigorously; an estimated 5,000 participated. Among them were more than a dozen from Amherst County, including Shadrack Battles, who enlisted and served three years, and Will Hartless, who first joined a militia unit and was later drafted into the regular army from Amherst.

Following the 1782 English surrender at Yorktown, and as the United States and Britain discussed a peace treaty, the Virginia General Assembly rescinded its "no private manumissions" law of more than a century and passed a bill, promoted by Thomas Jefferson, making it lawful to emancipate slaves by "last will and testament, or by any other instrument in writing, under his or her hand and seal."[19] But there were important exceptions: slaves over the age of 45 or in poor health, males under 21, and females under 18 were to be supported by their former masters or his estate; and that estate could be sold to pay the costs if he failed to do so. These removed from the state the financial burden of supporting indigent slaves.

Typical of the libertarian sentiments which inspired post-war manumissions is the will written by James Hopkins of Amherst County. He was "anxious to alleviate the miserable state of those *my fellow mortals* whom the Supreme Creator and Governor of all hath put into my hands." Another, filed in Campbell County in 1792, read: "We, Charles Lynch, John Lynch, and Samuel Mitchell, *from a full Conviction that all men are by Nature free. . .* emancipate a Negro Woman named Nan, but seeing that she is above the age of forty five, We do enter ourselves as securities that she shall not become chargeable to the publick."[20] [Authors' italics]

EASIER SAID THAN DONE

So successful and so popular was this new law that the number of Virginia's free blacks jumped from a few thousand prior to the Revolution to 12,866 in 1790, by far, the largest population in the country at the time. Ten years later, it was 20,493 and would be 30,570 in another decade. And still the numbers grew, and whites were worried.

Emancipation as an ideal was all well and good, but no one had counted on there being so many new freedmen; even the federal government was soon tightening the reins on the burgeoning free black population. Congress allowed only white aliens to be naturalized, again prohibited free coloreds from serving in the militia, and refused to hire them in the postal department, reasoning that was fertile ground for them to spread insurrection and subversion through legitimate contact with other people.

In Virginia, as in the rest of the country, much of this growth was taking place in urban settings, particularly the new towns which were founded along the frontier after the war and afforded freedmen greater job opportunities. Soon city officials in both North and South complained of "the large numbers of free blacks flock[ing] [in] from the country . . ."[21] The countryside had its own problems: where few people moved from their birth area and once residents knew their neighbors—white, black, or Indian—now there were many strangers.

Within a decade of loosening manumissions, Virginia whites were nervous enough to begin restrictions once more, particularly after the bloody uprisings in Saint-Domingue that ultimately led to the formation of Haiti. Thousands of free coloreds fled that island for Southern states, fueling resentment over the size of their numbers and kindling the fear that they carried rebellious ideas with them.

Virginia's first step in tightening control over its own population came in 1793, when the General Assembly required that "to restrain the practice of negroes going at large . . . free Negroes or mulattoes shall be registered and numbered in a book to be kept by the town clerk, which shall specify name, age, color, status and by whom, and in what court emancipated . . . Every free Negro shall once in every three years obtain a new certificate." A second act forbade free blacks from entering the state; if they did so, they would be deported to the place from which they had come. Five years later, they were forbidden to give their certificates of freedom to slaves, an aid to runaways.

Still, these were not strong enough legal shackles, as Virginia learned in 1800 when a slave carpenter named Gabriel Prosser led an unsuccessful but terrifying uprising in the Richmond area, in which the Haitian refugees were suspected of involvement.[22] The Legislature—which met in that city—promptly asked Gov. James Monroe to confer with Pres. Thomas Jefferson about acquiring and establishing a colony, well away from Virginia, for what they termed obnoxious and dangerous persons, that is, free and/or insurrectionary blacks and other coloreds. But their negotiations were secret and so never gathered public support.

HIS RIGHT TO FREEDOM

In 1806, the General Assembly approved two major laws which further tightened these restrictions. One prohibited free Negroes from carrying a firearm without a license and remained in effect until 1832 when, following the Nat Turner rebellion, permission to carry guns, with or without a license, was withdrawn.

The second statute was much more far-reaching; passed on January 25th, it took effect on May 1, 1806 and would remain in effect until the end of the Civil War. It specified that "if any slave hereafter emancipated shall remain within this commonwealth more than twelve months after his or her right to freedom shall have accrued, he or she shall forfeit all such right, and may be apprehended and sold by the overseers of the poor of any county or corporation [city] in which he or she shall be found, for the benefit of the poor of such county or corporation."

Suddenly liberation, once the most sought-after of gifts from a master, had become an instrument for separating families. Hereafter, registration of free coloreds had to note that the person was free himself or was descended from ancestors who were free before May 1, 1806. A freedman could still petition the General Assembly and ask permission to remain in Virginia. These documents often cited advanced age or, in the case of women, being past the age of child-bearing; the petitioner's industry and value to the community; and testimonials from white acquaintances. (See Chapter 4.)

Free coloreds had always held the right to own non-white slaves themselves and, previous to passage of the 1806 law, some had taken advantage of the post-Revolution manumission laws to set free their chattel. Philip J. Schwarz, in a 1987 article, noted that "between 1790 and 1806, free blacks constituted from 13 to 39 percent of emancipators in such diverse locations as York, Isle of Wight, Spotsylvania, *Amherst*, Powhatan, Amelia, and Charlotte Counties."[23]

But the number of slaveowners increased dramatically after 1806. How many true "commercial" slaves were held by blacks and Indians is not known, but most historians believe that those free coloreds not bound by the act—those who were free prior to 1806—became caretaker masters, purchasing family members and retaining them as slaves to comply with the letter of the law and yet circumvent it to keep relatives together.

"SO MISCHIEVOUS A CLASS"

The numbers of American free coloreds grew with every passing decade, much of it by natural increase. From 1790 to 1830, federal census data shows that Virginia and Maryland had the two largest populations, which increased 480% from nearly 21,000 to over 100,000. Pennsylvania and New York were the largest in the North, growing an astonishing 738% (from 11,000 to nearly 83,000) in the same period. Connecticut, Delaware, and North Carolina also ranked in the "top ten" every decade. Not until 1830 did the free colored population of a Midwestern state grow enough to appear in that ranking: Ohio's 9,568 freedmen reflected its position as a favored destination for those forced to leave eastern states.

Understandably, these and other states began to restrict the size and movements of free persons of color. Those bordering Virginia [Delaware, Illinois, Indiana, Kentucky, Maryland, Missouri, North Carolina, Ohio, and Tennessee], which new freedmen could most easily reach, quickly moved to prohibit their permanent residence. Many Northern and Midwestern states—some of which had just recently abolished slavery and didn't want more trouble—barred them from serving on juries or in the militia. Even Delaware, generally the most lenient toward free coloreds, required evidence of good behavior. The Missouri Compromise of 1820-1821 brought the issue further into the forefront, since the new state's proposed constitution forbade free blacks from entering Missouri for any reason. Congress approved the agreement with the condition that it not be construed to exclude any citizen from the enjoyment of privileges to which he was entitled, a sop to the abolitionists that proved nothing. Of course, with the 1821 ruling from the U. S. Attorney General[24] that Virginia's free coloreds were not American citizens, it became even more of a moot point.

Soon, with the total free black population in the country more than 200,000, their situation became increasingly restrictive everywhere. In 1821, the New York legislature removed property qualifications for white male voters but required colored males to post a $250 property bond before voting, and more states barred their entry. Because of this national climate of distrust and fear, freed slaves compelled to leave Virginia often had difficulty finding areas where they could live peacefully and with some degree of acceptance. So overwhelming had been the resulting number of their petitions for exemptions to remain in the state that, in 1819, the General Assembly gave county courts "the authority to allow peaceful and industrious freedmen of good character to remain in the state." [The Assembly would take that power back after Nat Turner's Rebellion and then return it again to local courts in 1837 after being once more inundated with petitions.]

In Virginia itself, the 1806 law and subsequent 1807 federal ban on slave imports certainly slowed the number of new freedmen but did little to curb the free black population as a whole: by 1830, it was approaching 50,000, with no end in sight, partly due to natural increase.[25] Another problem was the declining value of cropland, worn out by nearly two centuries of intensive tobacco farming. The economic solution for many plantation owners was to sell their more valuable slaves and set the others free, which created a "deluge" of freedmen with no place to go.

"THEIR NATIVE LAND"

Virginians began to return to what seemed a simple solution to the whole problem: get rid of the free coloreds by sending them . . . someplace else. It was an idea that had been discussed by the various English colonies as early as 1714, given the abundance of unsettled and public lands: America's "Wild Lands." Virginia had even tried to obtain part of the Louisiana Territory for a freedmen's colony, following the failure of its 1800 negotiations with Washington on that very topic.

Nor was colonization espoused only by Virginians. The Union Humane Society in Ohio (est. 1815) stated publicly that Negroes should be moved "beyond the pale of the white man." New Jersey minister, Princeton graduate, and colonization supporter Robert Finley argued that "everything connected with their condition, including their color, is against them,"[26] and northern missionary Samuel J. Mills maintained that "we must save the Negroes or the Negroes will ruin us."[27] Africa was the favored choice of most colonization advocates since it prevented free Negroes from making "common cause" with Indians and others to overthrow whites in this country and left no American asylum for runaway slaves. Finley was among those who also believed that Americans owed a debt to Africa, since "our fathers brought them [slaves] here," which could be repaid by returning "a population partially civilized and Christianized."

Repeatedly, Virginia's General Assembly sought a federally funded colony in the early years of the 19th century. Finally, slaveholder and legislator Charles Fenton Mercer took up the cause. In 1816 he learned of the abortive 1800 discussions, educated himself on the subject, and introduced, late that year, resolutions in the Assembly asking the federal government to set aside land in the North Pacific states for a freedman's colony. It was amended to include the African Coast as a possible site and passed: "The General Assembly of Virginia has sought to obtain an asylum beyond the United States for free persons of color, but has been frustrated: They now avail themselves of a period when peace has healed the wounds of humanity . . . to renew this effort."[28]

Charles Mercer was forthright about his reasons for sponsoring the bill: it would relieve the state of a dangerous population, increase slave values by reducing supply, and allow owners like him, who wished to free slaves but could not afford the expense of transporting them, to do so "without manifest injury to their country [state]."[29]

The Virginia chapters of the American Colonization Society [organized 1817 as the American Society for Colonizing the Free People of Color of the United States] became quite active; even the legislature, frantic to solve the free Negro dilemma, contributed funds. (In Amherst County, a few slaveowners such as Samuel M. Garland donated land.) The Society, however, was not shy about declaring its opinion of those it was to serve. Its first annual report likened free coloreds to "banditti, consisting of the degraded, idle, and vicious free blacks [who] sally forth from their coverts, beneath the obscurity of night, and plunder . . . They infest the suburbs of the towns and cities, where they become the depository of stolen goods."[30] Even proponents such as Robert Finley saw the whole point of the project as the "gradual separation of the black from the white population" and, consequently, the eventual elimination of slavery.

The Society acquired land in Africa and selected a site for a capitol they named Monrovia in honor of then-President James

Monroe. The first ship sailed to Liberia in 1821, but the efficacy of the solution was still being debated on the eve of the Civil War: fewer than 15,000 American free coloreds altogether are estimated to have emigrated.

John C. Rutherford, representative in the Virginia legislature from Goochland County, delivered his "Speech on the Removal from the Commonwealth of the Free Colored Population" in 1853 and summed up the concerns of previous decades: "Though as a class, they [the free coloreds] be idle, ignorant, degraded and immoral, filling our courts with culprits and our penitentiary with convicts, consuming more than they produce and diminishing rather than adding to the wealth of the state, yet there is little probability that their removal would be urged, if slavery did not exist among us. *In the delicate relations between master and slave, they are a disturbing element*." [Authors' italics]

Others, however, were contemptuous of colonization as the solution. In his 1859 book published by the American Anti-Slavery Society, Rev. James Freeman Clarke[31] pointed out the obvious dichotomy and bitterly described America's attitude: "The Free Colored People of the United States occupy an unfortunate and exceptional position. They stand among us, yet not of us. We know less of them than we know of the people of France and Italy. Born in the midst of us, as their fathers and grandfathers were before them, we yet talk occasionally about sending them back to 'their native land'—meaning Africa . . . (General [Andrew] Jackson's father was an Irishman, but what would he have said if we had proposed sending him back 'to his native soil'?) . . . both at the North and at the South, the free colored people are regarded as pariahs, if not as outlaws. Belonging to a race whom we persist in holding as slaves, we dislike them because we are unjust to them."[32]

In Virginia, where the white population was often barely more than that of slaves, free coloreds represented an additional three or four per cent that could tip the numerical scales in favor of blacks. In the natural way of things, as whites saw them, colored persons were inferior and suitable only for a subservient position: therefore, they were slaves. But the very existence of free Negroes disproved this argument and established that not all coloreds were or had to be slaves—just as John C. Rutherford had said.

Nor was this attitude of superiority prevalent only in Virginia. In Indiana, colored passengers had to produce evidence of their freedom before riding on trains. Pennsylvania disenfranchised blacks in 1838. The 1840 U. S. Census listed "insane and idiots" for the first time and declared that free Negroes were more prone to such conditions than slaves. And Representative Henry Murphy of New York favored laws to keep anyone from bringing them to the free states; they would, he feared, pollute white blood and eventually destroy themselves anyway because of their vicious natures.[33]

NAT TURNER

Much of this "official" rhetoric surrounding slavery and freedmen evolved in the 1830s and 1840s, as America's free black population grew even more rapidly.[34] In Virginia, two other factors marked the beginning of the most restrictive period in history for free blacks.

First was Nat Turner's Rebellion in Southampton County, Virginia on August 22, 1831. Fifty-seven whites were killed—more than in any other slave revolt—in an uprising led by an unlettered slave preacher. Reaction was swift in America's largest slaveholding state. Free Negroes, believed to be the instigators, were rounded up, and some were even killed. The General Assembly passed many new laws (some reiterating earlier statutes) with a long list of prohibitions. Freedmen who remained in Virginia illegally could be sold; no religious gatherings were permitted, nor possession of firearms. They were barred from owning slaves except spouses, children, or those gained "by descent" [inherited], and slaves and free coloreds who wrote or printed anything hinting at insurrection were to be whipped. Freedmen were also denied the right to trial by jury, except in cases where the death penalty was possible, and were instead to be tried by courts of oyer and terminer, as slaves were. The colonization movement gained new strength; two years after the revolt, the Legislature appropriated the large sum of $18,000 annually for the next five years to transport free coloreds to Liberia and to sustain them. In 1834 the state again forbade their entry into Virginia from any other state or a foreign country.

The most amazing result of Nat Turner's revolt, however, was the slavery debate in the Virginia Legislature in January and February 1832—the only time that a southern state openly and officially discussed the complete elimination of slavery within its bounds. (Cooler minds would say, in hindsight, that the issue should have been debated much later, after the hysteria, fear, and excitement had died down.) The gist of the argument was that slaves posed such an exceptional threat to Virginians that the state should exercise its power of eminent domain to confiscate and remove this private property in the interest of public safety. The proposal was defeated but neither side won, for slavery advocates also failed to pass a resolution *in favor of* the institution. The final document was an indecisive condemnation of slavery and a weak protest that it was too impractical to do anything about it.[35]

The second factor that influenced slavery rhetoric in this period was agricultural change. By 1840, Virginia and other Southern states had pulled out of an agricultural depression, thanks to new technology and practices such as marl fertilizers, diversified crops, implements like McCormick's reaper, and the gradual abandonment of tobacco as the main cash crop. At the same time, manufacturing was on the rise; Virginia began a series of internal improvements, including the James River & Kanawha Canal, to aid the development of industry. All this meant a changing role for slaves. Their brute labor was not as important in the "new" agriculture and, because of the federal ban on importation which had cut off a cheap supply, they could make more money for their owners outside the fields. Many were sold profitably to the cotton plantations farther south. Slave sales significantly reduced the number of bondsmen in Virginia and established a new industry: the itinerant slave traders. Traveling agents for these companies collected slaves to be shipped south. Franklin and Armisted, for example, a Louisiana firm, had a number of agents throughout Virginia, including Thomas Hundley in Amherst.[36]

Many slaveowners also hired out their slaves to manufacturers and filled their place in the fields with cheaper free Negroes.[37] This situation created a dilemma for whites, since their *official* distrust of colored freedmen as a whole had not changed. Because freedmen were important to their economy, providing a cheap and available labor force that was an alternative as well as an addition to slave labor, whites developed a legal system so complicated that, often, they were caught in their own snares. Rev. Clarke went so far as to compare the free coloreds to the Jews of medieval Europe: "hated and trampled on, they were still needed; they were an essential element in the business of society."[38]

And unlike the political propaganda that portrayed Negroes as shiftless, lazy, and thieving, most whites who had contact with colored freedmen knew them to be generally hardworking and law-abiding. So while the politicians enacted and orated, many whites simply ignored the laws that were not to their liking or financial advantage and developed an accommodating relationship with the free black population in their midst.

LAWS AND MORE LAWS

Legally, then, the reins on free coloreds grew ever tighter. Any who left Virginia to be educated could not return; local patrols were free to break into their homes and search for weapons; and special taxes were levied on male free Negroes, with the monies usually going to a colonization fund. They were forbidden to sell, prepare, or administer drugs, and any free Negro caught performing abortions with the aid of a drug went to prison. They could not keep ordinaries or even purchase spirits without an affidavit from three or more justices of the peace, affirming their good character. It was unlawful to assemble for the purposes of learning to read and write. Freed slaves could even choose to return to enslavement and had the right to select a master.

Fear grew so intense that laws specific to certain counties with larger black populations appeared on the books. These were all in the Tidewater, the coastal region which extends inland to Richmond, where the proportion of slave to white was quite high and where most free blacks were located. This section was also more urbanized than western Virginia, producing large population groups compressed into small, easily accessible areas. [See Appendix, Table M][39]

In Accomac and Richmond, for example, a free Negro could not sell certain agricultural products without a written statement from two white persons that he had raised the product himself. Free coloreds in Middlesex could not keep a dog without a license.

Emancipated slaves in Accomac and Northampton, which together make up Virginia's once isolated Eastern Shore, were denied recourse to petition the legislature for permission to remain in Virginia once they were freed.

State law was validated on a national level with the Dred Scott decision in 1857 when Chief Justice Roger Taney reaffirmed earlier rulings that Negroes were not citizens. [See footnote 24.] Giving a legal history of American free blacks, Taney declared that the framers of the Constitution had never intended to include the descendants of slaves, that they had no rights the white man needed to respect. Everyone knew that, he wrote; it was an opinion "fixed and universal in the civilized portion of the white race."[40] (Where Taney's opinion left freedmen who had no slave heritage was left unsaid.)

Abolitionist John Brown's raid on Harper's Ferry, Virginia [later West Virginia] in the fall of 1859—which followed the announcement of Arkansas' expulsion of all free Negroes from that state—seemed poised to fix the last legal bricks imprisoning free coloreds in place. Overwhelming panic had ensued, for Harper's Ferry was an uprising led by a white man and aided publicly and enthusiastically by free Negroes. Legislators in almost every Southern state debated the wisdom of emulating Arkansas, and several actually passed bills to enslave every colored who did not leave. Fortunately, common sense prevailed, and those who had advocated this course soon found that most Southerners did not support the plan and actually considered it illegal and offensive.[41]

ACCOMMODATION

How did this rigid legal framework surrounding free persons of color actually work on a local level in Virginia? Evidence indicates that state laws and rulings were often ignored, challenged, or adapted to suit local conditions, and that the extent to which this was true varied from an urban to a rural setting.

As noted earlier, the Tidewater was very restrictive, but this was not generally the case in western Virginia—the Piedmont which was the "frontier" of less than a century earlier. Here, as distinct from the transient cities of the coast, rural relationships tended to be older and more durable; consequently, a higher degree of acceptance and accommodation marked the black/white/Indian relationship.

That attitude led the Amherst Justices to react unfavorably when, in June 1861—one month before the Battle of Bull Run—Philip St. George Cock, "Colonel of Volunteers and commanding at Culpeper Court House," appeared before them. Cock had a requisition "for such able bodied Free Negroes as may be in the County of Amherst to be employed at the Camp of Menasses [sic] Junction in the erection of fortifications at that place." The Justices had no choice in the matter, so they appointed agents to oversee the required impressment and transportation. Yet it appears that they did not care for the order, since they stipulated that the agents were to execute it "in such manner as to cause as little irritation as possible and to interfere with the pursuits of said negroes as little as is compatible with the necessities of the state."

The smaller and more isolated population centers of the Piedmont also helped reduce both the possibility and the fear of slave uprisings, which urban whites continued to believe were organized by free blacks, despite the lack of evidence. In Amherst County, for example, the only known "rebellion" occurred in 1863 when several of Terisha Dillard's slaves murdered him. Though Dillard was known to have been a cruel master, the slaves were found guilty and hanged to discourage others from getting ideas, since so many white males by that time were in military service. But as in many other cases around the state, there was no evidence of freedmen being involved, nor were the County Court Justices so apprehensive about the alleged troublemakers in their midst as to even hint of the possibility.

Cases involving extreme punishment such as that meted out to the Dillard slaves became even more rare as the war progressed, and for a very practical reason: the county's agricultural labor force was shrinking fast. Many able-bodied male slaves had been hired out to essential industries; more were impressed by the state to work on public defenses. [That power had been granted to the Governor by the General Assembly in March 1863.] In addition, Amherst County death certificates from 1864 and 1865 show a surprisingly large number of slaves who had apparently been just recently freed.[42] The authors speculate that these manumissions point to a growing awareness on the part of Amherst slaveowners that the war was

probably not going to conclude in a manner
they rushed to free those chattel they could
further discussion of these death records.]

In this climate, the County Court
favorably to a January 1865 requisition
120 male Slaves between the ages of 1
ordered Sheriff Robert W. Snead to ascertain the
"liable to impressment." His report was not good news, as
Court subsequently explained to the Governor. Forty Amherst slaves had been impressed the preceding November to work one year and another 98 requisitioned to serve one month. The latter, reported the sheriff, had actually been kept 60 days and "are now Just returning home. Some have died in Service, and many of the others are so prostrated by disease as to be unable to render any Service." The state had already taken a large number of slaves, and more had been "hired to Iron Works in this and other counties, and work shops." Such hired hands could not be impressed, so the county's agricultural labor force was seriously diminished, which not only made fieldwork harder but lessened the number of slaves available for impressment. Amherst County, said its Justices, was also suffering the ravages of a severe drought and was "now in condition but illy prepared to Spare any further drain upon its agricultural labour, without Serious loss and injury." Snead was sent to Richmond to confer with "his Excellency William Smith the Governor of the State" and give him the Court's request.[43]

Apparently the Governor didn't agree with the county, for the next record shows the list of available owners and the number of slaves each was to furnish, with a note that John L. Turner, Jr., "a member of the reserve forces of the Confederate States" be appointed their superintendent. Another desperate requisition in March for 10% of all the county's male slaves, 18 to 55, was not even questioned.

In fact, these slave requisitions caused such agricultural hardship throughout the state that the General Assembly turned to free coloreds to work on Confederate fortifications. They were supposed to be paid and provided food, lodging, and medical care, but the quality of these amenities varied, as can be seen in the Amherst court records of July 1864 when the Justices championed unty's free blacks, whom they felt had been subjected to l and unjustified treatment by the state.

Acting on "information which it deems reliable," the Justices protested that "some of the free negroes recently called into the Confederate Service from this county . . . and placed at work on the public defenses near Richmond, have whilst thus employed been treated with great harshness, if not barbarity . . . [and though the Court does not wish to stray beyond its powers or to criticize others in the government, it] *feels it to be its duty to Shield its own citizens from oppression and wrong, and especially that class of all others, the most helpless and friendless*—It [the Court] therefore deems it proper to declare, that whilst it approves of the policy of calling into requisition whenever needed, the free negro labor of the country [state], and whilst it has always been willing to lend its aid in making that labor effective, it at the same time declares that it is repugnant to all the feelings of humanity . . . [as well as poor government] to treat these free negroes . . . with harshness and cruelty—On the contrary, such a course . . . will defeat the whole policy of the law and paralize [paralyze] every effort that might be made to render that labor effectual."[44] [Authors' italics]

Furthermore, as the Justices pointed out in this remarkable document, many of these same freedmen had worked on the defenses before "with cheerfulness and fidelity" when they were supervised by "discreet Persons" selected by the Court. This time, however, "most of them have deserted, fled to their homes, or to the mountains—Some of them bearing upon their bodies the marks of Severe Scourging, and all of them greatly alarmed and panic stricken." The Court appointed three men to personally "present to the Governor of this State" their protest and ask him to "take such action as in his opinion, Justice[,] patriotism and humanity may require."

The records do not give his response, but this document reveals several important facts about the ways in which free coloreds were viewed and treated in a rural area such as Amherst:

- County officials kept track of them, even when in other parts of the state.
- At a time when the Justices had many critical issues with which to deal, they yet considered the ill-treatment of the free blacks and Indians from Amherst important enough to

warrant the time and expense involved to protest, as well as the possibility that they would receive criticism from the state for doing so.

- Unlike the state and federal governments, Amherst Justices not only viewed their free coloreds as *citizens* and worthy of protection, but weren't afraid to say so in an official document.
- They also didn't hesitate to declare that these people, "the most helpless and friendless," were in that condition because of past wrongs done to them by those same governments.

Their defiance also illustrates the long-standing suspicion of mountain people for "government types" in the eastern part of the state, a suspicion that already dated back to the early 18th century when settlement began in the Piedmont (and still continues to some degree today). Richmond might make the rules, but local people would make them work to local advantage. Thus they accommodated the non-whites in their midst not just because it seemed right or charitable, but because it was convenient and didn't involve financial risk.

Chapter 2

"THE LAND CALLED THE MONOCANE"

The difficulty in discussing Amherst County's "free blacks" is that the term is misleading, for not all of them were Negro. A sizable portion of the people found in the county "Register of Free Blacks" and described in contemporary documents as persons of color were actually American Indians. Today, they have overcome centuries of less than pleasant relationships with Europeans and their descendants to re-build themselves as the Monacan Nation of their forebears.

THE ANCESTORS

Virginia's pre-colonial Indian tribes are designated by the language they spoke: Algonquian in the Tidewater (including the Powhatans), Iroquoian in the south and far west, and Siouan in the Piedmont. The Monacans fall into this last group.

Devotees of Hollywood "cowboy and Indian" movies probably think of the Sioux only as a western tribe, but archaeological evidence indicates they originated in the Ohio River Valley. In a loosely two-pronged migration centuries ago, one segment of the population traveled west to form those Siouan tribes of the western plains. A second migrated to the Carolinas, and from there, a smaller portion moved up into Piedmont Virginia and successfully occupied an enormous territory from the Fall Line [See footnote 12.] west into the Blue Ridge Mountains. This area extended south across the Piedmont from the Rappahannock to the James and Appomattox Rivers and comprised roughly the eastern part of modern West Virginia and the western half of Virginia.

One 17th century explorer who visited the Piedmont tribes described their history: ". . . the Indians now seated here are distinguished into several Nations . . . [they were] a people driven by the enemy from the Northwest, and invited to sit down here by an Oracle about four hundred years since [ago] . . . [they] had been led there by Manock, from whom they took their name."[45]

As many as a dozen or more tribes—all of whom spoke Siouan but with different dialects—formed a loose coalition known as the Monacan Confederacy for the dominant tribe. The Occaneechi and Saponi were along the upper Roanoke River; the latter had a village at Peaks of Otter in Bedford County. The Tutelo probably built Monahassanaugh in Nelson County [other sources say Nahyssan], and the Saponis established a village named Rassawek near the confluence of the James and Rivanna Rivers at Columbia [on the Goochland-Fluvanna County line]. Massinacack lay near Goochland Courthouse, Monasukapanough was north of the University of Virginia at Charlottesville, and Mowhemencho (possibly the main Monacan town) was at Manakin near Richmond, a location later taken over by Huguenots. Altogether there may have been at least a dozen palisaded towns. But exactly identifying any of these sites with a specific tribe is problematic because of shifting alliances and the people's extreme mobility.

By the time the Monacans and the English first met, the tribes had likely settled into a more settled lifestyle. Other Virginia natives called them "earth diggers" for their mining and processing of copper, an important trade item with other tribes.[46] They were also known for their ferocity and frequent raids into the Tidewater; Chief Powhatan regularly complained to the British that the Monacans swooped down upon his people every year "at the fall of the leafe" [autumn].

MONACAN SITES IN THE AMHERST AREA

The Sioux who traveled from Ohio to the Carolinas and Virginia carried with them a semi-nomadic tradition of moving seasonally to hunt, then returning to more permanent villages where they raised primarily corn, beans, and squash. In Amherst County, a hunting camp found on the Lee farm near Stapleton, on the James River, was excavated in 1970 by students from Central Virginia Community College under the direction of Bill McLeRoy, one of this book's authors. Probably used over the years by many small hunting groups, the site yielded few artifacts: a large soapstone pot, points, etc. Another site in the area, exposed after a 1985 flood, was later excavated and found to have been used from 900 to 1250 A.D.

McLeRoy also helped excavate a permanent village near Wingina in modern Nelson County on the banks of the James. This is thought to have been Monahassanaugh, one of the five major Monacan villages mapped in 1608 by Capt. John Smith of Jamestown fame. The excavation there revealed the foundations of at least thirteen round houses, cord-and-fiber-decorated pottery, nicely executed points, and mica sheets quarried across the James. Extensive croplands surrounding the town would have supported several hundred people.

No such large village has been found yet in Amherst County, although there are historic records of Indians—"peaceful Indians belonging to the Monagan [Monacan] tribe"—who camped in Madison Heights near the old "Horse Ford" (operated by John Lynch) as late as the 1780s. This location placed them squarely on an ancient trail long used by natives who crossed the James just below Percival's Island.

The Monacans buried their dead in 15-to-20 foot high earthen mounds, a custom surviving from their time in the Ohio Valley. The closest remaining one to Amherst is in Charlottesville, near the site of the Monasukapanough village. Thomas Jefferson recalled seeing a group of Indians who traveled out of their way in the 1750s to visit it and pay homage. He later excavated the mound, where he found bones "lying in the utmost confusion," and noted that it had been built with alternating layers of dirt and river rock.[47]

EARLY EUROPEAN CONTACT

The Monacan Confederacy's population is estimated to have been 10,000 at the beginning of the 17th century. [Its numbers had already begun to decline due to European contact, principally diseases brought by the Spanish and their livestock which had spread into North America via trading routes and against which the natives had no immunity.[48]] John Smith and Christopher Newport were the first English to visit the eastern Monacans while they were on several 1608 expeditions to search for gold, silver, and mineral deposits. They visited or heard of twelve towns: the five on the James River listed above (Monacan) and seven on the Rappahannock where the Manahoac lived. The Virginia Company's Lord Governor soon followed up on their report and authorized a mining expedition to travel above the Falls "into the land called Monocane 2 or 3 dayes Iourney [days' journey]."[49]

Those Monacans living closest to the coast were the first to feel the impact of British settlement and the first to be enslaved through military action. Soon, the Monacans and their allies were fighting on all fronts: the colonists to the east and south, and their old enemies the Iroquois who attacked from the north and west. The House of Burgesses even called for "annual expeditions from the sea to river heads to exterminate Indians" on lands the colonists wanted.[50] As the native population fell ever lower, smaller groups banded together and shifted their locations, usually to the west, trying to stay ahead of settlers, some finally forced to ask for protection from one aggressor—the British—against other enemies.

The western Monacans knew of threats to their east but were not themselves visited by Europeans until 1670, when German physician and explorer John Lederer reached them. He had been sent by Virginia's governor, Sir William Berkeley, to find a way over the Blue Ridge to the East India Sea [the Pacific Ocean] which the English were sure lay just on the other side of the mountains. Lederer made three trips and probably went through Amherst County while traveling up the James on his second visit.[51] He wrote that his Tidewater Indian guides, on first beholding the mountains where the Monacans lived, fell to the ground, "prostrating themselves in adoration, [and] howled out after a barbarous manner, 'Okiepaeze,' that is, 'God is Nigh,'" for they believed their supreme god Okaee resided in the clouds.

Bacon's Rebellion in 1676 brought an end to the centuries-old supremacy of Virginia's Indians, who were forced to sign the Treaty of Middle Plantation and swear their subjection to Great Britain. Among those native sovereigns signing the document was Shurenough, "King of the Manakins," whose sign resembled a large ornate E. Each tribe was to receive land, the right to hunt and fish, and protection from enemies, but there is no evidence that the Monacans ever received any of these benefits.[52]

In 1714, Gov. Alexander Spottswood offered the colony's Siouan tribes protection from escalating raids by the Iroquois. He ordered Fort Christianna built in Brunswick County [in "southside" Virginia] as a buffer fort on the frontier and kept the Monacans there for "safe-keeping" until 1721 when the British signed a peace treaty with the Iroquois that, theoretically, was to stop their attacks on the Monacans. Following their release from Christianna, now even more diminished in number, the various Siouan tribes dispersed. Many of the Tutelo and Saponi, for example, eventually traveled to New York where they were adopted by the Cayuga. Others moved to the Roanoke River valley. To English eyes, the Monacans appeared to simply fade away after leaving Fort Christianna; many Virginians thought they had all left the colony.

TO THE MOUNTAINS

Remnants of the once powerful confederacy, however, managed to survive. Most of the remaining Monacans and their confederates fled back into the Blue Ridge mountains to join those who had never left; in Amherst County, that refuge was principally on and near the rugged slopes of Tobacco Row Mountain and surrounding peaks, and along the James River. Isolated in hollows and valleys, they had little contact with whites, few of whom had ventured that far west.[53] This would have been familiar territory to the Monacans, both from earlier settlements before their internment in Christianna and from their longtime use of several major Indian roads which crossed Amherst County.[54] They also had ancient hunting grounds there, such as that on the north side of Buffalo Ridge, a long escarpment beginning east of the town of Amherst and extending northeast into Albemarle County, named for the once plentiful buffalo there. The first white settlers in the area would later refer to the grasslands there—which resulted from the Monacans' regular burning of it to drive out game for hunting and create grasses to attract more—as "The Savannahs" or "The Glades." [Glade Road, which began as an Indian trail through these hunting grounds, appeared on early maps of Amherst County and is still marked in Nelson.]

The Monacans' presence in the area was documented in 1742 when scouts encountered them while exploring the Amherst-Bedford-Campbell-Nelson region for a site to locate the Hat Creek Presbyterian Colony. They reported that some of the natives, particularly in Bedford, were quite willing to fight to retain their land, but others were more peaceful.[55] About the same time, Dr.

William Cabell, the first Englishman to settle along the Rockfish River, reported being attacked while marking the lines of his land grant. The Indians were understandably "much incensed" about his activity, but Cabell escaped by assuring them the marks were only to guide him back home. Lewis Evans' famous 1755 *Map of the Middle British Colonies* also showed Monacans and the Tuscarora who had joined them in the four-county area.[56]

For a few years, these peoples enjoyed their solitude deep in the frontier: from 1728 to mid-1731, county surveyors made only 49 surveys in all of Goochland County, which then included Albemarle, Amherst, and Nelson. But civilization soon caught up with the Monacans in the form of Tidewater planters moving west.

Dr. Cabell, whose land grant was described as being "in the last hunting ground of the Indian east of the Blue Ridge," had been the first; his properties stretched from Riverville north to Howardsville.[57] Hard on his heels came a flood of others, such as John Rucker and his sons who settled land from Harris Creek to Tobacco Row. Nicholas Davies patented large tracts in southern Amherst along the James where a trading post already existed at the mouth of the Pedlar River. Rev. Robert Rose and his sons built many homes along the Tye and Piney Rivers in the 1740s and 1750s, while John Carter, son of "King" Carter, received grants on the Buffalo and Piney Rivers. By 1739, James Warren had already opened copper mine shafts in The Glades area along Buffalo Ridge.

These men, and others like them who took an interest in old Amherst beginning in the 1730s, hoped to both make a home and turn a profit from the desirable new lands of the Piedmont. The terms of their land grants required them to settle people who would build houses, keep livestock, and pay taxes. So great was the rush to develop the region that much of the prime land was already taken by the late 1750s.[58] This quickly put enormous pressure on the Monacans, who—as Indians—had no legal title to the land they occupied.[59] By the time of the Revolutionary War, Amherst was no longer the frontier, and the Indians had been driven ever farther back into the mountains into small pockets of settlements, their hunting grounds farmed or mined, and their trails turned into public roads.

BUILDING A NATION

A number of Monacan forebears fought in the American Revolution. William and Thomas Johns[60] enlisted as privates March 1777 in a company of the 6th Virginia Regiment of Foot commanded by Capt. Samuel Jordan Cabell [Dr. William Cabell's son and a student at William & Mary College]. This was a rifle company, and the men "were expert marksmen, many exceeding six feet in height and powerful in person," who carried a tomahawk and long knife in addition to their rifle. The British called them "the shirt-men" for the homespun hunting shirts they wore, and they respected their sharpshooting abilities. Cabell's company were among the troops who crossed the icy Delaware River with George Washington and fought at the battles of Trenton and Princeton. The group was also one of "the eight rifle companies personally selected by Colonel Daniel Morgan" who helped bring about the surrender of General Burgoyne at Saratoga, and they endured the famous winter at Valley Forge. William Johns served through December 1777; Thomas re-enlisted for another year.[61]

Robert Johns, Jr. and Nathaniel Gutrey [Guthry, who later married Robert's sister Nancy], in Capt. William Tucker's militia company from Amherst County, served in the Continental Army in early 1781. Guthry was also a guard at the Albemarle Barracks, where British POWs from Saratoga were imprisoned.

William Hartless served in the Albemarle militia from 1779 to 1781, then was drafted into the Continental Army from Amherst County. John Johns is listed in Sweeney's *Amherst County, Virginia in the Revolution* as having been a soldier, along with John Redcross, William and Benjamin Evans, John and William Clark, and James Hartless, but no details are given of their service. [Pages 40-48]

But did they fight as whites or free persons of color?

On tax lists and pre-census "Heads of Households" registers, John Redcross is consistently described as white though later accounts [see below] maintain that he was clearly a full-blooded Indian. But by 1800, that had begun to change. He was not listed as a white male on the 1800 Lexington Parish tax roll, and the 1810 census showed him as a free man, other than white. Thomas Johns was white in 1785, 1790, and 1800 but was paying taxes as a free mulatto by 1822. William Johns does not appear in relevant records until 1800, where he was white; he, too, was "other than white" on the 1810 census. Robert was white in 1783 but does not appear in later records. His future brother-in-law Nathaniel Guthry appears to have been white from the few records available. James Johns does not appear in official records until 1810 and then as a free colored.

William Evans was white in surviving records until 1823, but Benjamin changed from being white in 1783 to mulatto in 1785. The Clarks were white in 1800 but had become mulattos a decade later. William Hartless was white in 1783, 1790, and 1800 but a mulatto in 1810; James was also white in 1800 and a free colored by 1820.

The apparent conclusion is that "whiteness" was easier to claim in the first few decades after the Revolution, but that changed in the 1790s as the state began to restrict once more its "colored" residents. [See Chapter 1.] Among the most humiliating laws was one passed in 1823 which declared the child of an Indian and the child, grandchild, and great-grandchild of a Negro to be mulattoes—a term that stripped both of their racial and ethnic heritage and was particularly galling to the Monacans, many whom were clearly "Indian:" "The older [people] were typical Indians of a rich copper color, high cheek bones, long, straight black hair, tall and erect in form . . .."[62] Nine years later (and shortly after Nat Turner's 1831 revolt), the General Assembly forbade slaves, free Negroes, and mulattoes to preach or "hold any meeting for religious purposes either day or night." They were also stripped of their right to own and carry firearms, an emotional blow to the Monacans who had a heritage of hunting and still supplemented their diet with game.

BEAR MOUNTAIN SETTLEMENT

[*Scores of researchers and descendants have not been able to sort out the Johns family lines in 18th and early 19th century Amherst. And neither have the authors. The narrative we have used below relies most heavily on the history accepted today by the Monacan Nation. However, we are troubled by inconsistencies and contradictions in records and printed sources. Sorting out the Johns' genealogy did not fall within the scope of this study, but we do want to note that there are some who question whether some of the Johns' wives—particularly Mary, the wife of Robert, Sr.—were actually Indian.*]

Today's Monacan community in Amherst County descends primarily from several Indian ancestors and white men who married Monacan (or one of their confederate tribes) women, a course of action advocated by leaders such as Thomas Jefferson, who believed Indian-white marriages were the most peaceful way to settle the frontier.[63]

Robert Johns[64] [circa 1720-1778] was the first to reach "old Amherst"—the county before it was divided in two—when he acquired land on Porridge [now Partridge] Creek in 1758 and more acreage a decade later. Robert brought with him to Porridge Creek his new wife Mary Gresham Johns,[65] the daughter of Thomas Gresham and an Indian woman also named Mary. Robert and Mary had ten or twelve children, and it was their son William (circa 1775-1863) who physically created the community known variously as the Johns, Bear Mountain, or Indian Settlement that is the heart of the Monacan tribe today.

John Redcross (circa 1770-1861) is considered a second founder of the Settlement. In 1783, his father (also John) was shown with 11 *whites* in his household, but Houck believes that the son and namesake "was probably the only pure-blooded Indian man in the original settlement" [page 66]; his name certainly suggests an Indian rather than European origin. Like the third founder, William Evans [see below], Redcross has been described as Cherokee, but the evidence does not support that, leading to speculation that he may have been Monacan or at least Siouan. John's son Paul was said to have looked like his father, ". . . every inch an Indian . . . straight as an arrow, long haired, with high cheek bones and copper skin."[66]

The third Settlement founder was William Evans, described by Edgar Whitehead in 1896 as Cherokee but shown in other records as white. In 1783 he had 6 whites and 1 black person in his household;[67] perhaps the latter was his Indian wife, whose name and history are unknown.

In 1790, Will Johns married Molly Evans, William's daughter. In 1807 he bought 57 acres on Tobacco Row Mountain, then put it up for collateral against a debt a few weeks later; he sold the property for $100 in 1810. If Virginia law prohibited, or at the least discouraged, free persons of color from buying real estate, as some sources indicate, how did Will—who appears on the 1810 census as a free colored—manage the purchase? The answer may well lie in the accommodations made on a local level which were discussed at the end of Chapter 1. The Johns family was regularly listed as *both* white and free colored on early census and tax lists for Amherst County, which created great confusion and often led local officials to make their own decisions concerning people they knew. (Will himself was a white male on the 1800 Lexington Parish roll and an "other [than white] free head of household" on the 1810 census.) In addition, several members of his family served in the American army during the Revolutionary War; Will's son Charles later fought in the War of 1812. [Charles moved to Bedford County.] All those factors, as well as respectable and peaceful relatives and a long acquaintanceship with him, undoubtedly smoothed his way through the county clerk's office.

In 1831 Will may have had the Indian Removal Act of the previous year preying on his mind, for it threatened the forcible removal of all American Indians from their ancestral homes in the East to the southwestern United States.[68] To avoid such a catastrophe, Johns made plans. In his first of two purchases, he bought 42 acres on Bear Mountain, which lies on the east side of Tobacco Row and may have been considered a sacred spot by earlier native inhabitants; today it is known that ancestral Monacans have lived on and near the peak for thousands of years. Two years later, Will paid Landon Cabell a dollar an acre for 400 adjoining acres.[69] Cabell's own home in (modern) Nelson County[70] contained an Indian cemetery and his mother was of Algonquian descent, so he was likely sympathetic to Will's desire to build a remote enclave—a hiding place—for his family. When completed, the Bear Mountain site stretched roughly south and west from the headwaters of Huff Creek, taking in the headwaters also of both Falling Rock Creek and a tributary of Harris Creek. It was ringed on three sides by High Peak and Cedar, Richardson, Kentucky, and Paul Mountains.

Will built "an humble dwelling in a little cove" on the east side of the mountain and farmed his land for the next two decades. During that time, he was joined by family and in-laws, including his father-in-law William Evans. His son Tarleton had married Eliza, the daughter of John Redcross, who also came to live on

Bear Mountain until his death in 1861. Sons Joshua (who died sometime between 1840 and 1856) and William B. and their families built homes as did Richard. Molly's sister Nancy moved to Bear Mountain with her husband Edward Branham; their son Edmund married Will Johns' only daughter Mary and joined the Settlement, too.

On New Year's Eve, 1856, Will deeded all the Bear Mountain lands to his children in exchange for $20 annual rent from each during the remainder of his life. Richard received 95 acres (which he sold two months later); William B., 109 acres; Tarleton, 96 acres and a house; Edith (Joshua's widow), 75 acres; and his son-in-law Edmund Branham, 92 ¼ acres.

At least one other Johns settlement in Amherst County lay only a few miles south of Bear Mountain on Johns Creek, which empties into the James River downstream from the ferry landing at Bethel [originally Davies' Lower Ferry and today Salt Creek]. A Monacan history states that the site was in existence by at least 1807 and was known as Oronoco for the type of tobacco grown there.[71]

BEVERLYTOWN

Bear Mountain and Oronoco were not the only Indian settlements based on blood ties. According to Monacan lore, some of the Beverly and Clark families—both surnames acknowledged by the tribe today as among their ancestors—lived in the Bear Mountain area at one time but later formed their own communities, though intermarriages between the groups continued. Others, such as Samuel Beverly, remained on Harris Creek between the Johns Settlement and Tobacco Row.

Beverlytown still appears on Amherst maps and is in the southwest corner of the county in the George Washington National Forest. If remoteness and security were the Beverlys' priorities, as they were with Will Johns, this location was well suited: it is completely surrounded by mountains, creeks, and the Pedlar River.[72] The family originated in adjacent Buckingham County and does not seem to have settled in Amherst before 1819 or 1820, though there were some earlier marriages with Monacan families. The community that still bears their name began when James F. Beverly and Isabella Williams[73] bought 100 acres on Brown's Creek and along the road to Pryor's Gap [modern County Road 607, designated Beverly Town Road] in 1834. This Beverly is probably the same as both James Beverly, who married Sarah Ann Taylor, and Frederick J. Beverly, whose wife was named Sarah Ann; he bought additional acreage on the creek a few months later and purchased Isabella's half interest in the original property in 1854. By 1860, Frederick had acquired a total of 500 acres, most of it unimproved but still worth $1,500, where he raised principally grains and tobacco.

The community's population peaked in the 1920s when more than a dozen related families lived there. "A number of families were landowners, some having acquired their property, it is said, in payment for taking the place of others called to service during the Civil War."[74] Photographs made of Beverlytown in 1924 show the residents living in small log cabins with fieldstone chimneys; the school, too, was a one-room log structure. The community had no electricity or paved roads.[75]

Two other Monacan settlements, Clark Town and Irish Creek, were formed in Rockbridge County, adjacent on the west to Amherst; Monacans settled in nearby Buena Vista, too. The Irish Creek group has been classified as "Rockbridge County Brown People," estimated in 1948 to include over 300 individuals.[76] Like Beverlytown, their populations peaked in the 1920s, when Virginia launched what has been called genocide against its Indian residents [see below].

"SHUT OUT FROM CONTACT AND INTERCOURSE"

The Monacans endured the decades prior to the Civil War as best they could, powerless to change the laws which classified them as blacks or mulattoes rather than Indians. They particularly scorned comparison to freed slaves for "they held themselves above the slaves;" some, in fact, owned slaves. A sympathetic writer later described this period: "Previous to the late war [the Civil War] these people were isolated and practically shut out from contact and intercourse [interaction] with the whites . . . there seemed to be no place for them, and no provision in the law for such a race as to schools . . . and to some extent they were cut off from Church privileges. The State law forbid the assembling of colored people unless specifically permitted by the county court, and under the control of whites, who had to be present . . . they became for the time, as they really were, a separate and distinct race and colony, and remained so until a few years before the late war. It is greatly to their credit that under such peculiar circumstances they did not become a settlement of thieves and murderers . . . [they were] shut out and hidden in the little coves of Bear mountain . . ..”[77]

Just before the Civil War, an elderly woman in the Johns Settlement contacted two white ministers in Amherst who had earlier arranged for area slaves to receive preaching. “Her life was coming to a close,” she told them, and she had not “heard the gospel preached nor hymns sung for 23 years.” The result was a brush arbor church “in the Indian reserve” where the ministers preached and buried the Monacan dead “until the war carried the evangelists into the Confederate army.”[78]

During this period, each county Commissioner of Revenue was required to file regular reports listing the free Negroes in his area for tax purposes. One of the few such lists that have survived for Amherst is from 1861. There are actually two versions of the list, differing somewhat, and they provide an interesting look at the Amherst Monacans. More than half were females. Of those whose occupations were listed—all men—the overwhelming majority, as might be expected, were farmers. The Beverlys had the highest number of skilled jobs: coopers, mechanics, and wheelwrights. Only one shoemaker, George Johns, was listed. The oldest, at 70 or 71, were Thomas Johns, Catharine Johns, and Creasy Branham.

During the Civil War, one family member reported that “many of their young men were drafted and carried to Petersburg and Richmond, to work on the Confederate fortifications.” [See Chapter 1.] It’s likely that few, if any, actually served as soldiers as their grandfathers had in the Revolutionary War.

Reconstruction left two painful legacies for the Monacans. Virginians began to distinguish between coloreds freed as a result of the war and those who were free before the war. The term used for the latter was “Free Issue,” in reference to the papers issued them by each county or city which proved they were free. In many of the counties containing such populations, this was quickly shortened to “Issue” or some variation. In Amherst, it came to refer primarily to those of Indian ancestry. This demeaning term is still used in the county, though much less so now than in recent decades.

The second legacy was education, or more specifically, the lack of it. Federal law required public schools for "coloreds" after the war, and Amherst County had several of these. But the Monacans refused to attend them, fearing it would only strengthen the perception that they were something other than Indian.[79] Not allowed to enter white schools, and refusing to enroll in black ones meant the continuation of high levels of illiteracy among Monacans. Houck writes that all this created two unfortunate consequences, one of which was to split further the county's population along racial lines and create even harder feelings between the groups. But it also began to segregate darker skinned Monacans from lighter ones and caused many to leave Amherst for other locations. [Page 77]

THE MISSION

In 1907, Rev. Arthur Gray came to Falling Rock Creek to begin an Episcopalian mission to the area Monacans. The white frame church he built the next year on land donated by a white neighbor is across the creek from the school and still in use today. [See footnote 79.] Gray sent several letters to the *Southern Churchman*, describing his work at Bear Mountain and the people to whom he ministered.

In appearance, he wrote, they were "a very rich brunette, with straight black hair and black eyes, and Caucasian features." Home was usually a 16 square foot cabin which held several families. His narrative of Monacan agricultural techniques is fascinating. "They raise tobacco in the [creek and river] bottoms and on new ground, and a little corn and oats on the hillsides. The hills are frequently too steep for any kind of wagon, so they put their produce on sleds and slide it down into the hollows." Their population was increasing, he added, and would soon be about 500 people.[80] They persistently referred to themselves as Indians, though they were not certain from which tribe(s) they descended.

LEGENDS OF CHEROKEES

In 1894, anthropologist James Mooney of the Smithsonian Institution's Bureau of American Ethnology was the first to examine the small, scattered Indian groups of Piedmont Virginia and to assert that many were Siouan, a radical idea in a day when people were familiar only with the western Sioux. In his *Siouan Tribes of the East*, Mooney declared that it was "extremely probable that the original home of the Siouan race was not the prairies of the west but amidst the eastern foothills of the southern Alleghanies [sic]." In 1914, David Bushnell, Jr. of Harvard's Peabody Museum wrote an article entitled *The Indian Grave: A Monacan Site in Albemarle County, Virginia*: "At the present time, there are living along the foot of the Blue Ridge, in Amherst, a number of families who possess Indian features and other characteristics of the aborigines. Their language contains many Indian words; but as yet no study has been made of the language. While these people may represent the last remnants of various tribes, still it is highly probable that among them are living the last of the Monacan."

Between the publication of these two academic studies, an article appeared in the Richmond, Virginia *Times* (April 19, 1896), written by Capt. Edgar Whitehead, a Confederate veteran from Amherst County. Not only was his wife a Cabell descended from Nicketti, but Whitehead had many interests in mining and tobacco which took him throughout the county; one of his tin mines was actually near the Clark settlement at Irish Creek. Consequently, he knew many of the Monacan leaders and wrote a sympathetic history and description of them. Unfortunately, the good captain had never read James Mooney's work, and he subscribed to the theory that the local Indians must be Cherokee, the largest and best known tribe in the mountains of Virginia and North Carolina.

As Whitehead presented it, Cherokees from North Carolina traveling to Washington, D. C. to "see the Great Father" [the President] or simply using old Indian roads through the area, happened upon Amherst and decided to settle there. Later generations embellished the legend by making the traveling Cherokees delegates going to urge Congress to rescind the Indian Removal Act of 1830. Yet another version makes the Amherst Indians descendants of Cherokees who escaped from the Trail of Tears and fled to the mountains. The legend of the Cherokee connection has persisted ever since, and there probably is some

Cherokee heritage in Amherst's surviving Indians since the tribe reached north into southwestern Virginia.[81]

THE EUGENICS "WARS"

A 1926 book added another theory to the origin of Amherst's Indians: they were descendants of prostitutes kicked out of neighboring Lynchburg after a church revival.[82] Such demeaning statements were, unfortunately, a staple of *Mongrel Virginians, The Win Tribe*: the Monacans were being used as ammunition in the eugenics "war."

Eugenics—improving the qualities of a race or breed through scientific breeding—became a hot topic in America after World War I.[83] The American Plant and Stock Breeders' Association, organized in 1904, had demonstrated how well the theory worked in agriculture, so why not, asked advocates, put it to work on the human race, too?[84] The Eugenics Record Office was established in New York in 1910 to study and quantify human traits.[85] The most potent question that arose was miscegenation—the mixing of races: "Is it a fact that any white race subject to continuous contact with the negro ultimately becomes mongrelized? When races intermix, does the inheritance of the more primitive, more generalized stock dominate the more specialized stock, or vice versa?"[86]

The ERO developed model legislation for establishing "racial purity" which was eagerly seized upon by Dr. Walter Ashby Plecker, Virginia's registrar of the Bureau of Vital Statistics, 1912-1946.[87] Passionate about the disgrace and evils of mulattoes, he urged the General Assembly to adopt the Racial Integrity Act in 1924 which mandated that anyone with "one drop" of Negro blood be classified as a Negro who could not, therefore, marry a white person. The original draft of the bill applied to Indian blood as well, but the resulting uproar from Virginia's white "aristocracy"—descendants of Pocahontas through her son by John Rolfe—caused a hurried change: anyone 1/16th or less Indian, and with no other non-white ancestry, was white.

Virginia's law also called for mental defectives and "degenerates" to be sterilized for the good of society.[88] And it was that which brought ERO-trained Dr. Arthur H. Estabrook to Amherst County to investigate a case concerning a Charlottesville woman, Carrie Buck, who had been committed to the Virginia Colony for Epileptics and Feeble-Minded, now the Lynchburg Training School. [Buck lost both her local case and her appeal to the U. S. Supreme Court and was the first person sterilized in Virginia under the 1924 law.] While in Amherst, Estabrook learned about the county's "Issues"—the WINs, as he would name them: White-Indian-Negro—and decided to study the group since they seemed a prime example of the evils of racial mixing.

MONGREL VIRGINIANS

Estabrook's study, undertaken with colleague Ivan E. McDougle from Goucher College and ERO field workers, took more than a year as the team interviewed "all living members of the Win tribe . . . time and again." They also photographed both people and settlements as part of the study.[89] Using ERO protocol, they gathered family pedigrees to demonstrate the degenerate characteristics which, they argued, the Wins were passing on, such as drunkenness, promiscuity, mental impairment, and sloth. [Family names were slightly changed in the book to "protect" identities.]

According to a promotional brochure, the resulting book, *Mongrel Virginians: The Win Tribe*, was purely scientific, "a careful and one of the most comprehensive studies ever published, of the effects of racial miscegenation . . . [it presents] facts which have a bearing upon one of the most momentous issues which the nation is facing, that of racial integrity . . . [it is] a dispassionate presentation of facts. No 'moral' is drawn, and no 'solution' attempted. The authors have not been concerned with racial or political propaganda. They hold no brief on behalf of the Racial Integrity Law, or against it."

To the contrary, however, both Estabrook and McDougle were ardent proponents of racial cleansing. They declared the Wins to be as much Negro as Indian, which incensed the Monacans. The book received some very critical reviews from the academic and scientific communities which termed it "racist drivel" and bad science. It also split the Monacan people, those who had been interviewed feeling betrayed and suspicious thereafter of anyone with a notebook and a camera. Some of their Amherst neighbors were also appalled. "One lays down the book," one said, "amazed at the want of sympathy for a neglected people .

. . its publication against a helpless people done fictitiously except to the initiated [a reference to the thinly disguised false names given interviewees] wherein they have no recourse or chance of denial or disclaimer is ruthlessly and heartlessly cruel."[90]

In 1928, Bertha Pfister Wailes, a 1917 graduate of Sweet Briar College in Amherst County, wrote her master's thesis on the tribe and tried to negate the influence of Estabrook and McDougle's book. Wailes had worked with groups such as Sweet Briar's YWCA, which volunteered to bring church and social activities to the Monacans, so she knew personally a number of them. In *Backward Virginians: A Further Study of the Win Tribe*, she maintained that their "degeneracy" was the result of poverty, unemployment, and lack of education.[91]

But negative reviews of Estabrook and McDougle's "study" didn't help the Monacans. Their troubles were only beginning, for Dr. Plecker used the book to further his own agenda.

GENOCIDE

Plecker believed absolutely that Virginia's Indians had long since ceased to be pure-blooded after generations of breeding with Negroes. To prove his point, he went back to late 18th and 19th century official records such as the free black registers, the 1823 law which defined a mulatto, and carefully selected histories, all of which labeled the Indians as blacks or mulattoes. He was incensed that these "mongrels" were trying to pass themselves off as anything but colored and even aspired to be registered as white. Their designation as "Indian" on the federal census was a lie, and he fumed when the 1920 U. S. Census listed 1,261 "Indians, Chinese, Japanese and all other races" in Virginia (304 in Amherst County).[92] He used the Racial Integrity Act to influence the 1930 census, pushing through the addition of a footnote which stated that the Indian category "includes a number of persons whose classification as Indians has been questioned." Some local census workers, however, objected to his high-handedness and reported 779 Indians in Virginia.

Plecker began a vendetta to officially expunge Indians from Virginia, altering birth, death, and marriage records to make them "colored" or "Negro" so they could not use the Indian designation "as a way station to whiteness." A lengthy warning notice was attached to the back of birth and death certificates, spelling out Plecker's arguments and including citations from *Mongrel Virginians*. There were no Virginia Indians unmixed with Negro blood, it stated; therefore, they would be listed as Negro or colored.[93]

A later registrar, who had known Plecker, called his actions "documentary genocide." Plecker was to Virginia's Indians, he said, what Hitler was to the Jews.[94]

PLECKER'S LIST

As early as 1925, Plecker began to single out the Amherst and Rockbridge Monacans, a total of about 800 people, because they were "giving us the most trouble, through actual numbers and persistent claims of being Indians."[95] They fought him vigorously, firing off angry letters to the Census Bureau, refusing to be classified as black, and taking the state to court—sometimes successfully. What really galled Plecker was that some white officials in Amherst, such as the 1930 census taker, were defying the law and continuing to register people as Indian. When World War II broke out and Virginia's Indians were drafted as Negroes, some Monacans filed suit and won the right to be "white" or "Indian." In December 1942, further enraged by that court action, Plecker sent a letter to all local registrars, physicians, public health officers, school superintendents, nurses, and court clerks which "set forth the determined effort to escape from the negro race of groups of 'free issues,' or descendants of the 'free mulattoes' . . . as distinguished from slave negroes."

When that didn't work, he sent those same people another letter. Now, he wrote in January 1943, the Bureau had realized "the great mistake [we] made in not stopping earlier the organized propagation of this racial falsehood. They [the Indians] have been using the advantage thus gained as an aid to intermarriage into the white race and to attend white schools, and now for some time, they have been refusing to register with war draft boards as negroes . . . Upon investigation we find that a few local registrars have been permitting such certificates [white birth certificates] to pass through their hands unquestioned and without warning our office of the fraud. Those attempting this fraud should be warned that they are liable to a penalty of one year in the penitentiary."[96]

To aid them in "determining just which are the mixed families, [the Bureau had] made a list of their surnames by counties and cities," which was attached. Known or suspicious cases were to be reported to the Bureau, and Plecker warned that he would reject any certificate bearing one of those surnames and showing the race as Indian or white. He concluded with another warning: 150,000 "other mulattoes in Virginia are watching eagerly the attempt of their pseudo-Indian brethren, ready to follow in a rush when the first have made a break in the dike."

His list of suspicious families from Amherst County was by far the longest and most detailed enumeration: "Adcock (Adcox), Beverly (this family is now trying to evade the situation by adopting the name of Burch or Birch, which was the name of the white mother of the present adult generation), Branham, Duff, Floyd, Hamilton, Hartless, Hicks, Johns, Lawless, Nukles (Knuckles), Painter, Ramsey, Redcross, Roberts, Southwards (Suthards, Southerds, Southers), Sorrells, Terry, Tyree, Willis, Clark, Cash, Wood."[97]

During this period, a number of Monacan families moved from Virginia, beyond Plecker's reach, to states where they could be registered as white or Indian. Others who remained "went underground," hiding their heritage. Some Indian words had long been part of the community's culture, but they faded from use after World War II as many feared continuing to use them.

At the state level, the 1943 warning notice was not removed from Virginia's birth and death certificates until 1972, five years after the U. S. Supreme Court struck down the Racial Integrity Act.

THE MONACANS TODAY

The 1980s saw the beginning of a native resurgence in Virginia which led to eight surviving tribes being recognized by the state as indigenous.[98] The Monacans had already begun organizing themselves the previous decade, and their story became public in 1984 when Lynchburg physician Peter W. Houck wrote *Indian Island in Amherst County*. In 1989, they elected the first chief of the new Monacan Indian Nation and were granted state recognition as an indigenous tribe; House Joint Resolution No. 390 noted that "a clearly documented settlement of Monacan descendants has existed at Bear Mountain in Amherst County for over 200 years."[99] The Nation's motto acknowledges the bitterness of the 20th century: "History Preserved Is Knowledge Gained." Its seal incorporates the three crossed arrows that were a colonial symbol for the Monacans as well as a bear for their home, Bear Mountain.

During the 1990s, they began an annual Powwow, proceeds from which have enabled them to buy land on Bear Mountain for future tribal use. [Part of the first purchase encompassed an old burying ground now known as the ancestral cemetery.] In conjunction with that campaign to regain some ancestral lands, the Episcopal Church gave the tribe the 7.5 acres on which its mission had been located since 1908; these buildings now house tribal offices. The old log school was placed on both the Virginia and National Register of Historic Places, restored, and re-opened as the Monacan Ancestral Museum in 1998, and some ancestors were brought back from other counties and reburied at Bear Mountain. At nearby Natural Bridge, the tribe built the Monacan Indian Living History Village and staffs it with costumed interpreters.[100]

The Nation even operates its own website, www.monacannation.com. In 2007, Monacans joined with Virginia's other tribes to celebrate the 400th anniversary of the first English settlement in America at Jamestown. And the General Assembly passed House Bill 2165 designating the new U. S. Highway 29 bypass from the town of Amherst to Campbell County as the Monacan Parkway.

The tribal register numbers approximately 1,400 people today, many of them out-of-state descendants of families who fled from Amherst after 1924.

The last official vestige of the Plecker era disappeared in 1997, with the aid of the Virginia Council on Indians, when the General Assembly ruled that any Virginia-born Indian whose certified birth certificate showed an incorrect racial designation could have it corrected without charge by the Bureau of Vital Statistics.[101]

BUFFALO RIDGE CHEROKEES

To further complicate sorting out the history of Amherst Indians, there is also a group which claims ancestry from the Cherokees, and the two populations overlap. The Cherokees were one of the largest Iroquoian tribes on the East Coast, whose territory stretched at one time from Georgia and Alabama to the Virginias. They adapted more easily to European culture than did other tribes and intermarried with both blacks and whites.

The "Buffalo Ridge Cherokees" of Amherst County—named for the escarpment where some of them settled—have been the subject of two books written by Dr. Horace R. Rice.[102] Rice contends that a population of both bi-racials and tri-racials [Indian, Indian/black, Indian/white, and Indian/black/white] moved from the Tidewater to the Piedmont in the middle 1700s. Their surnames were Beverly, Branham, Carter, Coleman, Evans, Harris, Hartless, Johns, Pinn, Redcross, Sizemore, and Sparrow.[103] The duplication with Monacan surnames is due to marriages between the two groups, confusion resulting from incomplete and inaccurate records, and perhaps even misinterpretation of those records.

Rawley (Raleigh, Rolly, and possibly Rowland) Pinn, as an example, was a Baptist minister from Lancaster County in the "Northern Neck" of the state. Anita Wills, a descendant who has written and lectured on Virginia's colonial free blacks, believes Rawley's family was of the Wicomico tribe of the Powhatan Confederacy, the mother a Cherokee and the father a Spanish/Indian. Rawley's wife Sarah was an Evans and may have been Saponi, and a brother is said to have married a Cherokee woman. Rawley moved to Amherst County sometime after 1774 and joined the militia. In 1781 he, John Redcross, and Benjamin Evans were part of the 2nd Virginia Cavalry and left Amherst on June 21, 1781 under the command of Maj. William Cabell, Jr. Between Amherst and Yorktown, they joined the troops of the Marquis de Lafayette, and all participated in the siege at Yorktown.[104]

In tax lists from the 1780s, Rawley Pinn was a free white tithable, but the 1790 census lists him as mulatto. He did own land on Partridge and Mill Creeks in the Buffalo Ridge area and was related by marriage to the Beverly, Clark, and Redcross families. A published Monacan history describes him as "an important figure in the group . . . who witnessed numerous marriages and land transfers among the people of the Indian community and whose children married into the group.[105]

Rawley Pinn exemplifies the difficulty in trying to trace Indian, black, and racially mixed individuals and make exact pronouncements about who they were. Was he Cherokee? Was he Algonquian? Was his wife a member of an allied Monacan tribe?

The publication of Dr. Rice's 1991 book spurred the formation of the United Cherokee Indian Tribe of Virginia, Inc., which has headquarters in Madison Heights in Amherst County. The membership includes not only descendants of the Buffalo Ridge people but those from Stonewall Mills on Blackfoot Creek in Appomattox County (directly across the James River from Partridge Creek). They have tried several times to obtain state recognition as an indigenous tribe but have failed thus far.

Chapter 3

THE AMHERST COUNTY REGISTER

The "Amherst County Register of Free Blacks, 1822-1864" was discovered accidentally in 1977 by one of the authors of this study, Sherrie McLeRoy. She was then director of the Amherst County Historical Museum and had obtained permission to inventory the holdings on that county in the closed stacks of the Virginia State Library in Richmond.[106] The leather-bound volume which contained the Register was labeled on the spine as "Index to Deeds, 1845-1850, Invested and Reversed." For no particular reason, she leafed through it and found that only a few pages had been used to index deeds, with the remainder being the Register.

The authors speculate that an older, possibly original, Register had fallen into such disrepair that, at some point after 1845, it was copied into a newer ledger, one that simply happened to be available. The entries begin only in 1822, and there is every possibility that there was—perhaps, still is—an earlier volume that dates to the passage of the registration law in 1793.

After discovering the Register and having it photocopied by the Library, the authors worked with several persons at Central Virginia Community College in Lynchburg to sort and classify the Register entries according to surname, age, color, and method of obtaining freedom. (In 1977-1978, the only computer available to do this task was a large mainframe which required punch cards.) The Register proved to contain information on nearly 400 free persons of color—Negro and Indian—who lived in Amherst County between 1822 and 1864.[107]

Over the next decade, the authors supplemented this core of data with material from census schedules (personal and agricultural), legislative petitions, tax records (county and state), county minute books, and county court records such as deeds, wills, marriages, and plats. For this 2007 revision, they also studied the records of the Death Records Indexing Project of the Virginia Genealogical Society, county commissioner of revenue records, additional years of county court order books, and dozens of pertinent historical and genealogical sites that have blossomed on the Internet.

In some cases, the authors looked for specific names that have been identified as belonging to the study group; in others, they looked for official designation that the person for whom the record was made was a person of color. Census schedules, for example, list race, while some county records noted that one or more of the parties involved were freemen. The original edition of *Strangers in Their Midst* contained information on 800 persons in addition to those in the Register. In this revision, the authors have added about 350 more (for a study group of 1,500 to 1,600 individuals) and expanded more than 100 previous entries.

ABOUT THE REGISTER

Chapter 1 describes the history of the registers, from the passage of the law requiring them in 1793. The style of a register entry changed in 1806 when the Virginia General Assembly ordered that slaves freed after May 1st that year had to leave the state within twelve months. As a result, the county court clerks, who kept the registers, were then required to note in the individual entries that a person had been free himself, or was born of parents who had been free, prior to 1806.

In 1834, even this was further restricted, and a free colored person could not register at all without the permission of the county court. Yet not until December 1850 did the Amherst Register entries begin referencing the court term at which an individual appeared to request registration. Moreover, the court's permission did not guarantee that the individual would be physically entered into the Register. Between January 1851 and July 1860, there are at least 46 occasions when the Court ordered that a person be registered or renewed, but the clerk never actually entered his name. Betsy Pinn, for example, appeared before the Amherst County Court three times and was approved three times: her name does not appear anywhere in the Register. Thirteen of these omissions occurred in April 1851, ten in July 1860. Those were the two years of the highest registration, so it is possible the clerks were simply overwhelmed.

Too much work may also be the reason why some registrations were entered late. Most of the time, the clerks completed their work within a few days or, at the most, months after the end of the court term. There are several instances, however, when a year elapsed. The Court ordered Delaware Scott to be registered in April 1851 but the entry is dated September 6, 1852, while William Scott's entry was eleven months late. Similarly, Washington Peters and W. H. Peters were approved in June 1856 but not entered until July 21, 1857.

Changes in handwriting indicate that at least four or five different people in the Amherst County Clerk's Office penned the entries over the years.

BLACK COMPLIANCE WITH THE LAW

The penalty for failing to register and to keep a copy of the registration was severe: freedmen who did not have that copy on their person at all times could be jailed or even sold into slavery.

Yet, in reality, less than a third of the known free coloreds in Amherst County ever registered. Not only did they ignore the law, but county authorities often failed to enforce it because of the time and cost connected with prosecuting unregistered coloreds.[108] State and national events which threatened the institution of slavery usually brought on a flurry of registrations which soon, however, died down.

In 1831 and 1832, for example, following Nat Turner's Rebellion, 24 free Negroes and Indians registered in Amherst County—more than 6% of *all* those who registered in the entire period, 1822-1864. Forty coloreds registered in 1851 (the second largest number of registrations in any single year), probably in response to the Compromise of 1850, the strengthening of the Fugitive Slave Act, and the passage of new legislation further restricting the travel of free blacks in and out of Virginia. During this period, Amherst court records also noted that the registrants had been granted leave to remain in the Commonwealth of Virginia. In January 1860, following John Brown's raid on Harper's Ferry, the Amherst Justices ordered the sheriff to prepare a list of all unregistered free coloreds living in the county, an action they took in response to an order of the General Assembly. Almost immediately thereafter, the county court records show a heavy influx of free persons petitioning the court to be registered or to have their registers renewed—77 in all, the single greatest number for any of the years the extant Register was kept.

The most restrictive acts governing free coloreds were passed between 1840 and 1860. It is no surprise, then, to find that 72% of all the entries in the Amherst Register occurred during these two decades. In addition, the law required registration every three years or upon a change in county of residence, but nearly 75% of the Amherst group who registered only did so once. Samuel Beverly, for example, did not register until 1850 at the age of 53.[109] Official records concerning him, however, date back to 1819. In those intervening years, Beverly paid taxes, married, filed deeds, and appeared on four federal census schedules, one of which valued his personal estate at $3,000. Clearly, Samuel Beverly was not an unimportant man in his community, nor was he unknown to white county officials during this time.

It is interesting to note that, of all the near 400 people registered, all but two dozen were born free.

WHITE COMPLIANCE

The law of 1806 placed those slaveowners who wished to emancipate their slaves in a difficult position, for they had to provide for their removal from the state and consider what would happen to those who did not wish to leave. Most slaveholders freed their human property in their wills, and as a result, those documents became increasingly long and complicated as the masters tried to cover every contingency.

London banker and entrepreneur Samuel Gist owned nearly a thousand slaves and extensive lands in Virginia but never visited the state. His will, probated in 1815 when Gist died at age 92, freed his slaves and ordered his trustees to buy land in Ohio where they could settle. [See glossary for more details.]

Some owners offered their slaves an option if they did not wish to leave Virginia after emancipation, but it came at considerable cost to the slave: remain a slave but *choose* a new master. Thomas Higginbotham of Amherst County did this in his will (probated 1834); if they wished to stay, "they may choose any of my Brothers or Sisters they are willing to serve." Higginbotham created a legal mess for his executors because his will did not mention how the emancipations and subsequent travel were to be funded. [See the legislative petition of Washington.]

Richard Smith, who freed Leanty and her children in his 1836 will, did the same. He stipulated that "my executor do apply to the Legislature by Petition on the behalf of the said Slaves, praying that an act may pass allowing them to reside in this state."

Failing that, Smith named two alternatives. If Leanty and her family chose to leave, the monies he had bequeathed them were to help them settle in their new home; his executor was to aid them "by his advice and better lights on the subject." If, however, they chose to stay in Amherst and return to slavery, he allowed them the "liberty freely to choose from amongst my blood relations." Although he couldn't legally force the new master, Smith hoped that he "will not only treat them humanely, but shew [sic] them all the favour allowed by the laws of the land or the useages [sic] of our Society, and . . . to appropriate the money which may go with them [the money he bequeathed the slaves] to their extraordinary comforts and convenience."[110] Smith's executor did file a successful petition in Leanty's name. [See below.]

John Warwick freed all his slaves in his will, probated in 1848. "The future condition of my slaves," he wrote, "has long been a subject of anxious concern with me, and it is my deliberate intention, wish, and desire that the whole of them be manumitted and set free *as soon after my demise as the growing crops shall be safe and the annual hires terminated*," an indication that Warwick was one of the many owners who hired out their slaves to other farmers or to factories. [Authors' italics]

Apparently, he had already started this process before he died, sending some of the slaves to a free state. He specified that the remainder emancipated in his will also go to a free state, preferably Indiana, and he left his entire estate "for the purpose of creating a suitable fund in the hands of my executors for their comfortable clothing, outfit, traveling expenses and settlement in their new homes."[111] However, before his wishes could be carried out, Indiana had barred the further admission of free Negroes.

Amherst County Court Clerk Arthur B. Davies freed his 15 slaves in his 1853 will and directed that a debt due him be collected and used for their transport to Liberia or a free state. Like Smith, he gave them the option to remain in slavery by choosing a new master from "amongst any of my Legatees hereinafter mentioned, and therefore to become their Slaves for life," parents making the decision for their young children.[112]

Madison Heights tavern keeper Sally Taylor, who freed her "servant man" William Henry Jefferson in her 1853 will, also left $100 for his move to Liberia or a free state. [See glossary for more.]

Daniel Day used some rather unsubtle pressure on his slaves. They were to be hired out for three years after his death, emancipated at that time, and the money they earned used to pay their way to Liberia. Those who chose not to go were to be sold, "but with the view of Aleviating [sic] their Condition to some extent, it is my will that they may . . . Select the person, or persons to whom they wish to be sold . . . and my Executors, if satisfied that the persons so Selected . . . are humane persons, may Ratify, and Sanction such Selections." Day's will was written in 1855 but not probated until mid-1862, so it is not clear what happened to the slaves.[113]

Some owners gave much thought to what would be best for their slaves after emancipation. In his will, written in 1859 with civil unrest on the horizon, Robert Tinsley agonized over their disposition. One, his mistress' (Tinsley's wife) favorite, "will be better off in her hands than any where else," presumably if conditions worsened. Several were too old to move. "The liberation of Archy and Lindsey must be postponed till the death of their mistress. This however is the less objectionable as the former has a wife and children that he may not care to leave, and Lindsey will be with his mother." Once free, the two men were to given $100 each and "removed to some place where they can enjoy their freedom." The rest of the slaves would also be freed after Mrs. Tinsley's death and "removed at the expence [sic] of my estate to . . . Ohio or some other of the Western States." They were to be settled in families on land the estate bought, given $100 each, "a Substantial Suit of Clothes each Suitable to the Season and plain provisions Sufficient for a year Supply." If this scheme proved impossible, the estate was to bear the cost of sending them to Liberia. Tinsley also left $1,000 to a friend who was to "act as the Counsel and next friend of my emancipated Slaves."

OFFICIAL COMPLIANCE

Though Amherst County justices defended the well-being of slaves and free coloreds when necessary, as discussed in Chapter 1, they could also be unyielding. The authors studied the County Court order books for 1828, 1851, 1856, 1859, 1860, 1861, 1864, and 1865 as they were years of high registration or important outside events. In these volumes are several instances where the Justices refused to renew registers, usually for lack of proof of residence in Amherst County, and required the person to remove at once. In 1851, Maria Peters applied to have her registration renewed, but the Justices, on learning that she was actually living in Lynchburg, refused her and ordered her to return to the city and register there. A month later, Madison Scott was also rebuffed, though the minutes do not record his actual place of residence.

The early months of 1851 must have been particularly tense when the Justices considered a third case. A man named Peatross had been jailed because he did not have his free papers on him as required by law. When it appeared that Peatross was registered in Caroline County, the Court ordered him to return there, but only after he had been hired out by the Amherst County sheriff to pay back his court costs and jail expenses.

But also evident from these court records is that Amherst free coloreds had access to that same court for justice and used it, seemingly without fear or obstacle. Mary Alexander sued her master for prolonging her period of apprenticeship (1851); William Flint filed a petition apparently charging his apprenticed master with cruelty (1856); and Bob sued his late master's administrators, alleging that they detained him as a slave (1856).

Matters of apprenticeship or residence were the most common court cases, but in another instance the Justices heard a motion from Nelson H. Clarke asking that they grant him a certificate establishing that he was white. This was possibly due to an 1833 law which gave county courts the right to issue such certificates to "any free white person of mixed blood, not being a free person, nor a free Negro;" such a ruling was sufficient to protect "such person against the disabilities imposed by law on free Negroes."[114]

And occasionally the Court heard matters involving whites with free coloreds. In 1856, for example, they sent a case on to the Grand Jury, which then indicted A. Leftwich, a white man, for "allowing an unlawful assembly of negroes on his lawn." Whether this was a religious gathering or one related to education or even for some other purpose altogether, was not stated in the records.

LEGISLATIVE RECOURSE

The county court was not the only source of justice available to free persons of color: the Virginia General Assembly could permit slaves freed after 1806 permission to remain in the state. That body reviewed dozens of petitions each year and seems to have granted as many as it denied. Their judgments were recorded in the official records as law, though sometimes there were conditions attached. Jacob Spengler was permitted to remain in Rockingham County "subject to revocation if guilty of an offense," a common stipulation. John Booker bought his freedom from his Petersburg master, but the Act of 1806 stopped the emancipation before it was final; he was conveyed to the man who owned his wife. The legislature ultimately recognized Booker's industry, since he had accumulated considerable property, and allowed him to remain in Petersburg unless he broke some law; in that case, he would be ordered to leave. Michael Smith was allowed to remain in the state to complete making the payments required to purchase his wife, a slave, but he was warned that he would lose his freedom if he overstayed the time the legislature had allowed him.[115] Female petitioners who asked to remain frequently stated their inability to have more children and thus add to the free colored population. Those persons who had worked to earn money to purchase their freedom made note of their industry.

The authors studied the six extant petitions from Amherst County, all of them in the manuscript collection of the Library of Virginia, which pertain to permission to stay in the state. [Transcripts are in the Individual Data section of the book.] The latest one is dated 1837, perhaps indicating that freed slaves didn't even bother to plead their cases in the restrictive decades prior to the Civil War. Some of these documents are written quite simply; the reader can almost hear the voice of the freedman. Others are couched in elaborate terms, implying that the petitioner was educated himself—an unlikely supposition for a former slave, forbidden education—or that the petition was written for him by an educated white person. In a few cases, such as Washington's, it is clear that the petition was prepared by the executor of the late master's estate.

The earliest Amherst petition dates from 1811 and was a joint request from nine members of the Dean and Floyd families, all of them "lately emancipated from a State of Slavery by the humanity of Miss Margaret Rose & Capt. Jno. N. Rose to whom they of right belonged." Interestingly, the white men who signed it in support noted "that they are so nearly white that they could not be taken to be mulattoes, where they were not known." All were born and raised in Amherst County, though some now lived in Nelson. "For their peaceable disposition & industrious habits" they hoped to be granted permission; unfortunately, their petition was rejected.

The next document (1814) states that the petitioner, John Charleston, bought his own freedom and had since, "by his exertion," purchased his wife and two children. Charleston "feels an anxious desire to emancipate his said wife and two children, was it not that the laws of this state prevent their residing therein when freed." His request was granted.

The language of these documents is often heartrending. Leanty and her children stated in an 1837 petition that they would rather remain "slaves of the white man" than to leave their home in Amherst County, "where they are knowing and are known." The children Mary and Henry even offered to "freely relinquish their claim in favor of their mother." Betsey Long of New Glasgow [Clifford], whose husband purchased her freedom while himself remaining a slave—"an act of generosity and magnanimity that cannot fail to challenge the admiration of your honorable body"—pleaded that forcing her to leave "would render the noble bounty of her husband, instead of a blessing, the most grievous of curses." At the least, she hoped to be allowed to stay "so long as her husband may live or remain a slave." This story had as happy an ending as possible: the legislature granted Betsey's request and her husband's owner later freed him. He appears in the Amherst Register (#179) in 1847, though she does not.

Perhaps the most eloquent of these statements came in the 1836 petition of Washington, born in Amherst County in 1793 and freed in 1835 upon the death of his master, Thomas Higginbotham. [See earlier section on "White Compliance."] He declared that he "loves the country where he was born and raised, in sight of the bigg [sic] mountains, and away from the Sea—That he wishes not to go to Liberia amongst strangers, a good country for the youthful, who can learn new things, manners and pursuits, and form new connections in life, but to him that time is passed [sic], he is too old to learn new things, manners or habits and he desires to form no new connections in this life."

The sixth petition was from Archibald Carey, a one-time hack driver in the neighboring city of Lynchburg, who acquired considerable property in both that city and in Amherst County "by honest labor." Carey seems to have been pessimistic about his chances for he requested that, if his petition to stay was denied, he be given five years to dispose of his property and move. That much the legislature considered "reasonable." He was aided in his search for a new home by several Lynchburg men who wrote recommendations for him: ". . . it is earnestly hoped that all good citizens will permit him to travel about through the country until he can find a place suitable for him to settle on." He eventually moved to North Carolina.

Two other legislative petitions filed by Amherst residents had a more lurid character. In 1834, Lucy Watts filed for divorce from her husband James, stating that he had deserted her, returned, left for five years in the Army (presumably the U. S. Army), and then took up with "the most vicious and corrupted part of Society. He became attached to a free woman of color [unnamed], and claimed her as his wife, and carried her away with him when he left Lynchburg where he had enlisted as a soldier."[116]

A second divorce petition came from William Howard in 1809. He had married Elizabeth Dean in 1806 expecting that she would prove "faithfull [sic] to her Bed and Board, and in all respects discharge the duty of a good and faithfull wife." Soon Howard heard that when he was away on business, "his House was the resort of the idle, the Vicious, and dicipated [dissipated]" and that Elizabeth "was engaged in the most brutal and licentious connections, having no regard to persons or Coular [color]."

Howard magnanimously disbelieved the reports until he returned home one night and found his wife "in Bed with a certain Aldridge Evans a man of couler, and reputed to be a mulattoe."[117]

VOLUNTARY ENSLAVEMENT

The General Assembly provided yet another option to freed slaves, as freed persons of color could petition and choose voluntarily to return to enslavement. This became particularly prevalent in the 1850s, though only two dozen or so are believed to have tried it. No such petitions are known from Amherst County, but some masters—such as Leanty's and Washington's—specified in their wills that, if the freed slaves' request to remain in Virginia was denied, they be allowed to choose new masters from the old one's family. In 1856, the legislature stipulated that any free Negro of mature, consenting age could petition the court for a master; his value would be appraised and half that amount paid by the master to the court. The act was amended five years later to reiterate that freed children of such slaves did not themselves also become slave. The master chosen was required to take care of the children until they were of mature age and then to pay them for services rendered to him.

The only case found by the authors that might pertain to this law is that of Henry Ann, who was freed with her mother Frances and brother Marcellus by Sally Taylor in 1853. Yet a *slave* named Henry Ann, of the correct age, died of unnamed causes in 1859. Is it the same young woman? If so, what prompted her return to slavery? The answers remain to be found.

CONFUSION AND AMBIVALENCE

The generally ambivalent attitude of local whites and blacks alike toward the registration laws can be seen in the registration histories of 33 freed slaves living in Amherst County. Only nine individuals—comprising two families, both headed by females (Leanty being one of them)—registered within a year after being freed. [For another eight, the date of freedom could not be determined.] Five years was the *minimum* period elapsing between date of freedom and the initial, or only, registration. Even Washington allowed eight years to pass after the granting of his petition before he registered.

The very people most likely to be careful and protective of their freedom—former slaves—generally disobeyed the registration law, even though this failure could have meant their reenslavement. And this behavior was common among all free coloreds in the county. Why? There are several possible explanations for their inaction.

White officials themselves may have poorly enforced the law, for whatever reason. Illiteracy among free coloreds would have meant, literally, ignorance of the law and its ramifications. Perhaps it was as simple a matter as not keeping track of the calendar. Finally, some individuals may have been suspicious of any effort by whites to regulate or control them further.

But there could also be another interpretation: they simply felt no coercion to obey the law. In such a case, other free coloreds, especially those who were born free and had never known slavery, would have felt relatively secure about their status in the Amherst community.

Chapter 4

DEMOGRAPHY OF THE RURAL FREE COLORED

Demographic data gleaned from available public records indicate that 19th century free persons of color in Amherst County were very similar to their white counterparts: mostly farmers, with an average household size of five or six, under fifty years of age, born locally, and living on a subsistence to moderate income level.[118]

FREE BLACK HOUSEHOLDS

One difference between the two populations, white and black, was in the comparative percentage of females. Women comprised 48% to 50% of the white population in Amherst County for the census years 1810 to 1860, but they were 49% to 56% of the free colored population, a trend found throughout the state.[119] Among *all* the Negroes and Indians in the county, both free and slave, the proportion of male to female was nearly even, with females being 49.4% to 50.7% of the total non-white population of Amherst.

Many of the free black households listed in the federal census schedules were nuclear families: father, mother, and children. A significant number, however, were extended, that is, they contained a third or fourth generation. Also present were single member households, childless couples, and families headed by females. As many as 6% of the free colored women in Amherst County were the heads of their households—at least according to the census taker—and their average family sizes ranged from 3.8 to 6.3 people over the period 1810-1860. Average family sizes for free coloreds as a whole were 4.9 to 6.8 individuals, with 16 being the actual size of the largest household found.

FREE PERSONS OF COLOR IN WHITE HOUSEHOLDS

The census records also illustrate an alternative way of life for some free coloreds, that of living in a predominantly white household. In some cases, this was a single individual working for a white employer and presumably receiving room and board in lieu of, or in addition to, wages; occasionally an entire family lived in these circumstances. Luther Porter Jackson, in his classic work *Free Negro Labor and Property Holding in Virginia, 1830-1860*, speculated that such free coloreds functioned in much the same manner as house slaves, particularly in the Tidewater where, in 1860, free coloreds comprised as much as a third of the total non-white population. Their employment, he continued, was either in the form of an apprenticeship where the colored earned a small wage, or more in the manner of a slave, where he was fed, clothed, and housed in return for services. [Pages 70-73]

Sometimes one or two free coloreds, usually males, were listed in white households that also included slaves. In fact, 78% of the 82 Amherst whites listing free coloreds in their households in the census years 1810 to 1840 also owned slaves, though there seems to be little correlation between their numbers. Richard Ellis, with the largest number of slaves on that list (61), only housed one free Negro, whereas Joseph Higginbotham, with 25 slaves, had the largest number of free coloreds (12). It was not uncommon, as the value of slaves rose, for owners to hire them out and replace slave labor on the farm with that of free coloreds, who were cheaper to employ. Whether that is the trend demonstrated in these census figures is unclear. But it is worth noting that these Amherst slaveowners apparently felt no qualms or concerns about their safety with this close proximity of free coloreds—supposedly prone to fomenting rebellion among slaves—to their slaves.

What is surprising is the number of free coloreds who followed this lifestyle. As many as 23% of the entire free black population of Amherst County lived in white households at varying times over the study period 1810 to 1860. This may be attributed to several factors: a perceived need for physical security, the financial inability to maintain an independent unit, or the presence of family members among the slaves of that household.

OCCUPATIONS

The variety of occupations engaging free coloreds—mostly males—in Amherst County is astonishing. According to Register, census, court, and county records, free Negroes and Indians held these jobs: assistant housekeeper, blacksmith, canal laborer, carpenter, chair maker, commerce, cooper, ditch digger/

ditcher, domestic, farmer/planter, housekeeper, jobbing, laborer/farm laborer, manufacturing/trade, mechanic, miller, navigation/boatman, painter/gardener, shoe/boot maker, spinner/weaver, washer, wheelwright, and woodchopper.

Census records prior to 1850 listed only general fields of occupation—agriculture, manufacturing, etc.—so it is difficult to make judgments about the proportion of skilled to non-skilled labor. Commissioner of Revenue lists for 1861 provided occupations for about a third of the people listed (in this case, all male). Most of the Amherst free coloreds on that list—70% to 75% of those for whom occupations were listed—were engaged in some form of agriculture, either as farmers themselves or as laborers on other farms. Farming was generally the major employment of free coloreds and whites, both in Amherst County and throughout Virginia.

Another 13% of free coloreds were engaged in some business or craft endeavor. The Dean and Floyd families, for example (whose legislative petition was described earlier in Chapter 3), were described by their white sponsors as "generally useful and industrious mechanicks [*sic*]." There were ten shoe makers discovered for the study period, several of them from the same family. Among the Tylers were four shoe makers, probably all related; 1860 found the head of the family, William, living in a white household which also included a white shoemaker. Could they have been running a business together, or was William an employee? There were also two Hill brothers and two Peters brothers who practiced the same craft, as well as three Beverlys—probably a father and two sons—who were wheelwrights.

A third major area of employment was navigation. Boatmen were important in an area such as Amherst, where planters relied heavily on the local river systems to transport their goods to market.[120] The peak year was 1840, when 10% of all the boatmen in Amherst County were free coloreds. But late in 1840, the James River & Kanawha Canal reached Lynchburg and began to supplant the independent boatmen. By 1850, only two free blacks were described as boatmen, and within ten years, there were none.

For women, domestic service of some type was the main employment; but the only accurate figures are from 1860, when 22 free colored women in Amherst County were listed in the census as domestics or housekeepers.

Sometimes freed slaves were set up in business by their former masters, as in the will of James Hopkins, probated in 1803. Tom, his blacksmith, was to be allowed to rent the smithy tools he had used while a slave at *Annandale*, Hopkins' plantation, and to apprentice a young slave to the trade.

THE WAGES OF THEIR WORK

How much money free coloreds made from these occupations is hard to determine. Extant personal property tax records from 1821 to 1850 show that the average tax paid by them during this period fluctuated regularly and ranged from 11.9¢ to 22.9¢. Most of the taxpayers were male, and they constituted less than a quarter of the total known male free colored population at the time. Most of them had only one type of taxable property, horses, for which they paid tax varying from 8¢ to 14¢ over the study period.

In 1860, the personal property tax system was changed, providing a more detailed listing of taxable property and showing the value of that property rather than just the tax paid on it. The number of free black taxpayers also jumped dramatically at the same time, from 42 in 1850 to 71 in 1860. As the free colored population in Amherst actually had declined by 32% in that decade, this may reflect more thorough tax collection, increased wealth of local free coloreds, or a greater awareness of and more careful watch over them.

The average value of their taxable property in 1860 was $89.15, the actual low and high being $0 and $1,610 respectively. It is possible, however, that the high figure belongs to a white man and skews the average. The entry for James Pendleton lists one male free negro at the beginning and one white male at the end and includes 16 slaves. So which was James Pendleton?

The second highest valuation recorded in 1860 was $525 for the property of Frederick J. Beverly, the probable founder of Beverlytown and known to be a free colored. He was a wheelwright [who made and repaired wheels and wheeled vehicles] and a successful farmer, raising both livestock and "truck" produce.

Among the more valuable households on the 1860 tax rolls was that of Henry A. Peters. He owned three horses worth $150, eight cattle valued at $65, sheep and/or hogs at $25, and enough furnishings (furniture, linens, dishes) to be worth $55; among the latter items was a clock. His aggregate value for tax purposes was $295. Compare that to Peters' 1860 census entry which lists him with real estate worth $875 and personal property valued at $575. Frederick Beverly also owned a clock; his aggregate value for taxes was $525, while his 1860 Agricultural Census entry states that Beverly's land alone was worth $1,500.

Typical of the free black "middle class" might be James Foster, a farmer. His 1861 estate inventory shows that his most valuable possession was a yoke of oxen, valued at $40. Minimal house furnishings included a cupboard, an "old bed," a dinner pot, and one chair; he had also raised a "small quantity of tobacco." Altogether, the estate was estimated by the appraisers to be worth $83.50.[121] Still, Foster was much better off than the majority of those listed on the tax rolls, whose aggregate value in terms of dollars was zero.[122]

FREE COLORED SLAVEOWNING

Using the personal property tax lists and the federal census schedules, 14 free colored slaveowners from Amherst County are found in the study period. The largest was James Pendleton with 16 slaves. [He may have been white; see above.] All the others owned five or fewer. Typically, these men were listed as owners for only a year or so, though the reason for that is not clear.

Richard Hartless' records show one of the longer periods of ownership, beginning with the 1810 census which lists him with five slaves. Ten years later, he still owned five; but since the census by that time broke the entries down by age and sex, it is evident that they may have been a family unit.

Turner Pinn's ownership of slaves was the longest and extended over a decade, from four slaves in 1829 to two in 1840. Luther Porter Jackson speculated that these were "true" slaves utilized by Pinn on his expanding farm.[123] If Pinn actually was a Buffalo Ridge Cherokee, as Horace Rice states, that would tend to corroborate Jackson, since it was not unusual for Cherokees to own slaves.

The taxable value of these slaves is also difficult to determine since the records simply show the quantity of taxable goods (such as three slaves and two horses) and the amount of tax owed. By using an average tax value of 12¢ for a horse, we can extrapolate taxes of 22¢ to 89¢ paid for each slave listed from 1821 to 1840. No records were found of free Negro slaveowners between 1841 and 1859, probably a reflection of the laws restricting them from holding slaves other than family members. Only two owners were found in 1860, one of them James Pendleton, whose identity is not certain; the other, Abram Martin, was definitely a free person of color.

The county's Death Records include a few more slaveowners. A total of four slaves owned by Sam Sparrow died in 1858 and 1859. Sparrow is a common free colored name, and it is possible this entry refers to Sampson Sparrow. A slave named Mealy Johns and an unnamed Johns slave both died in 1860; the owner's first name is difficult to read but appears to be Simpson Johns. Two other deaths in 1859 were listed in the slave column but are probably an error. [Marcellus Redcross, son of Paul Redcross, and Nancy Tyree, daughter of Wm. Tyler.]

BIRTH PLACES AND DATES

Places of birth were available for only 212 people from the entire study population. All of them were born in Virginia, 67% in Amherst County and 7.5% in adjoining Nelson County, which was formed from Amherst in 1807. As a whole, 98% were born west of Richmond, an indication perhaps that free blacks tended to move from their birth area less frequently than whites. This would be in accordance with the many laws prevailing in the early-to-mid-19th century which restricted their travel.

Birth dates, however, were more plentiful from census and death records and from the Register. Of the 1,013 birth dates determined, 17% of the study group were born prior to 1801. The birth rate then dropped off; only 172, or another 17%, were born in the first two decades of the 19th century, and 122 in the third decade. The largest and most dramatic rise then occurred: 42% of the study group was born between 1831 and 1850.[124] A sharp drop followed in the last decade before the Civil War with 104, or 11%, born between 1851 and 1860.

HEALTH

By using the Register and death records, it is possible to more closely examine the personal lives of the Amherst free coloreds.[125]

County registers contained detailed, sometimes minute, descriptions of individuals so they could be truly identified in the event of a question about their free status, hence the catalog of scars and marks that could be easily discerned in a quick examination. Whenever possible, the county clerk recording this information included a remark about the cause of the scar. A burn, for example, leaves a different scar from a cut, which in turn can be caused by a variety of sharp items.

The authors studied only those scars which were unusual or were accompanied by some brief explanation as to cause, and the result was revealing. As might be expected, men had more injuries than women, and many were incurred in daily work. Fingers were smashed under cart or wagon wheels, sharp "reap" hooks [curved blades used to harvest grains, etc. by hand] sliced fingers, and even a drawing knife [blade with a handle at each end for woodworking] could slide off and cut the user. Among the Amherst free men, we also found several instances of injuries resulting from a pistol shot or from gunpowder exploding close to the face. One blacksmith was missing his three upper front teeth, possibly a legacy from a cranky horse. Another man had been stomped by a horse and had the scars to prove it on his eyebrows and nose. Cuts from knives and axes were common. Three men were even missing body parts: a left hand cut off at the wrist (as well as the bottom of his right ear), a right eye missing, and a right arm lost just above the elbow.

There may even have been one example of a genetic trait. Three Tyler men all had little fingers that were crooked; Elizabeth Tyler, a sister and/or cousin, had this characteristic, too, but on only one hand. Possible examples of physical abuse also showed up in the analysis. Both William H. Jackson and his mother Judy Jackson carried scars from being hit by a blow to the head. Sam Arnold also had such a scar.

Only two people had pitted skin resulting from smallpox. One man had a shortened leg from white swelling, several carried scars of scrofula, and another had a speech impediment.

Among the women, burns were by far the most common injury, from dealing with fires every day used to cook food, wash clothes, and warm the house. Mary Beverly had a right eye that was nearly white, and she was partially blind in the same eye, no doubt from glaucoma. A few had cuts—one woman had even cut off the end of a finger with a knife or axe—but overall, that type of injury was much more common among the men.

CAUSES OF DEATH

Just over 100 persons could be certainly identified in death records as belonging to the study group. Sixty-three percent were males and the remainder females. The leading causes of death were pneumonia (10%), followed by diphtheria and "unknown causes" (16%). [See glossary for medical terms.] Consumption, fever, flux, old age, and typhoid fever took 35%. An additional third of the deaths were attributed to cold, colic, croup, dropsy, dysentery, heart disease, scrofula, spasms, suffocation, and whooping cough. [Suffocation took the lives of two month-old babies and was likely what we would today call Sudden Infant Death Syndrome.] The remainder of the causes ranged from apoplexy to St. Anthony's Fire to worms.[126] A number of these diseases tended to be seasonal. Pneumonia, for example, struck primarily in the coldest months, while flux, dysentery, and typhoid were summer killers.

As for age of death, these records also show a heartbreakingly high level of infant mortality: almost a third of the dead were three years old or less. Children and adolescents account for another third. Only 7% of the study group in these records died of "old age," 71 years or older.

Sometimes parts of entire families were killed when a virulent disease entered the household and spread from one person to another. In October and November of 1860, Fred Cousins lost three of his sons—aged 40, 20, and 18—to consumption (tuberculosis). Three Richeson children, ranging in age from 8 to 20, all died of a fever in May and June, 1864. The newly-freed Christian family lost three members in June and July, 1864: two to typhoid fever and one to colic. The most tragic deaths also happened in September and October of that year, when diphtheria swept through another family recently freed from slavery and killed five Rutherford boys and their sister. The youngest was a baby of only eight months, the oldest 14.

From the death records, another interesting fact emerged. Most of the entries included the name of the informant, the person who notified the county authorities of the death. From 1861 through 1863, records for Amherst are missing; but beginning in March 1864, there are over 60 entries where the informant is the deceased's *former owner*. Most of them are in 1864 and 1865, but listings still continued as late as 1867. The authors were unable to locate recorded deeds of manumission for *any* of the slaves involved.

What does that mean? First, it may indicate that owners glimpsing a less than optimistic future hastened to free their slaves before the war's end. Perhaps in the chaos of the times, they were unable or unwilling to spend the time to go into town and record a deed, simply giving the freedman a signed paper stating his manumission.

The former owner's presence in the listings also tells us that, in the midst of war and Reconstruction, he was keeping track of his "people," who were likely still living on or very close to his property.

Chapter 5

FARMING AND LAND OWNERSHIP

Most Amherst free coloreds were engaged in agriculture to some extent. Available records indicate that most of them were sharecroppers and lived on a subsistence level, able to meet the needs of their family unit only, and that just barely.

AGRICULTURAL CENSUS

But there were exceptions. A small number of Amherst free coloreds did own land and were commercial farmers who produced a significant surplus for sale or barter. Valuable information regarding them can be found in the 1850 and 1860 federal census records.[127]

For those two reporting years, the census included a separate agricultural schedule which listed the number of improved acres and heads of livestock, quantities (and in some cases, values) of crops, and value of machinery owned by the state's farmers. Among free Amherst County Indians and Negroes there are 13 such entries in 1850 and 21 in 1860. Six persons have entries in both years, including the following four individuals.

COMMERCIAL FARMERS

Tarleton Johns was especially successful. The value of his farm nearly tripled between 1850 and 1860, yet the amount of acreage actually declined. The value of his livestock also tripled, and he increased or doubled his crop yields. His most dramatic crop rise was in tobacco, from 750 pounds in 1850 to 4,000 pounds ten years later: clearly, a commercial venture. Johns also raised the standard crops of Indian corn, wheat, oats, Irish potatoes, and beans. He may have marketed some of his meat; in 1860 he listed $92 worth of slaughtered animals. What accounts for his success? The probable answer lies in another figure furnished by the Agricultural Schedule. The value of Tarleton Johns' machinery increased from a minimal $6 to $80, a thirteen-fold increase which most likely reflects his use of improved technology.

Edmund Branham was another commercial tobacco planter, increasing his yield over the decade from 1,000 to 3,000 pounds. He also may have sold butter (150 pounds in 1860) and meat ($105 worth of slaughtered animals.) Branham also invested in machinery, though his increase was only half that of Tarleton Johns'. Again, the farm size declined, in this case by more than a half, while the value of the land increased.

Samuel Beverly, on the other hand, had doubled the size of his farm on Harris Creek near Bear Mountain by 1860, and his 40 acres were valued at $2,100. Some of his crop yields declined as he seems to have concentrated on truck produce and tobacco. The 1850 census does not show that he was raising tobacco, but the 1860 schedule lists 3,400 pounds. Likewise, in 1860 Beverly was raising orchard products and had a market garden worth $40; he also sold beeswax and meat. Like Branham and Johns, he bought machinery, doubling his mechanical investment.

Frederick J. Beverly [whose exact relationship to Sam is unclear] had the largest free colored farm in the 1860 schedule. The bulk of his 513 acres on Brown's Creek at Beverlytown was unimproved, reducing the total value of the farm to only $1,500. Like Sam, Frederick apparently began raising tobacco in the 1850s; his 1860 schedule shows 2,000 pounds raised. And his increased use of farm machinery shows nearly as dramatic a rise as Tarleton Johns', from $15 to $155. Beverly raised and presumably sold orchard products, butter, beeswax, and honey.

These men typified the gains in property made by Virginia free coloreds between 1830 and 1860. Luther Porter Jackson's figures indicate that the amount of acreage and the number of farms and town lots they owned doubled in quantity and value over those thirty years, while the population grew only 20%. The significance of this gain is best seen in his assertion that Virginia's free negroes of 1860, proportionately, owned as much land as did all the state's "coloreds" in 1891. And he singled out Amherst County, noting that the free coloreds there had a 500% gain in acreage from 1830 to 1860, ranking the county high in terms of land ownership. [128]

EXPERIMENTING WITH OTHER CROPS

All four farmers raised quantities of tobacco, but how prevalent was it among other free colored farmers? All but three of the 28 farmers listed on the two agricultural schedules grew "the golden weed." Some produced as little as 400 pounds, probably enough to barter for other goods, but some raised 1,000 or more pounds.

As important as tobacco was, especially to the larger commercial farms, not everyone depended on it. In fact, Jackson notes two other areas of specialization among free colored farmers: hog and corn raising and truck gardening.[129]

James Clarke, Samuel Beverly, and William Peters together produced 77 pounds of wool, while Peter Curry and Henry Peters also raised sheep in addition to other grain crops. Judy Cousins was one of the more successful truck farmers; her market garden was valued at $500. She also produced 1,000 pounds of butter, 6 pounds of hops, and an astonishing $2,000 worth of slaughtered animals. The most valuable farm among the 28 free black farmers belonged to Samuel Scott; his 340 acres (200 of them improved) were valued at $7,000. His was also one of the highest yields of tobacco—4,000 pounds—which he probably raised on his acreage along the James River in the Porridge Creek area.

NEW TECHNOLOGY

The two decades prior to the Civil War were years of abundance for Virginia farmers due to a number of agricultural improvements. New marl fertilizers helped make the land richer and more productive. Tobacco continued to be the main cash crop though its decline was already beginning, while orchard products and grains became more popular. And new machinery such as McCormick's reaper, developed near Amherst County, made farming more efficient.

That the more successful Amherst free colored farmers took advantage of this new technology is evident from the 1850 and 1860 agricultural schedules. New crops such as buckwheat, flax, rye, and fruits began to appear next to the traditional oats, corn, and potatoes. The total value of the machinery owned by the 28 farmers quadrupled over the decade from $162 to $648. One notable exception to this rule among the commercial farmers was Judy Cousins, for whom no machinery is listed at all.

Livestock was still the backbone of the farm, serving as both draft animals and products. Most farmers had a milk cow or two and raised beef cattle; a few, unable to afford horses, worked oxen. Most of those who paid personal property taxes did so on horses or cattle and, occasionally, on sheep or hogs.

LAND OWNERSHIP

The majority of the Amherst free coloreds owned little beyond a horse, a few pigs, and some household goods; but at least 16 of them owned 100 or more acres in the county. Yet 13 of the 28 farmers listed in the agricultural schedules show no entry for lands owned, and a majority of the remaining study group also shows no evidence of land ownership, even those designated as farmers. These were probably tenant farmers, and they represent 90% to 95% of the total population being studied here. Tenancy was the most common way to acquire the use of land and enabled even the poor to farm enough land on which to live.

The similarity of some names between whites and blacks, and the uneven enforcement of the law, makes it difficult to determine land ownership through legal records. With the exception of a few surnames such as Branham, Johns, and Pinn, most of the Amherst free coloreds are hard to distinguish by name from whites unless the record clearly states they are non-white. Sometimes only a slight difference in spelling exists: Penn was generally white, Pinn colored. Even that minor distinction was often confused by harried or uneducated clerks.

There were, for example, two Samuel Scotts living in Amherst County at the same time, one a white doctor and the other a free Negro farmer. Because the deeds failed to recognize one of them as a "free man of color," it is impossible to sort out most of their legal records. In a society which legally regulated free coloreds as much as did 19th century Virginia, one might assume that legal records would carefully distinguish whites from blacks. But such was not the case. In only a few instances do the phrases "free person of color" or "colored person" occur in the Amherst deed books. Marriage records, wills, and plat books were the same.

That caveat aside, however, many of the deeds which are clearly those of free coloreds describe either inherited land, family relationships, or both. In 1778 Thomas Johns gave his brother Robert 100 acres "for love and affection;" the tract was part of 218 acres Thomas had inherited from their father Robert.[130]

Isabella Williams sold Frederick J. and Sarah Ann Beverly her half interest in 115 acres, as well as livestock and household goods, in exchange for "support" during her lifetime. [This deed is one of the few in which both parties are identified as "coloured persons."][131] The family ties here are harder to sort out. Evidence indicates that Frederick Beverly also appears in the records as James F. and James Beverly. [See page 37.] If so, he and Isabella bought the land together. Sarah Ann is probably Isabella's daughter, and the deed may indicate that they took care of her in old age.

The most unusual family land transaction involved William Johns and his six children. In 1856, William "surrendered" his property on Bear Mountain, totaling over 400 acres, and divided it equally among his five surviving children and the widow of a sixth. In return, they were each to pay him $20 rent per year during his lifetime.[132]

In some cases free negroes, especially freed slaves, acquired their property as a gift from a white person. In 1848 Sally Taylor freed Frances and her three children; five years later, she willed them a plot "adjoining what is known as the Quarry lot on the public road."[133]

Other free blacks applied for and received grants of land from the State of Virginia. Tobias acquired several hundred acres on "Hatt" [Hat] Creek in the late 1790s. Soloman Ritchey was given 170 acres on Pedlar River in 1803 and 150 acres on Staton's Creek in 1817.

Chapter 6

BRIEF HISTORY OF AMHERST COUNTY

Located on the eastern slope of Virginia's Blue Ridge Mountains, Amherst County is a land of rolling hills and ancient mountains, of fertile green valleys, clear rushing streams, and majestic waterways. The James River, which cuts east-west through the heart of Virginia and has played a major role in its history and development, forms the county's entire southern boundary, while the northern and northwestern borders are marked by the Tye and Piney Rivers. The floodplains of all three are similar: broad sweeps of rich sandy soil, built up by repeated floods, and nourished by the minerals and topsoil washed into them. They have been cultivated for hundreds, if not thousands, of years, by native tribes and later by European settlers.

The western side of the county is guarded by the high, shadowed mountains of the Blue Ridge, so called for the light blue, humid haze that hangs over them. Ranging from 3,000 to 4,000 feet above sea level in height, they are part of a larger chain forming the eastern side of the Great Valley of Virginia. Roughly paralleling them to the east is Buffalo Ridge, a much lower, more geologically worn outcropping composed of soft limestone, shales, and sandstones. Between these two lies a wide valley in which much of the settlement of Amherst County took place.

FRONTIER DAYS

The first white men to see the beauty of this land were 17th century explorers seeking new and untouched wilderness for hunting and trapping. [For the Indian history of the county, see Chapter 2.] Among them were the German emigrant and Quaker, John Lederer, who wrote several important accounts of his travels; Allen Tye, who gave his name to the Tye River; and a man now known only as Trader Hughes, who built a log trading port—probably the first permanent structure in Amherst County—in the forest behind the present Otter Lake.

Settlers were next. Their earliest communities in what is now Amherst County dated from the 1730s and 1740s and tended to follow an ethnic pattern: English in the west and east, Scots in the north and west.[134] A number of prominent Tidewater Virginians also invested in land here. One speculator was the English firm of Harmer and King, which established a largely German settlement at Nassau, which lay along Rucker's Run in modern Nelson County.

Then a part of Albemarle County, the area grew quickly as newly arrived immigrants from Europe, farmers, and restless coastal Virginians were lured there by the region's cheap, fertile land. They soon established tobacco as their major cash crop, transporting it down the James River by canoe to the markets at Richmond. Elegant houses, a prosperous economy, and a flourishing social life resulted. New Glasgow [now Clifford] became the area's social center and boasted a racetrack, taverns, and finely crafted homes. During the Revolutionary War, a supply depot for the Continental Army was also located in the town. Patrick Henry's mother and sister lived at *Winton* plantation, and even Thomas Jefferson was moved to predict that New Glasgow would one day rival New York in size and importance.

FORMATION OF AMHERST COUNTY

In 1761 the Virginia General Assembly recognized the rapid growth in this section of Old Albemarle County and carved out a new county, naming it Amherst in Honor of Sir Jeffrey Amherst, hero of Canada and a governor (non-resident) of Virginia. The courthouse was located at Cabellsville, now Colleen in Nelson County, but then the geographic center of the county and on the main stage road from the Carolinas to Washington and Philadelphia.

At about the same time, Anthony and Benjamin Rucker, two brothers from the Pedlar Mills area, improved upon the old double-dugout canoe, which had been used for several decades to transport hogsheads of tobacco and other goods by water. Their new "James River Batteau" found favor with many central Virginia tobacco planters—including Thomas Jefferson—and is believed to have been an inspiration for the later flatboat.

That development helped make Amherst tobacco an important product, and several English and Scottish firms became influential in the county's commercial and cultural life.

The Revolutionary War touched Amherst little, physically, though many of its men served in the Continental Army. [For free coloreds who served, see Chapter 2 and Individual Data Listings.] In 1776, Scottish soldiers captured before war was even officially declared were sent to Amherst and held as prisoners of war until being exchanged in 1778; at least one later returned to settle and still has descendants living there.[135] Some Hessian soldiers captured at Saratoga and imprisoned near Charlottesville escaped to Amherst County where they married local women and were welcomed as "valuable artizans [sic]." British loyalists, by contrast, were promptly investigated and, if found guilty, their property was seized and sold: Amherst alone realized almost half a million pounds sterling from such seizures. State authorities regularly requisitioned wagons, clothing, and food from county citizens for the soldiers; during the conflict, some necessary supplies such as salt were scarce and taxes high.

The conclusion of the war brought prosperity and further growth to the area. In the westward expansion that followed, the population of Virginia's mountainous interior grew rapidly. Tobacco, "the golden weed," remained the state's main cash crop; to more easily transport it to market, roads were built, ferries established, and the great waterway to the west—the James River and Kanawha Canal, the first navigation canal system in America—was begun. In only seven years, from 1783 to 1790, Amherst County's population jumped 29%; for the central part of the state as a whole, that figure was 40%.

DIVISION OF THE COUNTY

In 1807, the General Assembly further divided the region, the southern half retaining the name of Amherst County and the northern part becoming Nelson. A new county seat, Amherst Court House, was established at the small village of Five Oaks. Business continued to flourish, though the sharp rise in population began to taper off after the War of 1812, when many Virginians moved west into Kentucky and Tennessee. Miners extracted rich deposits of copper, iron, and slate from quarries throughout the county; hundreds of Irish workers poured in to build the Blue Ridge and the James River and Kanawha Canals, which ringed the southern and western boundaries. Resorts opened at several sulphur springs, and lumbermen began to commercially cut the great virgin forests of northern Amherst. Tobacco made the neighboring city of Lynchburg the second wealthiest for its size in the country, and that prosperity spilled over into Madison (Heights), located in southern Amherst on the bluffs above the James River.

SLAVERY AND CIVIL WAR

It was long believed that the percentage of slaves in western counties during the decades between the Revolution and the Civil War was relatively low, in comparison to the coast, due to different farming techniques and smaller plantations. If Amherst is a typical county, however, that belief is inaccurate. For the census years available between 1793 and 1860, slaves increased from 39% of Amherst's population to a high of 53% (1820) before declining to 45% on the eve of the Civil War.[136] Even as that population fluctuated, the free persons of color remained a constant 2%-to-3% of the county's inhabitants; in actual numbers, they nearly doubled until 1850. In the following decade, their numbers declined by nearly one-third.

Slaveowning was common in Amherst, and more than half of all households possessed slaves. The number of large slaveholders, however, was low; in 1850 and 1860, for example, only six people owned 80 or more slaves. Most owners held fewer than thirty and 50% of Amherst slaveholders owned five or fewer, probably house servants.[137]

When the Civil War erupted in 1861, Amherst was a typical central Virginia community. It was largely agricultural with an emphasis on tobacco as a cash crop, had a stable slave population of nearly 50% the total number of inhabitants, and nurtured the beginnings of an industrially based economy. There was little military action in the county during the war years except for Union general Hunter's abortive attempt in 1864 to capture Lynchburg, a valuable supply center for the Confederacy on Amherst's southern boundary. In proportion to its population, however, Amherst is said to have furnished more men to the South than any other county in Virginia.

But lack of military action did not mean lack of hardship. County court records referred to "these times of trial and difficulty" and "the mighty struggle in which we are now involved and upon the issue of which depends all that is most dear to free men." [August 1864] They go on to paint a bleak picture of the area's agricultural problems. Grain was scarce, the wheat crop a failure, and corn "very unpromising," all due to drought. Smallpox had been reported in the Temperance District, and salt—essential for preserving meat—was so scarce the Court voted in August 1864 to take out a loan for $25,000 (Confederate money, presumably) from an unspecified Lynchburg bank to buy supplies of it. The county was also paying stipends to needy families of Confederate soldiers. By November, matters had not improved. "The excessive drought of the past summer [has] reduced the crop so much that there is not Bread enough in the county for the consumers."

If the war spared Amherst military damage, its aftermath brought devastation. Southern capital invested in slaves was lost, Confederate paper money was worthless and hard cash non-existent, farms lay fallow, and the demand for Virginia's dark leaf tobacco declined as Kentucky developed its less expensive white burley tobacco.

INTO THE TWENTIETH CENTURY

In an attempt to rebuild the state's agricultural economy after the war, Virginia farmers experimented with other crops and discovered that the central Piedmont region was ideal for growing fruit trees. Peach and apple orchards appeared in Amherst, where they still constitute a major cash crop. The Ralls apple, first grown on Tobacco Row Mountain in the late 18th century, is a parent of the modern Fuji apple.

The James River and Kanawha Canal was abandoned when it became unprofitable, and its path became the route of the "iron horse" that supplanted it. A new courthouse was built in 1870 on the site of the original structure and, with a recent addition, still serves the county today. Libraries were established; the Elon facility (1915) is thought to be the oldest rural public library in Virginia. Among the many private schools established in this period was that at *Kenmore*, founded by Henry Aubrey Strode in 1873. Strode, who is buried in Amherst, became the first president of South Carolina's Clemson University in 1890. Sweet Briar College, an internationally recognized school for young women, opened in 1906 with a class of 36 students; its 3,000 acre campus encompasses the old *Locust Ridge* plantation of the 1790s. The county's first public high school was built in Amherst in 1912.

As Amherst moved into the 20th century, new railroad lines were built, and Monroe became a major yard. It was from there that Engine #1102 departed on a fateful September day in 1903 to go down in history as "The Wreck of the Old '97." Pedlar Dam was built in the first years of the 20th century to furnish water to Lynchburg, and a hydroelectric plant (1909) at Snowden—once on the old canal route—provided water to Bedford.

The timber industry became important again, though a major setback occurred in the 1920s when chestnut blight struck the forests. Many businesses then turned to pulpwood and veneer logs with such success that, in the 1950s, Amherst County ranked third in the state in production of pulpwood. One important lumber town of the early 20th century, Lowesville, enjoyed a brief resurgence in 1942 when it became a training area for American troops being sent to invade Sicily.

One county resident who achieved great fame in the mid and late 20th century was folk artist Queena Stovall (1887-1980), who began painting at the age of 62. Her "naive" paintings of life in Amherst County among both whites and blacks when she was young have hung in galleries and museums across the country, and she has been called the "Grandma Moses of Virginia."

For several decades (1940-1960), the county's population remained fairly stable at around 20,000. This began changing in the late 1960s and the 1970s when several major manufacturers began to locate there. By 1990 there were 28,000 residents, at least half of them located in southern Amherst, bordering on Lynchburg. Today the population has passed 32,000 and is predominantly white (78.3%), a vast difference from the 19th century. [Black: 19.7% American Indian: .8%]

Modern Amherst County has nearly 2,000 businesses producing everything from building steel to cuckoo clocks to plastic bags. Its northern half remains largely agricultural and rural, but even the most isolated settlements and homes now have electricity. The industrialized central and southern portions serve as "bedroom communities" where many residents travel to work in

Lynchburg or other counties. A significant number of retirees and "over-65s" call Amherst home, making up 15.2% of the population (11.4% for the state). Tourism brings many visitors, drawn chiefly by the Blue Ridge Parkway (National Park Service), which snakes through the western side of the county.

There has been a resurgence of interest in, and preservation of, the county's many 18th and 19th century buildings, though a few have been lost. The Amherst County Historical Museum was founded in 1976 to "explore the roots—the heritage—of Amherst County" and today has grown to encompass several historic buildings. The old James River Batteau, invented in Amherst, has also been revived in an annual festival and race which attracts thousands of spectators and several dozen homemade batteau and their crews who brave the river.

And despite Thomas Jefferson's faith, New Glasgow never became another New York.

But it sure is prettier.

Glossary: General Terms

Apprentice: a person legally bound, usually for a period of years, to learn a trade or profession.

County Court: in rural Virginia, this group of elected Justices not only governed the county and oversaw its daily management, but tried defendants and heard civil suits. They oversaw roads, probated wills, ordered deeds to be recorded, granted permits, appointed sheriffs, and authorized expenditures, among other duties. Today, in Amherst County, their successor is known as the Board of Supervisors and serves a strictly governmental purpose.

Court of Oyer and Terminer (literally, to hear and determine): a court that heard cases of felony and misdemeanor charges and made rulings on them. Also known as a called court. Slaves were tried for felonies only in these courts. There was no appeal of the court's decision.

Court order books: records of the proceedings and decisions of the county court.

Demography: description of a people or a community in terms of their social relationships and institutions, such as population, age, etc.

Ditcher: men who worked at such jobs as digging graves, gutters, drainage ditches, icehouses, canals, and dikes.[138]

Emancipate (noun: emancipation): to legally free an individual from slavery. A variation was "conditional manumission," in which a slave would be freed after a specified number of years of additional service. Usually this was to provide the master's spouse with support after his death.

Free colored, free black, free issue, free person of color: in antebellum legal terminology, this meant any non-white, non-Asian person.

Indentured servant: a person legally bound for a period of years to work for another as a servant, in exchange for passage to America. Indentures were almost completely under the control of their masters, and their contracts could be bought and sold. Like later slaves, runaway indentures were hunted and punished. Despite these hardships, an estimated 80,000 or more indentured servants made their way to Virginia in the colonial period.

Liberia: a country on the west coast of Africa.

Manumit (noun: manumission): to set free an individual from slavery.

Mestizo: a person with mixed Indian and Caucasian or black ancestry.

Mulatto: technically, a person with mixed Negro and Caucasian ancestry. In the Lower South, it meant any person of mixed ancestry, but in Amherst County, the term usually referred to someone of Indian or mixed Indian ancestry.

Ordinary: a tavern where food, liquor, and lodging were available. They were licensed and regulated by the county court.

Suffrage: the right to vote.

Tenant farmer: person who rents or pays some other fee for the land he farms.

Truck farm: one on which fruits and vegetables are grown in great quantities for sale in a market; also known as a market garden.

Virginia House of Burgesses: legislative body of the colony of Virginia; known by this name until the American War of Independence.

Virginia General Assembly: legislative body of the Commonwealth of Virginia; known by this name after the American War of Independence. Also referred to as the Legislature.

Glossary: Medical Terms

Apoplexy: a stroke, or paralysis due to a stroke.

Colic: spasms in the abdomen, which were painful but rarely fatal.

Consumption: an historic name for tuberculosis because it wastes away or "consumes" its victims.

Croup: an obstructive condition of the larynx or trachea which caused a barking cough and difficulty in breathing.

Diphtheria: Formation of a tough membrane in the throat which causes high fever, difficulty in breathing, and weakness. It was sometimes confused with scarlet fever or croup.

Dropsy: an abnormal collection of fluid in tissues and cavities, which can lead to congestive heart failure.

Dysentery: also known as bloody flux; an inflammation of the intestines.

Enteritis: inflammation of the bowels.

Flux: drainage or discharge of liquid from a body cavity, such as a hemorrhage or diarrhea.

Scrofula: one of the oldest documented infectious diseases. It is a tubercular infection of the lymph nodes which causes glandular swelling in the neck. It most commonly struck children and young adults.

St. Anthony's Fire: a contagious skin disease which produces bright red lesions.

Typhoid fever: an intestinal inflammation and ulceration—similar to typhus—which was once common in the summer and often fatal.

White swelling: also known as tuberculosis of the bone. A painful swelling of the bone, usually found in joints.

(For more information, see the "Research Aid for Death Certificates and Mortality Schedules" at *www.rootsweb.com.*)

Glossary: Geographic Locations in Amherst County

Bear Mountain: A peak just east of Tobacco Row Mountain; its southern end lies between Hicks Store and Crawfords Store.

Brown's Creek: Originates near the Rockbridge-Amherst County line west of Beverlytown and flows into the Pedlar River near Route 637.

Harris Creek: Originates at the base of Tobacco Row Mountain, flows south past Monroe, and empties into the James River opposite Treasure Island and the Rivermont section of Lynchburg.

Hat[t] Creek: Flows into the Tye River at Roseland in modern Nelson County.

Horsley's Creek: Originates west of Forks of Buffalo, on the north side of Tobacco Row Mountain, and flows into the Pedlar River at Pedlar Mills.

James River: Forms the entire southern boundary of Amherst County.

Juniper Creek: Originates east of Wright Shop and enters the James River south of Galts Mill and opposite Mt. Athos (in Campbell County).

Pedlar River: Headwaters are just south of Rockbridge/Amherst County line near Irish Gap. It flows south through the west side of the county until it reaches the James north of Holcombe Rock.

Porridge/Porrage Creek: Modern-day Partridge Creek, which originates south of Sweet Briar and flows into the James River at Stapleton. It appears on the 1751 Fry-Jefferson map of Virginia.

Rutledge Creek: Originates near Faulconerville, flows just east of Amherst, and empties into the Buffalo River.

Staton's Creek: Two forks originate just west of the modern Appalachian Trail and empty into the Pedlar River near Alto in the George Washington National Forest.

Stovall's Creek: Three forks come together west of Brightwell's Mill and flow into the James River at Stapleton.

Tobacco Row Mountain: The most visible range of peaks in the county, beginning near Agricola and stretching northeast. Highest peak is 2,932 feet. The surrounding area is known for fruit orchards.

Glossary: Amherst Officials and Residents Mentioned in the Records

Davies, Arthur B.: an attorney and Clerk of the County Court. Son of Nicholas Clayton Davies, who established Davies' Lower Ferry across the James River (now Salt Creek).

Garland, Samuel M. (1802-1880): an attorney and Clerk of the County Court. Member of the State Legislature, the Constitutional Convention of 1850-1851, and the Secession Convention of 1861. He married Dr. James Powell's daughter. His father was David Shepherd Garland, who owned *The Brick House* in Clifford and served in both the state legislature and Congress.

Gist, Samuel (ca. 1723-1808): wealthy London merchant, an original partner in the Dismal Swamp Co. (to drain that land), and absentee owner of plantations and slaves in Amherst, Goochland, Hanover, and Henrico Counties. His will provided that sales of his Virginia land would provide for his slaves, build houses and schools for them, and instruct them in the Christian religion. Of his nearly 1,000 slaves, 90% moved to Ohio after his death to form a colony, though some returned to Virginia. Today, the Gist Slave Settlement Foundation near Cincinnati sponsors an annual reunion of descendants of these slaves.

Hopkins, James, Sr. (?-1803): a wealthy landowner with property in Albemarle, Amherst, and Fluvanna Counties and an early vestryman of St. Anne's Parish, along with Thomas Jefferson. One of seven children of Arthur and Elizabeth Hopkins. Related to Jefferson, William Cabell, and "King" Carter. Married to Ann Sparks Hopkins. His will also provided for establishing a hospital for the poor and afflicted.

Powell, Dr. James: major landowner who helped settle Five Oaks, now the Town of Amherst.

Rose, Capt. John N. (1735-1802): eldest son of the pioneer Rev. Robert Rose. John inherited his father's *Rose Isle* plantation on the Tye River near Massies Mill in modern Nelson County; he also inherited half of his father's many slaves.

Rose, Margaret (1750-1828): daughter of Rev. Robert Rose. She lived near the modern town of Piney River in Nelson County.

Taylor, Sally (?-1862) (Mrs. John Taylor): owned a tavern in Madison Heights, on a bluff above the James River opposite Lynchburg. It was strategically located at the junction of a road leading down the gorge to Lynch's Ferry landing and a second road which ran north through another gorge to Scott's Ferry, farther up the James. Thomas Jefferson was reputed to have stopped there on his trips to *Poplar Forest* to visit several slaves he had once owned at *Monticello*. The tavern later burned, and nothing remains of the site today. (For more information, see the 1936 Works Progress Administration Historical Inventory of "Sally Taylor's Tavern.")

Transcript of the

AMHERST COUNTY REGISTER OF FREE BLACKS, 1822 – 1864

HOW TO USE THIS SECTION

This transcript is a verbatim copy made from the original hand-written document in the collection of the Library of Virginia. Spelling, capitalization, and punctuation have been preserved as they were. However, we have capitalized each name and printed it in **bold** ink to make it easier to find.

Be sure to check the individual listings which follow, too. Some people were certified by the County Court to be registered, but their names were never entered into the Register.

---

1 – 29 March 1822 – **DAVID COTTRELL** a Free Man of Colour aged about 28 years five feet nine inches high of yellowish complection has a small scar over the left eye a free man by birth and by occupation a waterman

2 – 29 March 1822 – **JOHN COUSIN** a Free Man of Colour aged about 25 years five feet Three quarter inches high of black complection and has a scar over the left eye and born free

3 – 29 March 1822 – **ALCY JOHNSON** a Free Woman of Colour aged about [blank] years five feet four inches high and has a scar on the right side of her face who was born free

7 – 19 April 1822 – **ESTHER NAPPER** a Free Woman of Colour aged about forty five years old & upwards five feet four & a half inches high dark complexion & her face scarred by the Small Pox

6 – 16 April 1822 – **SOLOMAN RITCHIE** This day appeared in the Clerk's Office of Amherst County Court. It appearing from the verified copy of Augusta County Court that said S. Ritchie a Negro man, aged about Fifty or Fifty one years of a black colour about five feet six inches high and formerly the property of Andrew Edwards, was regularly and properly liberated by the said Edwards, and that the said Ritchie is now a free man.

4 – 15 April 1822 – **BETSEY LACY** a free Woman aged about 24 years born free of low Stature has a mould [mole] in the palm of her left hand a scar on her neck and of dark complection [complexion]

5 – 15 April 1822 – **CATHARINE LACY** a free Woman aged about 22 Years was born free of middle stature has a scar on her forehead of black colour

8 – 23 May 1822 – **ANN HARRIS** a mulatto woman about five feet 4 ½ inches high who was eighteen years old on the 19th of March last and was born free No. 123

9 – 20 May 1822 – **THORNTON PETERS** a Freeman of Colour aged about 42 years five feet six inches high of a black complection [complexion] and has a scar on his face and was born free

10 – 22 August 1822 – **BENJAMIN H. CLARKE** a free man of colour aged twenty two years five feet eight inches high of a bright yellow complection grey eyes with a natural mark on his right cheek and was born free & by occupation a waterman

11 – 29 August 1822 – **ALEXANDER LARALL** a man of yellow complexion about five feet five inches high and about 25 years old who was born free as appears by the certificate of the Clerk of the Hastings Court for the City of Richmond

12 – 16 September 1822 – **WM [WILLIAM] BYAS** a free man of Colour commonly called Buck Hook aged about 23 about five feet eight or nine inches high with a scar over his left eye a bright mulatto born free

13 - 17 September 1822 – **REUBEN PETERS** a free man of Colour aged about 46 years five feet seven inches high has no apparent marks black complection [complexion] and born free

14 – 15 September 1822 – **RICHD [RICHARD] COOPER** a Mulatto Negro man of about the age of Twenty years and of small stature about five feet eight inches high have no apparent marks and born free

15 – 29 December 1822 – **SAWNEY MORRIS** a Mulatto Negro Man of about the age of Twenty two years Six months with Common Stature about five feet six inches high have a small speck in the right eye giving that eye the appearance of cros[s]ey[e]d & born free

16 – 4 February 1825 – **BENJAMIN SCOTT** a free Negro of a black complexion about 29 years of age about five feet eight inches high stout made born free. 2d [Second] copy given by order Ct. [Court] Decb. [December] 1830.

17 – 29 March 1825 – **ALEXANDER MOSS** a free born Mulatto Negro about 27 years of age 5 feet 5 ½ inches high a scar on the left wrist a scar over the left eye. 2nd copy given by order [of] Court Feb. 1837.

18 – 17 August 1825 – **BOB PAYNE** a free born Mulatto Negro about 32 years of age 5 feet high with a small rising over his right eye

19 – 31 January 1826 – **SCIPPES** a free Negro about the age of 80 years about five feet high set free by his Master George Holloway

20 – 20 August 1827 – **RICHARD ESEX** aged 50 years, black colour, about five feet 10 Inches high who was emancipated by a decree of the Superior Court of Chancery for the Richmond district

21 – 20 August 1827 – **MEREDITH GIBSON** aged 30 years black colour about five feet nine inches high who was emancipated by a decree of the Superior Court of Chancery for the Richmond district

22 – 18 September 1827 – **JACK FOSTER** aged about 23 years, a mulatto man of spare stature about five feet Ten Inches high who was born free, whose grandmother (named Priscilla) had her right to freedom established Together with her descendants by a decree of the Court of Amherst at June Court 1817

23 – ["Cert. Jan. 1829" is written at the side of this entry.] – **AMBROSE PAYNE** aged 28 years a Mulatto Man about five feet Ten Inches high with a large wart over his left eye whose mother named Sarah had her right to freedom established by the County Court of Amherst by a decree at June Court 1817

24 – 18 September 1827 – **CLOE PAYNE** aged 40 years a Mulatto Woman about five feet six inches high whose mother named Sarah had her right to freedom established by a decree of the Court of Amherst pronounced at June Court 1817

No. 25 Also **LUCINDA PAYNE** daughter of Cloe Payne aged 18 years a Mulatto Girl Also **MARY ANN PAYNE** daughter of Cloe Payne aged

14 years Also **SARAH JANE** an Infant suckling child of said Cloe Payne aged four months

26 – 24 September 1828 – **EVELINA HARRIS** Wife of James Harris aged 23 years a Mulatto of about five feet in h[e]ight who was born free being the daughter of Nancy Pinn wife of James Pinn

27 – 26 September 1828 – **TURNER PINN** a free man of dark brown complexion, about five feet ten inches high aged 46 years born free has a scar over the right eye

28 – 20 October 1828 – **SAUNDERS PINN** a free man of dark complexion about six feet in h[e]ight aged 22 years born free no marks or scars apparent on his face head or hands

29 – 20 October 1828 – **PATSY WILLIAMS** wife of Henry Williams a free Woman of Colour rather a dark mulatto about five feet high aged 36 – a scar on the back of the right hand seems to have been occasioned by a burn was born free

30 – 20 October 1828 – **JOICE PINN** wife of Turner Pinn a free woman of color rather light complexion about five feet in h[e]ight Stout built aged about forty five was born free

31 – 22 October 1828 – **ZACKARIAH FOSTER** a free man of color of dark complexion five feet five inches high of spare stature aged 21 years whose right to freedom may be seen by reference to the records of Amherst County Court wherein a decree was made at June Court 1817 in a suit between Priscilla vs Coppedge in relation to the Plts [Plaintiff's] title to freedom

32 – 27 October 1828 – **WILLIAM PINN** a free man of dark complexion about six feet & half an inch in h[e]ight of spare stature aged 23 years born free no marks apparent on his face head or hands

33 – 27 October 1828 – **RALEIGH PINN** a free man of dark complexion about five feet ten inches high aged 20 years – has a scar on his right cheek near his nose born free

34 – 27 October 1828 – **NANCY SCOTT** a free girl of color of dark brown complexion about five feet in h[e]ight aged fourteen years has a small scar occasioned by a burn on the upper joint of the third finger of the left hand born free

35 – 27 October 1828 – **SALLY SCOTT** a free girl of color aged 13 years dark brown complexion about five feet two inches in h[e]ight has no marks or scars apparent on her face head or hands born free

36 – 27 October 1828 – **POLLY PINN** a free woman of colour aged twenty three years rather dark mulatto complexion about five feet nine inches in height, has a mole in the left hand near the wrist. born free.

37 – 27 October 1828 – **JOHN PINN** a free man of colour aged twenty one dark brown complexion about five feet Eleven and a half inches in height has a small scar on the forefinger of the left hand – also on the middle finger of the same hand occasioned by cuts with a knife born free

38 – 27 October 1828 – **MARTHA JANE PINN** a free woman of colour, rather light complexion, stout built, about five feet two inches in hight [height] no scars apparent on her face head or hands – born free

39 – 20 January 1829 – **GEORGE CLARK** a free man of colour born free a light mulatto with straight hair five feet ten inches in h[e]ight with a scar on the middle of his forehead

40 – 14 August 1829 – **RICHARD TUPPENCE** a free man of light complexion (nearly white) light hair slightly curled five feet six inches and a half high with a small scar above the left eye – born free – aged Twenty five years

41 – 22 August 1829 – **SQUIRE JACKSON** a free black man emancipated by the last will and Testament of James Hopkins dec[ease]d – aged forty four years rather upwards of five feet seven inches in h[e]ight has a scar on the back of the left hand in the shape of a half moon also a scar above the left eye near the Temple

42 – 1830 – **LUCIND[A] PAYNE** daughter of Chloe Payne aged twenty one years born free a dark mulatto with a scar occasioned by a burn on the right side of the face below the cheek five feet three inches high (See former register, No. 25)

43 – 1830 – **CHLOE PAYNE** a Mulatto Woman aged 43 years born free with a scar between her eyebrows five feet two inches high (See No. 24) – also her infant child named **JAMES HENRY** aged six Months

44 – 1830 – **LEVI BRANHAM** son of Edward Branham free born aged thirty five a Bright Mulatto 5 feet six inches high with a scar across the back of his right hand

45 – 5 September 1831 – (See No. 31 same person heretofore registered) **ZACKARIAH FOSTER** a free Negro aged about 24 years, black complexion, 5 feet six & a half inches high, no scars apparent except a scratch on the back of his left hand. Certified Sept. Court 1831

46 – 11 October 1831 – **MARIA SPARROW** wife of Bartlet Sparrow formerly Maria Pinn a free Negro of light complexion daughter of Turner Pinn 29 years of age 5 feet 8 ½ inches high no scars apparent on her face head or hands

47 – 11 October 1831 – **SEGIS PINN** daughter of Turner Pinn a dark mulatto 5 feet 4 ¾ inches high 25 years of age no marks apparent on her face head or hands

48 – 11 October 1831 – **BETSY PINN** daughter of Turner Pinn a verry dark mulatto 5 feet 8 ¾ inches high 18 years of age with a scar occasioned by a cut with a knife on the joint of the third finger on the left hand and a mole on the left side of the face near the nose

49 – 11 October 1831 – **LAVINIA PINN** daughter of Turner Pinn verry light complexion for a Negro, or perhaps more properly a very dark Mulatto five feet 8 ¾ inches high about 16 years of age with a scar on the back of the right hand occasioned by a burn

50 – 21 November 1831 – **JUDITH FARRAR** daughter of Benjamin & Betty Whitesides of dark complexion 5 feet 5 inches high about 34 years of age with a scar under the left jaw and one on the neck on the left side

51 – 3 December 1831 – **HANNAH SCOTT** daughter of Nancy Scott light complexion for a Negro 5 feet 4 ½ inches high about twenty six years of age no marks or scars apparent. Certified December Court 1831

52 – 30 December 1831 – **PATRICK HENRY REDCROSS** a free man of Color, aged about twenty one years brown complexion five feet 4 ¾ inches high with a scar in the edge of his right eyebrow occasioned by a cut with an axe

53 – 30 December 1831 – **TURNER PINN JUN[IO]R** a free man of color aged about twenty one years dark brown complexion 5 feet 6 ½

inches high has a scar on the edge of right hand between little finger and the wrist occasioned by a cut with a Razor

54 – 7 March 1832 – **NANCEY B WILLIAM** a free woman of color, a bright mulatto five feet four & ¼ inches high, has a small scar over her left eyebrow daughter of Isabella Williams and free born – about nineteen years of age

55 – 15 May 1832 – **JUDY MORRIS alias BIAS** a free black woman five feet four & a half inches high no scars apparent on her face head or hands born free aged forty five years

56 – 15 May 1832 – **CAMILLA JANE MORRIS** alias BIAS a free black girl daughter of Judy Morris alias Bias no marks or scars apparent on her face head or hands born free on the 15th day of February 1817

57 – 15 May 1832 – **TOBIAS MORRIS alias BIAS** a free black boy complexion somewhat inclined to be light son of Judy Morris alias Bias no marks or scars apparent on his face head or hands, born free on the12th day of January 1819 four feet seven and a half inches high

58 – 15 May 1832 – **POLLY MORRIS alias BIAS** a free black girl four feet seven inches high daughter of Judy Morris alias Bias complexion somewhat inclined to be light, no marks or scars apparent on her face head or hands born free on the 9th day of March 1821

59 – 15 May 1832 – **LUCY ANN MORRIS alias BIAS** a free black girl three feet four inches high daughter of Judy Morris alias Bias, complexion inclined to be light no marks apparent on her face head or hands born free on the 1st day of May 1827

60 – 15 May 1832 – **ZELIUS MORRIS alias BIAS** a free black boy five feet seven inches high son of Judy Morris alias Bias has marks on the backs of both hands and on the backs of his fingers resembling small bumps in clusters – born free June 13th 1815

61 – 15 May 1832 – **JUDITH MORRIS alias BIAS** a free black girl two feet eleven inches high daughter of Judy Morris alias Bias no marks on her face head or hands born free on the 14th (?) day of January 1829

62 – 15 May 1832 – **WILLIAM CATO** a free black man of light complexion five feet nine & ¼ inches high Son of Sucky Cato no marks apparent on his face head or hands except the loss of three of the front

teeth in the upper Jaw, by trade a blacksmith, aged thirty seven years on the 4th of July next, born free

63 – 15 May 1832 – **SALLY CATO** wife of William Cato and daughter of Alley Jackson a dark mulatto no marks apparent on her face head or hands five feet four inches high free born aged about thirty six years

64 – 15 May 1832 – **JOHN WINTERS** son of Sally Cato formerly Sally Winters a boy of dark brown color five feet five inches high has a small scar over the right eye, another on the left cheek, several large scars on the right side of his head and has lost his right arm above the elbow. born free on the 22nd March 1818

65 – 15 May 1832 – **NANCY PAYNE** daughter of Sally Cato a mulatto girl a rather dark complexion three feet ten inches high no marks apparent on her face head or hands free born in the 5th day of April 1824

66 – 15 May 1832 – **ROBERT PAYNE** son of Sally Cato a mulatto boy three feet six inches high no marks apparent on his face head or hands born free on the 31st day of July 1826

67 – 15 May 1832 – **SARAH ANN ELIZABETH PAYNE** daughter of Sally Cato a bright mulatto girl three feet high no marks or scars apparent on her face head or hands born free on the 13th November 1829

68 – 15 May 1832 – **HEZEKIAH CATO** an infant son of Sally and William Cato a dark mulatto no marks or scars apparent on his face head or hands born free on the 1st day of February 1831

69 – 28 December 1833 – **JUDITH BRANHAM** daughter of Edward and Nancey Branham born free – aged about twenty five years a bright mulatto straight hair five feet one inch high no marks apparent on her face head or hands

70 – 20 January 1834 – **JAMES PETERS** son of Sarah Peters born free aged about twenty-two years a black man five feet six inches and a half high no marks apparent on his face head or hands

71 – 11 August 1834 – **CHRISTINA PINN** daughter of James Pinn and Jincey his wife free born aged about 19 years light complexion for a Negro five feet one inch high with 2 small scars on the forefinger of the left hand one above and one below the third joint and some moles or black spots on the face and hands

72 – 12 Mat 1835 – **SUSAN PETERS** daughter of Sally Peters born free aged 24 years a black woman five feet two and a half inches high with a mark on her right eyebrow the same being somewhat lighter than the skin adjoining

73 – 18 May 1835 – **ESTHER PETERS** daughter of Rebecca Peters born free aged 23 years five feet four inches high a dark mulatto with a small scar over the right eyebrow

74 – 16 November 1835 – **ORANGE JOHNSON** a free man of Color emancipated in the will of James Hopkins by the name of Orange aged 45 years. 5 feet 6 inches high. a mulatto rather dark with a scar on each eyebrow and one between the eyebrows

75 – 23 December 1835 – **MARIA PETERS** a free negro daughter of Sally Peters born free 5 feet 1 inch high complexion somewhat light no marks or scars apparent on her face head or hands except a small one on the left side of her forehead aged twenty one years

76 – 5 January 1836 – **ROBERT PINN** a free man of color light complexion for a Negro 5 feet Eight and a half inches high son of James & Jincey Pinn free born with a scar over his left eyebrow. Twenty three years of age

77 – 18 January 1836 – **NANCY JOHNSON** a free negro emancipated by the Will of James Hopkins by the name of Nancey forty years of age five feet six inches high with a small scar on her left cheek bone

78 – 25 May 1836 – **MARY ANN PAYNE** daughter of Chloe Payne born free a negro of light complexion aged twenty three years no marks or scars apparent upon her face head or hands five feet 4 inches high

79 – 5 January 1837 – **ROBERT EDENS** son of Anna Edens born free a mulatto man aged thirty eight years the forefinger of the right hand is stiff at the first joint and his head slightly bald. five feet three inches high

80 – 16 October 1837 – **HENRY** a mulatto man about twenty one years of age six feet three & a half inches high emancipated by the Will of Richard Smith Sen[io]r with a small scar in his right eyebrow

81 – 16 October 1837 – **LEANTE** a Negro woman about 50 years of age 5 feet 7 inches high emancipated by the Will of Richard Smith Sen[io]r no scars apparent on the face head or hands

82 – 16 October 1837 **MARY** a Negro woman of light complexion about twenty five years of age five feet six and a half inches high emancipated by the will of Richard Smith Sen[io]r no scars apparent upon her face head or hands

83 – 16 October 1837 – **BETSEY** an infant child of Mary who was emancipated by the will of Richard Smith Sen[io]r born since the decedents death a mulatto but not light for a child nine months old no scars apparent on her face head or hands

84 – 19 November 1838 – **JOHNATHAN F. ARNOLD** born on the 12th of March 1804 Six feet one and a half inches high a brown mulatto several scars on his right arm none on his face head or hands born free the son of Robert & Doshia Arnold

85 – 19 November 1838 – **DRURY H. ARNOLD** born 15th August 1809 five feet eight inches high a dark mulatto a scar on his left breast none apparent on his face head or hands the son of Robert & Doshia Arnold born free

86 – 18 September 1839 – **ANTHONY BEVERLY** 32 years of age son of Polly Beverly a dark mulatto 6 feet half inch high a scar on the right arm near the joint of the wrist occasioned by the cut of a knife and a scar on the left side of the face near the nose extending to the upper left born free

87 – 27 September 1839 – **JANE FIELDS** 22 years of age daughter of Milly Saunders, a dark mulatto – 5 feet 4 inches high – a scar on the right eyebrow & a scar on the right arm and on the forefinger of the right hand none others apparent – born free

89 – 2 November 1840 – **HENRY NAPPIER** About 32 years of age – son of Amy – of brown complexion – 5 feet 7 inches high – no scars apparent upon his face, head or hands – born free

90 – 16 January 1841 – **ABRAHAM JACKSON** About 46 years of age – Dark complexion – 5 feet 10 inches high – No scars apparent upon his face, head or hands – Emancipated by the Will of James Hopkins dec[eased]d

91 – 18 January 1841 – **RICHARD ESSEX** about 55 years of age – very dark complexion 5 feet 5 inches high – a scar on the inside of the left

arm, cut with a knife. Emancipated by the last will and Testament of Samuel Gist deceased late of the city of London

92 – 13 March 1841 – **GEORGE WASHINGTON LAFAYETTE PINN** About 20 years of age – Bright Mulatto – 5 feet 11 inches high – Scar over left eye – none apparent upon his head or hands – Son of Jincy Pinn – born free

93 – 13 May 1841 – **JAMES SHAVERS** of black complexion twenty seven years of age five feet eleven inches high, no scars perceivable on his head face or hands and free born

94 – 22 June 1841 – **TABA HUMBLES** Dark brown complexion – about 45 years of age – 5 feet & 3 Inches high – a Scar upon the breast, a scar on the right arm below the elbow – born free

95 – 14 December 1841 – **SARAH ANN GOOLSBY** daughter of Betsey Goolsby supposed to be about 18 years of age, a Bright mulatto, five feet 6 inches high, a scar between the upper lip and the nose – no other scars perceivable on her head face or hands – born free

96 – 11 November 1842 – **ADALINE FRANCES SNEAD** daughter of Susan Snead eighteen years of age, a bright mulatto 5 ft & 3 inches high no scars apparent on her head face or hands, one of her upper front teeth broken, also a wide space between two of her upper front teeth, born free

97 – 12 November 1842 – **PAUL alias PAUL JACKSON** black complexion, about 52 or 3 years of age 5 feet 10 inches high, a scar on each eyebrow and one across the nose, occasioned by the stamping of a horse, and an injury in the left knee – emancipated by the will of James Hopkins

98 – 22 November 1842 – **MARY alias MARY JACKSON** black complexion, about 5 feet 3 inches high, no scars visible on her head face or hands about 60 years of age, emancipated by the will of James Hopkins dec[ease]d

99 – 19 December 1842 – **SAMUEL B. SCOTT** Son of Samuel and Judith Scott, a bright mulatto, 22 years old. 5 feet ten & a half inches high, a scar on the right side of his neck produced by Kings evil or scrofula, and a scar on the right side of his face, a little below the corner of the mouth. born free

100 – 23 October 1843 – **ROBERT E. HOLLINSWORTH** a dark mulatto, emancipated by John H. Marye, about 23 years old, 5 feet 8 ¾ inches high, fleshy & stoutly made, a scar on the under part of his chin, a scar on the last joint of the thumb on the right hand and a film on the corner of the left eye – no other marks on head face or hands perceivable

101 – 8 November 1843 – **DORATHA ARNOLD** the wife of Robert Arnold, a bright mulatto – about 56 years of age – 5 feet 6 Inches high – a large scar on the breast, produced by a Cancer – No other marks on the head face or hands – Born free

102 – 8 November 1843 – **SARAH ANN HOLLINSWORTH** the wife of Robert E. Hollinsworth – the Daughter of Robert & Doratha Arnold – aged about 32 years – a Dark mulatto – 5 feet & 6 Inches high – No Scars apparent on the face, head, Arms or breast – Born free

103 – 8 November 1843 – **ROBERT W. ARNOLD** son of Robert & Doratha Arnold aged about 26 years – a Dark mulatto – 6 feet 2 ½ Inches high – a Small Scar on the right side of the neck – No other Scars apparent on the face, head, Arms, breast or hands – Born Free

104 – 8 November 1843 – **ANN MARIA ARNOLD** Daughter of Robert & Dortha Arnold – aged about 19 years – a bright Mulatto – 5 feet 6 Inches high – No Scar on the face, head, hands, Arms or breast – Born free

105 – 14 November 1843 – **JUDY JACKSON** wife of William Jackson a bright mulatto 4 feet one & a half inches high about 45 or 50 years of age a scar over the right eye occasioned by a blow, no other marks on head face or hands perceivable. born free

106 – 14 November 1843 – **JAMES ALEXANDER JACKSON** son of William Jackson dark complexion 5 feet 5 ½ inches high, a scar on the end of the middle finger of the left hand occasioned by a mash with cart wheel about 17 years of age. born free

107 – 14 November 1843 –**WILLIAM H. JACKSON** son of William Jackson, bright complexion 5 feet 3 ½ inches high a Scar on the left cheek occasioned by a blow, about 15 years old. born free

108 – 14 November 1843 – **ELIVISA JACKSON** daughter of William and Judy Jackson a bright mulatto about eleven years of age, 4 feet 8 inches high, no Scars on head face or hands perceivable – born free

109 – 14 November 1843 – **MARY JANE JACKSON** daughter of William & Judy Jackson of bright complexion 4 feet 1 inch high, a large scar extending across the middle & fore fingers occasioned by a Severe cut, middle finger stiff about eight years old. born free.

110 –15 November 1843 – **ELIZABETH WINTERS** wife of Edward Winters bright complexion 5 feet 8 inches high 24 years old cut on the chin. no other marks on the face hands or breast. born free

111 – 15 November 1843 – **JANE WINTERS** daughter of William & Nancy Winters dark complexion 5 feet 6 inches high a scar on the middle of the forehead about 31 years of age no other marks perceivable – born free

112 – 15 November 1843 – **LUCY WINTERS** daughter of William & Nancy Winters 5 feet 3 ¾ inches high aged about 41 dark complexion a cut on the middle [k]nuckle of the left hand no other marks perceivable. born free

113 – 15 November 1843 – **NANCY WINTERS** wife of William Winters bright coloured mulatto 71 years old 5 feet 5 inches high scar on the brow of the right eye occasioned by a cut no other marks perceivable. born free

114 – 18 November 1843 – **SAMUEL J. ARNOLD** son of Robert & Doratha Arnold about 17 years of age, 5 feet 5 ½ inches high dark complexion Scar on the left cheek bone occasioned by a blow a cut on the on the [k]nuckle of the first finger of the left hand. no other marks perceivable born free

115 – 18 November 1843 – **ROBERT I. ARNOLD** son of John Arnold 15 years old 5 feet ½ of an inch high dark complexion cut over his right eye. no other marks on his head face or hands born free

116 – 18 November 1843 – **DREWRY R. ARNOLD** son of John Arnold 14 years old 4 feet 4 ½ inches high dark complexion a large scar extending from the back of his neck down his left arm below the elbow, a small scar over the right Eye brow. born free

117 – 18 November 1843 – **EDWARD WINTERS** about 25 years old of black complexion 5 feet 11 ½ inches high. son of William & Nancy Winters, a scar on the fleshy part of the right hand between the fore

finger & the thumb, no other marks apparent on the head face or hands. born free

118 – 20 November 1843 – **JAMES JOHNS** about 63 years of age – Bright mulatto – 5 feet 3 ½ Inches high – A small scar on the forefinger of the left hand – no other Scars on the face, breast, arms or hands – Born free

119 – 20 November 1843 – **BETSEY TERRY** about 40 years of age – Bright mulatto – 5 feet 1 ¾ Inches high – a small mole on the right side of the neck – no Scars apparent on the face, head, breast, Arms or hands – Born free

120 – 20 November 1843 – **MARY TERRY** daughter of Betsey Terry – about 17 years of age – very Bright mulatto – 5 feet 7 ½ Inches high – A scar on the right cheek from a burn – No scars apparent on the breast arms hands or head – Born Free

121 – 20 November 1843 – **SALLY JOHNS** daughter of James Johns & Betsey Terry about 14 years of age – Bright mulatto – 4 feet 11 Inches high – A small scar on the left cheek near the mouth – none others apparent on the face, head, hands, Arms or breast – Born free

122 – 20 November 1843 – **JAMES JOHNS** son of James Johns & Betsey Terry about 10 years of age – Bright mulatto – 4 feet 4 ½ Inches high – A Scar on the top of the head – no other scar on the face Arms breast or hands – Born free

123 – 20 November 1843 – **CHARLES JOHNS** son of James Johns & Betsey Terry about 8 years old – Bright mulatto – 4 feet 2 inches high – A scar on the forefinger of the left hand – none others apparent on the face, Arms, breast or hands born free

124 – 20 November 1843 – **ARTHUR JOHNS** Son of James Johns & Betsey Terry about 6 years of age – Bright mulatto – An indistinct Scar over the left eye – none other apparent on the face, head, arms breast or hands Born free –

125 – 20 November 1843 – **MARGARET JOHNS** daughter of James Johns & Betsey Terry – about 5 years old – Bright mulatto – No scars apparent on the face, head, arms, breast or hands – Born free

126 – 20 November 1843 – **ARILLA JOHNS** daughter of James Johns & Betsey Terry – about 2 years old – Bright mulatto – 2 scars produced from burns on the breast & one on the neck – no others on the breast, arms, hands or face. Born free

127 – 20 November 1843 – **WILLIAM EVANS** Son of Betsey Terry – about 26 years of age – Bright mulatto 5 feet 10 inches high – A Scar on the left cheek bone – one on the right elbow. None others on the face, breast, hands or arms – Born free

128 – 21 November 1843 – **HEZEKIAH JOHNS** 5 feet 11 Inches high 23 years old dark complexion Stout made a cut on the forefinger of the right hand a small scar on the back of each hand a scar on the end of the middle finger of the right hand occasioned by mashing a cut on the fleshy part of the right hand. no other marks perceivable on hands face or arms born free

129 – 22 November 1843 – **EASOM PETERS** a free man of colour dark complexion 5 feet 6 inches high – 39 years old. a small scar occasioned by a cut on the left arm, no other scars perceivable on face hands or arms born free

130 – 18 March 1844 – **THOMAS WINTERS** free man of colour 5 feet 9 inches high, dark complexion 52 years old, a scar on the nose directly between the eyes – a scar on the right side of the forehead near the edge of the hair born free

131 – 18 March 1844 – **ELVIRA WINTERS** wife of Thomas Winters, free woman of colour 29 years old bright mulatto. born free, 5 feet 8 inches high, a scar on the wrist of each hand occasioned by a burn b[or]n free

132 – 18 March 1844 – **MARY WINTERS** daughter of Thomas & Elvira Winters bright mulatto. 8 years old, a scar on the forehead, born free

133 – 18 March 1844 – **LUCY ELLEN WINTERS** daughter of Thomas & Elvira Winters, bright mulatto – 6 years old born free

134 – 18 March 1844 – **VIRGINIA WINTERS** bright mulatto 4 years old, the daughter of Thomas & Elvira Winters, born free

135 – 18 March 1844 – **THOMAS WINTERS** son of Thomas Winters & Elvira Winters dark complexion 2 years old born free

136 – 18 March 1844 – **ROBERT WINTERS** son of Thomas & Elvira Winters – infant born free

137 – 13 April 1844 – **WILLIAM BRANHAM** Son of Creesey Branham, dark complexion 25 years old. 5 feet 6 ½ inches high – a sunken place on the Top of the head, a burn on the left side of his breast, a scar on the third joint of the third finger of the left hand, a cut between the first and second joint of the same finger done with a reep hook, a Splat in the end of the thumb on the same hand, a scar on the left side of the left leg (occasioned by the cut of an axe) between the Knee and ankle – born free

138 – 23 May 1844 – **WASHINGTON** a dark mulatto 6 feet ¼ inch high about fifty or fifty one years old, Emancipated by the will of Thomas Higginbotham dec[ease]d. a scar on the little finger of the left hand occasioned by a cut

139 – 15 July 1844 – **GUSTAVUS WINTERS** a bright mulatto, aged about 21 years, 5 feet 10 ½ inches high. a large scar between the eye brows, no other scars perceivable on face or hands – son of Milly Peters – born free

140 – 21 October 1844 & Certified at Octo[ber] Court 1845 – **MARY PAYNE** formerly **MARY WINTERS**, wife of Ambrose Payne a bright mulatto5 feet 7 inches high about 53 years old, a large scar on the inside of the right arm, extending from the elbow to wrist. no other scars visible on the head face or hands, born free

141 – 16 November 1844 – **PATTESON JOHNS** a free man, bright mulatto – 5 feet 8 inches high about 60 years of age a small scar under the left Jawbone, a rise (?) on under lip (?) cock eyed born free – no other marks [*NOTE: A loose draft copy of this entry, found in the back of the Register, gives Johns' name as Pattison, describes him as having a bright complexion and as being wall-eyed.*]

142 – 16 November 1844 – **EMALIZA M. JOHNS** daughter of Patteson & Judy Johns – very bright mulatto, 32 years old on the 1st day of Nov. 1844 – 5 feet 8 inches high a burn on the inside of the left [w]rist no other scars apparent on the face, hands or arms, born free

143 – 16 November 1844 – **JOHN PATTESON JOHNS** Son of Patteson & Judy Johns, very bright mulatto 20 years old on the 26th day of July 1844, 5 feet 5 inches high, a Small Scar on the forefinger of the right hand, no other marks apparent on face, hands or arms, born free

144 – 16 November 1844 – **PATTESON JOHNS JUN[IO]R** son of Emaliza M. Johns, very bright mulatto boy Strai[gh]t hair 10 years old in Sept 1844 – a Small Scar under the right Jawbone occasioned by a rising – born free – no other scars apparent on hands face or arms

145 – 16 November 1844 – **JUDY JOHNS** daughter of Emaliza M. Johns, very bright mulatto, 7 years old on the 4th day of November 1844, very Strai[gh]t hair – no scars apparent on her face hands or arms born free

146 – 16 November 1844 – **EMALINE FRANCIS JOHNS** daughter of Emaliza M. Johns bright mulatto 6 years old in May 1845, no Scars apparent on face, hands or arms – born free

147 – 16 November 1844 – **DICY DIANNA TERRY** daughter of Betsey Terry – very bright mulatto about 24 years of age 5 feet 4 inches high, a Scar on the forefinger of the left hand near the thumb a scar on the fleshy part of the Thumb, no other marks apparent on face hands or arms – born free

148 – 16 November 1844 – **MARY ELIZABETH TERRY** daughter of Dicy Dianna Terry, very bright mulatto 10 years old in September 1844 – a scar under the left eye – no other marks on face, hands or arms – born free [*NOTE: A loose draft copy of this entry, found in the back of the Register, gives her birthday as September 9th.*]

149 – 16 November 1844 – **JOHN TERRY** son of Dicy Dianna Terry very bright mulatto 7 years old the 21st April 1844 – burn on the back of the neck no other scars on his face arms or hands – born free [*NOTE: A loose draft copy of this entry, found in the back of the Register, gives his age as 21.*]

150 – 13 December 1844 – **RICHARD JOHNS** son of Emaliza M. Johns a very bright mulatto 4 years old on the 24th day of November 1844, strai[gh]t hair & black eyes, no marks upon face hands or arms – born free

151 – 15 March 1845 – **JULIANN PETERS** Daughter of Turza Peters, twenty three years old, very bright mulatto, 5 feet 5 inches high, a mole above the right corner of the mouth, no scars on face, hands or arms – born free

152 – 15 March 1845 – **EMILY JANE ARNOLD** wife of Drewry Arnold very bright mulatto, about 22 years old, Straight hair, 5 feet 3 inches high, black eyes, no scars on gave, hands or arms, born free

153 – 15 March 1845 – **JOSEPHINE PETERS** Daughter of Turza Peters, bright mulatto, very likely 17 years old the 6th day of May 1845, 5 feet 2 and ¾ inches high, very dark eyes, a scar over the left eye and another on the Centre of the forehead, No other Scars on face hands or arms born free

154 – 15 March 1845 – **SELDON M. PETERS** Son of Turza Peters, very bright Mulatto, 24 years old on the 12th day of June 1845, very bushy head of hair, no scars perceivable on his face, hands or arms – born free

155 – 15 March 1845 – **MANSFIELD PETERS** Son of Turza Peters, bright mulatto 5 feet 8 and 1/10 inches high, 18 years old, in November 1844, a wide space between the two front upper teeth – no scars on face hands or arms – born free

156 – 15 March 1845 – **TURZA PETERS** Daughter of Becka Peters Dark complexion, 40 years old, 5 feet 5 and 1/8 inches high – no scars on face, hands or arms – born free

157 – 15 March 1845 – **ELIZABETH ARNOLD** Daughter of Drewry and Emily Jane Arnold, Infant two years old, bright mulatto – born free

158 – 15 March 1845 – **MARY JANE ARNOLD** Daughter of Drewry & Emily Jane Arnold, Infant five months old – bright mulatto – born free

159 – 15 March 1845 – **NANCY THORNTON PETERS** Daughter of Turza Peters, bright mulatto 10 years old, Straight hair – no scars on her face or hands – born free

160 – 15 March 1845 – **NORVELLE PETERS** Son of Turza Peters, bright mulatto, 7 years old, the 6th day of November 1844, no scars on face, hands or arms – born free

161 – 15 March 1845 – **JOSIAH PETERS** son of Turza Peters, bright mulatto, five years old, on the 23rd day of August 1844, no scars on face or hands – born free

162 – 15 March 1845 – **JOHN OSCAR PETERS** son of Turza Peters, bright mulatto, 4 years old – born free

163 – 15 March 1845 – **VRGINIA PETERS** Daughter of Turza Peters, very bright mulatto, 5 feet 4 ¼ inches high, 15 years old, no scars on her face hands or arms, born free

164 – 21 October 1845 – **CHARLES LEWIS HENRY PAYNE** Son of Lucinda Payne, a free black Boy, 12 years old 20th Nov. 1845, very dark complexion, a Scar under the right eye, nappy hair – No other scars on his face or hands – born free

165 – 21 October 1845 - **MARTHAN ANN FRANCIS PAYNE** a Daughter of Lucinda Payne, a free girl, 8 years old 14th of Jan[ua]ry 1846, very black Skin – a wart on the inside of the right thumb. No scars on face or hands – born free

166 – 21 October 1845 – **CHARLOTTE ELIZABETH PAYNE** a Daughter of Lucinda Payne, age 6 years old, 25th of Jan[ua]ry. 1846, dark brown complexion, born free

167 – 21 October 1845 – **STEPHEN PAYNE** a Son of Lucinda Payne, 4 years old Aug. 1845 – dark complexion, large projecting forehead & big lips – born free

168 – 21 October 1845 – **TALBOT PAYNE** son of Lucinda Payne, 3 years old in May 1846 brown complexion – born free

169 - 21 October 1845 – **CAMILLA JANE PAYNE** a Daughter of Lucinda Payne, one year old

170 – 10 November 1845 – **RICHARD JOHNS** Son of Polly Johns, very bright mulatto, 5 feet 1o inches ¾ of an inch high, 32 years old in June 1846 – 3 Scars on the breast 2 large & 1 small occasioned by Biles, Stout made Quick spoken and born free

171 – 13 January 1846 – **JAMES HENRY PAYNE** Son of Cloe Payne – about 16 years of age – dark brown colour – No Scars apparent upon his face, hands or arms – born free – stoops in his shoulders

172 – 22 January 1846 – **SARAH JANE PAYNE** daughter of Cloe Payne – about 19 years of age – dark brown colour – 5 feet 2 ½ Inches high – No Scars apparent on her face, hands or arms – born free

173 – 17 November 1846 – **DAVID PETERS** Son of Rebecca Peters, Supposed to be 27 years old, dark complexion, 5 feet 4 Inches high, a Scar over the left eyebrow pointing to the nose, occasioned by a cut by falling upon an oven when very Small – black eyes and very thick Lips – no other Scars and born free

174 – 12 January 1847 – **JONATHAN F. ARNOLD JR.** Son of Jonathan F and Camilla J Arnold nine years old, dark complexion, no Scars perceivable on his face, hands or arms – born free

175 – 5 February 1847 – **WILLIAM BARNETT MORRISS alias BIAS**, Infant Son of Polly Bias alias Morriss dark complexion – born 5th Aug. 1844 and born free

176 – 21 June 1847 – **JOHN T. PINN** Son of Polly Pinn, a Bright mulatto, Five feet Seven and a half Inches high a Large Scar on the right Side of the face, another on the right arm between the wrist and Elbow another on the right hand below the wrist bone, all occasioned by burns, No other large or notable Scars on him – 21 years old and born free

177 – 19 July 1847 – **JONATHAN BEVERLY** aged about 62 years, 5 feet 10 inches high, dark complexion, a Scar on the left side of his bre[a]st produced by a burn, no other Scars on his face, hands, arms, or bre[a]st – born free

178 – 9 August 1847 – **GEORGE JEWELL** 29 years old, a bright mulatto, 5 feet 5 Inches and 5/8 of an Inch high, Stout made, Straight hair and black eyes, bald headed – a Scar on the Calf of the left leg produced by a cancer, a Scar on the left temple produced by a burn – born free – no other Scars on him

179 – 10 September 1847 & Certified Sept. C[our]t 1847 – **JAMES DILLARD** Manumitted by Charles A. Penn, Fifty three years old, a bright mulatto, 5 feet 7 Inches high, a mole on the right cheek, a Scar on the upper lip close up to the nose, black eyes, bushy hair, No other marks

180 – 18 October 1847 – **PERMELIA BRANHAM** daughter of Creasy Branham, a mulatto woman 33 years old 5 feet ¾ of an inch high, a Scar

on the left Side of the breast no other Scars on her hands face or arms. born free

181 – 18 October 1847 – **MARTHA JANE BRANHAM** daughter of Permelia Branham a light mulatto woman 16 years old, Straight hair black eyes no other marks or Scars on her face hands or arms – 5 feet one inch high, born free

182 – 20 March 1849 – **DELEWARE SCOTT** Son of Judith Scott dark mulatto 26 years old 5 feet 11 Inches high, no Scars on his face head or arms – born free

183 – 25 November 1850 (Reregistered) – **WILLIAM BRANHAM** son of Creasey Branham, dark complexion – aged 31 years – 5 feet 6 ½ Inches high, Sunken place on the top of his head – partly bald – a burn on the left side of his breast – a small scar on the third joint of the third finger of the left hand – a scar on the end of the thumb of the left hand – a scar on the side of the left leg between the knee & ancle [ankle] – born free

184 – 18 December 1850 – Renewed by order of December Court 1850 – **WASHINGTON** A dark mulatto, Six feet & ½ Inch high, about fifty Six years of age – A small scar on the little finger of the left hand – Hair partly grey – Emancipated by the Will of Thos. Higginbotham dec[ease]d & permitted to remain in this County by an order of Court, made on the 20th day of May 1844

185 – **JAMES FOSTER** – dark black negro – Five feet Seven and a half Inches high – no apparent Scars on his face, head & hands – 64 years of age, the son of Sella Foster

Amherst County Court December Term ordered to be registered – 186 – 19 December 1850 – **SAMUEL BEVERLY** Bright mulatto – Strai[gh]t hair, somewhat grey – Five feet, Six Inches & half – Fifty three years old no Scars apparent on his face head or hands – born free before the 1st day of May 1806 – Registered by order of Court made at December Court 1850

Amherst County Court December Term ordered to be registered – 187 – 19 December 1850 – **RHODA BEVERLY** wife of Saml Beverly – Bright mulatto – Strai[gh]t hair – Five feet three & half Inches high – Fifty three years of age – No Scars on her face, head or hands, born free before the 1st day of May 1806 - & Registered by order of Court made December Court 1850

188 – **DELAWARE BEVERLY** Son of Samuel & Rhoda Beverly – bright mulatto – hair brown & little inclined to curl – Five feet Seven ¼ inches high – Small Scar under his nose – no other Scars apparent on his face head or hands – Aged 25 years – Born of parents free before the 1st day of May 1806 And registered by order of Court made December Court 1850

Amherst County Court December Term 1850 ordered to be Registered – 189 – **TIMANDA BEVERLY** daughter of Samuel & Rhoda Beverly – Five feet ¾ Inches high, Bright mulatto – Straight black hair, Small Scar on the left side of her neck – Twenty two years old – Born of parents free before the 1st day of May 1806 – Registered by order of Court made December Court 1850

Amherst County Court December Term ordered to be registered – 190 – **SUSANNA BEVERLY** Daughter of Samuel & Rhoda Beverly – bright mulatto – Straight hair – Small scar under the right ear – No other scar apparent on her face, head, or hands – born free in the County of Amherst of parents free before the 1st day of May 1806 – Five feet 2 Inches & ¼ high, Registered by order of Court made December 1850 – near Twenty years old

Amherst County Court December Term 1850 ordered to be Registered – 191 – **FRANCES BEVERLY** Daughter of Samuel & Rhoda Beverly – bright mulatto – Straight black hair – Small mole on the right side of her neck – a small knot on the wrist of the right arm, Five feet, 3 inches high – going on 16 years of age – born in the County of Amherst of parents who were free before the 1st day of May 1806 – Registered by order of December Court 1850

Amherst County Court December Term ordered to be Registered – 192 – **SAMUEL BEVERLY JR** Son of Samuel & Rhoda Beverly – bright mulatto, straight black hair – Five feet Six Inches high going on 18 years of age – No Scars apparent on his face, head or hands – born in the County of Amherst of parents who were free before the 1st day of May 1806 & registered by order of December Court 1850

Amherst County Court December Term 1850 ordered to be registered – 193 – **ANDREW BEVERLY** Son of Samuel & Rhoda Beverly, bright mulatto, Straight hair, 5 feet & one inch high – a mole on his left cheek –

no other Scars apparent on his face head or hands – going on 14 years of age – born in the County of Amherst, of parents who were free before the 1st day of May 1806 – Registered by order of December Court 1850

Amherst County Court December Term ordered to be registered – 194 – **ALEXANDER BEVERLY** Son of Samuel & Rhoda Beverly – bright mulatto, straight hair – 4 feet Six Inches high – going on 12 years of age – Scar over the right eye – no other apparent mark on his face, head or hands – born in the County of Amherst, of parents who were free before the 1st day of May 1806 & Registered by order of December Court 1850

195 – **LEVI BRANHAM** Brown mulatto, Straight hair, somewhat grey – Five feet Six Inches high – 55 years of age – no scars apparent on face, head or hands – born in the County of Amherst of parents free before the 1st day of May 1806 – Register renewed by order at December Court 1850

Amherst County Court January Term 1851 ordered that . . . – 196 – **GEORGE WINTERS** a free man of Colour Registered in the Clerk's office of the County of Amherst by order of said Court made [blank] day of George Winters a free man of Color born in the County of Nelson five feet eleven ¼ inches high, dark skin, several Scars on his neck, Cut on the end of his nose cause[d] by Powder no other scars apparent on head, face or hands 43 years derived his freedom from ancestors free prior to the 1st of May 1806

Amherst County Court January Term 1851 – Virginia – County of Amherst to wit – 197 – Registered in the Clerks of the County of Amherst by order of said Court made the 20th day of January 1851 **JOHN KEY** a free man of Colour born in the County of King and Queen, bright mulatto 5 feet 6 ¾ Inches high small scar on left arm near the hand – no other scars apparent on head, face or hands – age 42 years – and by like order of Court it is certified that John Key derives his freedom from ancestors free prior to the 1st of May 1806

Amherst County Court January Term 1851 – Virginia – County of Amherst to wit – 198 – Registered in the Clerks office of the County Court of Amherst by order of said Court made 20th day of January 1851 – **JAMES HENLEY** a free man of Color born in the County of Amherst Dark complexion, five feet eight inches high scar on under lip, scar on left eye – burn on the thumb of left hand, no other scars apparent on head face or hands – Sixty five years of age, emancipated by the will of Wm.

D. Henley by his will admitted to record in the City of Norfolk on the 11th day of June 1838

Amherst County Court Jany Term 1851 – Virginia – County of Amherst to wit – 199 – Registered in the Clerks office of the County Court of Amherst by order of said Court made the 20th day of January 1851 **JAMES DONNER** a free man of Color born in the County of Amherst bright mulatto five feet six and ½ inches high no scars apparent on head face or hands. forty nine years old and by like order of Court it is certified that James Donner derived his freedom from ancestors free prior to the first of May 1806

Amherst County Court February Term 1851 – State of Virginia – County of Amherst to wit – 200 –Registered in the Clerks office of the County Court of Amherst by order of said Court made the 17th day of February 1851 **WILLIAM KEY** about thirty years of age a dark mulatto five feet ten inches high a scar on the middle finger on the inside of the joint of the right hand a scar below the root [?] of the forefinger of the left hand on the outside and a small scar on the middle of his forehead no other scars apparent on head face or hands born of ancestors free prior to the 1st of May 1806

Amherst County Court Feby Term 1851 – Virginia – County of Amherst to wit – 201 – Registered in the Clerks office of Amherst County Court of Amherst by order of said Court made February Term 1851 **WILLIAM H. PETERS** a Dark mulatto about five feet eight ¼ inches high a small scar on neck from a burn, large scar on first joint on right leg no other scars apparent on head face or hands about twenty one years of age no other scar or marks apparent on head face or hands born of ancestors free prior to the first of May 1806

Amherst County Court Feby Term 1851 – Virginia – County of Amherst to wit – 202 – Registered in the Clerks office of Amherst County Court by order of said Court made at the February Term 1851 **THOMAS PETERS** Son of Mildred Peters about twenty two years of age dark Mulatto, Scar on left side of his neck caused by a cut, a small mole on the left side of his nose no other scars apparent on head, face, or hands, born of ancestors free prior to the 1st of May 1806

Amherst County Court February Term 1851 – Virginia – County of Amherst to wit – 203 – Registered in the Clerks office of Amherst County Court by order of said Court made February Term 1851 **WASHINGTON PETERS** son of Mildred Peters Dark complexion about nineteen years of age five feet 6 ¼ inches high large scar on the left side of his neck caused by a [illegible], cut on [w]rist of right hand small burn on left hand, large scar on right knee caused by cut from Drawing Knife, no other apparent scars on head face or hands, born of parents free before the 1st of May 1806.

Amherst County Court February Term 1851 – Virginia – County of Amherst to wit – 204 – Registered in the Clerks office of Amherst County Court by order of said Court made the Seventeenth day of February 1851 – **ALLEN MERCHANT** born in the County of Amherst. Dark complexion five feet five inches high small scar on his forehead caused by a cut from wood no other scars apparent, son of Iris Merchant, about forty years of age born of ancestors free prior to the 1st of May 1806

Amherst County Court Feby Term 1851 – Virginia – County of Amherst to wit – 205 – Registered in the Clerks office of Amherst County by order of said Court made at the February Term 1851 **SUSAN MERCHANT**, wife of Allen Merchant, Daughter of James and Betsy Tuppence, born in Amherst County Dark mulatto about thirty three years of age five feet six inches high, a large brown Spot under left eye and several moles on her face, little finger of the left hand broken, no other scars apparent on head, face, or hands, born of ancestors free before the first of May 1806

Amherst County Court February Term 1851 – Virginia – County of Amherst to wit – 206 – Registered in the Clerks office of Amherst County Court by order of said Court made February Term 1851 **ZELIUS MORRISS** alias BIAS son of Judy Morriss alias Bias, Dark complexion, five feet seven and ¾ inches high, has marks on both hands and on the back of his fingers resembling small bumps in clusters 36 years of age no other scars apparent on head face or hands born of ancestors free prior to the 1st of May 1806

Amherst County Court February 1851 – Virginia – County of Amherst to wit – 207 – Registered in Clerks office of Amherst County Court by order of said Court made at the February Term 1851 **WILLIAM ESEX** a free man of colour born [*NOTE: This entry was incomplete and had been marked through.*]

Amherst County Court March Term 1851 – Virginia – County of Amherst to wit – 208 – Registered in the Clerks office of the County Court of Amherst by order of the said Court made the 17th day of March

1851 – **PERMELIA BRANNUM** a free woman of colour daughter of Creasey Brannum born in the County of Amherst brown complexion 5 feet one inch high – large scar on the left bre[a]st caused by a fall thirty seven years old, no marks apparent on head face or hands born of ancestors free prior to first of May 1806

Amherst County Court March Term 1851 – Virginia – County of Amherst to wit – 209 – Registered in the Clerks office of Amherst County Court by order of said Court made the 17th day of March 1851 **NANCY MAJORS alias NANCY EVANS** a free woman of dark complexion about seventy one years of age 5 feet 3 inches high a small scar in middle of breast small scar on right side of her neck no others scars or marks apparent on head face or hands emancipated by the will of Wm. Botts of Amelia County on 22nd day of the 7th month 1782

Amherst County Court March Term 1851 – Virginia – County of Amherst to wit – 210 – Registered in the Clerks office of Amherst County Court by order made at March Term 1851 – **MARY PETERS** a free woman of colour, daughter of Rachiel Peters Dark complexion – 5 feet one inch high scar on each elbow caused by a burn scar on left Jaw age about 26 year, born of parents free prior to the 1st May 1806

Amherst County Court March Term 1851 – Virginia – County of Amherst – 211 – **BARTLETT SPARROW** a free man of Colour born in Amherst County of parents free prior to the 1st of May 1806, Dark complexion, five feet 9 ½ inches high, small scar on right side of his neck forefinger on left hand broken, large scar on right hand caused by a cut from a Knife, no other marks apparent on head face & hands, about 54 years of age

Amherst County Court March Term 1851 – Virginia – County of Amherst to wit – 212 – Registered in the Clerks office of Amherst County Court by order of said Court made on the 17th day of March 1851 **JAMES SPARROW** Son to Bartlett and Mary Jane Sparrow born in Amherst County on 30th September 1830 of parents [free] prior to 1st of May 1806 Dark complexion, 5 feet eight and a half inches scar on first joint of first finger on left hand, no other marks or scars apparent on head face or hands short hair, black eyes about 21 years of age born of parents free prior to the 1st of May 1806

Amherst County Court March Term 1851 – Virginia – County of Amherst to wit – 213 – Registered in the Clerks office of Amherst of Amherst County Court by order of said Court made the 17th day of

March 1851. **SIMPSON SPARROW** Son to Bartlett & Mary J Sparrow born in the County of Amherst on the 15th of May 1833 of parents free prior to first of May 1806 brown skin Small scar between 4th & 5th fingers on left hand caused by a cut, long hair black eyes about 18 years of age 5 feet 8 ¼ Inches high

Amherst County Court March Term 1851 – Virginia – County of Amherst to wit – 214 – Registered in the Clerks office of said County Court by an order made on the 17th day March 1851. **TURNER SPARROW** son of Bartlett and Mary Jane Sparrow Dark complexion scar above right eye no other apparent marks on head face or hands, short hair black eyes 5 feet 9 inches born of parents free prior to the 1st of May 1806

Amherst County Court February 1851 – Virginia – County of Amherst to wit – 215 – Registered in the Clerks office of said Court by order made the 17th day of February 1851. **ALDRIDGE BEVERLY** [illegible] son [of] Polly Beverly born in Buckingham County Va bright mulatto strai[gh]t black hair scar over right eye caused by a cut from a nail, large scar on his [w]rist of the right hand caused by a cut from a Knife a large scar on the left hand caused by a Pistol Shot no other scars apparent on head face or hands about 23 years of age five feet nine inches high born of parents free prior to the first of May 1806

Amherst County Court March Term 1851 – Virginia – County of Amherst to wit – 216 – Registered in the Clerks office of said Court by order made on the 17th day March 1851. **PATRICK H. REDCROSS** son of John Redcross brown complexion, about 38 years of age, 5 feet 5 & ¾ Inches high scar over right eye by cut from an axe, small scar between eyes caused by cut from Reaphook, large dark spot under left eye, large scar on right arm near his elbow caused by a cut from a Knife, rather inclined to be bald, no other scars or marks apparent on head face or hands born in Amherst County of parents free prior to the first of May 1806

Amherst County Court March Term 1851 – Virginia – County of Amherst to wit – 216 – Registered in the Clerks office of Amherst County Court by order of said Court made on the 17th day of March 1851. **GEORGE JEWELL** a free man of Colour son of Viney Jewell, bright mulatto about thirty five years of age five feet five and ¾ inches high scar over left eye caused by a burn large scar on left leg between Knee and ancle [ankle] caused by a Cancer rather inclined to be bald, no other scars or marks apparent on head face or hands born in Amherst County of parents free prior to the 1st of May 1806

Amherst County Court March Term 1851 – Virginia – County of Amherst to wit – 217 – Registered in the Clerks office of Amherst County Court by order of said Court made the 17th day of March 1851 **WILLIAM TYLER** a free man of Colour, son [of] Sally Nicholas, Brown complexion 5 feet 5 ½ inches high about 29 years of age large scar between 1st & 2nd joint on forefinger of the left hand, caused by a cut from a Knife, born in the County of Fluvanna of Parents free prior to the 1st of May 1806

Amherst County Court March Term 1851 – Virginia – County of Amherst to wit – 217 – Registered in the Clerks office of Amherst County by order of said Court made on the 17th day of March 1851 **TABITHA BAUGH alias LOGAN** Daughter of Sukey Logan about 39 years of age bright mulatto 5 feet 2 ½ inches high dark place or spot under each eye, no other scars or marks apparent on head face or hands, born in Goochland County of parents free prior to the 1st of May 1806

Amherst County Court March Term 1851 – Virginia – County of Amherst to wit – 218 – Registered in the Clerks office of Amherst County Court by order of said Court made on 17th day of March 1851 **MARTHA JANE JEWELL** a free woman of Colour – Wife of Geo Jewell, Brown complexion 5 feet 2 inches high a small scar over right eye no other scars or marks apparent on head face or hands born in the County of Amherst of parents free prior to the 1st of May 1806

Amherst County Court March Term 1851 – Virginia – County of Amherst to wit – 219 – Registered in the Clerks office of said Court by order of Court made on the 17th day of March 1851 **BETSY SNEED** a free woman daughter of Susan Sneed 5 feet 3 ½ Inches high bright mulatto 3 large moles on right side of face and neck small scar on left hand near thumb no other marks or scars apparent on head face or hands about 30 years of age born in Nelson County of parents free prior to the 1st of May 1806

Amherst County Court April Term 1851 – Virginia – County of Amherst to wit – 220 – Registered in the Clerks office of said Court by order of Court made on the 21st day of April 1851 **DAVID MORRISS** a free man of Colour very dark complexion about 41 years of age, 5 feet 10 inches high, small scar on little finger, one on the 2nd joint of right arm caused by a burn no other scars or marks apparent on head face or hands, son of

Juda Morriss born in Campbell County of parents free prior to the 1st of May 1806

Amherst County Court April Term 1851 – Virginia – County of Amherst to wit – 221 – Registered in the Clerks office of said Court made on the 21st day of March 1851 [*NOTE: This is probably an error and should be April.*] **TOBIAS MORRISS** a free man of Colour son of Juda Morriss dark complexion about 26 years of age 5 feet 9 ½ inches high no scars apparent on head face or hands born in Campbell County of parents free prior to the 1st of May 1806

Amherst County Court April Term 1851 – Virginia – County of Amherst to wit – 222 – Registered in the Clerks office of said Court by order of Court made on the 21st day of April 1851 **ALFRED BAUGH** son of Tabitha Baugh very bright mulatto about 19 years of age five feet 4 ¼ Inches high no marks or scars apparent on head face or hands, born in Goochland County of parents free prior to the 1st of May 1806

Amherst County Court April Term 1851 – Virginia – County of Amherst to wit -223 – Registered in the Clerks office of said Court by order of Court made on the 21st day of April 1851 **NANCY TYLER** daughter of Tabatha Baugh about 15 years of age five [feet] one inch high brown complexion, no scars or marks apparent on head face or hands born in Fluvanna County of parents free prior to the 1st of May 1806

Amherst County Court April Term 1851 – Virginia – County of Amherst to wit – 224 – Registered in the Clerks office of said Court by order of Court made on the 21st day of April 1851 **JOHN TYLER** son of Tabatha Baugh brown complexion five feet 3 1/3 Inches high no scars or marks apparent on head face or hands about 17 years of age born in Fluvanna County of parents free prior to the 1st of May 1806

Amherst County Court April Term 1851 – Virginia – County of Amherst to wit – 225 – Registered in the Clerks office of Amherst County County [sic] Court by order of Court made on the 21st day of April 1851 **JAMES FOSTER** a free man of Colour, about 65 years of age very dark complexion five feet 7 ½ inches high no marks or scars apparent on head face or hands, Son of Benjamin and Lilla Foster, born in Amherst County of parents free prior to the 1st of May 1806

Amherst County Court Decem[ber] Term 1851 – Virginia – County of Amherst to wit – 226 – Registered in the Clerks office of Amherst County Court by order of said Court made on the 16th day of December

1851 **LEE BRANHAM** a free man of Colour, son of Nancy Branham a brown mulatto five feet five and ¾ inches high large scar on the inside of thumb of his left hand, no other marks or scars apparent on head face or hands, born in Amherst County of parents free prior to the 1st of May 1806

Amherst County Court April Term 1851 – Virginia – County of Amherst to wit – 227 – Registered in the Clerks office of Amherst County Court by order of said Court made on the 21st day of April 1851 **JOHN MORRISS** a free man of Colour son of Nancy Morriss a brown complexion fine black hair nearly and nearly [sic] straight, a Small scar on the back of each hand, five feet seven ½ Inches high, about forty one years of age, born in Chesterfield of parents free prior to the 1st of May 1806

Amherst County Court April Term 1851 – Virginia County of Amherst to wit – 228 – Registered in the Clerks Office of Amherst County Court by order of said Court made on the 21st day of April 1851. **WILLIAM FOSTER** a free man of colour, son of James Foster, brown complexion, black hair 15 years of age 5 feet 7 ¼ Inches high no marks or scars apparent on head face or hands born in Amherst County of Parents free prior to the 1st of May 1806

Amherst County Court April Term 1851 – Virginia – County of Amherst to wit – 229 – Registered in the Clerks office of Amherst County Court by order of said Court made on the 21st day of April 1851. **CHARLES FOSTER** a free boy of Colour son of James Foster brown complexion strai[gh]t black hair 13 years of age 4 feet 8 Inches high no scars or marks apparent on head face or hands born in Amherst County of Parents free prior to the 1st of May 1806

Amherst County Court April Term 1851 – Virginia – County of Amherst to wit – 230 – Registered in the Clerks office of Amherst County by order of said Court made on the 21st day of May 1851. [*NOTE: Probably should be April.*] **FRANCES KEY** a free woman of Colour daughter of Betsey Key a dark mulatto about forty two years of age, long strai[gh]t black hair, five feet four and ½ Inches high born in Nelson County of parents free prior to the 1st of May 1806

Amherst County Court February Term 1851 – Virginia – County of Amherst to wit – 231 – Registered in the Clerks Office of said County Court by an order made on the 17th day of February 1851 **SALLY KEY** daughter of Betsey Key bright mulatto 5 feet 3 ½ Inches high large scar on the left side of her neck caused by a burn no marks or scars apparent on head face or hands supposed to be about 35 years of age born in Nelson County of Betsey Key said Betsey born of parents free prior to the first of May 1806

Amherst County November Tern 1851 – Virginia – County of Amherst to wit – 232 – Registered in the Clerks office of said County Court by an order made on the 17th day of November 1851 **WILLIAM SCOTT** a bright mulatto 5 feet 9 ¾ Inches high black hair, large scar on the left side of his face caused by Scrofula – no other scars or marks apparent on head face or hands about 24 years of age born in Albemarle County of parents free prior to the 1st of May 1806

Amherst County Court April 21st 1851 – Virginia – Amherst County – 233 – Registered in the Clerks Office of said County Court by an order made on the 21st day of April 1851 **LUCINDA BRANHAM** of dark brown color – 5 feet 1 ½ inches high – straight black hair – No Scar on the face hands or arms – 23 years old – Born in the County of Amherst of parents free prior to the 1st of May 1806

Amherst County Court April 19th 1852 – Virginia – Amherst County – 234 – Registered in the Clerks Office of the County of Amherst, in the State of Virginia on the 19th day of April 1852 – **LIDDA JOHNS** – a bright mulatto – straight black hair – 5 feet 2 Inches high – A scar near the left wrist, produced by a cut – No other apparent Scars – Born in the County of Amherst of parents free prior to the 1st day of May 1806

Amherst County Court, August the 18th 1851 – Virginia – Amherst County – 235 – Registered in the Clerks Office of Amherst County, State of Virginia this 25th day of August 1852 by order of Court made on the 18th of August 1851 **ELIZABETH MORRISS** light brown complexion – black hair, somewhat curled – 19 years of age – 2 Small moles – one on the left side of the nose – the other on the left side of the upper lip – no other mark apparent upon the face, hands, or arms – 5 feet 4 ¾ Inches high – Born free in Amherst County of ancestors free prior to the [*1st*] day of May 1806

Amherst County Clerks Office Sept 6th 1852 – Virginia – Amherst County to wit – 236 – Registered in the Clerks Office of Amherst County, State of Virginia, by an order of Court made on the 21st day of April 1851 – **DELAWARE SCOTT** – a bright mulatto – 29 years of age – 5 feet 11 ½ Inches high – no marks apparent on his hands, face, or breast – born free in the County of Amherst of ancestors free before the 1st day of May 1806

Amherst County Court Clerks Office Octo 15 1852 – State of Virginia – Amherst County to wit – 237 – Registered in the Clerks Office of Amherst County Court, State of Virginia, by an order of Court made the 17th of November 1851 – **WILLIAM SCOTT** – a bright mulatto – 25 years of age – 5 feet 9 ½ Inches high – a Scar upon the left Jaw – no other marks apparent on his hands face or breast – Born in Albemarle County of ancestors free before the 1st day of May 1806

Amherst County Court Clerks Office Nov 18 1852 – Virginia – Amherst County to wit – 238 – Registered in the Clerks Office of Amherst County, State of Virginia, by an order of Court made the 15th day of November 1852 – **ELIZA JANE JOHNSON** – a bright mulatto – about 35 years of age – 5 feet one Inch high – a Small Scar under the left Jaw – no other marks apparent on his [sic] hands, face or breast – Born free in the County of Nelson, of ancestors free before the 1st day of May 1806

Amherst County Court Clerks Office Nov 21 1853 – 239 – Registered in the Clerks Office of Amherst County, State of Virginia, by an order of Court made the 21st day of November 1853 **FRANCES** a bright mulatto – about 33 years of age – 5 feet & ¼ Inch high – no marks apparent on her hands, face or breast – Emancipated by deed from Sally Taylor & Isaac R Reynolds, by deed dated the 20th day of January 1848 & recorded in the Clerks Office of Amherst County on [blank] day of [blank]

Amherst County Court Clerks Office, November 21st 1853 – 240 – Registered in the Clerks Office of Amherst County, State of Virginia, by order of County Court of Amherst, State of Virginia, made the 21 day of November 1853 **MARCELLUS** – a bright mulatto, Son of Frances – 15 years old the 4th of October 1853 – no marks apparent on his hands, face or breast – Emancipated in 1848 by Deed from Sally Taylor & Isaac R Reynolds

Amherst County Court Clerks Office, November 21st 1853 – 241 – Registered in the Clerks Office of Amherst County, State of Virginia, by order of County Court of Amherst, State of Virginia, made the 21st day of November 1853 **HENRY ANN** – a bright mulatto, daughter of Frances – 10 years of age – No marks apparent on her hand, hand face or breast – Emancipated in 1848 by Deed from Sally Taylor & Isaac R Reynolds

Amherst County Court Clerks Office, November 21 1853 – 242 – Registered in the Clerks Office of Amherst County, State of Virginia, by order of the County Court of Amherst, State of Virginia, made the 21st day of November 1853 **IMOGENE** – a bright mulatto – daughter of Frances – 4 years of age 10th of Jan[uar]y 1853 No marks apparent on her hands, face or breast – Emancipated in 1848 by deed from Sally Taylor & Isaac R Reynolds

Amherst County Court Clerks Office April 18 1854 – 243 – Registered in the Clerks Office of Amherst County, State of Virginia, by an order of the County Court of Amherst, made the 18th of April 1854 **SUSAN F JOHNSON** – a bright mulatto - Daughter of Betsy Johnson – 17 years old the 10th of July 1853 born in the County of Nelson State of Virginia, of ancestors free before the 1st day of May 1806 – 5 feet 4 ½ Inches high – No Scars apparent upon her hands, face, breast or arms

State of Virginia – Amherst County – 245 – Amherst County Court Clerks Office April 18th 1854 – Registered in the Clerks Office of Amherst County by an order of Court made 18 April 1852, **FRANCES ANN JOHNSON** – daughter of Susan F Johnson – born of ancestors free before the 1st day of May 1806 – in the County of Amherst, State aforesaid – aged 2 years May 1853 – Brown colour

State of Virginia – Amherst County – 246 – Amherst County Court Clerks Office Sept 27, 1854 Registered in the Clerks Office of Amherst County by an order of court made 18 Sept 1854 **LUCY ANN MORRIS alias TOBIAS** – daughter of Judith Morris alias Tobias – aged 25 years – dark complexion – a flesh mould on right arm – a small scar on the left wrist – no other marks apparent – 5 feet 2 ½ inches high – Born in Nelson County of ancestors free before the 1st day of May 1806

Amherst County Court Clerks Office – May 15th 1854 – Registered in the Clerks office of Amherst County State of Virginia, by an order of the County Court of Amherst made the 15th day of May 1854 **BETSY JOHNSON** a bright mulatto, aged about Forty Six years, born in the County of Nelson State of Virginia of ancestors free before the 1st day of May 1806 – 5 feet 3 ½ Inches high no scars apparent upon her hands, face breast or arms

Amherst County Court Clerks Office – May 15th 1854 – 248 – Registered in the Clerks office of Amherst County State of Virginia, by an order of the County Court of Amherst made the 15th day of May 1854 **LUCY JOHNSON** a bright mulatto, Daughter of Betsy Johnson, Fifteen years old 4th July 1854 – born in the County of Nelson State of Virginia, of ancestors free before the 1st day of May 1806 – 5 feet 6 ¾ Inches high – a flesh mould in front & near the left year [ear], a small scare [scar] on the forehead, no other marks apparent –

Amherst County Court Clerks Office Nov 24 1853 [?] – 249 – Registered [large blank space] **JUDITH COUSINS** – dark complexion – aged thirty years 4 feet 11 ¾ Inches high – two fore teeth missing in the upper jaw – born in the County of Goochland

Amherst County Court Clerks Office March 24 1856 – 250 – State of Virginia – Amherst County – Registered in the Clerks Office of Amherst County, made by an order of the County Court of Amherst at December Court 1855 **CYNTHIA LAWHORN** daughter of Lucinda Lawhorn a white woman of pure blood – about 23 years of age, born in the County of Amherst, whose father is a negro – her complexion is chocolate brown – hair straight & black 5 feet 2 ½ Inches high – No scars apparent on face or hands a small cut on wright arm

Amherst County Court Clerks Office April 18 1856 – 251 – Registered in the Clerks Office of Amherst County Court, by an order of Court made the 18 day of February 1856 **CAMILLA JANE MORRIS alias TOBIAS** – aged about 31 years, daughter of Judith Morris – Born in the County of Nelson, of ancestors free before the 1st day of May 1806 – dark complexion, 5 feet 3 ¼ Inches high – No scars apparent on her hands, face, breast or arms

Amherst County Court Clerks Office April 18 1856 – 252 – Registered in the Clerks Office of Amherst County Court, by an order of Court made the 18 day of February 1856 **McPHERSON ARNOLD** son of John Arnold & Camilla Jane Morris alias Tobias – aged 16 years, born in Amherst County, of parents whose ancestors were free before the 1st day of May 1806 – dark complexion 5 feet 6 ¼ Inches high – No Scars apparent on his hands face breast or arms

Amherst County Court Clerks Office Ap[ril] 23rd 1856 – 253 – Registered in the Clerks Office of Amherst County Court, by an order of Court made the 21st day of April 1856 **TOBIAS MORRIS** a free man of Colour, son of Judy Morris – dark complexion, about 31 years of age – 5 feet 9 ½ Inches high – no marks or scars apparent on his hands face, breast or arms – born in Campbell County, whose mother descended from ancestors free prior to the 1st day of May 1806

Clerks Office of Amherst County Court by an order made at April County Court 1856 **DAVID MORRIS** a free man of Colour – about 47 years of age dark complexion 5 feet 10 inches high – small scar on little finger, one on the 2nd joint of the right arm caused by a burn – no other marks or scars apparent on face, head, hands or arms – born in Campbell County and descended from ancestors free before the first day of May 1806

Amherst County Court Clerks Office April 23rd 1856 – 255 – Register Renewed, by an order of the County Court of Amherst, made on the 21st day of April 1856 **FRANCES KEY** a free woman of colour – a dark complexion mulatto – about 48 years of age – 5 feet 4 ½ Inches high – hair black & straight – no marks or scars apparent on head face or hands – born in Nelson County and descended from ancestors free before the 1st day of may 1806

Amherst County Court Clerks Office April 23rd 1856 – 256 – Register renewed in in the Clerks office of Amherst County Court, by an order of said Court made the 21st day of April 1856 **FRANCES** a bright mulatto, about 36 years of age 5 feet & ¼ Inches high – no marks apparent on her hands, face or breast – Emancipated by Deed from Sally Taylor & Isaac R Reynolds, recorded in the Clerks Office of Amherst County Court on the 21st day of February 1848

Amherst County Court Clerks Office April 23rd 1856 – 257 – Register renewed by an order of Amherst County Court, made on the 21st day of April 1856 **NANCY EVANS alias NANCY MAJORS** a free woman of dark complexion – about 77 years of age – 5 feet 3 inches high – a small scar in the middle of her breast – small scar on the wright side of her neck – no other scar or mark apparent on her head, face or hands – Emancipated by the Will of W Botts of Amelia County on 22nd day of the 7th month 1782

Amherst County Court Clerks Office April 23rd 1856 – 258 – Registered in the Clerks Office of Amherst County Court by an order of Amherst Court made the 21st day of April 1856 **BARTLETT SPARROW** a free man of colour, born in said County of parents free from the 1st day of May 1806 – of dark complexion, 5 feet 9 ½ inches – small scar on right side of his neck – fore finger on left hand broken – large scar on right hand caused by a cut from a knife, no other marks apparent on head face or hands, Sixty years of age

Amherst County Court Clerks Office April 23rd 1856 – 259 – Register renewed by an order of the County Court of Amherst, made the 21st day of April 1856 **IMOGANE** a free girl of Colour – daughter of Frances – about 7 years of age – a bright mulatto – no marks or scars apparent on her hands, face or breast – Emancipated by Deed from Sally Taylor & Isaac R Reynolds

Amherst County Court Clerks Office Ap[ril] 23rd 1856 – 260 – Register renewed by an order of the County Court of Amherst made the 21st day of April 1856 **MARCELLUS** a bright mulatto – Son of Frances – 17 years old the 4th October 1855 – No marks apparent on his hands, face or breast – Emancipated in 1848 by deed from Sally Taylor & Isaac R Reynolds

Amherst County Court Clerks Office May 20 1856 – 261 – Register renewed by an order of the County Court of Amherst made on the 19th day of May 1856 **WILLIAM KEY** about thirty seven years of age a darke mulatto five feet ten inches h[e]ight – a scar on the middle finger on the inside of the joint of the right hand, a scar below the root of the forefinger of the left hand on the out side, and a small scar on the middle of his forehead – no other scars apparent on his head face or hands – born of ancestors free prior to the 1st of May 1806

Amherst county Court Clerks Office May 20th 1856 – 262 – Register renewed by an order of the County Court of Amherst made the 19th day of May 1856 **GEORGE WINTERS** a free man of Colour, born in Nelson County, five feet Eleven and ¼ inches high, dark complexion, several scares [scars] on his neck, cut on the end of his nose caused by Powder, no other scars apparent on his head, face or hands age forty eight years, derived his freedom from ancestors [free] prior to the 1st of May 1806

Amherst County Court Clerks Office May 20th 1856 – 263 –Registered in the Clerks Office of Amherst County Court, by an order made by said Court on the 18 day of February 1856 **NATHAN TUPPENCE** a free man of colour, aged about 22 years, dark brown complexion – 5 feet 8 ½ Inches high – a small scar on the left arm – grey hairs in the top of his head – no other scars apparent on his head, face or hands – born in the County of Amherst of ancestors free before the 1st day of May 1806

Amherst County Court Clerks Office May 21 1856 – 264 – Registered in the Clerks Office of Amherst County Court, by an order made by said Court on the 19th of May 1856 **PLEASANT PETERS** a free man of colour, aged 23 years – black complexion – 5 feet 9 ¾ Inches high – no marks apparent on his head, face or hands – born in the County of Amherst of ancestors free before the 1st day of May 1806

265 – [large blank space] – **MARY ANN BEVERLY** a free woman of colour – bright mulatto – hair straight, 51 years of age – 5 feet & ¼ Inches high – Small mole on the right side of her neck

266 – [large blank space] – **MARTHA ANN BEVERLY** a free woman of colour – brown mulatto – hair straight 24 years of age – 5 feet 3 Inches high – Scar from a burn on left cheek

267 – [large blank space] – **WILLIAM JAMES ALEXANDER BEVERLY** a free boy of colour – brown mulatto – 19 years of age – 5 feet 6 Inches & ¼ high – Small scar on forehead

Amherst County Court Clerks Office July 5 1856 – 268 – Register renewed by the order of Amherst County Court June 17 1856 **SCIPIO SMITH** a free man of color, born free in Hanover County on the 25th of December 1800, of dark complexion, five feet nine inches high, and who has two scars on the back of his left hand, & one on his left wrist – one on his forehead over his right eye – one between his eyebrows, one on his right hand & a small wart on the inside of his left hand – derived his freedom from female ancestors free prior to 1st May 1806

Amherst County Court Clerks Office July 5 1856 – 269 – Registered renewed by the order of Amherst County Court July 17 1856 **SAWNEY STEWARD** a free man of color, born free in Bedford County on the day of [blank] 1828, of black complexion, five feet 6 ½ inches high, and who has a scar across his right knee pan and one on the leg just below

Amherst County Court Clerks Office Ju[?] [?] 1856 – 270 – Register renewed by the order of Amherst County Court June 16 1856 **ALDRIDGE BEVERLY** a free man of colour, born in Buckingham County a bright mulatto – strai[gh]t black hair – scar over the left eye, scar on the left hand, caused by a pistol shot; scar on the right wrist – no other scars apparent on head, face or hands – about 28 years of age – 5 feet 9 inches high born of female ancestors free prior to first May 1806

Amherst county court Clerks Office August 20 1856 – 271 – Register renewed by order of Amherst County Court August 18 1856 **JOHN MORRIS** a free man of colour, son of Nancy Morris – brown complexion & fine black hair & nearly straight – small scar on the back of each hand, no other scars or marks apparent on head face or hands – 5 feet 7 ½ inches high – 47 years of age, born in the County of Chesterfield of ancestors free before the 1st day of May 1806

Amherst County Court Clerks Office August 27 1856 – 272 – Registered by order of Amherst August Court 1856 **SOPHIA PADGETT** a free woman of colour – daughter of Sucky Padgett – bright complexion – hair straight – no scars apparent on face head or hands, 5 feet 3 ½ Inches – born in Amherst County of ancestors free before the 1st day of May 1806

Amherst County Court Clerks Office May 20 1856 – Register renewed by order of May Court 1856 **THOMAS PETERS** a free man of colour – about 26 years of age – Mulatto – Scar on left side of neck – Mole on nose – no other scars apparent on head, face or hands – 5 feet 6 ½ inches high – born in Amherst County & descended from ancestors free before the 1st day of May 1806

Amherst County Court Clerks [Office] October 20 1856 – 273 – Registered in the Clerks Office by order of October County Court **SARAH JANE JOHNSON** a free woman of colour daughter of Betsy Johnson, bright brown complexion – fine black hair, nearly straight – no scars apparent on her face, head or hands – born in the County of Nelson of ancestors free before the 1st day of May 1806 – 5 feet 2 ¾ Inches high – 15 years of age

Amherst County Court Clerks Office October 20 1856 – 274 – Registered in the Clerks Office by order of October County Court 1856 **ELIZA MILDRED JOHNSON** a free girl of colour, daughter of Betsy Johnson – bright brown complexion – fine black hair, nearly straight – no scars apparent on her face, head or hands – born in the County of Amherst of parents free before the 1st day of May 1806 – 13 years of age – 5 feet 2 ¾ Inches high

Amherst County Court Clerks Office February [blank] 1857 – Registered in the Clerks Office by order of February County Court 1857 **ELIZA JANE JOHNSON** a bright mulatto about 40 years of age – 5 feet one inch high – a small scar under the left jaw – no other marks apparent on her hands, face or breast – Born free in the County of Nelson - of ancestors free before the 1st day of May 1806

Amherst County Court Clerks Office March 6 1857 – 276 – Registered in Clerks Office by order of February County Court 1857 **JUDDY BIAS** dark complexion – about 23 years of age – 5 feet 4 Inches high – a small scar near the left wrist – no other scars or marks on head, face or hands – Born in the County of Amherst of ancestors free before the 1st day of May 1806

Amherst County Court Clerks Office March 16 1857 – 278 – Registered in Clerks Office by order of March Court 1857 **ELIZABETH BEVERLEY** a free woman of colour – bright mulatto – 23 years of age – small scar over left eye – small scar on wright hand – no other scars on head, face or hands – hair black & straight – 5 feet 4 Inches high – Born in Buckingham County of ancestors free before the 1st day of May 1806

Amherst County Court Clerks Office March 16 1857 – 279 – Registered in Clerks Office by order of March Court 1857 **JAMES PINN** a free man of colour – bright mulatto – 23 years of age – 5 feet 7 ½ Inches high – hair black & strai[gh]t – Scar on left arm no other scars on head face or hands – Born in Amherst of ancestors free before the 1st day of May 1806

Amherst County Court Clerks Office March 20 1857 – 280 – Register renewed by order of Amherst County Court Feb[ruar]y term 1857 **JOHN TURNER PINN** a free man of colour – bright mulatto – 31 years of age – 5 feet 7 Inches high – hair black & straight – large scar on right cheek from a burn – scar from a burn on right arm – no other scars apparent on head face or hands – Born in Amherst from ancestors free before the 1st day of May 1806

Amherst County Court Clerks Office March 20 1857 – 281 – Registered by order of Amherst County Court March Term 1857 **MARTHA ANN PINN** a free woman of colour – bright mulatto – straight black hair – 36 years old – 5 feet 4 ¼ Inches high – scar on right hand – dark spot on each cheek – scar on right side of face near mouth no other scars apparent on face head or hands – Born in Buckingham & descended from ancestors free before the 1st of May 1806

Amherst County Court Clerks Office April 15 1857 – 282 – Registered in the Clerks Office by order of March Court 1857 **BETSEY PETERS** bright mulatto – about 24 years of age – 5 feet 4 ¾ Inches high – no scars on head, face or hands – born in the County of Amherst & descended from ancestors free before the 1st day of May 1806

Amherst County Court Clerks Office July 21 1857 - 283 – Registered in the Clerks Office by order of June Court 1856 **WASHINGTON PETERS** Dark complexion – about 25 years of age 5 feet 6 inches high – Scar on right wrist near the hand – scar on left knee – no other scars apparent on face, head or hands – born in the County of Amherst of parents free before the first of May 1806

Amherst County Court Clerks Office July 22 1857 – 284 – Registered in the Clerks Office by order of Amherst County Court June Term 1856 – **W H PETERS** a bright mulatto – 27 years of age – Scar on neck from a burn – scar on right thigh – no other scars apparent on head face or hands, except scar on forehead – 5 feet 8 ½ inches high – born in the County of Amherst of ancestors free before the first day of May 1806

Amherst County Court Clerks Office June 23rd 1858 – 285 – Registered in the Clerks Office by order of Amherst County Court June Term 1858 **ACHILLES MASON** a bright mulatto – 26 years of age – two fingers on left hand injured – bone in right shoulder once broken – no other scars apparent – 5 feet 10 ¾ inches high – hair black & straight – born in Amherst County of Amherst of ancestors free before the first of May 1806

Amherst County Court Clerks Office November 27 1858 – 286 – Registered in the Clerks Office by order of Court made at November Term 1858 **MARY JANE SORRELL** bright mulatto – about 22 years of age – 5 feet high – Small Scar over right eye brow – no scars apparent on head, face or hands – born in the County of Amherst & descended from ancestors free before the 1st day of May 1806

Amherst County Court Clerks Office May 19 1859 – 287 – Registered in the Clerks Office by order of the County Court of Amherst made at May Court 1859 **ALEXANDER WARREN** bright mulatto – about 26 years of age – 5 feet 9 ¾ inches high – no scars of any note on his head, face or hands – right leg about 6 inches shorter than the left occasioned by the white swelling – born in the County of Amherst & descended from ancestors free before the 1st day of May 1806

Amherst County Court Clerks Office October 22 1859 – 288 – Register renewed in Clerks Office by order of October Court 1859 **HEZEKIAH CATO** a mulatto – 5 feet 8 inches high – 28 years of age – no scars apparent on head, face or hands – scar in right shin bone – born in Amherst County & descended from ancestors free before the 1st day of May 1806

Amherst County Court Clerks Office Jan[uar]y 10 1860 – 289 – Registered in the Clerks Office by order made at December Court 1860 [probably should be 1859] **SALLY ANN PETERS** of a dark brown complexion 5 feet 2 ½ inches high 33 years of age – no scars apparent on head, face or hands – born in Amherst County & descended from ancestors free before the 1st day of May 1806

Amherst County Court Clerks Office January 26 1860 – 290 – Registered in the Clerks Office by order of Amherst County Court made at December Court 1859 **MARY JANE** bright mulatto – Aged 28 years – 5 feet 3 inches high – black waiving hair – Small scar on right arm – no other scars apparent on head, face or hands – born in the County of Amherst and emancipated by deed from Nancy Simpson dated the 13th October 1859

Amherst County Court Clerks Office January 26th 1860 – 291 – Registered in the Clerks Office by order of Amherst County Court made at December Court 1859 **LUCY ANN** 12 years of age – brown strai[gh]t hair – 5 feet 2 inches high scar on right leg – no other scar on head, face or hands – born in the County of Amherst – daughter of Mary Jane – Emancipated by deed from Nancy Simpson by deed dated the 13th October 1859

Amherst County Court Clerks Office January 26th 1860 – 292 – Registered in the Clerks by order of Amherst County Court made at December Court 1859 **INDIANNA & MISSOURI** both bright mulattoes – no scars apparent on the head, face or hands of either, the first aged about 7 years & the other about 4 – both born in the County of Amherst & children of Mary Jane & emancipated by deed from Nancy Simpson dated the 13th October 1859

Amherst County Court Clerks Office February 8 1860 – 293 – Registered in the Clerks Office by order of Amherst County Court made at December Court 1859 **FRANK CRAIG** dark brown – 21 years of age – 2 Scars on left wrist – no other scars on head, face or hands – 5 feet 5 ¼ inches high – descended from ancestors free before the first [day of] May 1806

Amherst County Court Clerks Office Feb[ruar]y 11 1860 – 294 – Register renewed in the Clerks Office by order of Amherst January Court 1860 **TURNER SPARROW** dark complexion – 5 feet 11 ½ inches high – no scar apparent on face, head or hands – born in the County of Amherst of ancestors free before the 1st day of May 1806

Amherst County Court Clerks Office Feb[ruar]y 28 1860 – 295 – Register renewed by order of Amherst Feb[ruar]y Court 1860 **JAMES HENRY**

SPARROW dark complexion – aged 29 years – 5 feet 9 ½ inches no scars apparent on head, face or hands – born in Amherst County & descended from ancestors free before the 1st day of May 1806

Amherst County Court Clerks Office March 28 1860 – 296 – Registered in the Clerks [Office] by order of Amherst March Court 1860 **ELLEN FRANCES HARTLESS commonly called MASON** 21 years of age – bright mulatto – 5 feet ½ inch high – no scars apparent on head, face or hands – born in Amherst County & descended from ancestors free before 1st day of May 1806

Amherst County Court Clerks Office April 17 1860 – 296 – Registered in the Clerks Office by order of Amherst April Court 1860 **GEORGE JEWELL** bright mulatto – about 45 years of age – Scar over left eye – 5 feet 5 inches & a half high – no other scars apparent on head face or hands – descended from ancestors free before that 1st day of May 1806 & born in the County of Amherst

Amherst County Court Clerks Office April 16 1860 – 197 – Registered in the Clerks Office by order of April Court 1860 **ALEXANDER EVANS TAYLOR** a free man of color – mulatto complexion – 5 feet 9 inches high – Scar on his right fore arm & one on the back of the left wrist – 46 years of age – born in Richmond & descended from ancestors free before the 1st May 1806

Amherst County Court Clerks Office April 19 1860 – 298 – Register renewed by order of Amherst April Term 1860 **JUDITH COUSINS** dark complexion – aged thirty five years – 4 feet 11 ¾ inches high – two fore teeth missing in the upper jaw – born in the County of Goochland & descended from ancestors free before the 1st May 1806 – no marks apparent on head face or hands

Amherst County Court Clerks Office April 19 1860 – 299 – Registered by order of Amherst April Term 1860 **CLARA COUSINS** a free woman of colour – dark complexion – about 26 years of age – 5 feet ½ inch high – no marks apparent on head, face or hands – born in the County of Goochland & descended from ancestors free before the 1st day of May 1806

Amherst County Court Clerks Office Ap[ril] 19 1860 – 300 – Registered by order of Amherst April Term 1860 **PHOEBE COUSINS** a free Woman [of] colour – about 25 years of age – dark complexion – 5 feet 4 inches high – has a scar on her chin – and another scar on the thumb of the left hand – born in the County of Goochland & descended from ancestors free before the 1st May 1806

Amherst County court Clerks Office April 19 1860 – 301 – Registered in the Clerks Office by order of April Court 1860 **WILLIAM TYLER** a free man of colour – brown complexion – five feet 5 ½ inches high – about 45 years old – Scar on the fore finger of left hand – no other marks on face, head or hands – born in the County of Fluvanna & descended from ancestors free before the 1st day of May 1806

Amherst County Court Clerks Office April 19 1860 – 302 – Registered renewed by order of Amherst April Court 1860 **TABITHA BAUGH alias LOGAN** a free woman of colour – bright mulatto – about 48 years old 5 feet 2 ½ inches high no scar on face, head or hands – born in the County of Goochland & descended from ancestors free before the 1st day of May 1806

Amherst County Court Clerks Office April 27 1860 – 303 – Registered in the Clerks Office by order of April Court 1860 **RICHARD H BRANHAM** a free man of colour – about 26 years of age – bright complexion – Scar on fore finger of left hand – no other scars on face, head or hands – 5 feet 10 inches high – born in the County of Amherst & descended from ancestors free before the 1st day of May 1806

Amherst County Court Clerks Office May 4 1860 –304 – Registered in Clerks Office by order of April Court 1860 **FIELDING FOSTER** a free man of colour – 28 years of age – bright complexion – no Scar apparent on head face or hands – 5 feet 8 ¼ inches high – born in Amherst County & descended from ancestors free before the 1st day of May 1806

Amherst County Court Clerks Office May 4, 1860 – 305 - Registered in Clerks Office by order of April Court 1860 **JOHN FOSTER** a free man of colour – bright brown complexion – 21 years of age – Scar on middle finger of left hand – no other scar apparent on head, face or hands – 5 feet 9 inches high – born in Amherst & descended from ancestors free before the 1st day of May 1806 [*NOTE: "Renewed in 1863" is written across this entry.*]

Amherst County Court Clerks Office May 5 1860 –306 – Registered in Clerks Office by order of April Court 1860 **WILLIAM TYLER JR.** a free man of colour – 21 years of age – brown complexion – 5 feet 5 ½ inches high – little finger on left hand crooked – no other scar apparent on head, face or hands – born in Fluvanna & descended from ancestors free before the 1st day of May 1806

Amherst County Court Clerks Office May 5 1860 –307 – Registered in Clerks Office by order of April Court 1860 **HENRY TYLER** a free man of colour – 19 years of age – brown complexion – 5 feet 5 ¼ inches high – scar on back of right hand – no other scar apparent on head, face or hands – born in Fluvanna - & descended from ancestors free before the 1st day of May 1806

Amherst County Court Clerks Office May 7 1860 – 308 – Register renewed by order of April Court 1860 **WILLIAM FOSTER** a free man of colour – aged 25 years – brown complexion – 5 feet 9 ½ inches high – no scars apparent on head, face or hands – born in Amherst & descended from ancestors free before the 1st day of May 1806

Amherst County Court Clerks Office May 7 1860 –309 – Registered by order of April Court 1860 **EDWARD FOSTER** a free man of colour – aged 16 years – bright brown complexion – 5 feet 7 ¼ inches high – Small knot on each little finger – no other marks apparent on head face or hands – born in Amherst & descended from ancestors free before 1st day of May 1806

Amherst County Court Clerks Office May 7 1860 – 310 – Register renewed by order of April Court 1860 **JAMES FOSTER** a free man of colour – about 74 years of age – dark complexion 5 feet 7 ½ inches high – no scar apparent on head, face or hands – born in Amherst & descended from ancestors free before the 1st May 1806

Amherst County Court Clerks Office May 7 1860 –311 – Registered by order of April Court 1860 **OBEDIAH NUCKLES** a free man of colour – bright complexion – 5 feet 10 ¾ inches high – Small scar between eye brows – no other scar apparent on head, face or hands – born in Amherst & descended from ancestors free before the 1st day of May 1806

Amherst County Court Clerks Office May 8 1860 –312 – Registered by order of April Court 1860 **JORDINA BRANHAM** a free woman of colour – bright complexion – aged 19 years – no scar apparent on head, face or hands – 5 feet 2 ¾ inches high – born in Amherst & descended from ancestors free before 1st of May 1806

Amherst County Court Clerks Office May 1860 – 313 – Registered by order of April Court 1860 **PAULINA BRANHAM** a free woman of colour – bright complexion – aged 18 years – small scar on left cheek – no other scar apparent on head, face or hands – 5 feet 7 ½ inches high – born in Amherst & descended from ancestors free before 1st May 1806

Amherst County Court Clerks Office May 8 1860 –314 – Registered by order of April Court 1860 **CHRISTINA JOHNS** a free woman of colour – bright complexion –about 21 years of age – 5 feet ¾ inches high – small scar on left wrist – none other on head, face or hands – born in Amherst & descended from ancestors free before the 1st day of May 1806

Amherst County Court Clerks Office May 14 1860 – 315 – Registered by order of April Court 1860 **WILLIAM SCOTT** a free man of colour – bright complexion – about 32 years of age – scar on left cheek – scar under right cheek bone – no other scar apparent on head face or hands – born in Albemarle County & descended from ancestors free before the 1st May 1806 – 5 feet 10 inches high

Amherst County Court Clerks Office May 14 1860 – 316 – Registered by order of Ap[ri]l Court 1860 **FRANCES E BEVERLY** a free man of colour – bright complexion – 26 years of age – 5 feet 7 ¾ inches high scar on right arm – no other scars apparent on head, face or hands – born in Appomattox & descended from ancestors free before the 1st day of May 1806

Amherst County Court Clerks Office May 14 1860 – 317 – Registered by order of April Court 1860 **MARY BEVERLEY** a free woman of colour – bright complexion – 27 years of age – 5 feet 4 inches high – mole on neck & face – small scar on breast + one on thumb of right hand – small scar near left wrist – no other scars apparent on head, face or hands –born in Appomattox- Descended from ancestors free before the 1st of May 1806

Amherst County Court Clerks Office May 14 1860 – 318 – Registered by order of April Court 1860 **ISABELLA BRANHAM** a free woman of colour – bright complexion – about 45 years of age – 5 feet 1 inches high – mole on nose – no other marks apparent on head, face or hands – born in Amherst & descended from ancestors free before the 1st day of May 1806

Amherst County Court Clerks Office May 21 1860 – 319 – Registered in the Clerks Office by order of May Court 1860 **WILLIAM BRANHAM** a free man of colour – Bright complexion – 44 years of age – 5 feet 6 ½ inches h[e]ight Scar on first joint four [fore] finger of right hand & scar on thumb On left hand, burn on left side of breast – and Scar on left Side of Calf of left leg – no other marks or scars apparent on head face or hands – born in Amherst & descended from ancestors free before 1st day of May 1806

Amherst County Court Clerks Office May 21 1860 – 320 – Registered by order of May Court 1860 **JOSIAH PETERS** a free boy of colour 16 years of Age – bright complexion 5 feet 10 inches high – burn on right side of right hand, two black moles on left side of Neck, no other scars or marks apparent on head face or hands, born in Amherst & descended from ancestors free before the first day of May 1806

Amherst County Court Clerks Office May 21 1860 – 321 – Registered by order of May Court 1860 **ELIZABETH PETERS** a free woman of colour bright complexion, 5 feet & 1 ¼ inches high – aged 22 years, little finger on left hand cut off at 2d joint, scar on right corner of right eye, born in Amherst & descended from ancestors free before the 1st day of May 1806 [*NOTE: A loose draft copy of this entry, found in the back of the Register, describes her also as the wife of Thos. Peters and having a burn on the left side of her neck.*]

Amherst County Court Clerks Office May 21 1860 – 322 – Registered by order of May Court 1860 **MILDRED PETERS** a free woman of coulor [colour], dark complexion, aged 55 years, 5 feet 3 ½ inches high, Scar on left arm below elbow, No other Scars apparent on head face or hands – born in Nelson County & descended from ancestors free before the first day of May 1806 [*NOTE: A loose draft copy of this entry, found in the back of the Register, describes her as having a dark brown complexion.*]

Amherst County Court Clerks Office May 21st 1860 – 323 – Registered by order of Amherst County May Court 1860 **JOHN WINTERS** a free boy of colour – brown complexion, 16 years of age, 5 feet 6 ¼ inches high no scars apparent on head face or hands, born in Amherst – descended from ancestors free before the 1st day of May 1806

Amherst County Court Clerks Office May 21 1860 – 324 – Registered by order of May Court 1860 **ELIZABETH WINTERS** a free woman of colour Brown complexion – 16 years of age – 5 feet 4 & ½ inches high – Scar on first joint third finger on right hand – no other scars apparent on head face or hands, born in Amherst – Descended from ancestors free before the 1st day of May 1806

Amherst County Court Clerks Office May 21 1860 – 325 – Registered by order of May Court 1860 **MARY WINTERS** a free girl of colour, 14 years of age – 5 feet 2 ¼ inches high, Scar at the first joint of 3d & 4th fingers on left hand – Scar between eye brows no other scars apparent on head face or hands – born in Nelson County from ancestors free before the 1st day of May 1806 [*NOTE : A loose, draft copy of this entry, found in the back of the Register, describes her as having a bright complexion.*]

Amherst County Court Clerks Office May 21 1860 – 326 – Registered by order of May Court 1860 **WM H WINTERS** a free man of colour bright complexion – 19 years of age, 5 feet 6 ½ inches h[e]ight – Scar on right Side forehead, no other Scars apparent on head face or hand, born in Amherst – Descended from Ancestors free before the first day of May 1806

Amherst County Court Clerks Office May 21 1860 – 327 – Registered by order of May Court 1860 **LUCY WINTERS** a free woman of colour b[*r*]own complexion, 21 years of age – 5 feet 4 ½ inches high, no scars or marks apparent on head face or hands – born in Nelson County – Descended from ancestors free before the 1st day of May 1806 [*NOTE: A loose, draft copy of this entry, found in the back of the Register, describes her as never having been registered.*]

Amherst County Court Clerks Office June 27th 1860 –328 – Register renewed by order of Amherst June Term 1860 **FRANCES KEY** a free woman of colour, daughter of Betsey Key, dark complexion, about 51 years of age – strai[gh]t black hair, 5 feet four and ½ inches high born in Nelson County, from ancestors free before the 1st day of May 1806

Amherst County Court Clerks Office June 27 1860 – 329 – Register renewed by order of Amherst June Term 1860 **DAVID BIAS** a free man of colour – dark complexion, 50 years of age, little finger on right hand crooked at 2d joint – mole on back of left hand between little finger & wrist, no other scars or marks apparent on head face or hands, born in Campbell County from ancestors free before the 1st day of May 1806

Amherst County Court Clerks Office July 10 1860 –330- Registered by order of June Term 1860 **JANE EVANS** a free woman of color, bright complexion, 40 years of age, 5 feet 6 ½ inches high, Scar on the middle joint of fore finger, on left hand, straight black hair, born in Amherst County from ancestors free before the 1st day of May 1806

Amherst County Court Clerks Office May 25 1860 – 331 – Registered by order of May Court 1860 **LEVINA (?) PINN** a free woman of color – Brown Complexion, 5 feet 9 ¼ inches high – Scar on right wrist – one upper front tooth out – two moles on left side of lower lip – no other marks or scars apparent on head face or hands, born in Amherst, from ancestors free before the 1st day of May 1806

Amherst County Court Clerks Office May 25 1860 – 332 – Register renewed by order of Amherst County Court May Term 1860 **JOHN PINN** a free man of color, dark complexion, 48 years of age, 6 feet high, - Scar on little finger on right hand, and scar on middle first joint same hand – one on fore finger left hand – mole above right eyebrow – no other scars or marks apparent on head face or hands – born in Amherst from Ancestors free before the 1st day of May 1806

Amherst County Court Clerks Office May 25 1860 – 333 – Registered by order of May Court 1860 **EDMUND BRANHAM** a free man of color, bright complexion – aged 56 years, 5 feet 6 Inches high – fore finger broke at second joint on left hand, no other scars or marks apparent on head face or hands, born in Amherst & descended from Ancestors free before the 1st day of May 1806

Amherst County Court Clerks Office May 25 1860 – 334 – Register renewed by order of Amherst County Court May Term 1860 **MARY CATHARINE BEVERLY** a free woman of color, bright complexion, 19 years of age, 5 feet ¼ inches high, mark on right arm, between elbow & wrist – no other marks or scars apparent on head face hands or wrist, born in Appomattox from Ancestors free before the 1st day of May 1806 [*NOTE: Same entry, #334, follows, with this notation: "In witness whereof I have hereunto set my hand and affixed the seal of the said Court this 25th day of May 1860 & in the 84th year of the Commonwealth." Signed by Sam[uel] M Garland, Cl[er]k.*]

*Following this entry is a printed registration form from the City of Lynchburg registering **SAWNEY STEWART**, born in Bedford County in 1828. The form has been crossed through and the notation "Renewed" written across it with a date of June 17, 1851.*

Amherst County Could Clerks Office May 25 1860 – 335 – Registered by order of May Court 1860 **CAROLINE BRANHAM** a free woman of color bright complexion, aged 14 years, 5 feet 7 ¼ inches high – Scar under right ear – scar on third finger on right hand – no other scars or marks apparent on head face or hands born in Amherst & descended from ancestors free before the 1st day of May 1806

A loose, draft copy of the following entry was found in the back of the Register but was never officially entered: ***RITTY BEVERLY*** *– brown complexion, 50 years of age, 5 feet 2 inches high, no scars, born in Buckingham.*

Amherst County Court Clerks Office May 25 1860 – 336 – Register renewed by order of May Court 1860 **MARY BEVERLY** a free woman of color – brown complexion, 53 years of age, 5 feet 5 ½ inches high right eye ball nearly white, partially blind in right eye, no other marks or scars apparent on head face or hands –born in Buckingham – descended from Ancestors free before the 1st day of May 1806 [*NOTE: A loose, draft copy of this entry, found in the back of the Register, describes her right eye as nearly blind, getting white.*]

Amherst County Court Clerks Office May 25 1860 – 337 – Register Renewed by order of Amherst county Court May Term 1860 **MARIA SUSAN BEVERLY** a free woman of Color – bright complexion – 22 years of age, 5 feet 6 ½ inches high, Scar on right wrist, no other scars apparent on head face or hands, born in [blank] from ancestors free before the 1st day of May 1806 [*NOTE: A loose, draft copy of this entry, found in the back of the Register, describes her as born in Buckingham, registered in Nelson County in 1856, and gives her first name as Mary rather than Maria.*]

Amherst County Court Clerks Office July 12 1860 –338- Registered by order of June Court 1860 **JAMES CLARK** a free man of colour – dark brown complexion – 59 years of age – two fingers on right hand mashed at the end – right leg has been broke – born in Amherst & descended from ancestors free before the 1st day of May 1806 – 5 feet 7 ¼ inches high

Amherst County Court Clerks Office July 12 1860 –339- Registered by order of June Court 1860 **NELSON CLARK** a free man of colour – brown complexion – 67 years of age – 5 feet 11 ½ Inches high – born in Bedford – no scars apparent on head face or hands & descended from ancestors free before the 1st of May 1806

Amherst County Court Clerks Office July 12 1860 -340-Registered by order of June Court 1860 **NANCY WINTERS** a free woman of colour – dark complexion – 48 years of age – no scar apparent on head face or hands – 4 feet 10 inches high – born in Nelson County & descended from ancestors free before the 1st day of May 1806

Amherst County Court Clerks Office July 13 1860 – 341 – Register renewed by order of June Court 1860 **BETSY SNEAD** a free woman of colour, bright complexion, 5 feet 3 ½ inches high – three large moles on left side of face and neck, Small scar on left hand near the thumb – no other scars apparent on head face or hands – about 39 years of age, born in Nelson County – from ancestors free before the first day of May 1806

Amherst County Court Clerks Office July 16 1860 –342- Registered by order of June Court 1860 **EDITHA ANN PETERS** a free woman of colour – aged 33 years black complexion – Scar on forehead no other scar apparent on head, face or hands – 5 feet 2 ¼ inches high born in Amherst & descended from ancestors free before the 1st May 1806

Amherst County Court Clerks Office July 16 1860 –343- Registered by order of June Court 1860 **MARY ELIZABETH PETERS** a free woman of colour – aged 18 years – brown complexion – 5 feet 6 inches high no scar apparent on head face or hands – born in Amherst & descended from ancestors free before the first of May 1806

Amherst County Court Clerks Office July 23 1860 – 344 – Registered by order of July Court 1860 **TARLTON JOHNS** a free man of colour, bright complexion, 50 years of age – 5 feet 8 ¾ inches high mark under the breast on right side, no other marks or scars apparent on head face or hands – born in Amherst County from Ancestors free before the 1st day of May 1806

Amherst County Court Clerks Office July 23 1860 – 345 – Registered by order of July Court 1860 **CHARLES P JOHNS** a free man of colour – bright complexion, 27 years of age, 5 feet 7 ¼ inches high no scars apparent on head face or hands, born in Amherst County - from ancestors free before the 1st day of May 1806

Amherst County Court Clerks Office July 23 1860 – 346 – Registered by order of July Court 1860 **ESTRIDGE JOHNS** a free man of colour – bright complexion – 21 years of age – 5 feet 7 ½ inches high – no scars apparent on head face or hands – born in Amherst County from ancestors free before the 1st day of May 1806

Amherst County Court Clerks Office July 23 1860 – 347 – Registered by order of July Court 1860 **TARLTON JOHNS JR** a free boy of colour bright complexion – 16 years of age – 5 feet 3 ½ inches high, no scars apparent on head face or hands, born in Amherst County from ancestors free before the 1st day of May 1806

Amherst County Court Clerks Office July 23 1860 – 348 – Registered by order of July Court 1860 **PRESTON JOHNS** a free boy of colour, bright complexion, 13 years of age, 4 feet 9 ¼ inches high 2 small scars on fore finger on left hand 1st & 2d joints, and one on thumb, no other scars apparent on head face or hands, born in Amherst County, from Ancestors free before the 1st day of May 1806

Amherst County Court Clerks Office July 24 1860 – 349 – Register renewed by order of July Court 1860 **LEE BRANHAM** a free man of colour – brown complexion – 66 years of age – 5 feet 3 ¼ [?] inches high – Scar on inside of thumb on left hand, no other scars apparent on head face or hands – born in Amherst County from ancestors free before the 1st day of May 1806

Amherst County Court Clerks Office July 24 1860 – 350 – Registered by order of July court 1860 **MARY ANN PAXTON** a free woman of colour – bright complexion – 22 years of age – 5 feet 2 ¼ inches high – diseased with the scalled [?] head – no other marks or scars apparent on head face or hands – born in Amherst County from ancestors free before the 1st day of May 1806

Amherst County Court Clerks Office July 24 1860 – 351 – Registered by order of July Court 1860 **WILLIAM S JOHNS** a free man of colour – brown complexion, 27 years of age – 5 feet 8 inches high – small scar on fore finger left hand, no other scars apparent on head face or hands – born in Amherst County from ancestors free before the 1st day of May 1806

Amherst County Court Clerks Office July 25 1860 – 352 – Registered by order of July Court 1860 **WILLIAM B JOHNS** a free man of color [colour] – brown complexion, 57 years of age, 5 feet 9 ½ inches high – small scar on the end of 3d & 4th fingers on left hand – small scar between eye brows – no other scars apparent on head face or hands – born in Amherst county from ancestors free before the 1st day of May 1806

Amherst County Court Clerks Office July 25 1860 – 353 – Registered by order of July Court 1860 **JOSHUA JOHNS** a free man of color – bright complexion – 17 years of age – 5 feet 10 ½ inches high – small scar on 2d finger on left hand, no other scars apparent on head face or hands – born in Amherst County from ancestors free before the 1st day of May 1806

Amherst County Court Clerks Office July 25 1860 – 354 – Registered by order of July Court 1860 **PHILLIP JOHNS** a free boy of color, brown complexion – 15 years of age, 5 feet 11 ¼ inches high – stiff fore finger on right hand – no other marks or scars apparent on head face or hands – born in Amherst County from ancestors free before the 1st day of May 1806

Amherst County court Clerks Office July 26 1860 – 355 – Registered by order of July Court 1860 **REUBEN H WISE** a free man of color, bright Complexion, 34 years of age, 5 feet 7 ¼ inches high scar on end of 3rd finger on right hand – no other scars apparent on head face or hands, born in Amherst County from ancestors free before the 1st day of May 1806

Amherst County Court Clerks Office July 26 1860 – 356 – Registered by order of July Court 1860 **JOHN SHEPPARD** a free man of color bright complexion – 23 years of age – 5 feet 8 ¼ inches h[e]ight, Small scar on thumb on left hand – no other scars apparent on head face or hands, born in Amherst County from ancestors free before the 1st day of May 1806

Amherst County Court Clerks Office July 26 1860 – 357 – Registered by order of July Court 1860 **MARTHA JANE WISE** a free woman of color – 26 years of age – 5 feet 2 inches high – bright Complexion – no marks or scars apparent on head face or hands – born in Amherst County from ancestors free before the 1st day of May 1806

Amherst County Court Clerks Office July 26 1860 – 358 – Registered by order of July court 1860 **LOUISA JOHNS** a free woman of color – bright complexion – 17 years of age – 5 feet 4 inches high, no scars apparent on head face or hands – born in Amherst County – from ancestors free before the 1st day of May 1806

Amherst County Court Clerks Office August 2nd 1860 – 359 – Register renewed by order of May Court 1860 **JOHN TYLER** a free man of colour – bright complexion – 5 feet 6 ¼ inches high – no scars apparent on head, face, or hands – about 26 years of age – born in Fluvanna & descended from ancestors free before the 1st May 1806

Amherst County Court Clerks Office August 14 1860 – 360 – Registered by order of February Court 1860 **MARIA SPARROW** a free woman of colour – dark complexion – aged about 50 years – 5 feet 8 ½ inches high – scar over the right temple and one on the right side of the mouth – no other scars apparent on face head or hands – born in Buckingham County & descended from ancestors free before the 1st May 1806

Amherst County Court Clerks Office August 21st 1860 – 361 – Register renewed by order of August Court 1860 **SAMUEL CUSINS** a free man of colour dark complexion, 5 feet 8 ½ inches high, about 27 years of age, born in County of Goochland, Scar on the inside of left hand, one on the little finger of the same – right eye out, and impediment in speech, no other marks or scars of moment apparent on head face or hands, descended from ancestors free before the first day of May 1806

Amherst County Court Clerks Office Jan[uar]y 26 1859 – 362 – Registered in the Clerks Office by order of Amherst County Court made at December Court 1859 **GASTON OTEY** bright mulatto aged about one year, no scars apparent on head face or hands born in Amherst County, Son of Mary Jane, and emancipated by deed from Nancy Simpson, dated the 13th October 1859

Amherst County Court October Term 1860 – 363 – Registered by order of October Court 1860 **MARY SUSAN EVANS** a free woman of colour – bright complexion, aged 22 years, 5 feet 3 ¼ inches high, Scar on forehead above the nose, and burn on right shoulder – no other marks or scars apparent on head face or hands, born in Amherst County, and descended from ancestors free before the 1st day of May 1806

Amherst County Court Clerks Office June 20 1861 – 364 – Register renewed by order of June Court 1861 **SQUIRE JACKSON** a free man of Colour Dark Brown complexion aged about 61 years Five feet 7 inches high left hand cut off above the wrist and the under part of the right ear cut off – no other marks or Scars apparent on head face or hands

Amherst County Court Clerks Office July 15 1861 – 365 – Registered by order of Amherst County Court, July Term 1861 **WILLIAM WHITE** a free man of colour – Dark complexion – aged about 30 years 5 feet 8 inches high – scar over the left temple – No other scars on head, face or hands – born in Amherst County & descended from ancestors free before the first day of May 1806

Amherst County Court Clerks Office A[u]g[u]st 23rd 1861 – 366 – Registered by order of Amherst County Court August Term 1861 **RICHARD HERN** a free person of colour 33 years of age – 5 feet 11 ½ inches high brown complexion – pitted with the small pox – no other marks or scars apparent on head face or hands – born free & descended from ancestors free before the 1st day of May 1806

Amherst County Court Clerks Office August 25 1861 – 367 – Registered by order of Amherst County Court A[u]g[u]st Term 1861 **JOHN BEVERLEY** a free man of colour, about 37 years of age – Six feet high – Small scar on the wrist – no other scars or marks apparent on head, face or hands – bright brown complexion – born in Nelson County & descended from ancestors free before the 1st day of May 1806

Amherst County Court Clerks Office September 2nd – 368 – Registered by order of Amherst County Court August Term 1861 **SEGUS ANN SPARROW** a free woman of colour Brown complexion aged about 25 years 5 feet 6 inches high Scare [Scar] on the right hand & a Small Scare [Scar] on the right arm below the elbow no other Scares [Scars] on the head face or hand born free of ancestors who were free before the 1st of May 1806

Amherst County Court Clerks Office September 18 1861 – 369 – Registered by order of Amherst September Court 1861 **JOICY ANN MARIA SPARROW** a free woman of colour – aged 23 years – brown complexion – 5 feet 7 inches high – Scar on left arm from burn – also a small scar on wrist produced by cut – no other scars on head, face or hands – born in Amherst County & descended from ancestors who were free before the 1st of May 1806

Amherst County Court Clerks Office October 3rd 1861 – 370 – Registered by order of Amherst September Court 1861 **MARCELLUS** a bright mulatto – Son of Frances – 21 years of age the 4th of October 1860 – no marks apparent on head, face or breast – Emancipated in 1848 by deed from Sally Taylor & I. R. Reynolds 5 feet 7 Inches high

Amherst County Court Clerks Office December 17th 1861 – 371 – Registered by order of Amherst December Court 1861 **ELIZABETH THOMPSON** a free woman of colour, bright complexion – aged 21 years 5 feet 6 inches high – Small scar on neck & one on left arm above elbow – no other scars on head, face or hands – born in Amherst County & descended from ancestors free before the 1st of May 1806

Amherst County Court Clerks Office July 29 1862 – 372 – Registered by order of Amherst July Court 1862 **ELIJAH PETERS** a free man of colour – 22 years of age – 5 feet 7 ½ inches high – black colour – no scars on face, head or hands – born in Amherst County & descended from ancestors free before the 1st May 1806

Amherst County Court Clerks Office Nov 3 1862 – 373 – Registered in the Clerks Office of Amherst County under an order of the County Court of Amherst at Oct. Court 1862 **CYNTHIA LAWHORN** daughter of Lucinda Lawhorn, a white woman of pure blood, whose father is a negro – Said Cynthia Lawhorn is about 29 years of age – born in the County of Amherst – her complexion is chocolate brown – the hair is straight & black – about 6 feet high – No scar apparent on face or hands – small scar on right arm

Amherst County Court Clerks Office February 2nd 1863 – 374 – Registered in the Clerks Office by order of Amherst County Court at February Term 1863 **THOMAS PETERS** a free man of colour – dark complexion – 6 feet high – 22 years old – no scars apparent on head, face or hands – born in the County of Amherst & descended from ancestors free before the 1st of May 1806

Amherst County Court Clerks Office May 25 1863 – 375 – Registered in the Clerks Office of Amherst County Court by order made at May Court 1863 **ELIZA REDCROSS** a free woman of colour – bright complexion – 19 years old – 5 feet 5 ¼ inches high no scars apparent on head face or hands – left arm stiff – born in the County of Amherst & descended from ancestors free before the 1st of May 1806

Amherst County Court Clerks Office June 5 1863 –376 – Registered in the Clerks Office of Amherst Court by order made at May Court 1863 **JOHN N TYLER** a free boy of colour – Brown complexion – 19 years of age 5 feet 5 inches – No scars apparent on head face or hands – both little fingers crooked – born in the County of Fluvanna & descended from ancestors free before the 1st of May 1806

Amherst County Court Clerks Office June 5 1863 –377 – Registered by order of May Court 1863 **ELIZABETH TYLER** a free woman of colour – brown complexion – 21 years of age 5 feet 1 ¼ inches high – no scars apparent on head, face or hands – little finger on left hand crooked – born in Fluvanna & descended from ancestors free before the 1st of May 1806

Amherst County Court Clerks Office June 5 1863 –378 – Registered by order of May Court 1863 **JAMES TYLER** a free boy of colour – brown complexion – 19 years of age – 5 feet 5 ½ inches high – no scars apparent on head, face or hands – both little fingers crooked – born in Fluvanna County & descended from ancestors free before the 1st of May 1863

Amherst County Court Clerks Office June 5 1863 -379- Registered by order of May Court 1863 **JOHN TYLER** a free man of colour – dark complexion – about 45 years of age – 5 feet 6 ½ inches high – blind in left eye – both little fingers crooked – born in Fluvanna & descended from ancestors free before the 1st of May 1806

Amherst County Court Clerks Office June 5 1863 -380- Registered in Clerks Office by order [made] at May Term 1863 **LEVINIA GRAY** a free woman of colour – mulatto complexion – about 45 years of age – 5 feet 2 ½ inches high – no scars apparent on head, face or hands – born in Goochland & descended from ancestors free before the 1st of May 1806

Amherst County Court Clerks Office August 18th 1863 – 381 – Registered in the Clerks Office of Amherst County State of Virginia, by an order of the County Court of Amherst made the 17th day of May 1863 **LUCY JOHNSON** – a bright mulatto – Daughter of Betsey Johnson – 24 years old 4th July 1863 – born in the County of Nelson State of Virginia, of ancestors free before 1st day of May 1806 5 feet 9 Inches high – a flesh mould in front & near the left ear, a Small Scare [Scar] on the forehead, no other marks apparent

Amherst County Court Clerks Office Sept [blank] 1863 – 382 -Register renewed by order of August Court 1863 **JOHN FOSTER** a free man of colour – 24 years of age – Scar on middle finger of left hand – no other scar apparent on head, face or hands – 5 feet 9 ½ inches high – born in Amherst County & descended from ancestors free before the 1st May 1806

Amherst County Court Clerks Office Sept 22 1863 -383- Registered by order of September Court 1863 **ESSEX BIAS** a free man of colour – dark brown complexion – 5 feet 11 ½ inches high – 21 years of age – no scars apparent on head face or hands born in Amherst County & descended from ancestors free before the 1st May 1806

Amherst County Court Clerks Office Sept 22 1863 -384- Registered by order of September Court 1863 **TOBIAS** a free man of colour – dark brown complexion – 6 feet high 22 years of age – small scar under left eye – no other scars apparent on head face or hand – born in Amherst County & descended from ancestors free before the 1st May 1806

Amherst County Court Clerks Office Feb 11 1864 – 385 - Register renewed by order of January Court 1864 **CHARLES FOSTER** a free man of colour – light brown complexion – 30 years of age 5 feet 8 inches high – no scars apparent on head, face or hands born in the County of Amherst & descended from ancestors free before the 1st of May 1806

Amherst County Court Clerks Office March 17 1864 – 386 – Register renewed by order of February Court 1864 **ELIZA JOHNSON** a free woman of colour – bright complexion – about 45 years of age 5 feet 2 inches high – scar under left jaw – no other scars apparent on her head, face or hands – born in the County of Nelson & descended from ancestors free before the 1st of May 1806

Amherst County Court Clerks Office April 6 1864 – 387 – Register renewed by order of March Court 1864 **MARCELLUS** a bright mulatto – Son of Frances – 24 years of age – no marks apparent on head, face or hands – born in Amherst County, 5 feet 7 inches high – emancipated in 1848 by deed from Sally Taylor & I R Reynolds

Amherst County Court Clerks Office May 27 1864 – 388 – Registered by order of May Court 1864 **MALINDA BRANHAM** a free woman of colour – dark complexion – 45 years of age – little finger on right hand & thumb on left hand defective – no other marks apparent on head, face or hands – 5 feet high – born in Amherst County & descended from ancestors free before the 1st May 1806

Amherst County Court Clerks Office August 15 1864 -389-Register renewed by order of August Court 1864 **MARTHA ANN COUSINS** a free woman of color born in [blank] County on the 9th Nov 1835 – 5 feet 5 inches high, brown complection [complexion] Small Scar on right arm, 2 upper front teeth out – no other marks apparent on head face or hands and descended from ancestors free before the 1st day of May 1806

Amherst County Court Clerks Office Sept 19 1864 -390- Register renewed by order of Sept Court 1864 **JOHN MORRIS** a free man of Color, Son of Nancy Morris, brown complexion and fine black hair and nearly straight, Small Scar on the back of each hand, no other Scars or marks apparent on head face or hands, 5 feet 7 ½ inches high 55 years of age, born in the County of Chesterfield of ancestors free before the 1st day of May 1806

Amherst County Court Clerks Office September 19th 1864 – 391 – Register renewed by order of Sept Court 1864 **SOPHIA PADGETT** a free woman of color, daughter of Sucky Padgett bright complexion, hair straight, no scars apparent on face head or hands, 5 feet 3 ½ inches high, born in Amherst County of ancestors free before the 1st day of May 1806

Amherst County Court Clerks Office September 19 1864 – 392 – Register renewed by order of September Court 1864 **SCIPIO SMITH** a free man of color, born free in Hanover County on the 25th December 1800, of dark complexion, four feet nine inches high, and who has two scars on the back of his left hand, and one on his left wrist, one on his forehead over his right eye, one between his eyebrows, one on his right hand, and a Small wart on the inside of his left hand, derived his freedom from female ancestors free prior to the 1st May 1806

Amherst County Court Clerks Office Nov 28 1864 -393- Register renewed by order of Amherst County Court at its September term 1864 **MILLY JOHNSON** aged about 20 years, bright complexion 5 feet 6 inches high, little finger on right hand crooked, no other Scars apparent on head face or hands, born in the county of Amherst and descended from ancestors free before the 1st day of May 1806.

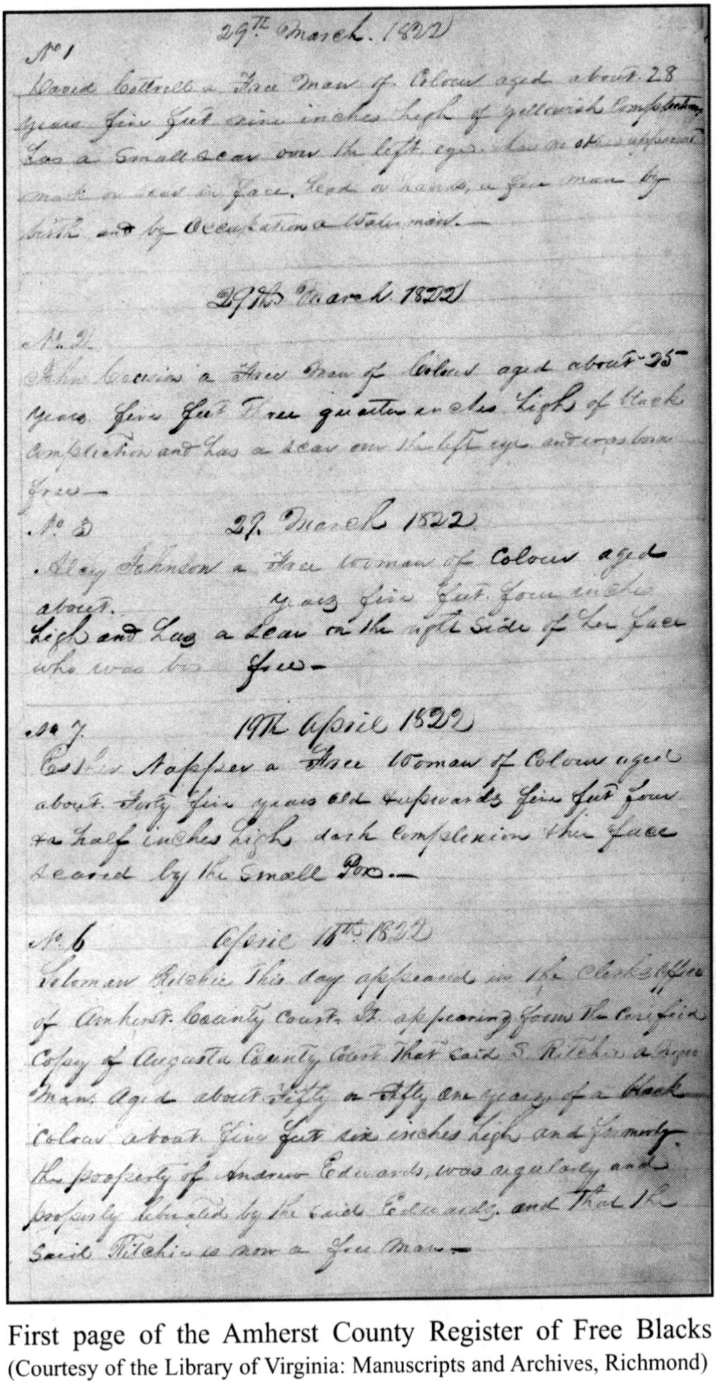
29th March 1822

No 1

David Cottrell a Free Man of Colour aged about 28 years five feet nine inches high of yellowish Complexion has a small scar over the left eye has no other apparent mark or scar in face, head or hands, a free man by birth and by Occupation a Waterman.—

29th March 1822

No 2

John Cousins a Free Man of Colour aged about 25 years five feet three quarter inches high of black complection and has a scar over the left eye and was born free—

No 3 29 March 1822

Alcy Johnson a Free Woman of Colour aged about years five feet four inches high and has a scar on the right side of her face who was born free—

No 7 19th April 1822

Esther Napper a Free Woman of Colour aged about forty five years old & upwards five feet four & a half inches high dark complexion the face scared by the Small Pox.—

No 6 April 18th 1822

Soloman Ritchie this day appeared in the Clerks office of Amherst County Court. It appearing from the certified Copy of Augusta County Court that said S. Ritchie a free Man aged about fifty or fifty one years of a black colour about five feet six inches high and formerly the property of Andrew Edwards, was regularly and properly liberated by the said Edwards, and that the said Ritchie is now a free Man—

First page of the Amherst County Register of Free Blacks
(Courtesy of the Library of Virginia: Manuscripts and Archives, Richmond)

Amherst County Courthouse, where the Register was kept
(Author photo)

"The bigg mountains" of Amherst County, about which some free coloreds wrote movingly
(Author photo)

A surviving slave cabin (since framed over) on the *Locust Ridge* plantation and now a Farm and Tool museum for Sweet Briar College
(Author photo)

Original school house (log section), circa 1868-1870, near Bear Mountain
(Author photo)

Monacan Ancestral Cemetery with original fieldstones and modern marker
(Author photo)

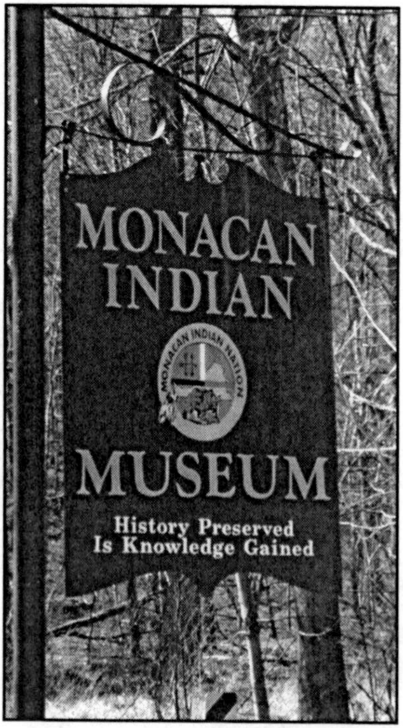

Sign marking the Monacan Indian Nation Museum on Kenmore Road near Amherst
(Author photo)

Indians and Free Blacks of Amherst County

INDIVIDUAL DATA

HOW TO USE THIS SECTION

Listings are alphabetical by last name. Please check the index for spelling variations.

Multiple entries exist for some names where it could not be determined whether the data listed was for the same person or another person with the same name. In those cases, data is listed separately rather than risk of attributing it incorrectly. Or there may be a note that the material represents more than one person. For example, the listing for "Betsey Beverly" includes four entries. There are at least two women by that name but it is impossible to sort them out; so all the entries are listed together, with a note that they apply to more than one person. Multiple entries for one person are indicated in the index by a page number in **bold** print.

Census records before 1850 listed only one name: that of the head of the household. All others were listed by age only. Agricultural census schedules for 1850 and 1860 list either the value of the crop/equipment or the quantity produced. A predecessor to the census was a listing of "Heads of Families," done in 1783 and 1785.

The information in the personal property tax records (1821-1840, 1850, and 1860) is reproduced here as it appeared in the original records in the Library of Virginia. Sometimes these records do little more than document an individual's existence. For tax lists from 1782 to 1820, see *www.freeafricanamericans.com* and look under "Amherst County: Personal Property Tax List 1782-1822."

Marriage records are listed under the name of the person who appeared first, alphabetically; both names are in the index.

Death certificate records list only blacks and mulattoes; post-Civil War include only those individuals identified there as freed slaves or persons recognized as being part of the study group.

On several occasions, the Commissioner of Revenue was required to prepare an annual list of free coloreds in his county, and their occupations, for tax purposes. The authors found only one for Amherst County: 1861. The Library of Virginia has two copies—possibly a draft (Form A) and a final form (Form B)—which contain many but not all of the same names. They list the sex, age, and occupation of the individuals.

Only the Court Order books for 1828, 1851, 1856, 1859, 1860, 1861 (all years of high registration numbers), 1864, and 1865 were examined by the authors.

Please bear in mind that entries prior to 1807 may refer to Nelson County, as it was part of Amherst until then.

KEY to Abbreviations:

CENSUS: Early:

HEADS OF FAMILIES (1783): lists whites and blacks only

HEADS OF FAMILIES (1785): lists "white souls" only

CENSUS through 1840:

fcm = free colored male, fcf = free colored female

fcms = free colored males, fcfs = free colored females

CENSUS 1850 and 1860:

Unless otherwise noted, last names for people are the same as that of the head of the household.

COMM. REV. A: Names on 1861 "draft" report of the Amherst County Commissioner of Revenue.

COMM. REV. B: Names on 1861 "final" report.

TAX LIST (1800) = Tax List for Lexington Parish, 1800.

Death Certificates which list birth or death in Amherst refer only to Amherst County, with no specific location given. "Informant" refers to the person providing the information to the recording authorities.

ADAMS, THOMAS

- HEADS OF FAMILIES (1783): 19 black.

AILSTOCK, ABSALOM

- CENSUS (1840): 2 fcm 10 to 24 years old, 1 fcm 36 to 55, 2 fcfs under 10, 2 fcfs 10 to 24, 1 fcf 36 to 55.
- PERSONAL PROPERTY TAX (1860): 1 male free negro over 16, 1 horse, 10¢ tax paid.

AILSTOCK, DAVID

- MARRIAGE REGISTER (1845): Married Sally Peters.

AILSTOCK, RUFUS

- CENSUS (1860): Rufus Ailstock (13, mulatto), Geo W Hamilton (18, white, farm laborer).

ALEXANDER, MARY

- COURT ORDER BOOK (July 1851): "On the motion of Mary Alexander a free coloured woman in the possession of Wm T Parrott and claimed by him as an apprentice a rule is awarded her against said Parrott to shew cause if any he can why said Mary shall not be discharged from his service said rule to be made returnable to the 1st day of August Court."

AMBLER, DICK

- DEATH CERTIFICATES (1867): Died in Amherst in September of old age at 95, a farmer, born in Culpeper, informant was his former owner P. St. Geo. Ambler. (*Pg 118, #2*)

AMBLER, FRANK

- DEATH CERTIFICATES (1865): Died in Amherst in March of pneumonia at age 25, born in Amherst, a farmer, his informant was his Hirer [employer] R. G. Scott. (*Pg 111, #7*)

AMBLER, MARY

- DEATH CERTIFICATES (1867): Died in Amherst in June of typhoid fever at age 2, born in Amherst, no parents listed, informant was her former owner P. St. Geo. Ambler. (*Pg 118, #3*)

APPLING, HENRY

- DEATH CERTIFICATES (1865): Died in Amherst in February of pneumonia at age 35, born in Amherst, a farmer, no parents listed, informant was his former owner David Appling. (*Pg 111, #1*)

APPLING, ROBIN

- DEATH CERTIFICATES (1865): Died in Amherst in September of pneumonia at age 63, a farmer, informant was his former owner David Appling (*Pg 111, #2*)

ARCHER

- COURT ORDER BOOK (February 1865): The Justices resolved themselves into a Court of Oyer and Terminer to hear the case of Archer, a slave belonging to a Mr. Sutphin, who was in jail for theft. He pled not guilty but was found guilty and ordered to receive 39 lashes immediately and another 39 if his owner didn't sell him. Three men were ordered to be paid for guarding Archer, "said guard being necessary because of the Jail of the county having been burnt."
- COURT ORDER BOOK (March 1865): To satisfy a suit amongst the Sutphin family, Archer was to be sold to the highest bidder and proceeds, minus expenses, distributed to the plaintiffs.

ARNOLD, DRURY H.

- MARRIAGE REGISTER (1841): Married Emily J Peters.

ARNOLD, ELIZABETH

- MARRIAGE REGISTER (1839): Elizabeth Arnold, daughter of Robert Arnold, married Edward Winters.

ARNOLD, ELVIRA ANN

- MARRIAGE REGISTER (1833): Married Thomas Winters.

ARNOLD, JOHN

- CENSUS (1830): 2 fcm under 10 years, 1 fcm 24 to 36, 1 fcf 10 to 24.

ARNOLD, McPHERSON

- COURT ORDER BOOK (February 1856): The Court ordered that he be registered, but there is no entry in that name.

ARNOLD, ROBERT

- CENSUS (1840): 4 fcm 10 to 24 years, 1 fcm 24 to 36, 1 fcm 55 to 100, 1 fcf 10 to 24, 1 fcf 24 to 36, 1 fcf 55 to 100.

ARNOLD, SARAH ANN

- MARRIAGE REGISTER (1842): Sarah Ann Arnold, "a free person of colour," married Robert E. Hollinsworth, "a free person of colour." She was the daughter of Robert Arnold, also "a free person of colour."

BARNE (?), JOHN

- CENSUS, DEATH (1860): 21 years old, free black male, born in Virginia – died in May of "disease of breath" after being sick 7 [?] days – occupation: "ditche[r]."

BARNES, MOSES

- DEATH CERTIFICATES (1867): Died in Amherst on December 27 of old age at 80, born in Amherst, a laborer, son of [?] and M. Barnes, informant was his former owner Wm. H. Barnes. (*Pg 118, #7*)

BARNETT, JANE

- CENSUS (1810): 1 free colored.

BATTLES, SHADRACK

- According to his pension application, Battles was born in 1746. At one time, he owned 200 acres on the Hardware River but sold it in 1775. He was a carpenter. On December 3, 1776, he enlisted for three years in Amherst County in Captain James Franklin's 10th Virginia Regiment [later Capt. Clough Shelton] and served for three years, fighting at Germantown, Monmouth, Savannah, and Brandywine before being discharged at Augusta, Georgia. There is no Register in Amherst County for Battles because he had moved to Albemarle County by 1822, when this journal begins. It is possible that his registration was included in an earlier and now missing volume. In 1820, at the age of 74, Battles applied for a pension for his military service, noting that he was no longer able to support himself and his 60-year old wife. (*Information from Backsights by Howard Newton, Jr. and Nathaniel Mason Pawlett; Amherst County, Virginia in the Revolution by Lenora Higginbotham Sweeny; an unpublished history of Amherst County by Lee Marmon; and www.freeafricanamericans.com.*)

BAUGH, ALFRED H.

- COURT ORDER BOOK (April 1851): The Court ordered that his registration be renewed, but there is no Register entry in that name.

BAUGH, JOHN

- COURT ORDER BOOK (April 1851): The Court ordered that his registration be renewed, but this person appears in his Register entries as John Tyler.

BAUGH, NANCY

- COURT ORDER BOOK (April 1851): The Court ordered that her registration be renewed; however, she appears in her Register entries as Nancy Tyler.

BENJAMIN

- MANUMISSION (January 21, 1793): Joshua Shelton freed his slaves Benjamin, Cato, and Jane. (*www.freeafricanamericans.com*)

BEVERLEY – see BEVERLY

BEVERLY, A.

- CENSUS, AGRICULTURAL (1860): value of machinery owned was $2 – 1 horse, 1 milk cow, 1 other cattle, 2 swine: total value of livestock was $75 – 150 bushels of Indian corn, 100 bushels of oats, 3,000 pounds of tobacco, 20 bushels of Irish potatoes – value of orchard products was $10 – value of market garden was $10 – 40 pounds of butter – value of slaughtered animals was $25

BEVERLY, ADOLPHUS

- COMM. REV. 1861 A: age 30, farmer.
- COMM. REV. 1861 B: age 30, wheelwright.
- WILL (dated January 18, 1883) (probated December 15, 1890) – All of his property was to be left to Leonah F. Burch and her five children (Richardson, Palentine, Emily, Alexander, and Adolphus). This was property inherited from his parents' estates. (*Will Book 23, pg 14*)
- INVENTORY (recorded April 7, 1891): 1 bay mare ($32.50), 1 bay mare ($15), 1 cow ($15), 1 wagon ($10), 1 buggy ($5), 1

plow ($0.25), 1 still and worm ($5), 1 lot of iron ($0.25), 1 mule spinnel ($0.50), 1 apple mill ($0.10), 1 bellows, anvil and vise ($1.50), 1 lot of gunsmith's tools ($2), 2 guns ($1), 1 lot of pistols ($0.50), 1 clock ($1), 1 fiddle ($0.05), 2 tables ($0.25), 1 lot of lumber ($0.25), 1 stove ($0.25) – total value: $96.46 (*Will Book 23, pg 113-114*)

- The above inventory was sold October 19, 1891 for $107.70. (*Will Book 23, pg 115*)

BEVERLY, ALDRIDGE

- COMM. REV. 1861 B: age 34, mechanic.

BEVERLY, ALEX

- PERSONAL PROPERTY (1860): 1 male free negro 21 to 55 years old, 1 cattle worth $10, household furnishings worth $15, aggregate value $25.
- COMM. REV. 1861 A: age 27, farmer.
- COMM. REV. 1861 B: age 23, farmer.

BEVERLY, AMANDA

- COMM. REV. 1861 A: age 24.
- COMM. REV. 1861 B: age 26.

BEVERLY, ANDERSON

- COURT ORDER BOOK (June 1851): "The Free Negro Anderson Beverly now confined in jail on a charge of unlawful shooting is allowed to be bailed by some justice of the peace in the amount of $50."

BEVERLY, ANDR[EW]

- PERSONAL PROPERTY TAX (1860): 1 male free negro 21 to 55 years old, 1 horse worth $50, aggregate value $50.
- COMM. REV. 1861 A: age 25, farmer.
- COMM. REV. 1861 B: age 24, farmer.

BEVERLY, ANTHONY/ANT

- CENSUS (1840): 1 fcm under 10 years of age, 1 fcm 24 to 36, 1 fcf 10 to 24.

BEVERLY, BAILEY

- CENSUS (1860): Bailey Beverly (45, mulatto), Aldridge (30, mulatto), Lucy (27, mulatto), Betsey (23, mulatto), Henry (14, mulatto), Aderson - (7, mulatto), Marcellus (3, mulatto), Wm. E. (1, mulatto), Willis (6, mulatto), Ben A. (3, mulatto), Mary (29, mulatto), Addison (5, mulatto), Spencer (3, mulatto), Geo. (2, mulatto), Wm. (1, mulatto), Delilah (48, mulatto)

BEVERLY, BETSEY

- [*NOTE: Several women are represented in these entries.*]
- CENSUS (1850): Betsey Beverly (50, mulatto), W. (25, mulatto, laborer), Jese (18, mulatto, laborer).
- COURT ORDER BOOK (April 1851): The Court ordered that she be registered, but there is no entry in that name.
- CENSUS (1860): Betsey Beverly (70, mulatto), Jas Pinn (17, black, $100 personal estate), Wm H Pinn (14, black), Jese Pinn (12, mulatto), John Pinn (11, mulatto), Bob Pinn (10, mulatto), Betsey Pinn (9, mulatto), Pattia Pinn (8, mulatto), Geo W Pinn (6, mulatto), Elderson Pinn (5, mulatto), Martha Pinn (2, mulatto).
- CENSUS, DEATH (1860): 80 years old, free mulatto female, born in Virginia, died in March of "dropsy of h[e]art" after being sick 7 days, occupation: domestic.
- COMM. REV. 1861 A: age 20.
- COMM. REV. 1861 B: also known as Polly, age 50.
- COMM. REV. 1861 B: age 23.

BEVERLY, CATHERINE

- COMM. REV. 1861 A and B: age 30.

BEVERLY, CHARLES

- MARRIAGE REGISTER (1827): married Mary Johns.
- PERSONAL PROPERTY TAX (1829): 1 horse, 8¢ tax paid
- CENSUS (1830): 1 fcm 36 to 55 years old, 1 fcf 10 to 24.
- CENSUS (1840): 2 fcm under 10 years old, 1 fcm 36 to 55, 2 fcfs under 10, 1 fcf 10 to 24, 1 fcf 36 to 55 - 2 people engaged in agriculture, 1 in commerce

BEVERLY, D.

- CENSUS (1860): Listed in the household of B. Staton, a white farmer: D. Beverly (37, mulatto, farmer, $100 personal estate) – C. (33, mulatto) – M. (11, mulatto) – L. (15, mulatto) – E. (9, mulatto) – E. A. (7, mulatto) – Peter (6, mulatto) – John (3, mulatto) – A. (21, mulatto, farmer) – M. (26, mulatto) – A. (24, mulatto, farmer) – J Terry (26, mulatto, farm labor)

BEVERLY, D.

- CENSUS, AGRICULTURAL (1860): value of machinery owned was $5 – 1 milk cow, 1 other cattle, 2 swine: value of livestock was $50 – 8 bushels of wheat, 100 bushels of Indian corn, 50 bushels of oats, 1,800 pounds of tobacco, 10 bushels of Irish potatoes, 20 pounds of butter – value of slaughtered animals was $20

BEVERLY, DELAWARE

- PERSONAL PROPERTY TAX (1850): 1 male free negro over 16 years old
- CENSUS (1850): Delaware Beverly (25, mulatto, farmer), Lafayette (6, mulatto), Polly (3, mulatto), Elizabeth (1, mulatto)
- CENSUS, AGRICULTURAL (1850): 50 improved acres, 60 unimproved acres: total value of land owned was $200 – total value of machinery owned was $4 – 1 milk cow, 10 swine: total value of livestock was $25 – 60 bushels of wheat, 125 bushels of Indian corn, 650 pounds of tobacco, 25 pounds of butter
- PERSONAL PROPERTY TAX (1860): 1 male free negro 21 to 55 years old, 2 cattle worth $20, household furnishings worth $30, aggregate value: $50.
- COMM. REV. 1861 A: age 35, farmer.
- COMM. REV. 1861 B: age 22, farmer.

BEVERLY, DELILA[H]

- COURT ORDER BOOK (April 1851): The Court ordered that she be registered, but there is no entry in that name.
- COMM. REV. 1861 A: age 40.
- COMM. REV. 1861 B: age 41.

BEVERLY, EADY PINN

- MARRIAGE REGISTER (1800): Married William Beverly.

BEVERLY, EDWARD

- COMM. REV. 1861 A: age 18.
- COMM. REV. 1861 B: age 19.

BEVERLY, ELIZABETH

- MARRIAGE REGISTER (1839): Elizabeth Beverly, daughter of Samuel Beverly, married Matterson Beverly.

BEVERLY, F. [?] T. [?]

- DEATH CERTIFICATES (1857): F. or T. Beverly, female, 7 months old, no date or cause of death listed, daughter of Jas. Sparrow and Louisa Pinn. (*Pg 67, #13*)

BEVERLY, FANNIE

- DEATH CERTIFICATE INDEX: Died April 12, 1890.

BEVERLY, FAYETTE/LAFAYETTE

- COMM. REV. 1861 A: age 14, farmer.
- COMM. REV. 1861 B: age 15.

BEVERLY, FRANCES

- MARRIAGE REGISTER (1827): Married Joel Branham.

BEVERLY, FRANCES

- MARRIAGE REGISTER (1852): Married Paulus Redcross.

BEVERLY, FRANCES

- COMM. REV. 1861 A: Female, age 23.
- COMM. REV. 1861 B: age 26.

BEVERLY, FRANCIS

- MARRIAGE REGISTER (1792): Married Mary Williams.

BEVERLY, FRANK

- COURT ORDER BOOK (February 1860): The Court ordered that his registration be renewed, but there is no entry in that name.
- CENSUS (1860): Frank Beverly (26, mulatto), Segus (23, mulatto), Susan (5, mulatto, born in Virginia), Wm. (3, mulatto), David (2, mulatto).
- COMM. REV. 1861 B: age 35, mechanic.

BEVERLY, FRANK C.

- COURT ORDER BOOK (April 1851): The Court ordered that he be registered, but there is no entry in that name.
- PERSONAL PROPERTY TAX (1860); 1 male free negro 21 to 55 years old, household furnishings worth 10¢.
- COMM. REV. 1861 A: no age listed, farmer.

BEVERLY, FRED

- DEATH CERTIFICATE INDEX: Died April 6, 1890.

BEVERLY, FRED C.

- COMM. REV. 1861 A: age 59, wheelwright.

BEVERLY, FREDERICK J. [See page 37.]

- MARRIAGE REGISTER (1829): James Beverly married Sarah Ann Taylor, daughter of Richeson Taylor.
- CENSUS (1830): 1 male 40 to 50 years old, 1 fcm 10 to 24, 1 fcm 24 to 36, 1 fcm 55 to 100, 2 fcfs under 10, 1 fcf 36 to 55.
- DEED (August 23, 1834): James Martin sold Frederick J. Beverly 35 acres on Brown Creek for $30. (*Deed Book V, pg 25*)
- DEED (March 17, 1834): Richard Crawford, attorney for Bennett A, Crawford, sold James F. Beverly and Isabella Williams 100 acres on Browns Creek (on the road to Pryor's Gap), also 13 ½ acres in the same location, for $300 (*Deed Book W, pgs 23-24*)
- PERSONAL PROPERTY TAX (1840): 2 horses, 16¢ tax paid
- CENSUS (1840): Fred J. Beverly (no numbers listed for household members) – 2 engaged in agriculture, 1 in manufacturing
- PERSONAL PROPERTY TAX (1850): 1 male free negro over 16 years old, 2 horses, etc., 20¢ tax paid

- CENSUS, AGRICULTURAL (1850): 20 improved acres, 50 unimproved acres, total value of land was $200 – total value of machinery owned was $15 – 2 horses, 2 milk cows, 2 working oxen, 3 other cattle, 23 swine, total value of livestock was $250 – 65 bushels of wheat, 250 bushels of Indian corn, 20 bushels of oats, 20 bushels of Irish potatoes, 250 pounds of butter, 30 pounds of beeswax and honey.
- DEED (April 8, 1854): Isabella Williams, colored woman, sold Frederick J. and Sarah Ann Beverly, colored persons, all of her interest in 115 acres on Browns Creek (a half interest), 1 sorrel mare, 1 black cow and yearling, household and kitchen furniture, and all of her other property for $5 and support during the lifetime of the said Isabella Williams. (*Deed Book CC, pg 254*)
- PERSONAL PROPERTY TAX (1860): 1 male free negro 21 to 55 years old, 5 horses worth $250, 12 cattle worth $120, household furnishings worth $75, sheep and hogs worth $75, 1 clock worth $5 – aggregate value of $525.00.
- CENSUS, AGRICULTURAL (1860): 70 improved acres, 443 unimproved acres, total value of land owned was $1,500 – total value of machinery owned was $155 – 4 horses, 5 milk cows, 5 other cattle, 25 swine: total value of livestock was $380 – 40 bushels of wheat, 370 bushels of Indian corn, 150 bushels of oats, 2,000 pounds of tobacco, 5 bushels of beans, 30 bushels of Irish potatoes, 300 pounds butter, 20 pounds of beeswax – value of orchard products was $50 – value of slaughtered animals was $70.
- DEED (March 7, 1862): For the purpose of providing for his wife Sarah Ann and their children, Frederick J. Beverly sold to James McMilmer all of his property and estate, to be held by McMilmer in trust for the payment of his debts and then for the support of his wife during her natural life. He gave Sarah the power and authority to dispose of the estate as she wished; if she died intestate, the estate was to be divided equally among the children. He did not sign this document but, instead, made his mark (*Deed Book FF, pg 108*)

BEVERLY, FREDERIC, Jr.

- COMM. REV. 1861 B: age 60, wheelwright.

BEVERLY, GEO.

- DEATH CERTIFICATE INDEX: Died April 8, 1890.

BEVERLY, GEO ANNA [Georgianna]

- DEATH CERTIFICATE INDEX: Died March 5, 1882.

BEVERLY, HENRY

- COMM. REV. 1861 A: age 45 or 48, cooper.

BEVERLY, HENRY

- COMM. REV. 1861 B: age 15.

BEVERLY, HENRY

- COMM. REV. 1861 B: age 16.

BEVERLY, INCY [LUCY?]

- COMM. REV. 1861 A: Female, age 26.

BEVERLY, ISABELLA

- COMM. REV. 1861 A: age 19.
- COMM. REV. 1861 B: age 20.

BEVERLY, JAMES

- CENSUS (1850): James Beverly (45, mulatto, carpenter), Sally (40, mulatto), Adolphus (20, mulatto, carpenter), Moab (17, mulatto, carpenter), Francis (15, mulatto), Josephine (12, mulatto), Isabella (10, mulatto), Richard (7, mulatto), Morris (4, mulatto), Geo W (2, mulatto), J M Jewel (22, white)

BEVERLY, JAMES F. [see Frederick J.]

BEVERLY, JEMINA[H]

- COMM. REV. 1861 A: age 42.
- COMM. REV. 1861 B: age 43.

BEVERLY, JESSE

- COURT ORDER BOOK (April 1851): The Court ordered that he be registered, but there is no entry in that name.

BEVERLY, JNO.

- DEATH CERTIFICATES (1867): Died in Amherst in June of a fever at age 2, son of N. and B. Beverly. (*Pg 118, #8*)

BEVERLY, JOHN

- CENSUS (1860): John Beverly (35, mulatto), Mary (30, mulatto), John (3, mulatto), Jas (5, mulatto), Lindsey (2, mulatto), Leannah Pinn (7, mulatto).
- COMM. REV. 1861 B: age 36, cooper.

BEVERLY, JOHN

- BOND (October 16, 1882): Lavinda Beverly and W. H. Pinn filed a $40 bond to qualify her as the administrator of her husband John's estate. (*Will Book 20, pg 379*)

BEVERLY, JOHN S.

- COURT ORDER BOOK (May 1860): The Court ordered that he be registered, but there is no entry in that name.

BEVERLY, JONATHAN

- PERSONAL PROPERTY TAX (1829): 1 horse, 8¢ tax paid.

BEVERLY, JOSEPHINE

- COMM. REV. 1861 A: age 21.
- COMM. REV. 1861 B: age 22.

BEVERLY, JUDITH/JUDY

- COMM. REV. 1861 A and B: age 25.

BEVERLY, JULIA

- DEATH CERTIFICATE INDEX: Died April 15, 1890.

BEVERLY, LOU

- DEATH CERTIFICATE INDEX: Died April 19, 1890.

BEVERLY, LUCY

- COMM. REV. 1861 B: age 32.

BEVERLY, MADISON

- CENSUS (1840): 1 fcm 24 to 36 years old, 2 fcfs 10 to 24 - 2 engaged in agriculture.

BEVERLY, MARIA

- COMM. REV. 1861 A: no age given.
- COMM. REV. 1861 B: age 22.

BEVERLY, MARY

- [*NOTE: There are several women represented here.*]
- CENSUS (1850): Mary Beverly (40, mulatto), Betsey (15, mulatto), Henry (5, mulatto)
- CENSUS (1860): Mary Beverly (60, mulatto), Martha (35, mulatto), Wyatt Jewell (109, mulatto), M. D. Jewell (8, mulatto)
- CENSUS, AGRICULTURAL (1860): 3 other cattle, 5 swine: total value of livestock owned was $45.
- COMM. REV. 1861 A: age 65.
- COMM. REV. 1861 B: age 66.

BEVERLY, MARY ANN

- CENSUS (1850): Mary Ann Beverly (43, mulatto), Catharine (16, mulatto), William J. (14, mulatto)
- CENSUS, AGRICULTURAL (1850): 55 improved acres, 65 unimproved acres: total value of land owned was $400 – total value of machinery: $2 – 200 bushels of Indian corn, 15 bushels of oats.

BEVERLY, MARY D.

- COMM. REV. 1861 A: age 49.

BEVERLY, MARY I.

- COURT ORDER BOOK (April 1851): The Court ordered that she be registered, but there is no entry in that name.

BEVERLY, MARY JANE

- COMM. REV. 1861 A: age 27.
- COMM. REV. 1861 B: age 28.

BEVERLY, MARY S.

- DEATH CERTIFICATES (1866): Died on November 8 of Whooping Cough, aged 1 year and 1 month, daughter of Aldridge and Rebecca Beverly, born in Amherst. (*Pg 115, #17*)

BEVERLY, MINNA

- COURT ORDER BOOK (April 1851): The Court ordered that she be registered, but there is no entry in that name.

BEVERL]Y, MOAB

- PERSONAL PROPERTY TAX (1860): 1 male free negro 21 to 55 years old, aggregate value $0
- COMM. REV. 1861 A: age 25, farmer.
- COMM. REV. 1861 B: age 28, wheelwright.

BEVERLY, MORRISS

- DEATH CERTIFICATES (1864): Died in Amherst in May 1864, born in Amherst, son of Saml. And F. J. Beverly. (*Pg 107, # 8*)

BEVERLY, NANCY

- DEATH CERTIFICATE INDEX: Died September 5, 1887.

BEVERLY, PATSEY

- COURT ORDER BOOK (February 1851): The Court ordered that her registration be renewed, but there is no entry in that name.

BEVERLY, PATSEY

- DEATH CERTIFICATE INDEX: Died February 5, 1886.

BEVERLY, PERMELIA

- MARRIAGE REGISTER (1844): Married Jefferson Ross.

BEVERLY, POLLY

- PERSONAL PROPERTY TAX (1829): 1 horse, 8¢ tax paid.

BEVERLY, POLLY

- CENSUS (1840): 4 fcm under 10 years old, 2 fcm 10 to 24, 3 fcfs 10 to 24, 2 fcfs 24 to 36, 1 fcf 55 to 100 - 7 engaged in agriculture, 2 in navigation.

BEVERLY, POLLY

- CENSUS (1860): Polly Beverly (55, mulatto), Eliza (25, mulatto), Hiram (7, mulatto), Aldridge (30, carpenter), Henry (16, mulatto), Lucy (35, mulatto).

BEVERLY, RHODA

- COMM. REV. 1861 A: age 60.
- COMM. REV. 1861 B: age 63.

BEVERLY, RICHARD

- COMM. REV. 1861 A: age 17.
- COMM. REV. 1861 B: age 16.

BEVERLY, RITTA

- COMM. REV. A: Female, age 45.
- COMM. REV. 1861 B: age 50.

BEVERLY, R. M.

- DEATH CERTIFICATE INDEX (1872): Died May 2, 1872.

BEVERLY, ROB

- DEATH CERTIFICATE INDEX: Died March 4, 1886.

BEVERLY, SALLIE

- DEATH CERTIFICATE INDEX: Died March 20, 1896.

BEVERLY, SAM

- DEATH CERTIFICATE INDEX: Died April 4, 1890.

BEVERLY, SAM/SAMUEL

- PERSONAL PROPERTY TAX – (1823): 1 male free negro, 1 horse, 12¢ tax paid – (1824): same – (1825): 2 horses: 24¢ tax paid – (1826): 1 male free negro, 1 horse: 12¢ tax paid – (1827): same – (1828): same – (1829): same - 10¢ tax paid.
- MARRIAGE REGISTER (1819): Married Rhoda Terry.
- CENSUS (1830): 4 fcm under 10 years old, 1 fcm 24 to 36, 3 fcfs under 10, 1 fcf 24 to 36, 1 fcf 36 to 55, 1 fcf 55 to 100.
- DEED (January 6, 1838): Lewellen J. and Sarah Ann Reynolds of Alleghany County sold Samuel Beverly 201 acres on Harris Creek for $600. (*Deed Book W, pg 283*)
- CENSUS (1840): 3 fcm under 10 years old, 2 fcm 10 to 24, 1 fcm 24 to 36, 1 fcm 36 to 55, 2 fcfs under 10, 1 fcf 10 to 24, 1 fcf 36 to 55 – 4 engaged in agriculture – 1 insane
- PERSONAL PROPERTY TAX (1840): 1 horse, 8¢ tax paid – (1850): 1 male free negro over16, 1 horse, etc., 10¢ tax paid
- CENSUS (1850): Samuel Beverly (53, mulatto, farmer, $600 real estate), Roda (52, mulatto), Tymanda (24, mulatto), Swany (19, mulatto), Frances (15, mulatto), Samuel (16, laborer), Alexander (12, mulatto), Edward (10, mulatto)
- CENSUS, AGRICULTURAL (1850): 100 improved acres, 101 unimproved acres: total value of land was $600 – total value of machinery was $50 – 1 horse, 4 milk cows, 2 working oxen, 8 other cattle, 33 swine: total value of livestock was $150 – 140 bushels of wheat, 400 bushels of Indian corn, 100 bushels of oats, 10 bushels of Irish potatoes, 50 pounds of butter.
- PERSONAL PROPERTY TAX (1860): 1 male free negro 21 to 55 years old, 2 male persons over 16, 1 horse worth $100, 8 cattle worth $50, household furnishings worth $100, 11 sheep/hogs worth $15 – aggregate value: $265.00.

- CENSUS (1860): Samuel Beverly (63, mulatto, $1,000 real estate, $3,000 personal estate), Rody (64, mulatto), T. (27, mulatto), E. (18, mulatto)
- CENSUS, AGRICULTURAL (1860): 200 improved acres, 200 unimproved acres: total value of farm was $2,100 – total value of machinery was $100 – 3 horses, 4 milk cows, 1 other cattle, 14 swine: total value of livestock was $460 – 60 bushels of wheat, 200 bushels of Indian corn, 200 bushels of oats, 3,400 pounds of tobacco, 1 bushel of beans, 30 bushels of Irish potatoes, 20 bushels of sweet potatoes, 40 pounds of butter, 1 ton of hay, 12 pounds of beeswax – value of market gardens was $40 – value of orchard products was $50 - value of slaughtered animals was $150.
- DEED (November 30, 1860): Samuel M. Garland (the commissioner appointed by the County Court in the case of Pryor versus Pryor) conveyed to Samuel Beverly, for $1, the title to 196 acres involved in the suit; Beverly had actually purchased the land from Pryor at an earlier date. (*Deed Book EE, pg 468*)
- COMM. REV. 1861 A: age 60, farmer.
- COMM. REV. 1861 B: age 62, farmer.
- DEED (May 2, 1862): Samuel and Rhoda B. Beverly, free persons of color, sold 25 acres to Martin D. Tinsley for $125.00. The land was on the road from Hix's Grocery to Tinsley's. Both Samuel and Rhoda made their marks instead of signing their names. (*Deed Book FF, pg 115*)
- DEED (May 2, 1862): Martin D. and Emily Tinsley sold to Samuel Beverly, a free man of color, for $125.00, the same tract conveyed above, with the stipulation that the line fence shall be kept in repair by the parties owning the land. (*Deed Book FF, pg 116*)
- WILL (dated September 1, 1877) (probated December 19, 1881): ". . . being now an old man but in full possession of my mind and judgment think it wise and prudent to make such disposition of my estate . . . Having made what I possess by my industry and honesty it is my will that all my just debts be paid." All of his estate was to go to his "beloved wife Rhoda" and at her death to be divided equally among the nine lawful grandchildren. (*Will Book 20, pgs 223-224*)
- INVENTORY (recorded December 30, 1881): 1 milk cow ($18), 1 waggon ($13), farmers utensils ($4.50), house and [illegible] ($10), 2 beds ($32), 1 set of chairs ($4), 1 press

($2.50), 1 sideboard ($3), 1 bureau ($4), 2 tables ($5), 1 gun ($5), 2 trunks ($2). (*Will Book 20, pgs 264-265*)

BEVERLY, SAMUEL

- DEATH CERTIFICATE INDEX: Died February 18, 1877.

BEVERLY, SAMUEL

- DEATH CERTIFICATE INDEX: Died November 25, 1881.

BEVERLY, SAMUEL, JR.

- PERSONAL PROPERTY TAX (1860): 1 male free negro 21 to 55 years old, 1 horse worth $50, household furnishings worth $10 – aggregate value: $60.
- CENSUS (1860): S. Beverly, Jr. (27, mulatto, farm labor), E. L. (38, mulatto), V Suthers (11, mulatto).
- COMM. REV. 1861 B: age 21.

BEVERLY, SARAH A.

- COMM. REV. 1861 A: age 50.
- COMM. REV. 1861 B: age 53.

BEVERLY, SEFUS/SEGIS/SEJUS ANN

- COMM. REV. 1861 A: Female, no age given.
- COMM. REV. 1861 B: age 44.

BEVERLY, SUSAN

- COMM. REV. 1861 B: age 12.

BEVERLY, SUVINA [?]

- COMM. REV. 1861 B: Female, age 35.

BEVERLY, TH[OMA]S

- COURT ORDER BOOK (November 1856): The Grand Jury presented a bill against Ths. Beverly "for committing a fornication in the County of Amherst with Betsey Peters, a free woman of colour, within the last 6 months."

BEVERLY, TIMANDA/TIMANDY

- COMM. REV. 1861 A: Female, age 23.
- COMM. REV. 1861 B: age 29.

BEVERLY, WASHINGTON

- CENSUS (1850): Washington Beverly (29, mulatto, carpenter), Frances (29, mulatto), Elvira (3, mulatto), Martha (18, mulatto), Wm. (26, mulatto, farmer), Aldridge (27, mulatto, farmer), Betsey (29, mulatto), Jese (23, mulatto, farmer), James (3, mulatto), John (2, mulatto).

BEVERLY, WM.

- COURT ORDER BOOK (April 1851): The Court ordered that he be registered, but there is no entry in that name.

BEVERLY, WILLIAM

- PERSONAL PROPERTY TAX—1823: 1 male free negro, 1 horse, 12¢ tax paid – 1825: 2 horses, 24¢ tax paid.

BEVERLY, WILLIAM

- MARRIAGE REGISTER (1800): Married Eady Pinn.

BIAS – See also BYASS

BIAS, DAVID

- CENSUS (1850): David Bias (30 [?], black, laborer), Frances (22, black), Elizabeth (20, black), James H. (14, black), John (12, black), Toby (10, black), Esex (9, black), Wiatt (7, black), Geo. (6, black), Jane (5, black).

BIAS, FANNY

- CENSUS (1860): Fanny Bias (41, black, washer, $35 personal estate), Washington (40, black, laborer), Toby (20, black, laborer), E. (18, black, laborer), W. (16, black, laborer), Geo. (11, black), E. (8, black), E. A. (7, black), Eliza (26, black), A. (6, black), James (2, black), L. (75, black).

BIAS, JOHN

- DEATH CERTIFICATES (1859): Died of pneumonia at age 21, son of David Bias, "a free negro." (*Pg 81, # 8*)

BIAS, TOBI

- DEATH CERTIFICATE INDEX: Died March 26, 1875.

BIASS, JOHN

- TAX LIST (1800): 1 white male over 21, 1 horse.

BIASS, ROLING

- TAX LIST (1800): 1 white male over 21, 3 horses, 2 slaves over 16.

BIRD, RICHARD

- CENSUS (1850): Richard Bird (42, black, laborer), Hannah (38, black), Mildred (20, black), Wm. (19, black, laborer), Ann M. (18, black), John (15, black, no occupation), Mary (12, black), Sally (8, black).

BOB

- COURT ORDER BOOK (May 1856): Bob Tapscott's administrators "alledging that he was unlawfully detained as a slave by the D[e]f[endan]ts."

BOST, CALVIN

- DEATH CERTIFICATES (1865): Died in Amherst in September of dropsy at age 20, no parents or informant listed. (*Pg 111, # 22*)

BOST, EZEKIEL

- DEATH CERTIFICATES (1865): Died in Amherst in January of B. Fever [Bilious Fever?] at age 15, no parents or informant listed. (*Pg 111, #20*)

BOST, JOHN

- DEATH CERTIFICATES (1865): Died in Amherst in September, unborn, aged 2 months [premature?], no parents or informant listed. (*Pg 111, #21*)

BRANHAM, AMAZA ANN

- MARRIAGE REGISTER (1846): Married John C. Noel.

BRANHAM, BALINDA

- CENSUS (1850): Balinda Branham (28, mulatto), Alison (1, mulatto), Wm Adcock (37, white, no occupation)

BRANHAM, BE[R]LINDA

- COURT ORDER BOOK (June 1851): The Court ordered that her registration be renewed, but there is no entry in that name.
- COMM. REV. 1861 A and B: age 35.

BRANHAM, BETSEY

- MARRIAGE REGISTER (1825): Betsey Branham, daughter of Creasey Branham, married James Foster.

BRANHAM, CAROLINE

- COMM. REV. 1861 A: age 18.
- COMM. REV. 1861 B: age 15.
- COURT ORDER BOOK (October 1864): The Court ordered that she be registered.

BRANHAM, CHESH [?]

- DEATH CERTIFICATE INDEX: Died September 1886.

BRANHAM, CHESLEY

- DEATH CERTIFICATE INDEX: Died October 2, 1887.

BRANHAM, CHRISTIANNA

- COMM. REV. 1861 B: Female, age 54.

BRANHAM, CHRISTIANNA

- COMM. REV. 1861 B: Female, age 22.

BRANHAM, CHRISTOPHER

- PERSONAL PROPERTY TAX (1850): 1 male free negro.
- CENSUS (1850): Christopher Branham (49, mulatto, born in Virginia) was listed in the household of A. C. Harrison (white, hotelkeeper).

BRANHAM, CREASEY

- [*NOTE: There are at least two women in these entries.*]
- CENSUS (1830): 1 fcm under 10 years of age, 1 fcf under 10, 2 fcfs 10 to 24, 1 fcf 36 to 55.

- CENSUS (1850): Creasey Branham (36, mulatto), Wm. (28, mulatto, farmer), Lucinda (22, mulatto), Marshal (5, mulatto), Winston (3, mulatto), Francis Evans (22, mulatto), Seadney Evans (5, mulatto), Leathy Evans (3, mulatto).
- COURT ORDER BOOK (June 1851): The Court ordered that her registration be renewed, but there is no entry in that name.
- COMM. REV. 1861 A: Female, age 70.

BRANHAM, EADY

- CENSUS, AGRICULTURAL (1850): 50 improved acres, 35 unimproved acres, total value of land owned was $120 – total value of machinery was $2 – 3 swine worth $8 – 20 bushels of wheat, 30 bushels of rye, 75 bushels of Indian corn, 20 bushels of oats, 500 pounds of tobacco

BRANHAM, EDMOND

- DEATH CERTIFICATES (1885): Died in the Courthouse District of Amherst on August 2 of rheumatism at age 84, parents not listed, informant was his son Richd Branham. (*Pg 2, #16*)

BRANHAM, EDMOUND

- MARRIAGE REGISTER (1825): Edmound Branham, son of Creasey Branham, married Mary Louise Johns, probably the daughter of Will and Molly Johns.

BRANHAM, EDMUND

- MARRIAGE REGISTER (1790): Edmund Branham married Nancy Evans, the daughter of William Evans, sister of Molly Evans, and an Indian woman. (From *Indian Island in Amherst County*)

BRANHAM, EDMUND

- PERSONAL PROPERTY TAX (1840): 1 horse - 8¢ tax.
- PERSONAL PROOPERTY TAX (1850): 1 male free negro over 16, 1 horse, etc. - 10¢ tax paid.
- CENSUS (1850): Edmund Branham (46, mulatto, farmer), Mary E. (19, mulatto), Richard H. (17, mulatto, laborer), Judith (14, mulatto), Indianna (8, mulatto), Polvia (6, mulatto), Caroline (5, mulatto).
- CENSUS, AGRICULTURAL (1850): 150 improved acres, 250 unimproved acres, total value of land owned was $500 – total value of machinery: $5 – 1 horse, 2 milk cows, 4 other cattle, 18 swine, total value of livestock was $125 – 30 bushels of wheat, 100 bushels of Indian corn, 1,000 pounds of tobacco, 100 pounds of butter

- DEED (December 31, 1856): William Johns surrendered all of his land to his children, reserving the right to collect $20 rent annually from each of them for support during his lifetime. Edmund was married to Johns' daughter, and their portion was 92 ¼ acres on Harris Creek where he was then living, on the east side of Bear Mountain on the north fork of Harris Creek. (*Deed Book DD, pgs 340-341*)
- DEED: see Judith Branham: Deed, 1858.
- PERSONAL PROPERTY TAX (1860): 1 male free negro 21 to 55 years old, 1 horse worth $45, 6 cattle worth $80, household furnishings worth $25 – 7 sheep/hogs worth $15 – aggregate value: $165.
- CENSUS (1860): Edmund Branham (55, mulatto, farmer, $819 real estate, $150 personal estate), Caroline (13, mulatto), Orlena (5, mulatto).
- CENSUS, AGRICULTURAL (1860): 40 improved acres, 59 unimproved acres, total value of farm was $800 – total value of machinery: $30 – 1 horse, 2 milk cows, 2 working oxen, 2 other cattle, 1 sheep, 16 swine, total value of livestock was $170 – 99 bushels of wheat, 250 bushels of Indian corn, 3,000 pounds of tobacco, 6 bushels of beans, 10 bushels of Irish potatoes, 150 pounds of butter – value of slaughtered animals: $105.
- COMM. REV. 1861 B: age 57.
- COMM. REV. 1861 A: age 45, farmer.

BRANHAM, EDMUND

- ESTATE (November 17, 1885): Otto L. Evans qualified as administrator of Edmund Branham's estate. (*Will Book 21, pg 238*)

BRANHAM/BRANNUM, EDWARD

- HEADS OF FAMILIES (1783): 1 white person.
- HEADS OF FAMILIES (1785): 3 white persons.
- TAX LIST (1800): 1 white male over 21, 1 horse.
- CENSUS (1810): 3 free colored persons.
- CENSUS (1820): 2 fcms 14 to 25 years old, 1 fcm 26 to 44, 1 fcm over 45, 2 fcfs under 14, 1 fcf 14 to 25 – 2 engaged in farming.
- PERSONAL PROPERTY TAX (1822): 1 horse -14¢ tax.
- PERSONAL PROPERTY TAX (1826): "Edward Brannum Senr." – 1 free male, 1 horse – 12¢ tax.
- CENSUS (1830): 1 fcm 55 to 100 years old, 1 fcf under 10, 1 fcf 10 to 24, 1 fcf 36 to 55.

BRANHAM, EDWARD

- CENSUS (1840): 1 fcm under 10 years old, 1 fcm 10 to 24, 1 fcm 36 to 55, 2 fcfs under 10, 1 fcf 24 to 36 – 1 engaged in agriculture.

BRANHAM, ELIZA

- COMM. REV. 1861 B: age 26.

BRANHAM, ELIZABETH

- COMM. REV. 1861 B: age 25.

BRANHAM, ELY

- PERSONAL PROPERTY TAX (1821): 1 horse –14¢ tax (1824): same -12¢ tax (1825): same.

BRANHAM, GROVER

- DEATH CERTIFICATE INDEX: Died August 9, 1887.

BRANHAM, HENRY

- COMM. REV. 1861 B: age 13.

BRANHAM, INDIANNA

- COURT ORDER BOOK (April 1860): The Court ordered that she be registered, but there is no entry in that name.

BRANHAM, JAMES

- MARRIAGE REGISTER (1802): Married Elizabeth Whitten

BRANHAM, JAMES

- COMM. REV. 1861 B: age 15.

BRANHAM, JANE

- COMM. REV. 1861 B: age 26.

BRANHAM, JOEL

- CENSUS (1830): 1 fcm 10 to 24 years old, 2 fcfs under 10, 1 fcf 10 to 24, 1 fcf 24 to 36.
- PERSONAL PROPERTY TAX (1831): 1 mulatto, 1 horse – 6¢ tax.
- CENSUS (1840): 1 fcm 24 to 36 years old, 2 fcfs under 10, 3 fcfs 10 to 24, 1 fcf 36 to 55 – 2 engaged in agriculture.
- PERSONAL PROPERTY TAX (1840): 2 horses-16¢ tax.
- CENSUS (1850): Joel Branham (40, mulatto, farmer), Mary J. (23, mulatto), Martha (20, mulatto), Evaline (17, mulatto), Drury (14, mulatto), Varilla (14, mulatto).
- PERSONAL PROPERTY TAX (1850): 1 male free negro over 16 years old, 1 horse, etc. – 10¢ tax.

BRANHAM, JORDENA

- COMM. REV. 1861 A: Female, age 22.
- COMM. REV. 1861 B: age 23.

BRANHAM, JUDITH (JUDY)

- DEED (May 12, 1858): William Johns conveyed to Judy Branham, daughter of Edm[un]d Branham, all his household and kitchen furniture, reserving its use and enjoyment during his lifetime. He did this in consideration of his affection for his granddaughter Judith and as compensation to her for her care of him in his old age. (*Deed Book EE, pg 65*)
- CENSUS (1860): Judy Branham (23, mulatto, housekeeper) was listed in the household of John W. Rucker (white, planter).

BRANHAM, KITT

- CENSUS (1860): Kitt Branham (65, mulatto, laborer) was listed in the household of John Thompson, Jr. (white, lawyer). (*See also Squire Jackson.*)

BRANHAM/BRANNUM, LEVI/LEVY

- CENSUS (1850): Levy Brannum (54, mulatto, laborer), Elizabeth (30, mulatto), Mary (7, mulatto).
- CENSUS (1860): Levy Branham (66, mulatto, farmer), Eliza Ponton (30, mulatto), Mary Ann Ponton (22, mulatto), Dolly Ponton (4, mulatto), Milly Ponton (1, mulatto).
- CENSUS, AGRICULTURAL (1860): 1 swine worth $4 – 50 bushels of Indian corn, 745 pounds of tobacco, 6 bushels of Irish potatoes, 20 pounds of butter – value of slaughtered animals: $16.
- COMM. REV. 1861 B: age 65, farmer.

BRANHAM, MATILDA

- MARRIAGE REGISTER (1826): Married Joseph Huggart.

BRANHAM, MITTIE

- DEATH CERTIFICATE INDEX: Died August 1888.

BRANHAM, NANCY

- MARRIAGE REGISTER (1841): Nancy Branham, daughter of Joel Branham, married Jackson Noel.

BRANHAM, NANCY

- MARRIAGE REGISTER (1804): Married Sam[ue]l B. Mitchell.

BRANHAM, PAULINE

- COMM. REV. 1861 B: age 17.

BRANHAM, PERMELIA

- MARRIAGE REGISTER (1830): Married Jefferson Rowsey.

BRANHAM, POLLY

- MARRIAGE REGISTER (1810): Polly Branham, daughter of Edward and Nancy Branham, married James Johns.

BRANHAM, POLLY

- MARRIAGE REGISTER (1823): Married Wm. G. Vest.

BRANHAM, RICHARD

- COMM. REV. 1861 A: age 25, farmer.
- COMM. REV. 1861 B: age 30.

BRANHAM, RICHARD H.

- PERSONAL PROPERTY TAX (1860): 1 male free negro 21 to 55 years old, household furnishings worth $25 – aggregate value $25.
- CENSUS (1860): Richard Branham (26, mulatto, farmer, $20 personal estate), Christianna (22, mulatto), Geo. M.(5, mulatto), Beauford (2, mulatto), Mary (7 months, mulatto), Seaton Johns (18, mulatto).
- CENSUS, AGRICULTURAL (1860): value of machinery owned: $6 – 2 swine worth $10 – 50 bushels of Indian corn, 30 bushels of oats, 2,700 pounds of tobacco, 7 bushels of Irish potatoes – value of slaughtered animals: $12.

BRANHAM, SALLIE

- DEATH CERTIFICATE INDEX: Died August 15, 1896.

BRANHAM, W. G.

- CENSUS, AGRICULTURAL (1860): 1 horse, 2 swine, total value of livestock was $15.

BRANHAM, WILLA [?]

- DEATH CERTIFICATE INDEX: Died May 7, 1892.

BRANHAM, WILLIAM

- [*NOTE: There are at least two men by this name.*]
- PERSONAL PROPERTY TAX (1850): 1 male free negro over 16 years old.
- PERSONAL PROPERTY TAX (1850): 1 male free negro over 16 years old.
- PERSONAL PROPERTY TAX (1860): 1 male free negro 21 to 55, household furnishings worth $20 – aggregate value $20.
- CENSUS (1860): Wm. (42, black, farmer), L. J. (30, mulatto), J. A. (16, mulatto), G. S. (12, mulatto), A. (7, mulatto), A. M. (5, mulatto), Jane (2, mulatto), C. P. (2 months, black).
- COMM. REV. 1861 A: age not given, farmer.
- COMM. REV. 1861 B: age 30, cooper.

BRIDGET

- CENSUS (1850): Bridget (76, black) was listed in the household of Benjamin J. Rucker, Overseer of the Poor.

BROWN, HENRY

- DEATH CERTIFICATES (1867): Died in Amherst on April 25 of dropsy at age 18, born in Amherst, a laborer, son of [?] and S.

Brown, informant was his former owner Daniel E. Bailey. (*Pg 118, #6*)

BURKS, SAMUEL

- HEADS OF FAMILIES (1783): 7 blacks.

BYAS/BYASS, DAVID

- COMM. REV. 1861 A: age 51, farmer.
- COMM. REV. 1861 B: age 50, mechanic.

BYAS/BYASS, ELIZABETH

- COMM. REV. 1861 B: age 25.

BYAS/BYASS, ESEX/ESSEX

- COMM. REV. 1861 A: age 16, farmer.
- COMM. REV. 1861 B: age 18.

BYAS/BYASS, FANNY

- COMM. REV. 1861 B: age 50.

BYAS/BYASS, FRANCES

- COMM. REV. 1861 A: Female, age 45.

BYAS/BYASS, GEORGE

- COMM. REV. 1861 A: age 12, farmer.
- COMM. REV. 1861 B: age 14.

BYAS/BYASS, JAMES

- HEADS OF FAMILIES (1783): 3 white persons

BYAS/BYASS, JOHN

- Listed in *Amherst County, Virginia in the Revolution* as having served in the military. (Page 40)
- HEADS OF FAMILIES (1783): 7 whites.

BYAS/BYASS, JUDY/JUDITH

- COMM. REV. 1861 A: age 79.
- DEATH CERTIFICATES (1864): Died in Amherst in May of old age at 80, born in Amherst, wife of Toby Byas, informant was her son Toby Byas. (*Pg 107, #7*)

BYAS/BYASS, LARKIN

- Listed in *Amherst County, Virginia in the Revolution* as having served in the military. (Page 40)
- HEADS OF FAMILIES (1783): 5 whites.
- HEADS OF FAMILIES (1785): 6 white persons.
- TAX LIST (1800): 2 white males over 21, 2 horses.
- CENSUS (1810): all whites.

BYAS/BYASS, MARIA

- COMM. REV. 1861 A: age 40.

BYAS/BYASS, MARY

- COMM. REV. 1861 B: age 12.

BYAS/BYASS, MONA [*?*]

- COMM. REV. 1861 B: Female, age 40.

BYAS/BYASS, OBEDIAH

- Listed in *Amherst County, Virginia in the Revolution* as having served in the military. (Page 40)
- HEADS OF FAMILIES (1783): 1 white person.

BYAS/BYASS, TOBY

- [*NOTE: There are at least two men by this name.*]
- CENSUS (1850): Toby Byas (40, black, laborer).
- COMM. REV. 1861 A: age 41, farmer.
- DEATH CERTIFICATES (1864): Died in Amherst in April of old age at 85, born in Amherst, a farmer, husband of Judy Byas, informant was his son Toby Byas. (*Pg 107, #6*)

BYAS/BYASS, TOBY, Jr.

- COMM. REV. 1861 A: age 18, farmer.
- COMM. REV. 1861 B: age 22.

BYAS/BYASS, WYATT

- COMM. REV. 1861 B: age 16.

CAMPBELL, JO.

- CENSUS (1840): 1 fcm under 10 years old, 1 fcm 24 to 36, 2 fcfs under 10, 1 fcf 10 to 24, 1 fcf 36 to 55 – 2 engaged in manufacturing.

CAREY, ARCHIBALD (ARCHER) (ARCHY)

- PERSONAL PROPERTY TAX (1829): 2 horses-16¢ tax (1831): same -12¢ tax.
- LEGISLATIVE PETITION (December 27, 1833): "The Honorable the Speaker and the Members of the Legislature of Virginia, the Undersigned Petitioners respectfully represent that they are informed and believe that Archy—known by the name of Archy Higginbotham or Archy Carey is a free man of color, and emancipated by Thomas Higginbotham and who is now residing in the County of Amherst and State of Virginia is a Person of good character, honest deportment and without exception in his behavior, he is regarded by all who known him as a respectable worthy man—He has by honest labor acquired real estate in Lynchburg of considerable value and a tract of land of considerable vale in the County of Amherst: he is deemed by all his acquaintances as not only harmless in disposition and conduct, but praiseworthy and he is justly esteemed by all who know him—he has a wife and children—and the undersigned regard it as a hardship that he should be

compelled to leave the State of Virginia—or if compelled to leave it, they think it right that a reasonable time should be allowed him to dispose of his estate, collect its proceeds and make provisions for his removal. The undersigned therefore respectfully petition your Honorable Body to permit by law the said Archy to remain in the State of Virginia and if that cannot be done to permit him to remain in the county of Amherst—or if that should be deemed unwise to allow him a reasonable time to dispose of his estate, collect the proceeds and prepare for removal which would require something like five years.—They respectfully ask that the most liberal indulgences and relief should be extended to him by the Legislature and as is duly bound they will ever pray."

- This petition was signed by 135 persons; attached to it were several corroborating letters of support: "The undersigned citizens of Lynchburg in Virginia, take pleasure in testifying to the respectability and good conduct of Archy Carey, a man of color. He has lived in this place from his boyhood . . . He has been employed here, for the last ten years or more, as a hack-driver; and in that capacity stands higher than any one else who has ever lived in this part of the world."
- The Legislature's response to Carey's petition: "Petition to remain—rejected. Petition for time to sell property etc. Reasonable."
- Letter from Thomas L. Stevens of Milton, North Carolina (May 1830): "Archy Carey, a free man of colour has called on a number of Gentlemen and exhibited unquestionable testimonials of a fair character from Gentlemen of Lynchburg, Va. In consequence of which the gentlemen of this state have agreed so far as they have been consulted, that as long as his conduct comports with his recommendation, they will not enforce the law against him. The substance of the law is, that after 20 days notice he must leave the State, or will be subject to pay 500 dollars and be sold for a term not over 10 years."
- Letter from Ammon Hancock of Lynchburg, Va. (May 20, 1830): "Archer Carey, a man of color the bearer of this note was emancipated a few years ago by Thomas Higgin-botham on account of his uniform good conduct while a slave & being compelled to leave this state on account of the severity of the laws relative to free negroes is now in pursuit of a home & it is earnestly hoped that all good citizens will permit him to travel about through the country until he can find a place suitable for

him to settle on and protect in any way they would any other good citizen."

- Letter from James Saunders of Lynchburg, Va. (January 2, 1832): "Archer Carey is compelled to seek a residence out of Virginia in consequence of the laws of the state not allowing free persons of color, who have acquired their freedom to remain in it. He visits North Carolina for the purpose of obtaining a residence there. After which it is his object to return here, where he has valuable property and accounts, and settle his business . . . There is not an honest or more upright man under the sun. He is exemplary in all his deportment—industrious, obedient, humble and obliging . . . "
- Letter from Ammon Hancock to Archy Carey in North Carolina: "Archy—I have had an offer of $800 for your house & lot and wish you write me word by return mail whether you will take that price or not. My opinion is that you had better take that price. Property is low here of every description and your property will decline in value renting it to such as have been renting it."
- PROBATE: Amherst County Court (June 1842): "The court doth commit the estate of Archy Carey to Nelson Crawford Sh[eri]ff of this County to be by him administered according to law[,] said Cary having been dead more than three months." [*NOTE: This entry was repeated on page 147 but the words "been dead" are scratched out and "departed this life" written instead.*] (*Will Book 11, pg 129*)

CARTER, CHARLES, Estate of

- HEADS OF FAMILIES (1783): 5 black persons.

CARTER, LOUISA

- CENSUS (1860): Mary S. Pamplin (white ?), Segus A. Pamplin (white ?), Louisa Carter (17, mulatto), Geo Carter (11, mulatto)

CARTER, SOPHIA

- DEATH CERTIFICATES (1865): Died in Amherst on December 12 of consumption at age 45, born in Amherst, informant was her former owner Ann Smith. (*Pg 115, #23*)

CASH, REBECCA

- DEATH CERTIFICATES (1867): Died in Amherst on August 7 of scrofula at age 58, born in Amherst, daughter of [?] and R. Cash, wife of Jo Cash, informant was her former owner D. H. Page. (*Pg 118, #15*)

CASHWELL, BETSY

- DEATH CERTIFICATE INDEX: Died August 4, 1874.

CASHWELL, BETTY

- DEATH CERTIFICATE INDEX: Died September 3, 1884.

CASHWELL, BLANCH

- DEATH CERTIFICATE INDEX: Died December 1, 1894.

CASHWELL, DICK

- DEATH CERTIFICATE INDEX: Died December 26, 1894.

CASHWELL, GEO.

- DEATH CERTIFICATE INDEX: Died November 25, 1884.

CASHWELL, HENRY

- HEADS OF FAMILIES (1783): 1 white person.

CASHWELL, HENRY

- DEATH CERTIFICATE INDEX: Died February 15, 1888.

CASHWELL, JANICE [?]

- DEATH CERTIFICATE INDEX: Died June 2, 1876.

CASHWELL, JOHN

- CENSUS (1850): John Cashwell (45, mulatto, farmer), Betsey (14, mulatto), Milly (11, mulatto), Wm. (9, mulatto), Catharine (7, mulatto), Caroline (5, mulatto), Peter (6, mulatto), John (3, mulatto).

CASHWELL, JOHN

- CENSUS (1850): John Cashwell (38, mulatto, farmer), Mary (37, mulatto), 7 children
- COURT ORDER BOOK (April 1851): Mary Cashwell, the wife of John, and her children were permitted to remain in Amherst County until "next fall."
- COURT ORDER BOOK (October 1860): "On the motion of John Cashwell (& his wife Mary & their children), a free man of colour, the acting Justices are ordered to be summoned to next Court, to consider his application to remain in this County for a limited time."

CASHWELL, MARY

- CENSUS (1860): Mary Cashwell (47, black, housekeeper, $650 personal estate), Betty (23, mulatto, domestic), Milly (20, mulatto, domestic), Wm. (17, mulatto, laborer), Catharine (16, mulatto, domestic), Peter (14, mulatto), Caroline (13, mulatto), John (10, mulatto), Mary J. (8, mulatto), Richard (7, mulatto), Va. (5, mulatto), Saml. (1, mulatto).

CASHWELL, MOLLIE

- DEATH CERTIFICATE INDEX: Died December 1896.

CASHWELL, PETER

- HEADS OF FAMILIES (1783): 10 white persons.

CATO, SALLY PAYNE

- MARRIAGE REGISTER (1830): Sally Payne married Wm. Cato, a free man of colour and a blacksmith by trade, from Rockbridge County; his father was also a "Free man of colour."

CATO, WILLIAM

- CENSUS (1830): 1 fcm under 10 years old, 1 fcm 36 to 55, 2 fcfs under 10, 1 fcf 36 to 55, 1 fcf 55 to 100.

CHARLESTON, JOHN

- LEGISLATIVE PETITION (October 13, 1814): To the Hon[ora]ble Speaker & members of the General Assembly of Virginia; Your petitioner John Charleston a man of Colour, aged forty seven years and now a resident of Amherst County, begs leave humbly to represent that some several years past, by the aid and kind interference of a friend he was enabled to procure his freedom for the sum of One hundred and ten pounds, which said sum he has long since paid and satisfied, and by his exertions and economy he has since been enabled to purchase his wife Ursley and her two children two [sic] wit Asberry and Caroline for which he gave Ninety pounds and who are now Slaves and belonging to your petitioner, who feels an anxious desire to emancipate his said wife and two children, was it not that the laws of this state prevent their residing therein when freed—Your Petitioner therefore prays that a law may pass allowing the said Ursley, Asberry, and Caroline to reside in this State, on condition that they are set free by your petitioner, and he as in duty bound will ever pray—John Charleston."
- Letter signed by 47 persons: "We whose names are hereto annexed, have been for many years past (many of us personally) and all with his Character that he has for years occasionally been in the Counties of Campbell, Amherst and Nelson, and has for about two years past resided and now does in the County of Amherst near Lynchburg, that he conducts himself, not only as an industrious and honest Citizen, but is considered as a man of fair Character and Moral rectitude, and finally has conducted himself so as to merit the good will of the Citizens of the County aforesaid and that they in his behalf unite in praying that this honorable body may pass a law agreeable to his petition as above stated by him."
- The Legislature's response to Charleston's petition: "reasonable, Bill drawn."
- CENSUS (1820): 2 fcms under 14 years old, 1 fcm 45 and up, 1 fcf under 14, 1 fcf 26 to 44 – I engaged in agriculture.

CHRISTIAN, CHARLES

- DEATH CERTIFICATES (1865): Died in Amherst in April of scarlet fever at age 3, informant was his former owner C. R. [A.?] Christian. (*Pg 111, #35*)

CHRISTIAN, IDA

- DEATH CERTIFICATES (1865): Died in Amherst in September of scrofula at age 17, no parents or informant listed. (*Pg 111, #47*)

CHRISTIAN, JOHN

- DEATH CERTIFICATES (1864): Died in Amherst in July of typhoid fever at age 1, born in Amherst, no parents listed, informant was his former owner C. B. Christian. (*Pg 107, #23*)

CHRISTIAN, JORDAN

- DEATH CERTIFICATES (1864): Died in Amherst in July of colic at age 17, a farmer, no parents listed, informant was his former owner C. B. Christian. (*Pg 107, #24*)

CHRISTIAN, MARGARET

- DEATH CERTIFICATES (1864): Died in Amherst in June of typhoid fever at age 17, born in Amherst, no parents listed, informant was her former owner C. B. Christian. (*Pg 107, #22*)

CHRISTIAN, MARTHA

- DEATH CERTIFICATES (1867): Died in Amherst in September of burns at age 5, born in Amherst, daughter of [?] and P. Christian, informant was her former owner M. M. Pendleton. (*Pg 118, #16*)

CHRISTIAN, ROB

- DEATH CERTIFICATES (1865): Died in Amherst in October of pneumonia at age 50, a farmer, born in Amherst, informant was his former owner C. R. [A.?] Christian. (*Pg 111, #34*)

CLARK, ALEX

- COMM. REV. 1861 A and B: age 20.

CLARK, ANDREW JACKSON

- MARRIAGE REGISTER (1840): Andrew Jackson Clark married Manervy Peters, daughter of Reuben Peters.

CLARK, CAROLINE

- COMM. REV. 1861 B: age 13.

CLARK, CORDELIA

- COMM. REV. 1861 A: age 12.

CLARK, ELLEN

- COMM. REV. 1861 A: age 23.
- COMM. REV. 1861 B: age 24.

CLARK, FRANCES

- COMM. REV. 1861 A: Female, age 40.
- COMM. REV. 1861 B: age 41.

CLARK, GEORGE

- MARRIAGE REGISTER (1821): Married Jane Johns.
- PERSONAL PROPERTY TAX (1822): 1 free mulatto, 1 horse – 14¢ tax.

CLARK, HORACE

- PERSONAL PROPERTY TAX (1860): 1 male free negro 21 to 55 years old – aggregate value $0.
- COMM. REV. 1861 A: age 23, farmer.

CLARK, JAMES

- TAX LIST (1800): 1 white male over 21, 2 horses. [*This may not be the same person as below.*]
- CENSUS (1810): 9 free coloreds.

CLARK, JAMES

- MARRIAGE REGISTER (1826): Married Jane Peters.

CLARK, JAMES

- COMM. REV. 1861 A: age 60, farmer.
- COMM. REV. 1861 B: age 61, farmer.

CLARK, JAMES, Jr.

- COMM. REV. 1861 A: age 18, farmer.
- COMM. REV. 1861 B: age 19.

CLARK, JAMES, Sr.

- PERSONAL PROPERTY TAX (1860): 1 male free negro 21 to 55 years old, 3 horses worth $175, 7 cattle worth $75, household furnishings worth $25 – aggregate value $275.

CLARK, JANE

- COMM. REV. 1861 A and B: age 45.

CLARK, JOHN

- CENSUS (1810): 4 free coloreds.

CLARK, LOISA

- MARRIAGE REGISTER (1805): Loisa Clark, a widow, married Charles Johns of Bedford County.

CLARK, MAHALA

- COMM. REV. 1861 A: Female, age 16.

CLARK, MARY E.

- COMM. REV. 1861 A: age 14.
- COMM. REV. 1861 B: age 15.

CLARK, MATILDA

- COMM. REV. 1861 B: age 17.

CLARK, MICAJAH

- [*NOTE: There appears to have also been a white Micajah Clark; only those records which could be identified positively as those of a free negro are included here.*]
- CENSUS (1810): 3 free coloreds.
- CENSUS (1820): 4 fcm under 14 years old, 1 fcm 26 to 44, 1 female free colored under 14, 1 fcf 26 to 44, 1 male slave 14 to 25 – 2 engaged in agriculture.
- PERSONAL PROPERTY TAX (1824): 1 free mulatto, 1 horse – 12¢ tax.

CLARK, NELSON

- PERSONAL PROPERTY TAX (1860): 1 male free negro over 55 years old, a cattle worth $15, household furnishings worth $15 – aggregate value: $30.
- COMM. REV. 1861 A: age 55, farmer.
- COMM. REV. 1861 B: age 57.

CLARK, NELSON H.

- MARRIAGE REGISTER (1840): Married Frances Mason.
- COURT ORDER BOOK (April 1851): "The application of Nelson H. Clark for a certificate that he is a white man is continued until next court."
- COURT ORDER BOOK (June 1851): The applications of A. Terry, N. H. Clark, and O. Knuckles were continued until the next court. [*NOTE: There was no further mention of Clark's petition in 1851.*]
- CENSUS (1860): Nelson H. Clark (66, mulatto, planting, $200 personal estate, born in Virginia), Frances E. (40, mulatto), Nelson M. (18, mulatto, laborer), Elisha A. (17, mulatto, laborer), Susan J. (15, mulatto, domestic), Pheba J. (12, mulatto), Zach (10, mulatto), Elijah A. (9, mulatto), Alfred M. (6, mulatto), Rebecca (4, mulatto), Jese Mason (80, race left blank, retired shoemaker).
- CENSUS, AGRICULTURAL (1860): value of machinery owned: $72 – 1 milk cow, 4 working oxen, 2 other cattle, 3 swine, value of livestock was $232 – 16 bushels of rye, 20 bushels of Indian corn, 50 bushels of oats, 2,000 pounds of tobacco, 20 bushels of Irish potatoes, 75 pounds of butter, 1 ton of hay, 3 bushels of flaxseed – value of orchard products: $68 – value of slaughtered animals: $64.

CLARK, PARTHENA/PARTHENIE

- COMM. REV. 1861 A: Female, age 21.
- COMM. REV. 1861 B: age 22.

CLARK, PRESTON

- COMM. REV. 1861 A: age 35, farmer.
- COMM. REV. 1861 B: age 36.

CLARK, SUSAN

- COMM. REV. 1861 A: age 30.
- COMM. REV. 1861 B: age 31.

CLARK, WILLIAM

- TAX LIST (1800): *There are two William Clarks: one with 4 white males over 21 and 5 horses, and one with 2 white males over 21 and no horses. This may not be the same person in the next entry.*
- CENSUS (1810): 9 free coloreds.
- CENSUS (1820): 1 fcm 14 to 25 years old, 2 fcms 26 to 44, 1 fcm 45 and up, 1 fcf 14 to 25, 2 female slaves 26 to 44 – 4 engaged in agriculture.

CLARKE, ANDREW JACKSON

- PERSONAL PROPERTY TAX (1850): 1 male free negro over 16 years old, 1 horse etc. – 10¢ tax.

CLARKE, DEBBIE [?] M.

- CENSUS, DEATHS (1860): 12 [?] years old, free mulatto female, born in Virginia, died in April of a cold after being sick 6 weeks.

CLARKE, JAMES

- CENSUS, AGRICULTURAL (1860): 100 improved acres, 130 unimproved acres, total value of land owned was $800 – total value of machinery: $70 – 1 horse, 3 milk cows, 3 other cattle, 6 sheep, 4 swine, total value of livestock was $160 – 7 bushels of wheat, 60 bushels of rye, 100 bushels of Indian corn, 2,600 pounds of tobacco, 10 pounds of wool, 50 pounds of butter – value of orchard products: $45 – value of slaughtered animals: $56.

CLARKE, PRESTON

- PERSONAL PROPERTY TAX (1850): 1 male free negro over 16 years old, 1 horse etc. – 10¢ tax.
- PERSONAL PROPERTY TAX (1860): 1 male free negro 21 to 55 years old, 8 horses worth $100, household furnish-ings worth $25, sheep/hogs worth $25 – aggregate value: $150.
- CENSUS (1860): Preston Clarke (30, mulatto, farmer, $500 real estate, $200 personal estate, born in Virginia), Susanna (37, mulatto), Wm. J. (7, mulatto), Sarah (5, mulatto), John (4, mulatto), N. A. (2, mulatto).

COCKOLATE [?], WILLIAM

- PERSONAL PROPERTY TAX (1850): 1 male free negro over 16 years old.

COISE [?], JOHN

- CENSUS (1850): John Coise [?] (25, mulatto, carpenter), Mary Ann (24, mulatto).

COLE, DAVID

- CENSUS (1850): David Cole (35, black, laborer), Mary (30, black). [*NOTE: This listing appears twice.*]

COLEMAN, GABRIEL

- DEATH CERTIFICATES (1864): Died in Amherst on March 22 [disease illegible] at age 48, a farmer, no parents or informant listed. (*Pg 107, #17*)

COLEMAN, PAULINE

- DEATH CERTIFICATES (1865): Died in Amherst in April of scrofula at age 8, born in Amherst, no parents listed, informant was former owner W. E. Coleman. (*Pg 111, #48*)

COLEMAN, ROBERT L.

- MARRIAGE REGISTER (1827): Married Frances A. Pinn.

COLEMAN, SUSAN

- DEATH CERTIFICATES (1864): Died in Amherst in February, no cause of death or age listed, born in Amherst. (*Pg 107, #18*)

COOPER, ALFRED

- PERSONAL PROPERTY TAX (1860): 1 male free negro 21 to 55 years old, 2 cattle worth $25, household furnishings worth $35 – aggregate value: $60.
- COMM. REV. 1861 A: age 36, farmer.
- COMM. REV. 1861 B: age 37, farmer.

COOPER, BARTLETT

- CENSUS (1850): Bartlett Cooper (50, mulatto, laborer), Ann (50, mulatto), Mary (24, mulatto), James (21, mulatto, no occupation), Saml. (20, mulatto, no occupation), Eliza (18, mulatto), Bartlett (14, mulatto), Rebeca (13, mulatto), Emily (10, mulatto), Susan (8, mulatto), Roda (6, mulatto), Henry (5, mulatto), Elmira Evans (20, mulatto), Permelia Evans (13, mulatto), Jane Evans (10, mulatto).

COOPER, DAVID

- PERSONAL PROPERTY (1860): 1 male free negro 21 to 55 years old – aggregate value: $0.
- CENSUS (1860): David Cooper (25, mulatto, occupation illegible).
- COMM. REV. 1861 A and B: no age given, farmer.

COOPER, ELIHU

- PERSONAL PROPERTY TAX (1860): 1 male free negro 21 to 55 years old – aggregate value: $0.
- COMM. REV. 1861 A: age 30, farmer.
- COMM. REV. 1861 B: age 31, farmer.

COOPER, HANNAH

- COMM. REV. 1861 A and B: age 50.

COOPER, JOHN

- [*NOTE: There are at least two men represented here.*]
- CENSUS (1810): 6 free coloreds.
- CENSUS (1810): 4 free coloreds.
- CENSUS (1820): 1 fcm 26 to 44 years old, 4 fcfs under 14, 1 fcf 14 to 25 – 1 engaged in agriculture.
- CENSUS (1830): 1 fcm 55 to 100 years old, 1 fcf under 10, 1 fcf 10 to 24, 1 fcf 55 to 100 years.
- PERSONAL PROPERTY TAX (1823): 1 free mulatto, 2 horses – 24¢ tax (1824): 1 free mulatto, 1 horse – 12¢ tax (1828): same (1829): same – 10¢ tax (1831): same – 6¢ tax.

COOPER, PATSY

- CENSUS (1830): 3 fcm under 10 years old, 1 fcm 10 to 24, 1 fcf 10 to 24, 1 fcf 36 to 55.

COOPER, Unnamed Female

- COMM. REV. 1861 B: age 35.

COOPER, VIRGIL

- PERSONAL PROPERTY TAX (1850): 1 male free negro over 16 years old, 1 horse etc. – 10¢ tax.

COOPER, WESLEY/WILLIAM WES[T]LEY

- MARRIAGE REGISTER (1845): Married Juliann Peters.
- PERSONAL PROPERTY TAX (1850): 1 male free negro over 16 years old, 1 horse etc. – 10¢ tax.
- PERSONAL PROPERTY TAX (1860): 1 male free negro over 55, 1 horse worth $30, cattle worth $20, household furnishings worth $25, shhep/hogs worth $5 – aggregate value: $80.
- COMM. REV. 1861 A: age 55, farmer.
- COMM. REV. 1861 B: (William Cooper), age 56, farmer.

COOPER, WINSTON

- PERSONAL PROPERTY TAX (1860): 1 male free negro 21 to 55 years old – aggregate value: $0.
- CENSUS (1860): Winston Cooper (24, mulatto).
- COMM. REV. 1861 A: age 25, farmer.
- COMM. REV. 1861 B: age 29, farmer.

COUSIN, JOHN

- CENSUS (1830): 1 fcm 36 to 55 years old, 2 fcfs 10 to 24, 1 fcf 24 to 36.
- CENSUS (1850): John Cousin (45, mulatto, laborer), Mary Cousin (40, mulatto), Margaret Cousin (16, mulatto).

COUSINS, CLARA

- COMM. REV. 1861 A: age 25.
- COMM. REV. 1861 B: age 27.

COUSINS, ENOCH

- DEATH CERTIFICATES (1860): "a Free Negro," died in November of consumption at age 20, born in Amherst, son of Fred Cousins, informant was his sister Judy Cousins. (*Pg 98, #25*)

COUSINS, ENOCH

- COMM. REV. 1861 A: age 20.

COUSINS, FRED

- DEATH CERTIFICATES (1860): "a Free Negro," died in October of consumption at age 18, born in Amherst, son of Fred Cousins, informant was his sister Judy Cousins. (*Pg 98, #24*)

COUSIN[S], HENRY

- PERSONAL PROPERTY TAX (1860): 1 male free negro 21 to 55 years old – aggregate value: $0.
- COMM. REV. 1861 A: age 21.

COUSINS, HENRY

- DEATH CERTIFICATES (1860): "a Free Negro," died in October of consumption at age 40, born in Amherst, son of Fred Cousins, informant was his sister Judy Cousins. (*Pg 98, #23*)

COUSIN[S], JUDDY

- CENSUS (1860): Juddy Cousin (37, black, domestic), Clary (23, black, domestic), Feaby (20, black, domestic).
- CENSUS, AGRICULTURAL (1860): 1 milk cow, 3 swine, total value of livestock was $30 – 4 bushels of beans, 100 bushels of Irish potatoes, 30 bushels of sweet potatoes, 1,000 pounds of butter, 6 pounds of hops – value of market gardens: $500 – value of slaughtered animals: $2,000.

COUSINS, JUDITH

- COMM. REV. 1861 A: age 22.
- COMM. REV. 1861 B: age 36.

COUSINS, MARTHA ANN

- AMHERST COUNTY COURT (August 1864): The Court ordered that she be registered.

COUSINS, PHOEBE

- COMM. REV. 1861 A: age 23.
- COMM. REV. 1861 B: age 24.

COUSINS, SUSAN E.

- CENSUS (1850): Susan E. Cousins (8, mulatto, born in Virginia) was listed in the household of Benjamin McCary (white, farmer) along with Wm. Johnson (20, mulatto, laborer).

COUSINS, WALTON

- COMM. REV. 1861 B: Male, age 12.

COY [?], ANTHONY

- CENSUS (1810): 7 free coloreds.

CRUMP, FRANK

- CENSUS (1820): 1 fcm 26 to 44 years old, 2 fcfs under 14, 1 fcf 14 t0 25.

CURRY, MARY

- CENSUS (1810): 7 free coloreds.
- CENSUS (1830): 1 fcm 10 to 24 years old, 1 fcf 55 to 100.

CURRY, PETER

- PERSONAL PROPERTY TAX (1860): 1 male free negro 21 to 55 years old, 3 horses worth $125, cattle worth $50, household furnishings worth $35, sheep/hogs worth $35 – aggregate value: $245.
- COMM. REV. 1861 B: age 50, farmer.
- LAW ORDER BOOK (August 22, 1864): "On the petition of Peter Curry, Stating that he is illegally in custody by Van [?] Otey provost marshal of the Confederate States of America at the post [of] Lynchburg A Writ of Habeas Corpus ad Subj[??]dium is granted him; directed to the said Van Trump Otey provost marshal as aforesaid commanding him to have the body of the petitioner before this court on Wednesday next at ten o'clock together with the day and cause of his capture [?] and detention. (*Law Order Book No. 7, Amherst Circuit Court, 1860-1868, pg 133*)

CURRY, Unnamed Female

- COMM. REV. 1861 B: age 48.

DAMERON, GEO.

- DEATH CERTIFICATES (1865): Died in Amherst in June of bronchitis at age 2, born in Amherst, no parents listed, informant was his former owner Malaki Dameron. (*Pg 111, #40*)

DAVIS, GEO. W.

- DEATH CERTIFICATES (1864): Died in Amherst in May of a fever at age 6, born in Amherst, son of Geo. W. and Virginia Davis. (*Pg 107, #26*)

DAVIS, MARY

- DEATH CERTIFICATES (1865): Died in Amherst in March of a fever at age 7 months, born in Amherst, daughter of G. W. and Virginia Davis. (*Pg 111, #41*)

DAVIS, RANCH [RANAL?]

- DEATH CERTIFICATES (1867): Died in Amherst in June of heart disease at age 45, born in Amherst, a farmer, husband of Resetta [*?*] Davis, informant was his former owner H. L. Davis. (*Pg 118, #20*)

DEAN, BETTY

- LEGISLATIVE PETITION (December 4, 1811): "To the Hon[ora]ble the Speaker and Members of the Gen[era]l Assembly of Virginia—The Petition of Betty Dean, Franky Dean, Billy Dean, John Dean, Henry Dean, Daphne Dean, Samuel Floyd, Frank Floyd, and Mitchell Floyd humbly sheweth that they have been lately emancipated from a State of Slavery by the humanity of Miss Margaret Rose & Capt. Jno. N. Rose, to whom they of right belonged; and being very desirous from many weighty considerations to remain in this State, (but being informed that by the existing laws of the Country they are prohibited from that previledge unless by a special interference of your Honble Body,) they beg leave in the most humble & respectful manner to solicit that favor at your hands. Your Petitioners were born and raised in the County of Amherst & and they now reside part of them in that County & the rest of them in the County of Nelson and for their peaceable disposition, & industrious habits, which they hope they will be able to make appear to the satisfaction of your Honble body, they rest in the hope that their prayer will be granted and that a law will pass allowing them to remain in this state and to enjoy such rights & previledges as are allowed to free Citizens of this Commonwealth."
- Affidavit signed by 14 persons: "We whose names are hereunto subscribed do certify that we have for many years been acquainted with the certain [?] Petitioners, that they have ever been peaceable & inoffensive in their Disposition, as far as we know or believe, that they are generally useful & industrious Mechanicks & we are fully [illegible] that they will at no time

become chargeable to the State, that they are so nearly white that they would not be taken to be mulattoes where they were not known & upon the whole we are of the opinion that no injury could result to allow them the previledge of remaining in this State—Given under our hands this [blank] day of Nov. 1811."

- The Legislature's response: petition rejected.

DEANE, MARY

- MANUMISSION (August 1, 1785): Ann Rose freed Mary Deane, one of her female slaves. (*www.freeafricanameri-cans.com*)

DICK

- COURT ORDER BOOK (April 1860): "On the motion of Dick a free man of colour residing at Bethel, the Court doth order that all the acting Justices of this County be summoned to attend here on the 1st day of June Court next to consider his application to remain in this State & reside in this County."

DILLARD, ONEY/ONEZ/ONLY

- MARRIAGE REGISTER (1790): Oney Dillard, the daughter of William Dillard, married John Johns. [*NOTE: According to Indian Island in Amherst County, he was the son of Robert Johns and his wife Mary, an Indian.*]

DRUMMOND, MILLY

- DEATH CERTIFICATES (1865): Died in Amherst in November of unknown causes at age 58, informant was her former owner whose name was illegible. (*Pg 111, #39*)

DUMUCK, JOHN

- CENSUS (1850): John Dumuck (17, black) was listed in the household of John F. Hix (white, merchant).

DUNCAN, FLEMING

- MARRIAGE REGISTER (1795): Fleming Duncan married Sally Johns, whose guardian was John Richeson.

DUNCAN, FLEMING H.

- TAX LIST (1800): 1 white male over 21, 1 horse, and 1 slave over 16. [*NOTE: This may not be the same person as in the entry above.*]

DUNLAP, DANIEL

- CENSUS (1850): Daniel Dunlap (44, mulatto, laborer on canal), Hannah (43, mulatto), Virginia (17, mulatto), Henderson (15, mulatto), Anderson (14, mulatto), James (12, mulatto), Caroline (11, mulatto), Jane (10, mulatto), Richard (9, mulatto).

ESSEX, JOHN

- PERSONAL PROPERTY TAX (1850): 1 male free negro over 16 years old.

ESSEX, RICHARD

- COURT ORDER BOOK (October 1819): "Upon application of Richard Essex and Meredith Free Negroes of Colour who were part of the Slaves belonging to the estate of Sam[ue]l Gist Dec[ease]d to be allowed the liberty of residing within this Commonwealth. It appearing to the Court that a majority of the acting Justices of this County have been summoned to hear this application and that Notice thereof has been posted up at the front door of the Courthouse more [?] than five weeks of this County and that the law in relation thereto has been in every respect complied with, and upon hearing said application, it being satisfactorily proved to the Court that the said Essex and Meredith are Negroes of extraordinary merit and that their general good character and conduct have been unexceptionable therefore the Court do grant permission to the said Essex and Meredith to reside within this County as free Negroes as long as they support such characters as above and do not in any manner violate the laws relating to free Negroes making application of this sort."

ESSEX, RICHARD

- PERSONAL PROPERTY TAX (1824): 1 free negro, 1 horse - 12¢ tax (1827): same (1828): same (1829): same – 10¢ tax (1831):– 6¢ tax (1850): 1 male free negro over 16 years old.

ESSEX, RIC[HAR]D

- CENSUS (1860): Ricd Essex (80, black, farm laborer) was listed in the household of Willis Gillispie (white, farmer).

ESSEX, WILLIAM

- COURT ORDER BOOK (February 1851): The Court ordered that his registration be renewed; but there is only one Register entry in that name, and it is incomplete.
- PERSONAL PROPERTY TAX (1860): 1 male free negro 21 to 55 years old – aggregate value: $0.
- COMM. REV. 1861 A: age 38, farmer.
- COMM. REV. 1861 B: age 39, ditcher.

EUBANK, SAM

- DEATH CERTIFICATES (1866): Died in Amherst in May of pleurisy at age 71 or 79, informant was his former owner Thos. A. Eubank. (*Pg 115, #35*)

EVANS, [Illegible]

- CENSUS (1810): 9 free coloreds.

EVANS, AMBROSE

- CENSUS (1810): 6 free coloreds.

EVANS, ANDERSON

- CENSUS (1820): 3 fcms under 14 years old, 1 fcm 14 to 25, 1 fcm 26 to 44, 4 fcfs under 14, 1 fcf 14 to 25, 1 fcf 26 to 44 – 1 engaged in manufacturing.

EVANS, BENJAMIN

- HEADS OF FAMILIES (1783): 6 white persons.
- HEADS OF FAMILIES (1785): 6 mulattoes.
- CENSUS (1790): 6 mulattoes – 1 building other than a dwelling.

EVANS, BETS[E]Y

- COURT ORDER BOOK (December 1856): "It is ordered that any two of the Overseers of the Poor bind out according to law Betsy Evans a free girl of colour, daughter of Jane Evans, to John Pryor, Jr."
- CENSUS (1860): Betsey Evans (15, mulatto) was listed in the household of Mary S. Pryor (white).

EVANS, CHARLES

- CENSUS (1810): 1 free colored.

EVANS, ETHLY

- MARRIAGE REGISTER (1828): Ethly Evans married Albert Terry, son of Dicey Terry.

EVANS, FOSTER

- CENSUS (1810): 9 free coloreds.

EVANS, FRANKEY [?]

- CENSUS (1810): 4 free coloreds.

EVANS, HENRY A.

- CENSUS (1810): 2 free coloreds.
- CENSUS (1820): 1 fcm 45 years and up, 1 fcf 45 years and up – 1 engaged in agriculture.
- PERSONAL PROPERTY TAX (1821): 1 horse– 14¢ tax (1822): same.
- CENSUS (1830): 1 fcm 55 to 100 years old, 1 fcf 55 to 100.

EVANS, JANE

- CENSUS (1810): 4 free coloreds and 1 white female.
- CENSUS (1820): 1 fcm under 14 years old, 2 fcms 26 to 44, 1 fcf 26 to 44, 2 fcfs 45 years and up.

EVANS, JANE

- CENSUS (1860): Jane Evans (40, mulatto, farm hand) was listed in the household of Wm. Staton (white, planter), along with Sandra Evans (3, white).

EVANS, JOHN

- CENSUS (1820): 1 fcm under 14 years old, 1 fcm 26 to 45, 1 fcf under 14, 1 fcf 14 to 26 – 1 engaged in agriculture.

EVANS, MARY

- PERSONAL PROPERTY TAX (1826): 1 free mulatto, 2 horses – 24¢ tax (1827): 1 free mulatto, 1 horse – 12¢ tax (1828): same.

EVANS, MARY

- COMM. REV. 1861 B: age 25.

EVANS, MOLLY

- CENSUS (1810): 2 free coloreds.

EVANS, POLLY

- CENSUS (1840): 1 fcf 10 to 24 years old, 1 fcf 24 to 36, 1 fcf 36 to 55 – 2 engaged in agriculture.

EVANS, SARALLA [?]

- CENSUS (1860): Saralla [?] Evans (7, mulatto) was listed in the household of Elizabeth Lawhorne (mulatto).

EVANS, THOMAS

- MARRIAGE REGISTER (1795): Thomas Evans, a blacksmith, married Anna Pinn, the daughter of Rolly and Sarah Pinn.
- CENSUS (1810): 7 free coloreds.

EVANS, WILLIAM

- [*NOTE: This may represent more than one person.]*
- HEADS OF FAMILIES (1783): 6 white persons, 1 black.
- HEADS OF FAMILIES (1785): 7 white persons.
- TAX LIST (1800): 1 white male over 21, 3 horses, 1 slave over 16, and 2 slaves 12 to 16. [*NOTE: This may not be the same person.*]
- PERSONAL PROPERTY TAX (1823): 1 free mulatto, 1 horse – 12¢ tax (1824): same (1826): same.

EVANS, WILLIAM

- CENSUS, AGRICULTURAL (1860): value of machinery owned: $5 – 1 horse, 1 milk cow, value of livestock was $35 – 50 bushels of Indian corn, 900 pounds of tobacco, 10 bushels of Irish potatoes, 20 pounds of butter – value of slaughtered animals: $24.
- COMM. REV. 1861 B: age 27, farmer.

FERRER, DAVID

- PERSONAL PROPERTY TAX (1831): 1 free negro, 1 horse – 6¢ tax.

FIELD[S], JOHN

- PERSONAL PROPERTY TAX (1850): 1 male free negro over 16 years.
- PERSONAL PROPERTY TAX (1860): 1 male free negro over 55 years old, 1 horse worth $5, 2 cattle worth $15, household furnishings worth $30 – aggregate value: $50.
- CENSUS (1860): John Fields (60, mulatto), Betsey (40, mulatto), Susan (8, mulatto).
- COMM. REV. 1861 A: age 60, farmer.
- COMM. REV. 1861 B: age 65, farmer.

FIELDS, JOHN

- DEATH CERTIFICATE INDEX: Died September 29, 1873.

FLETCHER, DOLLY

- DEATH CERTIFICATES (1865): Died in Amherst in November of old age at 90, born in Amherst, no parents listed, informant was her former owner Sidney Fletcher. (*Pg 112, #11*)

FLETCHER, SUCKEY

- DEATH CERTIFICATES (1864): Died in Amherst in June of old age at 100, born in Amherst, no parents or informant listed. (*Pg 107, #40*)

FLINT, WILLIAM

- COURT ORDER BOOK (April 1856): Wm. Flint versus Thos. G. Hill – entry was illegible but apparently had to do with Hill's mistreatment of Flint.
- COURT ORDER BOOK (March 1856): "On the motion of William Flint a free negro heretofore apprenticed to Thomas G. Hill who filed his petition and complaint in writing, it is ordered that the said Thos. G. Hill be summoned to appear here at the next court to answer the complaint aforesaid & that he do not presume to beat or mistreat him on this account."
- COURT ORDER BOOK (May 1856): The Court refused to cancel the indentures of apprenticeship and rejected the Plaintiff's [Flint's] petition. Thomas Hill was permitted to transfer Flint's bond to someone else.

FLOYD, EDWARD

- PERSONAL PROPERTY TAX (1827): 1 free mulatto, 1 horse – 12¢ tax.

FLOYD, JOHN

- CENSUS (1850): John Floyd (30, mulatto, carpenter), Eliza (38, mulatto), 4 unnamed children.

FLOYD, MITCHELL

- CENSUS (1820): 2 white females 10 to 15 years old, 1 white female 16 to 18, 1 male free negro 26 to 44 – 1 engaged in agriculture.

FLOYD, SAMUEL

- CENSUS (1820): 2 fcms under 14 years old, 1 fcm 14 to 25, 1 fcm 26 to 44, 2 fcfs under 14, 1 fcf 14 to 25 – 1 engaged in agriculture.
- PERSONAL PROPERTY TAX (1823): 1 free mulatto, 1 horse – 12¢ tax (1829): same – 10¢ tax (1831): same – 6¢ tax
- CENSUS (1850): Saml Floyd (80, mulatto, carpenter), Eliza Floyd (34, mulatto), 5 unnamed children.

FLOYD, SAMUEL, Jr.

- PERSONAL PROPERTY TAX (1831): 1 free mulatto, 1 horse – 6¢ tax.

FORTUNE, JOHN

- MILITARY SERVICE: enlisted as a substitute from Amherst County during the American Revolution. (*www.freeafricanamericans.com*)

FOSTER, BETSEY

- COURT ORDER BOOK (April 1851): The Court ordered that her registration be renewed, but there is no entry in that name.
- COMM. REV. 1861 A: age 45.

FOSTER, BETSY

- DEATH CERTIFICATES (1860): A free woman, died in May of unknown causes at age 60, informant was her son Fielding Foster. (*Pg 99, #38*)

FOSTER, CHAS. W.

- COMM. REV. 1861 B: age 26.

FOSTER, FIELDING

- COMM. REV. 1861 B: age 32, farmer.

FOSTER, FRANCES

- COMM. REV. 1861 B: Female, age 17.

FOSTER, JAMES

- [*NOTE: There is more than one person represented here.*]
- CENSUS (1820): 2 fcms 14 to 25 years old, 1 fcm 26 to 44, 1 fcm 45 years and up, 2 fcfs 26 to 44 – 2 engaged in agriculture.

- PERSONAL PROPERTY TAX (1821): 2 horses – 27¢ tax (1826): 1 free mulatto, 1 horse – 12¢ tax (1827): same (1828): same (1840): 2 horses – 16¢ tax (1860): 1 male free negro over 55 years old, 1 horse worth $35, 2 cattle worth $40, household furnishings worth $20, 3 sheep/hogs worth $5 – aggregate value: $100.
- CENSUS (1830): 1 fcm 24 to 36 years old, 1 fcf under 10, 1 fcf 10 to 24.
- CENSUS (1840): 3 fcm under 10 years old, 1 fcm 10 to 24, 1 fcm 36 to 55, 1 fcf 10 to 24, 1 fcf 24 to 36 – 3 engaged in agriculture.
- CENSUS (1840): 2 fcm under 10 years old, 1 fcm 24 to 36, 2 fcfs under 10, 1 fcf 24 to 36 – 1 engaged in agriculture.
- CENSUS (1850): James Foster (64, black, farmer), Betsey (34, black), Nancy (21, black), Phillip (18, black), Wm. (16, black, laborer), Charles (12, black), Polly (9, black), Paulus (4, black), Sophiah (1, black), John (10, black), Edward (6, black).
- CENSUS, AGRICULTURAL (1850): 15 improved acres, 35 unimproved acres, total value of land owned was $100 – total value of machinery: $45 – 1 horse, 1 milk cow, 2 working oxen, 2 other cattle, 7 swine, total value of livestock was $40 – 15 bushels of wheat, 30 bushels of Indian corn, 1,000 pounds of tobacco, 45 pounds of butter.
- CENSUS (1860): James Foster (68, black, farmer, $150 real estate, $100 personal estate), Eliza Foster (23, mulatto, housekeeper).
- COURT ORDER BOOK (April 1860): The Grand Jury presented cases against Jas. Foster and other unnamed free negroes for not having their free papers.
- DEATH CERTIFICATES (1860): A free man, died in August of unknown causes at age 67, a farmer, husband of Betsy Foster, informant was his son Fielding Foster. (*Pg 99, #37*)
- INVENTORY (April 12, 1861): 1 yoke of oxen ($40), 1 horse ($25), 1 lot of old ploughs ($2), 1 plough and 2 collars ($1.25), 1 cupboard and table ($1.50), 1 old bed ($0.50), 1 log chain and 2 wedges ($2), 1 dinner pot ($0.50), 1 chain ($0.75), old saddle harness ($2.50), old wagon ($2.50), small quantity of tobacco ($5). (*Will Book 16, pg 75.*)
- COMM. REV. 1861 A: age 65, farmer.

FOSTER, JOHN

- PERSONAL PROPERTY TAX (1823): 1 free mulatto, 1 horse – 12¢ tax.

- COMM. REV. 1861 B: age 22, farmer.

FOSTER, JORDENA

- COMM. REV. 1861 B: Female, age 25.

FOSTER, LUCRETA [?]

- COMM. REV. 1861 B: Female age, 20.

FOSTER, NANCY

- MARRIAGE REGISTER (1850): Nancy Foster, daughter of James Foster, married Delaware Scott.

FOSTER, PHILLIP

- PERSONAL PROPERTY TAX (1850): 1 male free negro over 16 years old.
- CENSUS (1860): Phillip J Foster (38, mulatto, farmer), Wm. (24, mulatto, farm laborer), John (22, mulatto, farm laborer), Charles (19, mulatto, farm laborer), Edward (16, mulatto, farm laborer), Paulus (11, mulatto), Sophia (10, mulatto), Jordana (21, mulatto), Frances (16, mulatto), Wm. B. (1, mulatto), Ben J. C. Stinnett (1, white).

FOSTER, POLLY A.

- DEATH CERTIFICATES (1857): Died in December of whooping cough at age 16, daughter of James and Betsy Foster. (*Pg 77, #19*)

FOSTER, WILLIAM

- COURT ORDER BOOK (April 1851): The Court ordered that the registration of Wm Foster, son of James and Betsy Foster, be renewed; but there is no Register entry in that name prior to 1851.
- PERSONAL PROPERTY TAX (1860): 1 male free negro 21 to 55 years old – aggregate value: $0.
- COMM. REV. 1861 A: age 27, farmer.
- COMM. REV. 1861 B: age 28, farmer.

FRANCES – see KURL, FRANCES

FULAR [?], JOHN

- CENSUS (1850): John Fular [?] (55, mulatto), Peter (40, mulatto), Frank (18, mulatto), Mary (1, mulatto).

GANNAWAY, PAUL

- DEATH CERTIFICATES (1865): Died in Amherst in October of typhoid fever at age 22, born in Amherst, a farmer, no parents listed, informant was his former owner [?] Gannaway. (*Pg 112, #22*)

GARLAND, [?]

- DEATH CERTIFICATES (1864): Died in Amherst on January 10 of pneumonia at age 18, born in Amherst, no parents or informant listed. (*Pg 107, #38*)

GARLAND, EDMUND

- DEATH CERTIFICATES (1865): Died in Amherst in April of consumption at age 22, born in Amherst, no parents listed, informant was his former owner S. M. Garland. (*Pg 112, #17*)

GARLAND, JORDAN

- DEATH CERTIFICATES (1865): Died in Amherst in April of consumption at age 22, born in Amherst, no parents listed, informant was his former owner S. M. Garland. (*Pg 112, #16*)

GARLAND, LINCOLN

- DEATH CERTIFICATES (1864): Died in Amherst in April of a fever at age 2, informant was his former owner Saml. M. Garland. (*Pg 107, #46*)

GARNER, JOS.

- MARRIAGE REGISTER (1802): Jos. Garner married Only (Oney, Onez) Dillard Johns, widow of John S. Johns and daughter of William Dillard.

GEORGE

- DEATH CERTIFICATES (1881): Died in the courthouse District of Amherst County on January 7 of burns at age 80, unmarried, no parents listed, informant was the Overseer of the Poor. (*Pg 2, #68*)

GILBERT, JAMES

- PERSONAL PROPERTY TAX (1831): 1 free mulatto, 1 horse – 6¢ tax.

GILL, RICH'D.

- COMM. REV. 1861 A: age 30, farmer.

GO[W]ING, WILL[IAM] [H.]

- CENSUS (1820): 2 female slaves 45 years and up, 2 fcms under 14, 1 fcm 14 to 25, 1 fcm 26 to 44, 1 fcm 45 years and up, 1 fcf under 14, 1 fcf 14 to 25 – 1 engaged in agriculture. [*NOTE: This entry appears twice.*]
- PERSONAL PROPERTY TAX (1829): 2 horses – 16¢ tax.
- DEED (April 5, 1838): In consideration of his friendship for Martha Jane Snead, the daughter of his wife, John Vier sold the following to Wm. Gowing for $5: 1 sorrel mare, 1 yoke of oxen, 3 cows, 2 calves, 17 hogs, and household and kitchen furniture. (*Deed Book W, pg 274*)

- DEED (November 22, 1842): In consideration of his affection for his youngest brother Phillip Going, James W. Going sold the following to Wm. G. Going: 1 grey mare and colt, 1 bay mare. (*Deed Book Y, pg 344*)
- DEED (February 24, 1844): Wm. Going was the administrator of the estate of James Evans. This transaction involved 300 to 330 acres "where Wm Going lives," adjoining the copper mining and furnace company. (*Deed Book Z, pg 109*)

GOODE, WILLIAM

- HEADS OF FAMILIES (1783): 7 blacks.

GOODRICH, HOLLAND

- CENSUS (1820): 1 male slave under 14 years old, 1 female slave under 14, 1 female slave 14 to 25, 3 fcms 26 to 44 – 2 engaged in agriculture.
- PERSONAL PROPERTY TAX (1823): 1 free negro, 2 horses – 24¢ tax (1824): same.
- BILL OF SALE (July 26, 1824): Holland Goodrich, "a free man of colour," sold the following to Thos. Coppedge, Jr.: 1 grey mare ($20), 1 black mare, blind ($5), and 1 red cow ($9.50). Total sale was $43.87. Goodrich made his mark. (*Deed Book Q, pg. 124*)

GOODWIN, MOSES

- DEATH CERTIFICATES (1865): Died in Amherst in March of pneumonia at age 30, born in Amherst, a farmer, no parents listed, informant was his former owner M. C. Goodwin. (*Pg 112, #27*)

GUE, BELINDA

- MARRIAGE REGISTER (1815): Married Obediah Nuckles.

GUNN, LINDSAY

- PERSONAL PROPERTY TAX (1824): 1 free mulatto, 1 horse – 12¢ tax (1826): 1 free mulatto, 2 horses – 24¢ tax (1827): 1 free mulatto, 1 horse – 12¢ tax (1828): same (1829): 1 free mulatto, 2 horses – 20¢ tax (1831): same – 12¢ tax.

GUNN, MINNY

- CENSUS (1830): 1 fcf 55 to 100 years old.

GUTHRY, NATHANIEL

- MARRIAGE REGISTER (1790): Nancy Johns, daughter of Mary Johns, married Nathaniel Guthry.

HARDING, GROVES, Estate of

- HEADS OF FAMILIES (1783): 7 black persons.

HARIE [?], REUBEN

- CENSUS (1860): Reuben Harie [?] (30, mulatto, planter, $65 personal estate), M. J. (female, 25, mulatto).

HARLOE, NATHANIEL

- Listed in *Amherst County, Virginia in the Revolution* (70) as having property impressed and filing claim for it in 1782.
- HEADS OF FAMILIES (1783): 10 blacks.
- HEADS OF FAMILIES (1785): 11 white persons.

HARRIS, MARTIN

- DEATH CERTIFICATES (1864): Died in Amherst in January of unknown causes at age 14 days, born in Amherst, parents name illegible. (*Pg 108, #7*)

HARRISS, WILLIAM

- CENSUS (1830): 1 fcm under 10 years old, 1 fcm 24 to 36, 1 fcf 10 to 24.
- CENSUS (1840): 1 fcm under 10 years old, 1 fcm 10 to 24, 1 fcm 36 to 55, 2 fcfs under 10, 1 fcf 10 to 24, 1 fcf 24 to 36 – 2 engaged in agriculture.

HARTLESS, BENJAMIN, Jr.

- PERSONAL PROPERTY TAX (1829): 2 horses – 16¢ tax.

HARTLESS, HENRY

- *[NOTE: There are at least two persons represented here.]*
- April 2, 1782: was reimbursed by Amherst County Court for 20 pounds bacon and 275 pounds beef provided to the Army. (*www.freeafricanamericans.com*)
- HEADS OF FAMILIES (1783): 9 white persons, 1 black.
- HEADS OF FAMILIES (1785): 9 white persons.
- TAX LIST (1800): 1 white male over 21, 6 horses (1 stud), 3 slaves over 21, 1 slave 12 to 16.
- CENSUS (1820): 1 male slave 14 to 25 years old, 1 female slave 26 to 44, 2 fcms under 14, 1 fcm 26 to 44, 1 fcf 26 to 44 – 3 engaged in agriculture.
- CENSUS (1820): 1 fcm under 14 years old, 2 fcms 14 to 25, 2 fcms 45 years and up, 4 fcfs under 14, 2 fcfs 14 to 25, 1 fcf 45 years and up – 2 engaged in agriculture.

HARTLESS, HENRY C.

- CENSUS (1860): Listed in the household of Mary S. Hartless (32, white) were Leana F. Hartless (14, white), Emily I. Hartless (2 months, white), Henry C. Hartless (8 months, mulatto).

HARTLESS, JAMES

- TAX LIST (1800): 1 white male over 21, 1 horse.

- CENSUS (1820): 1 fcm 26 to 44 years old – engaged in manufacturing.

HARTLESS, JANE

- CENSUS (1840): 1 fcm 24 to 36 years old, 2 fcfs 10 to 24, 1 fcf 55 to 100 – 3 engaged in agriculture, 1 insane.

HARTLESS, JOHN

- CENSUS (1820): 3 fcms under 14 years old, 1 fcm 26 to 44, 3 fcfs under 14, 1 fcf 26 to 44 – 1 engaged in agriculture.

HARTLESS, NANCY

- CENSUS (1850): Listed in the household of Elias Martin (white, farmer) were: Nancy Hartless (35, mulatto), Betsey (16, mulatto), Ellen (10, mulatto), Mary (5, mulatto), Lucy (3, mulatto), Ellis (2, mulatto), Balinda (6 months, mulatto)

HARTLESS, PETER

- MILITARY SERVICE: applied for his pension in Amherst in 1832, at the age of 80. He was born in Caroline County and enlisted there circa 1778; moved to Amherst County in 1787. (*www.freeafricanamericans.com*)
- TAX LIST (1800): 1 white male over 21, 1 horse.
- CENSUS (1810): 3 free coloreds.
- CENSUS (1830): 1 fcm 10 to 24 years old, 1 fcm 55 to 100, 1 fcf 24 to 36, 1 fcf 55 to 100.

HARTLESS, RICHARD

- TAX LIST (1800): 1 white male over 21, 1 horse, and 1 slave over 16.
- CENSUS (1810): 5 free coloreds, 5 slaves.
- CENSUS (1820): 1 male slave under 14 years old, 1 male slave 14 to 25, 1 female slave under 14, 2 female slaves 14 to 25, 2 fcms under 14, 1 fcm 14 to 25, 1 fcm 45 years and up, 2 fcfs under 14, 1 fcf 26 to 44, 2 fcfs 45 years and up.

HARTLESS, SUSANNA

- MARRIAGE REGISTER (1812): Susanna Hartless, "a free mulatto," married Reuben Peters, "a free negro."

HARTLESS, WILL/WILLIAM

- MILITARY SERVICE: applied for a pension for his service in Amherst County Court in 1832. He was born in Caroline county and moved to Amherst at age 23. He joined the Albemarle militia in 1779 but was drafted from Amherst in 1781. He was taxable in Amherst County 1782-1821. He is listed as a head of household in the 1783 census. (*www.freeafricanamericans.com*)
- HEADS OF FAMILIES (1783): 1 white person.
- TAX LIST (1800): 1 white male over 21, 3 horses.

- CENSUS (1810): 13 free coloreds.
- CENSUS (1820): 1 white female 26 to 44 years old, 1 fcm under 14, 1 fcm 26 to 44, 2 fcm 45 years and up, 2 fcfs under 14.

HARVIE, MARTHA

- Listed in *Amherst County, Virginia in the Revolution* (70) as having property impressed and filing claim for it in 1782.
- HEADS OF FAMILIES (1783): 11 blacks.

HARVIE, RICHARD

- Listed in *Amherst County, Virginia in the Revolution* (70) as having property impressed and filing claim for it in 1782.
- HEADS OF FAMILIES (1783): 16 blacks.

HARVIE, WM.

- HEADS OF FAMILIES (1783): 6 black persons.

HENRY ANN

- DEATH CERTIFICATES (1859): Died at age 16, no cause of death listed, a slave. [*NOTE: See Kurl, Frances.*] (*Pg 85, #39*)

HIGGINBOTHAM, ARCHY

- LEGISLATIVE PETITION (December 27, 1833): Requested permission to remain in Virginia.
- CENSUS (1840): 1 white female 5 to 10 years old, 1 white female 20 to 30, 1 fcm under 10, 1 fcm 36 to 55, 2 fcfs 10 to 24, 1 fcf 36 to 55, 1 female slave 55 to 100 – 2 engaged in agriculture.

HIGGINBOTHAM, CARTER

- DEATH CERTIFICATES (1864): Died in Amherst in March of typhoid fever at age 16, a farmer, no parents or informant listed. (*Pg 108, #6*)

HIGGINBOTHAM, JANE

- CENSUS (1830): 3 fcm 10 to 24 years old, 1 fcm 36 to 55, 2 fcfs under 10, 1 fcf 24 to 36, 1 fcf 36 to 55.

HIGGINBOTHAM, WESLEY

- CENSUS (1840): 1 fcm 24 to 36 years old, 1 fcf under 10, 1 fcf 24 to 36 – 1 engaged in manufacturing.

HILL, P.

- CENSUS (1860): P Hill (35, mulatto, shoemaker), S Hill (35, mulatto, shoemaker), Bill Nuckles (10, mulatto).

HILL, PATRICK [H.]

- [*NOTE: There are several men by this name.*]
- PERSONAL PROPERTY TAX (1860): 1 male free negro 21 to 55 years old, household furnishings worth $10 – aggregate value: $10.

- CENSUS (1860): Patrick Hill (45, mulatto, shoemaker), Sally Nuckles (28), Wm Nuckles (11), Jas Peters (49, black, farm laborer).
- COMM. REV. 1861 A: age 45, farmer.
- COMM. REV. 1861 B: age 45, shoemaker.

HILL, RANDAL/RANDOLPH

- [*NOTE: There are probably two men represented here.*]
- CENSUS (1850): Randolph Hill (69, black, ditcher).
- PERSONAL PROPERTY TAX (1860): 1 male free negro over 55 years old – aggregate value: $0.
- COMM. REV. 1861 A: age 64, farmer.
- COMM. REV. 1861 B: age 65, ditcher.

HIX, BILLY

- DEATH CERTIFICATES (1864): Died in Amherst, no other information, informant was his former owner B. Hicks. (*Pg 108, #10*)

HOPKINS, JOHN

- HEADS OF FAMILIES (1783): 3 black persons.

HOWARD, WILLIAM

- HEADS OF FAMILIES (1783): 13 black persons.

HOWARD, WILLIAM, Estate of

- HEADS OF fAMILIES (1785): 0 persons.

HUMBLES, JOYCE

- MARRIAGE REGISTER (1807): Married Turner Pinn.

HYLTON [HELTON], JACK

- PERSONAL PROPERTY TAX (1823): 1 free negro, 1 slave, 2 horses – 71¢ tax (1824): 1 free negro, 1 horse – 12¢ tax (1826): same.
- CENSUS (1830): 1 fcm 55 to 100 years old, 1 fcf 55 to 100.

IRVING, CHARLES

- HEADS OF FAMILIES (1783): 36 black persons.

JACKSON, ABRAHAM

- MANUMISSION: Will of Dr. James Hopkins. (Written October 31, 1802) (Probated May 16, 1803). ". . . My Will & desire is That so soon after my Decease as may be Convenient all the Negroes I die possessed of may be Carryed to Amherst Court House & that the s[ai]d. Court may Judge of their Respective Ages & have the same together with their Respective Names Committed to Record at the Charge of my Estate . . . and thereafter according to the said Judgment the said Negroes shall each & every one of them be Emancipated set free—that is to say—the Males when they shall Respectively attain the Age of Forty four years agreeable to the Judgment of the sd. Court—and the Females when they shall Respectively attain the age of Forty years by the same Judgment—But with this One Exception that my Negro Woman Patty shall & may be liberated & set free at the Age of thirty six by the sd. Judgm[en]t & also that whereas my Negro Woman Old Judy doth at present far exceed either of those Ages, Therefore she shall not be carry'd to Court to be Judged but it is my wish & desire that my wife may keep her in her present Station (Cook) with sufficient assistants, so long as she may be able to discharge it & for which she shall be allowed wages not less than Six Dollars Cash to be paid her annually on each Xmas Day . . . Provided nevertheless with respect to this Article of Emancipation that if at any time circumstances should arise which in the opinion of my Executors . . . [may] render it dangerous either to my own Family or to the Country at large if such Negroes should be emancipated at that time, then in such case . . . [the Executors] may delay or suspend the Emancipation of such Negroe or Negroes untill in their opinion the same may be done with safety . . .." The rest of the will leaves specific instructions for possible circumstances that might arise and for several of Hopkins' black watermen and carpenters. (*Deed Book 4, pgs 86-110*)

- INVENTORY of Dr. Hopkins' Estate (November 1, 1804): Among the inventory were 26 slaves, who were listed and appraised at their market value. These included Paul [Jackson] (£120), Mary [Jackson] and child (£100), Abra[ha]m [Jackson] (£100, Nance[y] [Johnson] (£100), and Squire [Jackson] (£130). (*Will Book 4, page 269*)

JACKSON, ANDERSON

- CENSUS (1850): Anderson Jackson (50, mulatto, laborer), Sally (29, mulatto), Reuben (25, mulatto, laborer), June (24, mulatto), Mary (21, mulatto), Richard (19, mulatto, laborer).

JACKSON, BILLY

- MARRIAGE REGISTER (1823): Billy Jackson, whose guardian was Kiah Jackson, married Judith Johns, "a woman of colour," the daughter of James Johns.

JACKSON, DANIEL

- MARRIAGE REGISTER (1840): Daniel Jackson married Sejus (Segis) Pinn, the daughter of Turner Pinn.

JACKSON, HEZEKIAH

- PERSONAL PROPERTY (1831): 1 free mulatto, 1 slave – 25¢ tax.

JACKSON, SQUIRE

- DEATH CERTIFICATE INDEX: Died December 1, 1894.

JACKSON, WILLIAM

- [*NOTE: Several men are represented here.*]
- MILITARY SERVICE: served as a "free man of color" from Amherst in the American Revolution but was living in Bedford County at the time he applied for pension. (*www.freeafricanamericans.com*)
- CENSUS (1830): 2 fcm under 10 years old, 1 fcm 10 to 24, 1 fcf 10 to 24.
- CENSUS (1840): 2 fcm 10 to 24 years old, 1 fcm 36 to 55, 2 fcfs under 10, 1 fcf 24 to 36, 1 white male 70 to 80 – 6 engaged in agriculture.
- CENSUS (1850): Listed in the household of Samuel Boyers (white, wheelwright) were: Wm Jackson (15, mulatto, no occupation, born in Virginia), John (14, mulatto), Henry (9, mulatto), James (5, mulatto).
- CENSUS (1850): Wm Jackson (50, black, laborer on canal), Ann (45, black), Mary (28, black), Ann (20, black), John (16, black, no occupation), James (15, black, no occupation), Eliza (14, black), Jane (13, black), Saml (10, black), Richd (9, black), Margaret (8, black), Martha (6, black), Wm Cooper (25, black), John Cooper (18, black), Anderson Cooper (13, black).

JEFFERSON, WILLIAM HENRY

- MANUMISSION: Will of Sally Taylor, Article 2 (1853): "I hereby emancipate my servant man, William Henry Jefferson, and direct Executor shall pay him one hundred dollars, to enable him to remove to Liberia or some one of the free states of this Union." (*Will Book 16, pg 196*)

JENKINS, JAMES

- PERSONAL PROPERTY TAX (1850): 1 male free negro over 16 years old.

JEWEL, GEORGE W.

- MARRIAGE REGISTER (1838): George Jewel married Martha Pinn, daughter of Turner Pinn.
- CENSUS (1840): total of 2 in the household, 1 engaged in agriculture.
- PERSONAL PROPERTY TAX (1860): 1 male free negro 21 to 55 years old – aggregate value: $0.

- CENSUS (1860): Geo. Jewel (45, mulatto, farm laborer) was listed in the household of G W Foster (white, farmer).
- COMM. REV. 1861 A: age 41, farmer.
- COMM. REV. 1861 B: age 42, farmer.

JEWEL, MARTHA

- COMM. REV. 1861 A: no age given.
- COMM. REV. 1861 B: age 40.

JOHNS, ADELIA

- DEATH CERTIFICATE INDEX: Died May 18, 1887.

JOHNS, BARTLETT

- COURT ORDER BOOK (May 1802): Bartlett Johns versus John Gregory. Upon petition, the case was continued until next Court.

JOHNS, BETSEY

- CENSUS (1850): Betsey Johns (60, mulatto), Obediah (30, mulatto), Granville (10, mulatto), John Gue (65, mulatto, farmer).

JOHNS, CATHARINE

- CENSUS (1850): Catharine Johns (60, mulatto), Thomas (59, mulatto, farmer), Joshua (7, mulatto), Philip (6, mulatto), Frances (5, mulatto), Brunettir (4, mulatto), Francis Wise (26, mulatto).
- COMM. REV. 1861 A and B: age 70.

JOHNS, CHARLES

- Son of William Johns – served in the War of 1812. (*Amherst County Indians* by Edgar Whitehead)

JOHNS, CHARLES B.

- PERSONAL PROPERTY TAX (1860): 1 male free negro 21 to 55 years old – aggregate value: $0.

JOHNS, CHARLIE

- DEATH CERTIFICATE IDEX: Died October 17, 1890.

JOHNS, CHRISTIANNA

- COMM. REV. 1861 A: age 21.

JOHNS, D.

- COURT ORDER BOOK (December 1859): The Commonwealth versus D. Johns, alias Knuckles: The Defendant, a free man of colour, was charged with unlawfully keeping firearms. He was found guilty and remanded to jail, with no bail, until February Court.

JOHNS, DARCAS

- DEATH CERTIFICATES (1874): Died in Temperance Township of Amherst County on August 28 of inflammatory rheumatism at age of 39, born in Amherst, daughter of John and Jennie Crawford, wife of Saml. Johns. (*Pg 1, #33*)

JOHNS, DEANY

- DEATH CERTIFICATES (1882): Died in the courthouse District of Amherst in July of croup at age 2, daughter of Estridge and Paulina Johns. (*Pg 4 index, #35*)

JOHNS, EADY/EDY

- CENSUS (1850): Eady Johns (37, mulatto), Wm Tyry (26, mulatto, no occupation), Martha Johns (19, mulatto), Lyda Johns (16, mulatto), Christian Johns (10, mulatto), Sally Johns (8, mulatto), Louisa Johns (7, mulatto), Seaton Johns (2, mulatto), Wm Johns (1, mulatto).
- COMM. REV. 1861 A: age 50.
- DEATH CERTIFICATES (1879): Died in the Courthouse District of Amherst County on April 10 of "a rising" at age 70, born in Amherst, daughter of Wm. And Dicy Terry, informant was her friend Edmond Branham. (*Pg 2, #50*)

JOHNS, EDITH

- INHERITANCE (September 30, 1857): Report of monies received and distributed by Nelson Hicks, trustee for Edith Johns and children. (1) Paid $20 to Wm. Johns, Sr. on January 1, 1858. (2) Paid $2.04 in 1857 taxes on land. (3) Paid $20 to Wm. Johns, Sr. on January 1, 1859 (4) Paid $2.04 in land taxes for 1858 and 1859 (5) Distributed $7.34 principal and .23 interest to each of the following: Edith Johns, William Johns, Christianna Johns, Martha Jane, Sarah Johns, Arianna Johns, and Louis A. Johns. – Report confirmed and recorded April 20, 1863. (*Will Book 16, pg 242-243*) [The $20 paid annually to Wm. Johns, Sr. resulted from a stipulation he made when conveying his Bear Mountain property to his children in 1856.]

JOHNS, EDITH TERRY

- DEED (1856): William Johns divided his property on Bear Mountain among his children. Edith, the widow of William's son Joshua, received his share, 75 acres. (*Deed Book DD, pg 338*)
- COURT ORDER BOOK (July 1860): The Court ordered that she be registered, but there is no entry in that name.

JOHNS, ELIZA

- COURT ORDER BOOK (July 1860): The Court ordered that she be registered, but there is no entry in that name.

JOHNS, ESTREDGE

- COMM. REV. 1861 A: age 21.

JOHNS, ESTRIDGE

- GUARDIANSHIP (October 20, 1890): Estridge Johns and Ro. A. Pendleton filed $20 bond to qualify Johns as guardian of "Courtney Johns his infant child." (*Will Book 22, pg 489*)
- GUARDIANSHIP (November 17, 1890): Estridge Johns and Ro. A. Pendleton filed $20 bond to qualify Johns as guardian of "his infant child Rosa Johns." (*Will Book 22, pg 487*)

JOHNS, FRANCES

- [*NOTE: Several women are represented in this material.*]
- MARRIAGE REGISTER (1794): Frances Johns, daughter of Robert and Mary Johns, married James McCabe.
- COMM. REV. 1861 A: age 13.
- COMM. REV. 1861 A: age 38 [*probably the wife of Wm. B. Johns*]

JOHNS, FRANCES A.

- COURT ORDER BOOK (July 1860): The Court ordered that she be registered, but there is no entry in that name.

JOHNS, GEORGE

- COMM. REV. 1861 A: age 36, shoemaker.

JOHNS, GEORGE W.

- PERSONAL PROPERTY TAX (1860): 1 male free negro 21 to 55 years old, household furnishings worth $10 – aggregate value: $10.

JOHNS, JAMES

- CENSUS (1810): 4 free coloreds.
- PERSONAL PROPERTY TAX (1821): 1 horse – 14¢ tax (1822): 1 free mulatto, 1 horse – 14¢ tax (1823): same – 12¢ tax (1824): 1 free mulatto, 2 horses – 24¢ tax (1825): 4 horses – 48¢ tax (1827): 1 free mulatto, 1 horse – 12¢ tax (1829): same – 10¢ tax (1831): same – 6¢ tax.

JOHNS, JAMES D.

- PERSONAL PROPERTY TAX (1822): 1 horse – 14¢ tax (1823): 1 horse – 12¢ tax (1824): same (1825): same (1826): same.
- MARRIAGE REGISTER (1824): James D. Johns married Frankey Tinsley, daughter of George M. Tinsley.
- DEED (December 19, 1825): Lorenzo Lyon sold James D. Johns his 1/8 interest in an undivided tract he [Lyon] inherited from the estate of Joshua Tinsley. The land was located on the Pedlar River, and Lyon sold it to Johns for $35. (*Deed Book R, pgs 152-153*)
- CENSUS (1830): 1 fcm 10 to 24 years old, 1 fcm 36 to 55, 4 fcfs under 10, 1 fcf 10 to 24, 1 fcf 24 to 36.

- DEED (September 22, 1831): Frances and James D. Johns sold her interest in the estate of her father George M. Tinsley for $160; at this time, they were living in Campbell County. Both signed their names rather than making their marks. (*Deed Book T, pg 502*)
- CENSUS (1840): 3 fcm under 10 years old, 1 fcm 55 to 100, 1 fcf under 10, 3 fcfs 10 to 24, 1 fcf 36 to 55, 1 fcf 55 to 100 – 4 engaged in agriculture – 1 insane.

JOHNS, JEFFERY

- CENSUS (1830): 1 white female 40 to 50 years old, 3 fcm 10 to 24, 1 fcm 55 to 100, 2 fcfs under 10, 1 fcf 10 to 24.

JOHNS, JOHN

- CENSUS (1840): 1 fcm 24 to 36 years old, 1 fcf 24 to 36 – 2 engaged in agriculture.

JOHNS, JOHN A.

- TAX LIST (1800): 1 white male over 21, 2 horses, 1 slave over 16, and 2 slaves 12 to 16.
- COURT ORDER BOOK (December 1801): Oney Johns, the widow of John A. Johns, qualified as the administrator of his estate.

JOHNS, JOHN J.

- PERSONAL PROPERTY TAX (1850): 1 male free negro over 16 years old.
- PERSONAL PROPERTY TAX (1860): 1 male free negro 21 to 55 years – aggregate value: $0.
- CENSUS (1850): John J. Johns (32, mulatto, farmer), Rachel (27, mulatto), Samuel (8, mulatto), Parthenia (7, mulatto), Alfred (6, mulatto), Wm. (5, mulatto), Erastus (3, mulatto).

JOHNS, JOHN P.

- CENSUS, AGRICULTURAL (1850): 38 improved acres, 60 unimproved acres, total value of land owned was $120 – value of machinery: $3 – 2 milk cows, 3 other cattle, 5 swine, total value of livestock was $60 – 40 bushels of wheat, 150 bushels of Indian corn, 50 bushels of oats, 500 pounds of tobacco, 17 bushels of Irish potatoes, 100 pounds of butter.

JOHNS, JOHN S[HEPHERD]

- MARRIAGE REGISTER (1825): John S. Johns married Caroline Tinsley, daughter of Anson Tinsley.
- PERSONAL PROPERTY TAX (1825): 1 horse - 12¢ tax (1828): 1 slave, 2 horses - 71¢ tax (1829): 1 horse - 10¢ tax.
- DEED (December 22, 1829): Anson Tinsley, in debt to Elijah Davies for $1,098, took out a deed of trust with Maurice H.

Garland and John S. Johns, pledging 158 acres of land on Harris Creek, an additional 33 and 72 acres elsewhere, his slaves Betsey (aged 30), Judy (25), and Amey (17), 2 horses, 1 ox cart and yoke of steers, 3 cows, 6 sheep, 4 pigs, plantation tools, 4 beds, 1 desk, 1 cupboard, 1 chest of drawers, 1 folding table, 2 square tables, 8 chairs, all his other furniture, his crops of corn and tobacco, and his interest in his wife's father's estate. (*Deed Book T, pgs 48-49*)

- POWER OF ATTORNEY (January 22, 1844): John S. Johns appointed Wm. R. Tinsley his power of attorney to receive for him $160 from the estate of his mother, Naomah Garner of Amherst County. Tinsley was also to demand Johns' share of the estate of David Tinsley. Johns was then living in Lincoln County, Tennessee. On March 20, 1844, he recovered $69.41. (*Deed Book Z, pg 123*)
- COURT ORDER BOOK (July 1860): The Court ordered that he be registered, but there is no entry in that name.

JOHNS, JOSHUA

- MARRIAGE REGISTER (1828): Joshua Johns married Edith Terry, daughter of Dicey Terry.
- PERSONAL PROPERTY TAX (1829): 1 horse – 8¢ tax.
- CENSUS (1840): 1 fcm under 10 years old, 1 fcm 10 to 24, 1 fcm 24 to 36, 5 fcfs under 10, 1 fcf 10 to 24, 1 fcf 24 to 36 – 3 engaged in agriculture.

JOHNS, JOSHUA

- COMM. REV. 1861 A: age 17.

JOHNS, LEWIS H.

- PERSONAL PROPERTY TAX (1821): 1 horse – 14¢ tax (1822) same (1823): 2 horses – 24¢ tax (1825): 1 horse – 12¢ tax (1826): same (1827): same
- MARRIAGE REGISTER (1822): Married Susan Simpson

JOHNS, MALLORY

- [*NOTE: According to* <u>*Indian Island in Amherst County*</u>*, Mallory was William Johns' nickname.*]
- COURT ORDER BOOK (March 1802): Mallory Johns versus Caleb Watts in a suit for slander. William Thurmond was summoned to show cause why he should not be fined for failing to appear as a witness for Johns. Case continued until May Court.
- COURT ORDER BOOK (May 1802): Regarding above case. Johns failed to appear in court. The Court ruled that Caleb Watts recover 5 shillings damages plus costs from Johns.

- CENSUS (1810: 1 free colored
- PERSONAL PROPERTY TAX (1821): 1 horse – 14¢ tax (1823): 1 free mulatto, 1 horse – 12¢ tax (1828): same (1829): same – 10¢ tax (1831): same – 6¢ tax.

JOHNS, MARTHA A.

- COMM. REV. 1861 A: age 21.

JOHNS, MARY

- HEADS OF FAMILIES (1783): 7 white persons, 5 black.
- HEADS OF FAMILIES (1785): "7" is written off to one side with no other designation. "Mary Johns" appears on the list in three different places.
- CENSUS (1790): 7 free coloreds and 1 building other a dwelling. (*NOTE: This entry appears twice; the second lists only one building.*)

JOHNS, MARY

- COURT ORDER BOOK (July 1860): The Court ordered that she be registered, but there is no entry in that name.

JOHNS, MARY

- COMM. REV. 1861 A: age 14.

JOHNS, MEALY

- DEATH CERTIFICATES (1860): Died in December, a slave, informant was her owner Simpson Johns [?]. (*Pg 7 index*)

JOHNS, MIMY

- DEATH CERTIFICATES (1879): Died in the Courthouse District of Amherst County on August 27 at age 78. (*Pg 2 index, #55*)

JOHNS, NANCY D.

- MARRIAGE REGISTER (1813): Nancy D. Johns, daughter of Onez [Johns] Garner, married Charles Tyler.

JOHNS, NATHAN

- CENSUS (1840): 1 fcm under 10 years old, 1 fcm 24 to 36, 1 fcf 24 to 36, 1 fcf 36 to 55, 1 female slave 55 to 100 – 3 engaged in agriculture, 1 engaged in navigation.

JOHNS, PATSY

- TAX LIST (1800): 0 white males over 21, 2 horses, 1 slave 12 to 16 years old.
- COURT ORDER BOOK (April 1810): Patsy Johns versus Richard and Bennett Tinsley in a case of debt. Case continued until next court.
- COURT ORDER BOOK (September 1810): The Court ordered that Patsy Johns recover £52 plus costs from the Tinsleys.

JOHNS, PATTE[R]SON

- [*NOTE: See Johns, William, first entry.*]
- PERSONAL PROPERTY TAX (1821): 1 horse – 14¢ tax (1822): same (1823): 1 free mulatto, 1 horse – 12¢ tax (1824): same (1829): same – 10¢ tax (1831): same – 6¢ tax (1840): 1 horse – 8¢ tax.
- CENSUS (1830): 1 fcm under 10 years old, 1 fcm 10 to 24, 1 fcm 36 to 55, 1 fcf 10 to 24, 1 fcf 36 to 55.
- CENSUS (1840): 1 fcm under 10 years old, 1 fcm 10 to 24, 1 fcm 36 to 55, 2 fcfs under 10, 1 fcf 24 to 36, 1 fcf 36 to 55–3 engaged in agriculture, 1 insane.

JOHNS, PAULINA

- DEATH CERTIFICATES (1881): Died in the Courthouse District of Amherst County in September of kidney disease at age 38, daughter of Edmond and Mary Branham, wife of Estridge Johns. (*Pg 2 index, #67*)

JOHNS, PHILIP

- COMM. REV. 1861 A: age 15.

JOHNS, P. I.

- COURT ORDER BOOK (July 1860): The Court ordered that he be registered, but there is no entry in that name.

JOHNS, POLLY

- MARRIAGE REGISTER: Polly Johns, daughter of Patsy Johns, married James Ownbey.

JOHNS, RICHARD

- CENSUS (1840): 1 fcm 24 to 36 years old – engaged in agriculture.
- CENSUS (1850): Richard Johns (36, mulatto, farmer).
- CENSUS, AGRICULTURAL (1850): 30 improved acres, 35 unimproved acres, total value of land owned was $110 – value of machinery: $3 – 1 horse, 1 milk cow, total value of livestock was $50 – 60 bushels of wheat, 140 bushels of Indian corn, 20 bushels of oats, 600 pounds of tobacco, 25 pounds of butter.
- PERSONAL PROPERTY TAX (1850): 1 male free negro over 16 years old, 1 horse etc. – 10¢ tax.
- DEED (February 21, 1857): Richard Johns sold to Reuben H. Wise and Ob[*e*]diah Nuckles, for $200, 95 acres "sold" to him by his father William in 1856. Johns made his mark. (*Deed Book DD, pg 361*)

JOHNS, ROBERT

- LAND GRANT: Virginia Land Office (September 28, 1758): Robert Johns of Albemarle County was granted 92 acres on both sides of the north branch of Porrage [now called Partridge] Creek. [*NOTE: At this time, Amherst County had not yet been split off from Albemarle; that would take place in 1761.*]
- LAND GRANT: Virginia Land Office (July 14, 1769): Robert Johns of Amherst County was granted 218 acres on Porridge [Partridge] Creek.
- LAND GRANT: Virginia Land Office (July 14, 1769): Robert Johns of Amherst County was granted 30 acres on the south side and adjoining Porridge [Partridge] Creek.
- ESTATE: Amherst County Court (November 1779): William Boothe and Judith, his wife; John Richardson and Mary, his wife; Robert Johns; William Johns; Jesse Johns; Nathaniel Booth and Elizabeth, his wife; John Richardson, acting for infant Martha Johns; Francis Johns; John Alexander Johns; Nancy Johns; and William Booth acting for infants Salley Johns and Bartlett Johns sued Mary Johns (widow and administratix of Robert Johns, Sr.) and Robert's heir Thomas Johns for an accounting of the senior Johns' estate. A committee of three appointed by the Court would "have the authority to divide the Estate of her said Husband having regard to her Dower." (Lenora Higginbotham Sweeny, *Amherst County, Virginia in the Revolution*, page 86)

JOHNS, ROBERT

- TAX LIST (1800): 1 white male over 21.

JOHNS, ROBERT, Jr.

- MARRIAGE REGISTER (1779): Robert Johns, son of Robert and Mary Johns, married Elizabeth Lyon, daughter of Elisha Lyon.
- HEADS OF FAMILIES (1783): 3 white persons.

JOHNS, SAM

- DEATH CERTIFICATES (1879): Died in the Courthouse District of Amherst County in February of rheumatism at age 70, husband of Mimy Johns. (*Pg 2 index, #54*)

JOHNS, SUSAN

- COMM. REV. 1861 A: age 22.

JOHNS, TARL[E]TON

- PERSONAL PROPERTY TAX (1840): 1 horse – 8¢ tax.

- CENSUS (1840): 4 fcm under 10 years old, 1 fcm 10 to 24, 1 fcm 24 to 36, 1 fcf under 10, 1 fcf 24 to 36 – 3 engaged in agriculture.
- BILL OF SALE (June 2, 1842): Tarleton Johns sold the following items to Eliza Redcross [whom he later married] for $58.50: 1 sorrel horse, 1 black cow, 1 heifer, 1 bull yearling, 1 sow and 6 pigs, 1 feather bed, bedstead and furniture, 1 walnut cupboard, 1 pot, 1 oven, plantation utensils (2 plows, 3 hoes, and 1 sett plow). Both Johns and Redcross made their marks. (*Deed Book Y, pg 389*)
- PERSONAL PROPERTY TAX (1850): 1 male free negro over 16 years old.
- CENSUS (1850): Tarleton Johns (38, mulatto, farmer), Eliza (43, mulatto), Charles (19, mulatto, laborer), Susan (16, mulatto), Claiborne (13, mulatto), Shepherd (13, mulatto), Estredge (9, mulatto), Polly (8, mulatto), Tarleton (3, mulatto), Preston (2, mulatto), Mahala Redcross (7, mulatto), Eliza Redcross (5, mulatto).
- CENSUS, AGRICULTURAL (1850): 20 improved acres, 100 unimproved acres, total value of land owned was $200 – total value of machinery: $6 – 1 horse, 2 milk cows, 2 other cattle, 8 swine, total value of livestock was $70 – 50 bushels of wheat, 15 bushels of rye, 250 bushels of Indian corn, 40 bushels of oats, 750 pounds of tobacco, 30 bushels of Irish potatoes, 100 pounds of butter.
- PERSONAL PROPERTY TAX (1860): 1 male free negro 21 to 55 years old, 2 horses worth $100, 6 cattle worth $60, household furnishings worth $25, 9 sheep/hogs worth $15 – aggregate value: $200.
- CENSUS (1860): Tarleton Johns (57, mulatto, farmer, $576 real estate, $255 personal estate), Eliza (50, mulatto), Wm. C. (23, mulatto, laborer on farm), Estred (21, mulatto, laborer on farm), Mary (19, mulatto, domestic), Tarleton, Jr. (16, mulatto, farm laborer), Preston (13, mulatto), Eliza Redcross (17, mulatto, assistant housekeeper), Nathan Redcross (6 months, mulatto).
- CENSUS, AGRICULTURAL (1860): 60 improved acres, 36 unimproved acres, total value of land owned was $576 – total value of machinery was $80 – 2 horses, 1 milk cow, 2 working oxen, 3 other cattle, 16 swine, total value of livestock was $215 – 99 bushels of wheat, 515 bushels of Indian corn, 50 bushels of oats, 4,000 pounds of tobacco, 3 bushels of beans, 40 bushels of

Irish potatoes, 1 bushel of sweet potatoes, 60 pounds of butter – value of slaughtered animals: $92.

- COMM. REV. 1861 A: age 50, farmer.
- WILL (written June 29, 1863) (filed for probate August 17, 1863): After all his just debts were paid, the estate was to go to his wife and children. The property was to be kept together until the children were of age and then divided. Samuel M. Garland [Clerk of the Amherst County Court] was appointed executor. Tarleton Johns made his mark on the document. (Will Book 16, pg 412)

JOHNS, TARLTON

- PROBATE (February 21, 1888): Jno. L. Lee and S. B. Walker filed $800 bond for Lee to qualify as administrator of estate of Tarlton Johns. (*Will Book 22, pg 48*)

JOHNS, TARLTON, Jr.

- COMM. REV. 1861 A: age 15.

JOHNS, THOMAS

- According to a family website, Thomas enlisted March 4, 1776 at Amherst Courthouse and served in Capt. Samuel Cabell's company, seeing action in several major battles. He was discharged from service March 1778 and later moved to Kentucky, where he died.
- DEED (December 18, 1778): Thomas Johns conveyed to Robert Johns, from his love and affection for his said brother Robert and to fulfill the desire of their late father (also called Robert), 100 acres on Porrage [now Partridge] Creek. This land was part of the 218 acres left to Thomas by their father, who died intestate. Thomas Johns made his mark. (*Deed Book E, pgs 111-112*)
- MARRIAGE REGISTER (1779): Thomas Johns, son of Robert Johns and his Indian wife Mary [according to Indian Island in Amherst County], married Nancy Mehone, daughter of Daniel Mehone. [On the 1800 Lexington Parish Tax List, Daniel Mahone is listed as a white male over 21.]
- DEED (June 4, 1782): Thomas Johns and his wife (who were then living in Cumberland County) sold to James Franklin of Amherst County for £430 the tract on Rutledge Creek where "William Johns' overseer lived.' (*Deed Book G, pg 200*)
- HEADS OF FAMILIES (1785): 5 white persons.
- LAND GRANT: Virginia Land Office (November 20, 1792): Thomas Johns of Amherst County was granted 200 acres on the north branches of Stovall's Creek.

- LAND GRANT: Virginia Land Office (November 20, 1792): Thomas Johns of Amherst County was granted 124 acres on both sides of Porage [now Partridge] Creek.
- DEED (June 17, 1793): Thomas and Nancy Johns of Amherst County sold to John Jenkins 200 acres on Stovall's Creek for £35. (*Deed Book G, pgs 229-230*)
- TAX LIST (1800): 1 white male over 21, 1 horse.
- DEED OF TRUST (January 23, 1801): Thomas Johns owed Brown Rives & Co. of New Market, Virginia £120. He took a deed of trust with Daniel Higginbotham and secured it with 7 cattle, 16 hogs, 1 sorrel mare, 3 beds and furniture, and all his other household furnishings. (*Deed Book I, pgs 24-246*)
- PERSONAL PROPERTY TAX (1822): 1 free mulatto, 1 horse – 14¢ tax.
- CENSUS (1840): 2 fcm 10 to 24 years old, 1 fcm 55 to 100, 1 fcf 10 to 24, 1 fcf 36 to 55 – 5 engaged in agriculture.

JOHNS, THOMAS

- PERSONAL PROPERTY TAX (1850): 1 male free negro over 16 years old.

JOHNS, THOMAS

- CENSUS (1860): Thos. Johns (70, mulatto, farmer, $20 personal estate), Catharine (66, mulatto), Frances A. (12, mulatto).
- COMM. REV. 1861 B: age 71.

JOHNS, THOMAS

- COURT ORDER BOOK (July 1860): The Court ordered that he be registered, but there is no entry in that name.
- COMM. REV. 1861 A: age 70, farmer.

JOHNS, THOMAS, Jr.

- MARRIAGE REGISTER (1807): Thomas Johns, son of Thomas Johns, married Nancy Laine, daughter of William Laine.

JOHNS, Unnamed Slave

- DEATH CERTIFICATES (1860): Died February 15, owned by Simpson Johns [?]. (*Pg 7 index*)

JOHNS, WILLIAM

- [*NOTE: This is likely the father of Robert Johns, Sr. and Thomas Johns, Sr.*]
- DEED (July 28, 1775): Carter and Elizabeth Braxton sold William Johns 243 acres on the north side of Rutledge Creek for £202 and 16 shillings. (*Deed Book D, pgs 300-301*)

- INVENTORY AND ESTATE (1777): Thomas Johns filed bond as administrator of the estate of William Johns. (*Will Book 1, pgs 323-324*)
- INVENTORY (1777): 5 fatt [sic] hogs, 3 sows, 7 shoats, 1 sorrel horse, 1 mare, 1 yoke of oxen, 3 cows and yearlings, 2 steers and yearlings – 3 axes, 3 grub[b]ing hoes, 4 hilling and weeding hoes [for tobacco cultivation] – 8 ½ bar[r]els of corn, damaged, a parcel of fodder – a pair of steelyards, a raw hide, a parcel of flax, nails, a cutting ax[e], a handax[e], a man's saddle and bridle - 2 juggs [sic], 4 bottles, a parcel of pewter knives and forks, 3 books – a walnut chest, 7 chairs, 1 table, a bed and furniture, 1 gun – a negro fellow, Pompey – a wench, Dinah – Aggy – Milly – Bett, a girl – Susannah and her child Tabby. Total value of inventory was £523. (*Will Book 1, pg 340*)

JOHNS, WILLIAM OR PATTERSON

- TAX LIST (1800): 1 white male over 21.

JOHNS, WILLIAM

- [*NOTE: William Johns, the son of Robert Johns and his Indian wife Mary, was a founder of the modern Monacan Indian settlement on Bear Mountain. According to Indian Island in Amherst County, he also went by the nickname of Mallory; see that entry. In the following entries, we have listed only items having to do with the Tobacco Row/Bear Mountain area as these are the only ones we can be reasonably certain pertain to him.*]
- DEED (November 19, 1807): Caleb Wilsher sold William Johns 57 acres on Tobacco Row Mountain for £18. (*Deed Book L, pg 348*)
- DEED OF TRUST (December 13, 1807): William Johns conveyed 57 acres on Tobacco Row Mountain to Isaac Tinsley, Jr. to secure payment for a debt he owed Richard Burks. (*Deed Book L, pg 89*)
- DEED (October 15, 1810): William Johns sold Richard Burks 57 acres on Tobacco Row Mountain for $100. (*Deed Book L, pg 402*)
- DEED (December 31, 1856): William Johns conveyed all his property on Bear Mountain to his children, reserving the right to collect $20 annually from each of them as rent for support during his lifetime. The portions were as follows: Richard Johns (95 acres), William B. Johns (109 acres), Tarleton Johns (96 acres, including a house), Edith Johns, widow of Joshua (75 acres), and Edmund Branham (92 ¼ acres). (*Deed Book DD, pgs 334-341*) [*NOTE: This is the deed that establishes the Bear*

Mountain community that is so important in the later history of the area residents.]

- INVENTORY (August 11, 1863): Appraisement of property: 1 [pie]safe and contents ($10), 1 Bed & Furniture ($5), 1 Wheal [spinning wheel?] ($2), 1 Square Table ($1), 1 Pot & Hooks & Potrack ($3), 1 Skillet & Lid ($1), 1 pair of G[??] ($2.50), 1 Chic[k]en ($2.50), 1 Cattle ($2), 1 Bay Mare ($5), 1 Brindle Cow ($100), 1 P[??] Bull ($35), Total $169.00. (*Will Book 16, pg 404*)

JOHNS, WILLIAM

- [*NOTE: There are several men named William Johns who are represented in the following material, which is listed chronologically and with no attempt to distinguish one from another. Some of these entries, such as the will, are almost certainly that of man listed above.*]
- DEED OF TRUST (March 20, 1815): To secure payment of a bond due to J. & R. Ellis, William Johns conveyed to Thos. N. Eubank various livestock, household furnishings, etc. (*Deed Book M, pg 622*)
- CENSUS (1820): 4 fcms under 14 years old, 1 fcm 14 to 25, 1 fcm 26 to 44, 1 fcf under 14, 1 fcf 14 to 25, 1 fcf 26 to 44.
- PERSONAL PROPERTY TAX (1821): 2 horses – 27¢ tax (1822): 1 free mulatto, 3 horses – 41¢ tax (1823): 1 free mulatto, 2 horses – 24¢ tax (1824): same (1825): same (1826): same (1827): same (1828): same (1829): 1 free mulatto, 3 horses – 30¢ tax (1831): same – 18¢ tax (1840): 2 horses – 16¢ tax (1850): 1 male free negro over 16 years old.
- CENSUS (1830): 4 fcm 10 to 24 years old, 1 fcm 55 to 100, 1 fcf 10 to 24, 2 fcfs 55 to 100.
- CENSUS (1840): 1 fcm 10 to 24 years old, 1 fcm 55 to 100, 1 fcf 55 to 100, 1 fcf over 100, 1 male slave under 10, 1 female slave 24 to 36 – 4 engaged in agriculture.
- CENSUS (1850): Wm. Johns (73, mulatto, farmer), Wm., Jr. (21, mulatto, laborer).
- CENSUS, AGRICULTURAL (1850): 30 improved acres, 48 unimproved acres, total value of land owned was $150 – total value of machinery: $3 – 1 horse, 1 milk cow, 2 other cattle, 13 swine, total value of livestock was $40 – 40 bushels of wheat, 150 bushels of Indian corn, 400 pounds of tobacco, 30 bushels of Irish potatoes, 50 pounds of butter.
- CENSUS, AGRICULTURAL (1850): 25 improved acres, 40 unimproved acres, total value of land owned was $150 – total value of machinery: $4 – 2 milk cows, 1 other cattle, 5 swine, total value of livestock was $100 – 70 bushels of wheat, 100

bushels of Indian corn, 20 bushels of oats, 700 pounds of tobacco.

- CENSUS (1860): Wm. Johns (88, mulatto, farmer, $200 real estate, $50 personal estate), Chas. T. (28, mulatto, farm laborer).
- COMM. REV. 1861 A: age 50, farmer.
- WILL (written February 7, 1861) (filed for probate April 20, 1863): After all his just debts were paid, his granddaughter Judith Branham was to receive 1 bay mare, 1 cow, all his household furnishings, and all of his estate left after payment of his debts. Edmund Branham was named executor. (*Will Book 16, pg 307*)

JOHNS, WILLIAM

- PERSONAL PROPERTY TAX (1860): William, son of Joshua Johns – 1 male free negro 21 to 55 years old – aggregate value: $0.
- COMM. REV. 1861 A: son of Josh, age 60, farmer.

JOHNS, WILLIAM B.

- Son of William Johns, born February 19 (?), 1799. In 1896, he was 97 and living on the farm of Adolphus Coleman. (*Amherst County Indians* by Edgar Whitehead)
- CENSUS (1830): 1 fcm 10 to 24 years old, 2 fcfs under 10, 1 fcf 24 to 36.
- DEED OF TRUST (December 9, 1839): William B. Johns was surety for Tarleton Johns in various debts that he [Tarleton] owed to Nicholas Hicks. William secured these with the following: his land and crops of tobacco and corn, 2 horses, 3 cows, 1 heifer, 1 red ox, 7 hogs, 3 beds and furniture, 6 chairs, 1 cupboard and folding table, and all the debts due to him [William]. (*Deed Book X, pg 183*)
- DEED OF TRUST (February 17, 1840): William B. Johns was surety for Tarleton Johns in various debts he [Tarleton] owed to Marble Stinnette. William secured these with the following: 2 horses, 2 cows, 2 yearlings, 3 feather beds and furniture, 1 folding table, 1 poplar cupboard, 6 split bottom chairs, 7 hogs, his crops of corn and tobacco, and his [William's] interest in the land held by his father, William Johns. (*Deed Book X, pgs 236-237*)
- CENSUS (1840): 1 fcm under 10 years old, 1 fcm 36 to 55, 3 fcfs under 10, 1 fcf 10 to 24 – 2 engaged in agriculture.
- PERSONAL PROPERTY TAX (1850): 1 male free negro over 16 years old.

- PERSONAL PROPERTY TAX (1860): 1 male free negro over 55 years old, 2 horses worth $50, 1 cattle worth $20, household furnishings worth $20, sheep/hogs worth $20, aggregate value: $100.
- CENSUS, AGRICULTURAL (1860): 50 improved acres, 3 unimproved acres, total value of land owned was $212 – 1 horse, 1 milk cow, total value of livestock was $40 – 50 bushels of Indian corn, 600 pounds of tobacco, 2 bushels of Irish potatoes, 15 pounds of butter – value of slaughtered animals: $65.
- COMM. REV. 1861 A: age 57, farmer.
- COMM. REV. 1861 B: age 58, farmer.

JOHNS, WILLIAM CLAIBORNE

- COURT ORDER BOOK (July 1860): The Court ordered that W. C. Johns be registered, but there is no entry in that name.
- COMM. REV. 1861 A: age 22, farmer.
- MARRIAGE REGISTER (1867): Wm. Claiborne Johns, colored, age 30, son of Tarlton and Eliza Johns, a farmer, married M. F. Parker, age 23.

JOHNS, WILLIAM J.

- CENSUS (1850): Wm. J. Johns (47, mulatto, farmer), Sopha (20, mulatto), Wm. (15, mulatto), Susan (9, mulatto).

JOHNS, WILLIAM, Jr.

- PERSONAL PROPERTY TAX (1829): 1 free mulatto, 1 horse – 10¢ tax (1831): 1 horse – 6¢ tax (1840): 1 horse – 8¢ tax (1850): 1 male free negro over 16.

JOHNS, WILLIAM P.

- PERSONAL PROPERTY TAX (1860): 1 male free negro 21 to 55 years old, household furnishings worth $25 – aggregate value: $25.
- COMM. REV. 1861 A: age 28, farmer.

JOHNS, WILLIAM S.

- CENSUS, AGRICULTURAL (1860): 35 bushels of Indian corn, 1,860 pounds of tobacco, 80 pounds of butter – value of slaughtered animals: $25.

JOHNS, WILLIAM T.

- CENSUS (1860): Wm. T. Johns (31, mulatto, planter, $50 real estate, $10 personal estate), Frances Sauler (34, white, domestic), Willis Sauler (8, white), Edward Sauler (3, white), [illegible] Ann Sauler (2, white), Martha Sauler (1 month, white).

JOHNSON, BETSEY

- CENSUS (1860): Betsey Johnson (79 [*?*], mulatto), Molly (17, mulatto), Cassandra (12, mulatto), Wm. (6, black), Martha (2, black), Luther (4, mulatto).
- CENSUS, AGRICULTURAL (1860): 1 horse, 1 milk cow, 1 other cattle, 3 swine, total value of livestock was $75 – 15 bushels of wheat, 100 bushels of Indian corn, 5 bushels of oats, 450 pounds of tobacco, 4 bushels of beans, 20 bushels of Irish potatoes, 200 pounds of butter – value of slaughtered animals: $80.
- COMM. REV. 1861 A: age 45.

JOHNSON, CASSANDRA

- COMM. REV. 1861 A: age 12.

JOHNSON, FRANK

- PERSONAL PROPERTY TAX (1850): 1 male free negro over 16 years old.

JOHNSON, LUCY

- CENSUS (1860): Lucy Johnson (21, mulatto, domestic), Fielding (6, mulatto), Bettie (3, mulatto), Lucy F. (1, mulatto), Margaret Fix [*?*] (25).
- COMM. REV. 1861 A: age 23.

JOHNSON, MILDRID

- COMM. REV. 1861 A: age 18.

JOHNSON, MILLY

- COURT ORDER BOOK (October 1864): The Court ordered that she be registered.

JOHNSON, SARAH

- COMM. REV. 1861 A: age 20.

JONES [?], JAMES

- CENSUS (1820): 1 fcm under 14 years old, 1 fcm 14 to 25, 2 fcms 45 and up, 1 fcf 14 to 25.

JONG [?], ELIZABETH

- CENSUS (1830): 1 fcf 24 to 36 years old.

KENT, JENNY

- DEATH CERTIFICATES (1865): Died in Amherst in September of old age at 85, informant was her former owner Wm. Kent. (*Pg 113, #2*)

KENT, KITTY

- DEATH CERTIFICATES (1866): Died in Amherst in March of dropsy at age 30, born in Amherst, informant was her former owner Wm. Kent. (*Pg 116, #65*)

KEY, FRANCES

- COURT ORDER BOOK (April 1851): The Court ordered that her registration be renewed, but there is no entry in that name prior to 1851. [*NOTE: It is possible she had previously registered in another county.*]

KEY, JOHN

- CENSUS (1850): John Key (42, mulatto, farmer), Esix (95, mulatto, no occupation), Wm. (35, mulatto, laborer on farm).
- COURT ORDER BOOK (January 1851): The Court's instructions to register John Key note that he was born in King William County; however, the final Register entry says King and Queen County.

KEY, NANCY

- COURT ORDER BOOK (March 1851): The Court ordered that her registration be renewed, but there is no entry in that name. [*NOTE: It is possible she had previously registered in another county.*]

KEY, SALLY

- COURT ORDER BOOK (February 1851): The Court ordered that her registration be renewed, but there is no entry in that name prior to 1851. [*NOTE: It is possible she had previously registered in another county.*]

KEY, WILLIAM

- COURT ORDER BOOK (February 1851): The Court ordered that his registration be renewed, but there is no entry in that name prior to 1851. [*NOTE: It is possible he had previously registered in another county.*]

KNUCKLES, NATHAN

- COMM. REV. 1861 A: age 50, farmer.

KNUCKLES, OBADIAH

- COMM. REV. 1861 A: age 35, farmer.

KNUCKLES, OBEDIAH

- DEED (August 31, 1835): John Bias of Amherst County deeded to his "natural son Obadiah Knuckles" 100 acres of land where Bias then lived. (*Deed Book V, pg 327*)
- DEATH CERTIFICATES (1866): Died in Amherst in June of dropsy at age 87, born in Amherst, son of John and Mary Knuckles. [*NOTE: According to a family website, Knuckles was actually the natural son of John Bias. It also states that he is on the roll of Monacan Indians.*] (*Pg 116, #62*)

KNUCKLES, SUSAN

- COMM. REV. 1861 A: age 25.

KURL, FRANCES

- DEED OF MANUMISSION (written January 20, 1848) (filed with the Court on February 21, 1848): Sally Taylor, wife of John Taylor, of Amherst County, with the consent of her trustee Isaac R. Reynolds, freed Frances and her children Marcellus and Henry Ann, as well as their future increase, "to enjoy the rights and priviledges [sic] of free persons and never to be held in a State of Slavery." Taylor also freed Martha and Doctor, but their freedom was to be effective only after her own death and that of her husband John. (*Deed Book AA, pgs 177-179*)
- WILL OF SALLY TAYLOR (1853): "I give to my servant maid, Frances and her Heirs forever the lot next above and adjoining what is known as the Quarry lot on the public road. Frances has heretofore been emancipated and is entitled to remain in the Commonwealth by permission of the County Court of Amherst." (*Will Book 16, pg 196*)

LEANTY

- MANUMISSION: Will of Richard Smith (written April 5, 1836) (filed for probate May 16, 1836): ". . . It is my will and desire that my Slaves Leanty a Woman about forty five years of age, Mary her Daughter and Henry her son be and they are hereby manumitted, them and the increase of the females which may at any time after the date hereof be born unto them . . . I give [to them] . . . in equal portions any residue arising from the sales of my perishable Estate . . . [and also] Two hundred dollars out of the proceeds of the Sale of my Lands . . . It being suggested by my legal adviser, that Slaves manumitted like the foregoing are forbidden by the laws of the Commonwealth [of Virginia] to remain therein beyond the term of twelve months, this being the case: It is my desire that my Executors do apply to the Legislature by petition on behalf of the said Slaves, praying that an act may pass allowing them to reside within the State. If upon application to the proper tribunal leave cannot be obtained . . . then it will be a subject left to the judgment and discretion, of rather choice, of the said Leanty, Mary and Henry to remove themselves without the limits of the Commonwealth, to such place or places as they may be enabled to enjoy their freedom, or to remain within it, and they and their posterity to be Slaves of some person or persons. If they decide upon removal then I desire that my Executors shall appropriate to their use the pecuniary legacies herein before given to the purposes of such removal, and the settlement of themselves in the Country they may emigrate to, and in the selection of which I desire that my Executors may aid them by their advice and better lights on the subject. If . . . they prefer to remain here and be Slaves then it is my will and desire that [they] be left at liberty freely to choose from amongst my blood relatives their Master or Masters, Mistress or Mistresses as they and each of them shall see fit . . . In this latter case altho' I cannot impose any legal conditions upon the title and ownership which will accrue to the selected relation or relations yet I will make the request that such relation or relations will not only treat them humanly [sic], but show them all the favor allowed by the Laws of the Land or the useages [sic] of our Society and as far as may be to appropriate the moneys [sic] which may go with them to their extraordinary comforts and convenience . . .." In this will, Smith left 10 other slaves to his two nephews. (*Will Book 9, pgs 226-227*).

- LEGISLATIVE PETITION (January 25, 1837): "The Humble Petition of Leanty a freed woman of color about forty five years of age, and of Mary her daughter and Henry her son, also free persons of color, respectfully state that they were heretofore the slaves of Richard Smith, Sen., of the County of Amherst, and served him in that character with great fidelity, insomuch that the said Smith . . . made, declared and published his last will and testament, and a short time thereafter departed this life, wherefore the said Will was duly served and recorded . . . and Richard Smith, Jr., a nephew of the testator who was appointed one of the Executors thereof . . . [he attaches a copy of the will, etc. to this petition] . . . . [Transcripts of sections of the will follow.] Your Petitioners state that the Executor of the will of their late and beloved master has assented to their freedoms which will be evidenced by his uniting in this their Petition . . . and they are advised that now the time permitted them to remain here pursuant to the existing laws, has commenced to run against them, and that it now behooves them humbly to ask your body to suffer them to remain and reside within the limits of the Commonwealth—Your petitioner Leanty states that from her age she cannot be expected to give birth to any other child or children, and that she is convinced [?] that for that reason the policy of the laws on the subject would be less influenced by permitting her to remain, and your petitioners Mary and Henry if it be that your body cannot or will not intend it [permission to remain] to all, do hereby freely relinquish their claim in favor of their mother and all of them . . . will shortly say that they were all born and raised in the County of Amherst, that they love the place of their nativity, where they are knowing and are known, they love the neighborhood and neighbors who knew and loved their late master, they are ignorant and unlettered, and desire not to be cast amongst strangers to them, although they might set out for that new home as free as was their late master, and that journey might put them amongst persons of their own color, and conscious as was the desire of their late master to better their condition . . . They freely declare their purpose rather than to tear themselves from the place and the people they know first, and latest in life, and where alone they can expect to find contentment, it is their settled purpose to return again under the provisions of their master's will, into voluntary servitude, to be again the slaves of the white man, in preference to quitting their home and county. They will not disguide [disguise] the fact that they could remain here pursuant to the bounteous gift of their late master, it could be to them far preferable, but if your honorable body wills otherwise, they submit with resignation, and shall be content to return to their late condition. They therefore pray that an act may pass authorizing all, each or any of them to remain within the limits f the Commonwealth and as is duly bound they will ever pray." Signatures of witnesses and the declaration of Richard Smith, Jr. follow. [*NOTE: This petition apparently was approved, as Leanty and her family appear in the Amherst Register.*]

LITCHFORD, WM.

- DEATH CERTIFICATES (1857): Died August 16 of flux at age of 8, born in Amherst, son of P. F. and Sarah Litchford. (*Pg 73, #23*)

LONG, BETSEY

- LEGISLATIVE PETITION (January 25, 1837): "The Petition of Betsey Long a free woman of color, Respectfully Shows: That your petitioner was heretofore the slave of Mrs. Long of the County of Amherst, and whilst her slave [she] became the wife of James Dillard, a mulatto slave then belonging to Thomas Alderidge, and now the property of Joseph Penn of the said County. Your petitioner and her husband have lived together as man and wife for a period but little short of twenty years, during all which time they have discharged the various duties growing out of the relationship of husband and wife, and of slaves with a fidelity, which has attracted the admiration of the community in which they lived. Your Petitioner since her marriage, has given birth to but one child, now a boy nearly seventeen years of age, and she is informed that it is the opinion of the physician, who officiated at his birth, that she will never give birth to another child. Your petitioner further sheweth [sic], that her husband James Dillard has by the kindness and indulgences of his master, been enabled out of his little, yearly annual savings to accumulate the sum of Six Hundred Dollars, which in the month of December last, he appropriated to the purchase of your petitioner's freedom, he himself consenting to remain in bondage so that your petitioner is indebted for her emancipation to an act of generosity and magnanimity that cannot fail to challenge the admiration of your honorable body. Your petitioner further sheweth that without the interpretation of your honorable body, under the existing laws, she will be compelled to leave the State within twelve months and thereby sever the connubial tie which has so long and so hapily [sic] united herself and her husband which would render the noble bounty of her husband, instead of a blessing the most grievious [sic] of curses: she therefore prays that your honorable body would enact a law to authorize her to remain in the Commonwealth of Virginia, if not indefinitely at least so long as her husband may live or remain a slave. Your petitioner is advised that consideration of her Sterility the prayer of her petition is Esp[ecially] in conflict with the policy of the laws that would be that of a female in a different condition, and she is advised that the means by which her emancipation was accomplished, cannot fail to attract to her petition the most favorable consideration of your honorable body. She is advised that the citizens about Amherst Courthouse where she once resided, and about New Glasgow [now Clifford] where she now resides, will concur in her petition and will approve the passage of the law herein prayed for—And as is duly bound your petitioner will ever pray."

- Attached to the petition is a list of 125 people urging its passage. However, there is no notation as to the legislature's action, and Betsey Long does not appear in any other documents that the authors studied.
- According to www.freeafricanamericans.com Betsey married Revolutionary War veteran Benjamin Viers, a free colored man who enlisted in Henry County in 1775. They lived in Amherst for 5 years, then moved to Gallia County, Ohio in 1827.

MABRY, JOHN

- CENSUS (1850): John Mabry (29, black, laborer).

MARKET, ALLEN

- CENSUS (1850): Allen Market (39, black, boatman), Susan (30, black), Eliz. (3, black), Richd. Turpin (7, black), Catharine Howard (18).

MARTIN, ABRAM

- PERSONAL PROPERTY TAX (1860): 2 male free negroes 21 to 55 years old, 3 horses worth $300, 10 cattle worth $70, household furnishings worth $75, 2 slaves, 20 sheep/hogs worth $20 – aggregate value: $475 – 1 white male over 21.

MARTIN, SYLVUS

- CENSUS (1860): Sylvus Martin (24, mulatto), [illegible] Martin (male, 5 months, mulatto).

MARY JANE

- MANUMISSION: Deed of Nancy Simpson (written October 13, 1859): "For divers [various] good and sufficient reasons, I do hereby emancipate & forever set free my slave woman named Mary Jane aged about 28 years –I do emancipate and forever set free my slave girl named Lucy Ann daughter of Mary Jane and aged about 12 years—also Indianna the daughter of said Mary Jane aged about 7 years—also Missouri daughter of said Mary Jane aged about 4 years—also Gaston Otey son of said Mary Jane aged about 9 months—all said emancipated slaves are bright mulattoes—are my property & are hereby emancipated, released from slavery & forever set free."
- Following this record was a description of the freed slaves: Mary Jane (28, bright mulatto, small scar on right arm, black waving hair, 5 feet 3 inches), Lucy Ann (12, bright colour, almost white, 7, no scars), Missouri (bright colour, almost white, 4, no scars).
- WILL OF NANCY SIMPSON (written May 6, 1862) probated September 15, 1862): She made provisions for the slaves she'd freed in 1859. "I feel it to [be] my duty to make some provision for their removal & Settlement elsewhere—And to that end, I hereby devise to my Executor hereafter named, three hundred dollars to be expended & used for the benefit of Said emancipated Slaves on their removal & Settlement elsewhere, as he may think best." She left the rest of the estate to her daughter and named Samuel M. Garland her Executor. (*Will Book 16, pgs 151-152*)

MASON, ACHILLES

- PERSONAL PROPERTY TAX (1860): 1 male free negro 21 to 55 years old.

MASON, JESE

- PERSONAL PROPERTY TAX (1827): 1 free mulatto, 1 horse – 12¢ tax.
- CENSUS (1830): 1 fcm under 10 years old, 1 fcm 10 to 24, 1 fcm 36 to 55, 2 fcfs under 10, 1 fcf 10 to 24, 1 fcf 36 to 55, 1 fcf 55 to 100.
- CENSUS (1840): 1 fcm 10 to 24 years old, 1 fcm 55 to 100, 1 fcf under 10, 2 fcfs 10 to 24, 1 fcf 36 to 55 – 3 engaged in agriculture.

MASON, LAWRENCE

- Received bounty land for serving in North Carolina militia during War of 1812. He was taxable in Amherst County 1787-1821 and listed as a head of household in the 1810 census with 3 "other free." (*www.freeafricanameri-cans.com*)

MASON, PETER

- PERSONAL PROPERTY TAX (1850): 1 male free negro over 16 years old, 1 horse etc. – 10¢ tax.
- PERSONAL PROPERTY TAX (1860): 1 male free negro 21 to 55 years old, 1 horse worth $50, 1 cattle worth $15, household furnishings worth $20 – aggregate value: $85.
- CENSUS (1850): Peter Mason (37, mulatto, laborer), Deannah (38, mulatto), Valentine (10, mulatto), John (8, mulatto), Josephine (6, mulatto), Polly (4, mulatto), Susan (3, mulatto), Judith (2, mulatto), Jese (15, mulatto).
- COMM. REV. 1861 A: age 50, farmer [?].

MASSIE, BILL

- DEATH CERTIFICATES (1864): Died in Amherst in March of pneumonia at age 21, born in Amherst, no parents listed, informant was his former owner Chas. Massie. (*Pg 108, #37*)

MASSIE, HARRIET

- DEATH CERTIFICATES (1865): Died in Amherst in July of flux at age 13, informant was her former owner Charles Massie. (*Pg 113, #13*)

MASSIE, JANE

- DEATH CERTIFICATES (1865): Died in Amherst in September of heart disease at age 17, informant was her former owner Charles Massie. (*Pg 113, #12*)

MASSIE, MARY

- DEATH CERTIFICATES (1865): Died in Amherst in July of flux at age 1, informant was her former owner Charles Massie. (*Pg 113, #14*)

MASSIE, ROBERT

- DEATH CERTIFICATES (1865): Died in Amherst in February of a cold at age 19, no parents listed, informant was his former owner Charles Massie. (*Pg 113, #11*)

MATTHEWS, GEORGE

- DEATH CERTIFICATES (1864): Died in Amherst in November of consumption at age 30, born in Amherst, no parents listed, informant was E. A. Matthews.(*Pg 108, #33*)

MATTHEWS, WM.

- DEATH CERTIFICATES (1864): Died in Amherst in October of influenza at age 5, born in Amherst, no parents or informant listed. (*Pg 108, #45*)

MAYS, JUNE

- DEATH CERTIFICATES (1865): Died in Amherst in January of cancer at age 55, born in Amherst, no parents or informant listed. (*Pg 113, #25*)

McCOY, LOUISA

- COURT ORDER BOOK (May 1851): The Court ordered that her registration be renewed, but there is no entry in that name.

McDANIEL, DAVE

- DEATH CERTIFICATES (1864): Died in Amherst in July of flux at age 3, born in Amherst, no parents or informant listed. (*Pg 108, #34*)

McDANIEL, EDWARD

- DEATH CERTIFICATES (1865): Died in Amherst in June of flux at age 2, born in Amherst, son of Sylla McDaniel, informant was his former owner Lindsey McDaniel. (*Pg 113, #22*)

McDANIEL, FRANKY

- DEATH CERTIFICATES (1864): Died in Amherst in March of colic at age 75, born in Amherst, no parents listed, informant was her former owner Lindsey McDaniel. (*Pg 108, #42*)

McDANIEL, HARRIETT

- Died in Amherst in January of "a complaint" at age 33, born in Amherst, no parents or informant listed. (*Pg 108, #35*)

McDANIEL, WILSON

- DEATH CERTIFICATES (1865): Died in Amherst in June of flux at age 5 months, born in Amherst, son of Sylla McDaniel, informant was his former owner Lindsey McDaniel. (*Pg 113, #23*)

MERCHANT, ALLEN

- COURT ORDER BOOK (February 1851): The Court ordered that his registration be renewed, but the only Register entry in that name is 1851. [*NOTE: It is possible he had previously registered in another county.*]

MERCHANT, SUSAN TUPPENCE

- COURT ORDER BOOK (February 1851): The Court ordered that her registration be renewed, but the only Register entry in that name is 1851. [*NOTE: It is possible she had previously registered in another county.*]

MER[R]EDITH, WILLIAM

- HEADS OF FAMILIES (1783): 18 black persons.
- HEADS OF FAMILIES (1785): 8 white persons.

MINOR, LAURA

- DEATH CERTIFICATES (1865): Died in Amherst in July of consumption at age 16, born in Amherst, daughter of Chas. And Lucy Minor, informant was her former owner Lindsey McDaniel. (*Pg 113, #21*)

MOORE, MARY

- DEATH CERTIFICATES (1864): Died in Amherst in October of flux, no age given, born in Amherst, daughter of Henry and Joicy Moore. (*Pg 108, #41*)

MORRISS, CAMILLA JANE alias TOBIAS, CAMILLA JANE

- COURT ORDER BOOK (January 1851): The Court ordered that she be registered, but the only Register entry in that name is May 1832.
- COURT ORDER BOOK (February 1856): The Court ordered that she be registered.

MORRISS, DAVID

- COURT ORDER BOOK (April 1851): The Court ordered that his registration be renewed, but his name does not appear in the Register until 1851. [*NOTE: It is possible he had previously registered in another county.*]

MORRISS, ELIZABETH

- COURT ORDER BOOK (August 1851): The Court ordered that her registration be renewed, but her name does not appear in the Register until 1852. [*NOTE: It is possible she had previously registered in another county.*]

MORRISS, JAMES

- COURT ORDER BOOK (August 1851): The Court ordered that his registration be renewed, but there is no entry in that name. [*NOTE: It is possible he had previously registered in another county.*]

MORRISS, JOHN

- CENSUS (1850): John Morriss (40, mulatto, carpenter) was listed in the household of Robert Tinsley (white, clerk and lawyer).
- COURT ORDER BOOK (April 1851): The Court ordered that his registration be renewed, but the earliest Register entry in that name is 1851. [*NOTE: It is possible he had previously registered in another county.*]
- COURT ORDER BOOK (August 1851): The Court ordered that his registration be renewed, but the earliest Register entry in that name is 1851. [*NOTE: It is possible he had previously registered in another county.*]
- COURT ORDER BOOK (September 1864): The Court ordered that his registration be renewed.

MORRISS, JUDITH alias BIAS, JUDITH

- COURT ORDER BOOK (January 1851): The Court ordered that she be registered, but there is no Register entry in that name.

MORRISS, WM.

- DEATH CERTIFICATES (1864): Died in Amherst in October of diphtheria at age 1, born in Amherst, son of Geo. And Esther Morriss. (*Pg 109, #1*)

MORRISS [alias BIAS], ZELIUS/ZELOUS/ZELUS

- COURT ORDER BOOK (February 1851): The Court permitted him to remain in Virginia [indicating he was a freed slave] and renewed his registration.
- COURT ORDER BOOK (June 1856): The Court ordered that his registration be renewed, but there is no entry in that name in 1856.
- COURT ORDER BOOK (February 1860): The Court ordered that his registration be renewed, but there is no entry in that name in 1860.
- COMM. REV. 1861 A: age 35, farmer.

MOUNTCASTLE, ANN

- DEATH CERTIFICATES (1864): Died in Amherst in May of pneumonia at age 15, born in Amherst, no parents listed, informant was her former owner Tansy Mountcastle. (*Pg 108, #44*)

MUNDY, CARRY

- DEATH CERTIFICATES (1864): Died in Amherst in September of diphtheria at age 5, born in Amherst, no parents listed, informant was her former owner Alex Mundy. (*Pg 108, #43*)

NAPIER, SICILY [CECILY?]
- CENSUS (1830): 1 fcm under 10 years old, 1 fcf 10 to 24, 1 fcf 24 to 36.

NAPPIER, CHARLES
- PERSONAL PROPERTY TAX (1822): 1 free negro, 2 horses – 27¢ tax (1823): 1 free negro, 1 horse – 12¢ tax (1826): same (1827): same (1828): same

NAPPIER, HENRY
- CENSUS (1830): 1 fcm 10 to 24 years old.

NUCKLES, L. J.
- CENSUS (1860): L. J. Nuckles (3, mulatto).

NUCKOLS, DAVID
- PERSONAL PROPERTY TAX (1850): 1 male free negro over 16 years old.
- CENSUS (1850): David Nuckols (35, mulatto, bootmaker).

NUCKOLS, NATHAN
- PERSONAL PROPERTY TAX (1850): 1 male free negro over 16 years old.
- PERSONAL PROPERTY TAX (1860): 1 male free negro 21 to 55 years old, 1 cattle worth $15, household furnishing worth $20 – aggregate value: $35.

NUCKOLS, OBEDIAH
- PERSONAL PROPERTY TAX (1821): 1 horse – 14¢ tax (1822): same (1823): same – 12¢ tax (1824): same.
- PERSONAL PROPERTY TAX (1860): 1 male free negro 21 to 55 years old, 1 horse worth $100, household furnishings worth $25, 6 sheep/hogs worth $10 – aggregate value: $135

PADGETT, SOPHIA
- COURT ORDER BOOK (September 1864): The Court ordered that her registration be renewed.

PALMORE, JOHN
- CENSUS (1820): 1 fcm under 14 years old, 1 fcm 26 to 44, 1 fcf under 14, 1 fcf 14 to 25 – 1 engaged in agriculture.
- CENSUS (1830): 2 fcms under 10 years old, 1 fcm 55 to 100, 1 fcf 36 to 55.

PARRISH, REUBEN
- DEATH CERTIFICATES (1867): Died in Amherst in December of unknown causes at age 78, a farmer, born in

Amherst, husband of Miley Parrish, informant was his former owner N. B. Layne. (*Pg 119, #54*)

PAXTON, STERLING

- CENSUS (1850): Sterling Paxton (18, mulatto) was listed in the household of Alfred Paxton (white, farmer).

PAYNE, AMBROSE

- PERSONAL PROPERTY TAX (1824): 1 free mulatto, 1 horse – 12¢ tax (1827): same.

PAYNE, CHLOE

- CENSUS (1840): 1 fcm 10 to 24 years old, 1 fcf 10 to 24, 1 fcf 24 to 36, 1 fcf 36 to 55 – 3 engaged in agriculture.

PAYNE, FOSTER

- DEATH CERTIFICATES (1864): Died in Amherst in March of scrofula at age 50, a farmer, born in Amherst, no parents listed, informant was his former owner Saml. S. Payne. (*Pg 109, #9*)

PAYNE, ROBERT [BOB]

- PERSONAL PROPERTY TAX (1824): 1 free mulatto – 12¢ tax (1827): same.

PEATROSS, JOHN

- COURT ORDER BOOK (February 1851): "On the motion of Peatross a freeman of colour confined in the Jail of this County for want of free papers, It appearing to the Court from a letter written by the Clerk of Caroline County directed to the Jailer of this County which is in these words, D[ea]r Sir, I have examined the register of free negroes as far back as 1830. I find one man by the name of John Peatross registered in 1832. he is described as of dark complexion about 21 years of age five feet 3 ½ Inches high and has lost three of his toes on his left foot. It will not be in our power to issue the papers again without satisfactory proof to the Court that the original has been lost and an order to the Court to that effect. Very respectfully Wm. A. Pendleton DC, the Court doth order that said Peatross be released from prison and after being hired out to pay Jail fees and other charges according to law he be permitted to return to Caroline County with a copy of this order."

PENDLETON, JAMES

- PERSONAL PROPERTY TAX (1860): 1 male free negro 21 to 55 years old, 7 horses worth $875, 10 cattle worth $150, household furnishings worth $250, 16 slaves, 30 sheep/hogs worth $60 – aggregate value: $1,610 – 1 white male over 21.

PENDLETON, LAURA

- DEATH CERTIFICATES (1864): Died in Amherst in September of "Hooping Cough" at age 2, born in Amherst, no parents listed, informant was her former owner J. [I.?] S. Pendleton. (*Pg 109, #11*)

PENDLETON, MICAJAH

- DEATH CERTIFICATES (1864): Died in Amherst in November of pneumonia at age 6, born in Amherst, no parents listed, informant was his former owner M. M. Pendleton. (*Pg 109, #10*)

PETERS, ANN

- CENSUS (1860): Ann Peters (45, black, domestic) is listed in the household of Meredith Coffey (white, overseer).

PETERS, CLARA A.

- PERSONAL PROPERTY TAX (1860): [blank] male free negro 21 to 55 years old, 1 horse worth $50, 3 cattle worth $35, household furnishings worth $20, sheep/hogs worth $10 – aggregate value: $115.
- COMM. REV. 1861 A: age 45.

PETERS, DAVID

- COURT ORDER BOOK (February 1851): The Court ordered that his registration be renewed, but there is no entry in that name for that date.

PETERS, E[A]SOM

- CENSUS (1830): 1 fcm under 10 years old, 1 fcm 24 to 36, 1 fcf under 10, 1 fcf 10 to 24.
- CENSUS (1840): 2 fcm under 10 years old, 2 fcm 10 to 24, 1 fcm 24 to 36, 1 fcf 24 to 36 – 3 engaged in agriculture, 2 engaged in manufacturing and trade.

PETERS, EDITHA

- COURT ORDER BOOK (February 1851): The Court ordered that her registration be renewed, but there is no entry in that name.

PETERS, ELIJAH

- PERSONAL PROPERTY TAX (1860): 1 male free negro 21 to 55 years old – aggregate value: $0.
- COMM. REV. 1861 A: age 21, farmer.

PETERS, ELIZABETH

- COURT ORDER BOOK (May 1860): The court ordered that her registration be renewed, but there is no entry in that name before 1860. [*NOTE: It is possible that she registered previously in another county.*]

PETERS, HENRY A.

- PERSONAL PROPERTY TAX (1850): 1 male free negro over 16 years old.
- PERSONAL PROPERTY TAX (1860): 1 male free negro 21 to 55 years old, 3 horses worth $150, 8 cattle worth $65, household furnishings worth $50, sheep/hogs worth $25, 1 clock worth $5 – aggregate value: $295.
- CENSUS (1860): Henry A. Peters (33, mulatto, farmer, $875 real estate, $575 personal estate), Lucy J. (28, mulatto), Gerome V. (4, mulatto), Henry C. (2, mulatto).
- COMM. REV. 1861 A: age 33, farmer.

PETERS JAS.

- CENSUS (1860): Jas. Peters (17, black) is listed in the household of Curtis Gill (white, farmer).

PETERS, JOE

- COMM. REV. 1861 A: age 16.

PETERS, JOHN

- COMM. REV. 1861 A: age 14.

PETERS, LUCY J.

- COMM. REV. 1861 A: age 27.

PETERS, MARIA

- COURT ORDER BOOK (February 1851): The application of Maria [blank] to be registered in this county is rejected.
- COURT ORDER BOOK (February 1851): Maria Peters, who had registered in 1836 [actually, it was 1835], applied for a renewal of her registration. It was refused because the Court determined that she was living in Lynchburg at the time. The Court ordered the Clerk to give her a copy of her former registration, as well a copy of this order, and she was to return to Lynchburg. [*According to Free Blacks of Lynchburg, Virginia, 1805-1865, she registered there on August 7, 1851. She was born in Amherst County in 1821 and "derived her freedom from ancestors free prior to May 1, 1806."*]

PETERS, MARTHA

- CENSUS (1860): Martha Peters (40, black), Laura (9, black).

PETERS, MARY

- COURT ORDER BOOK (March 1851): The Court ordered that her registration is renewed, but the earliest entry in that name is 1851. [*NOTE: It is possible she registered previously in another county.*]

- CENSUS (1860): Mary Peters (22, black), Martha (4, mulatto), and Jane (4 months, black) were listed in the household of C. C. Dillard (white, farmer).
- COMM. REV. 1861 A: age 20.

PETERS, MILDRED/MILLY

- CENSUS (1850): Milly Peters (45, mulatto), Mary (10, mulatto), Josiah (6, mulatto), Paul (4, mulatto), Robert (12, mulatto), Wm. (11, mulatto).
- COURT ORDER BOOK (May 1860): The Court ordered that the registration of Mildred Peters be renewed, but the earliest entry in that name is 1860. [*NOTE: It is possible she registered previously in another county.*]
- COMM. REV. 1861 A: age 55.

PETERS, PAUL

- COMM. REV. 1861 A: age 15.

PETERS, PLEASANT

- PERSONAL PROPERTY TAX (1821): 1 horse – 14¢ tax (1822): 1 free negro, 1 slave, 1 horse – 67¢ tax (1823): 1 free mulatto, 1 slave, 2 horses – 71¢ tax.

PETERS, PUG [?]

- COMM. REV. 1861 A: Female, age 18.

PETERS, RACH[I]EL

- CENSUS (1830): 4 fcfs under 10 years old, 1 fcf 10 to 24.
- CENSUS (1840): 1 fcm under 10 years old, 3 fcfs 10 to 24, 1 fcf 24 to 36 – 4 engaged in agriculture.
- CENSUS (1850): Rachel Peters (54 [?], mulatto), Betsey (20, mulatto), Pleasant (18, black, laborer), Joe (6, black), Frances (4, mulatto), and Julia (2, mulatto) were listed in the household of James Powell (white, doctor).
- COURT ORDER BOOK (June 1851): The Court ordered that the registrations of Rachiel Peters and her children Sally and Betsey be renewed, but there are no Register entries in those names.

PETERS, R[E]UBEN

- DEED (August 8, 1818): Henry and Jane Hartless, Richard and Mary Hartless, Wm. And Nancy Wilson, John and Mary Clark, Reuben and Susannah Peters, James and Isbell Graham, Moriant [?] Hartless, [illegible], Joseph and Nancy [illegible] and Nathaniel and Patsy Cooper sold to Wm. Hartless for 6 shillings, 58 ½ acres on the north fork of the Pedlar River. (*Deed Book O, pgs 293-294*)

- DEED (August 8, 1818): The same parties sold Wm. Hartless 330 acres on Horsley's Creek for £295. (*Deed Book O, pgs 295-296*)
- DEED (August 12, 1818): Wm. And N. Hartless, Richard and Mary Hartless, James and Isbell Graham, Henry and Jane Hartless, Wm. And Nancy Wilson, and John and Tabitha Cooper sold John Clark, Joseph Gaines, Reuben Peters, and Nathaniel Cooper 82 acres on the headwaters of the Pedlar River, plus 53 acres adjoining that tract, for $2. (*Deed Book O, pgs 331-332*)
- CENSUS (1820): 1 fcm 26 to 44 years old, 4 fcfs under 14, 1 fcf 14 to 25, 1 fcf 26 to 44 – 1 engaged in agriculture.
- PERSONAL PROPERTY TAX (1821): 2 horses – 27¢ tax (1822): 1 free negro, 3 horses – 41¢ tax (1823): 1 free mulatto, 2 horses – 24¢ tax (1824): same (1825): same (1826): same (1827): same (1828): 1 free negro, 3 horses – 36¢ tax (1829): 1 free mulatto, 2 horses – 20¢ tax (1831): same – 12¢ tax (1840): 4 horses – 32¢ tax
- DEED (April 8, 1823): John and Mary Clark of Ohio sold Reuben Peters 141 acres on the headwaters of the Pedlar River and on the south side of "the blue ridge" for $60. (*Deed Book R, pgs 39-40*)
- CENSUS (1830): 1 fcm under 10 years old, 1 fcm 36 to 55, 1 fcf under 10, 4 fcfs 10 to 24, 1 fcf 36 to 55.
- DEED (February 20, 1837): Patsy Cooper, the widow of Nathan Cooper, sold Reuben Peters her undivided 1/5 interest in 140 acres on "the top of the Blue Ridge of Mountains" for $35. Part of the tract was in Rockbridge County and had belonged to her father James Hartless. (*Deed Book W, pg 183*)
- DEED (May 24, 1838): William, John, and Polly Jarvis of Rockbridge County sold Reuben Peters 142 acres for $1. The tract had belonged to James Hartless and was "where Reuben Peters now lives on the headwaters of the Pedlar River." (*Deed Book W, pg 460*)
- DEED (October 19, 1839): Joseph, James, and Elizabeth Jarvis of Rockbridge County sold Reuben Peters and Patsey Cooper their interest in the lands of James Hartless, where Peters and Cooper then lived, for $48. (*Deed Book W, pg 461*)
- CENSUS (1840): 1 fcm under 10 years old, 1 fcm 10 to 24, 1 fcm 55 to 100, 2 fcfs under 10, 3 fcfs 10 to 24, 1 fcf 24 to 36, 1 fcf 36 to 55 – 3 engaged in agriculture.

- PERSONAL PROPERTY TAX (1850): 1 male free negro over 16 years old, 3 horses – 30¢ tax.
- DEED (October 1, 1852): Reuben and Susan Peters gave their children Clara and Henry Peters 142 acres "where we now reside" and all their personal property: cows, sheep, hogs, utensils, etc. The children in return would furnish their parents with "good and sufficient waring [wearing] apparel, food lodging and washing will protect attend to them in sickness and in every way to make them as comfortable as their circumstances will admit." Both Reuben and Susan made their marks. (*Deed Book BB, pg 385*)

PETERS, SALLY

- [*NOTE: This probably represents several women.*]
- COURT ORDER BOOK (March 1851): The Court ordered that her registration be renewed, but there is no Register entry by that name in any year.
- COURT ORDER BOOK (May 1856): The Court ordered that she be registered, but there is no entry in that name.
- CENSUS (1860): Sally Peters (32, mulatto), Jas. (13, mulatto), Jane (16, mulatto), and Elijah (21, black) were listed in the household of James Powell (white, doctor).
- COURT ORDER BOOK (January 1860): "Sallie Ann Peters a free woman of colour came into Court & requests the Court to bind out her son James Peters aged 14 years to James Powell & her daughter Mary Jane peters aged [blank] to Caroline Powell & her Sister Frances Peters aged 13 years to said C. Powell—It is therefore ordered by the Court that they [be] bound out according to law."
- COMM. REV. 1861 A: age 30.

PETERS, SUSAN

- COURT ORDER BOOK (June 1856): "On the motion of Susan Peters who made oath thereto according to law & together with Eldridge Peters, Seaton Peters & William Peters her securities entered into & acknowledged a bond in the penalty of $300 . . . A certificate is granted her for obtaining a probate of the last will & testament of William Peters dec[ease]d . . .."
- CENSUS, AGRICULTURAL (1860): 150 improved acres, 150 unimproved acres, total value of land owned was $$3,000 – total value of machinery: $10 – 1 horse, 3 milk cows, 4 other cattle, 5 swine, total value of livestock was $130 – 15 bushels of wheat, 60 bushels of Indian corn, 1,500 pounds of tobacco, 1 bushel of beans, 5 bushels of Irish potatoes, 10 bushels of sweet potatoes,

75 pounds of butter – total value of orchard products: $10 – total value of slaughtered animals: $32.

- INVENTORY OF ESTATE (May 2, 1877): 1 bedstead and bedclothes ($14), 1 trundle bed ($0.50), 1 bed and mattress ($7), 1 lot bedclothes ($2), 6 chairs ($3), 1 trunk ($1.50), 1 cupboard and contents ($3), 1 lot sundries ($1.50), 1 feather bed ($8) - total value: $40.50 – Debt against Wm. Peters ($20), rent for 1876 ($80), debt for Chas. Myers ($10), cash on hand ($3.50), rent of place for 4 months ($26.66), debt due from W. J. Peters ($30). (*Will Book 19, pg 270*)
- DISPOSAL OF ESTATE: Wm. Peters bought all items in the inventory. (*Will Book 19, pg 271*)

PETERS, THOMAS

- [*NOTE: At least two men are represented in these entries.*]
- COURT ORDER BOOK (February 1851): The Court ordered that his registration be renewed, but the earliest Register entry in that name is 1851. [*NOTE: It is possible he previously registered in another county.*]
- CENSUS (1860): Thos. Peters (25, black, $75 personal estate), Paige (female, 20, mulatto), Ellen (1 month), Wm. Key (40, ditcher).
- CENSUS (1860): Thos. Peters (20, black), John Peters (16, black).
- CENSUS, AGRICULTURAL (1860): 1 milk cow, 3 swine, total value of livestock was $45 – 40 bushels of Indian corn, 1,000 pounds of tobacco.
- COMM. REV. 1861 A: age 23, farmer.
- COMM. REV. 1861 A: son of Martha, age 20.

PETERS, TURZA /TURYA

- CENSUS (1840); 3 fcm under 10 years old, 2 fcm 10 to 24, 1 fcf under 10, 4 fcfs 10 to 24, 1 fcf 36 to 55 – 5 engaged in agriculture.

PETERS, WASHINGTON

- COURT ORDER BOOK (February 1851): The Court ordered that his registration be renewed, but the earliest Register entry in that name is 1851. [*NOTE: It is possible he previously registered in another county.*]
- PERSONAL PROPERTY TAX (1860): 1 male free negro 21 to 55 years old – aggregate value: $0.
- CENSUS (1860): Washington Peters (26, mulatto, shoe and boot maker, $50 personal estate), Wm. Peters (28, mulatto, shoe and boot maker, $10 personal estate).

- COMM. REV. 1861 A: age 25, shoemaker.

PETERS, WILLIAM
- COMM. REV. 1861 A: age 27, shoemaker.

PETERS, WILLIAM H.
- [*NOTE: At least two men are represented in these entries.*]
- COURT ORDER BOOK (February 1851): The court ordered that his registration be renewed, but the earliest Register entry in that name is 1851. [*NOTE: It is possible he previously registered in another county.*]
- PERSONAL PROPERTY TAX (1860): 1 male free negro 21 to 55 years old – aggregate value: $0.
- PERSONAL PROPERTY TAX (1860): 1 male free negro 21 to 55 years old, 2 horses worth $200, 2 cattle worth $20, household furnishings worth $0 – sheep/hogs worth $10 – aggregate value: $230.
- CENSUS, AGRICULTURAL (1860): total value of machinery owned: $50 – 1 milk cow, 3 other cattle, 14 sheep, 12 swine, total value of livestock was $278 – 75 bushels of rye, 75 bushels of Indian corn, 75 bushels of oats, 1,200 pounds of tobacco, 47 pounds of wool, 8 bushels of Irish potatoes, 26 bushels of buckwheat, 50 pounds of butter, 2 tons of hay – value of homemade manufactures: $8 – value of slaughtered animals: $35.
- COMM. REV. 1861 A: age 23, farmer.

PIERCE, HENRIETTA
- DEATH CERTIFICATES (1865): Died in Amherst in May of croup at age 1, no parents listed, informant was former owner J. T. Pierce. (*Pg 113, #34*)

PIERCE, WM.
- DEATH CERTIFICATES (1865): Died in Amherst in September of croup at age 1 year and 6 months, no parents listed, informant was his former owner J. T. Pierce. (*Pg 113, #33*)

PINN, BETSEY/BETSY
- [*NOTE: These entries may represent several women.*]
- COURT ORDER BOOK (April 1851): The Court ordered that she be registered, but there is no Register entry in that name for this or subsequent dates.
- COURT ORDER BOOK (February 1860): The Court ordered that her registration be renewed.
- COURT ORDER BOOK (May 1860): The Court ordered that she be registered.

- COMM. REV. 1861 A: age 35.

PINN, IDA

- DEATH CERTIFICATE INDEX: Died January 16, 1892.

PINN, JAMES

- [*NOTE: These entries may represent more than one man.*]
- MARRIAGE REGISTER (1799): James Pinn married Nancy Redcross, daughter of John Redcross.
- TAX LIST (1800): 1 white male over 21.
- CENSUS (1810): 6 free coloreds, 1 slave.
- MARRIAGE REGISTER (1812): Married Jane Cooper.
- DEED (July 21, 1817): James and Jinsey Pinn sold Turner Pinn 108 acres, where Turner was then living, for $1. James had purchased it from Wm. Chick. Both James and Jinsey made their marks. (*Deed Book N, pgs 349-350*)
- DEED (July 21, 1817): James and Jincy Pinn and Turner and Joyce Pinn sold Reuben Carver 112 acres on Porage [Partridge] Creek, where James then lived, for $100. All four Pinns made their mark. (*Deed Book N, pgs 351-352*)
- DEED (July 21, 1817): John and Turza London sold James Pinn 130 acres on Porage [Partridge] Creek for $1,000. (*Deed Book N, pg 354*)
- DEED (January 19, 1818): James London sold James Pinn 19 acres on Porage [Partridge] Creek for $360. (*Deed Book N, pgs 463-464*)
- DEED (May 19, 1820): Reuben and Polly Norvell sold James Pinn 145 acres on the east side of the Glade Road for $1,700. (*Deed Book O, pgs 698-699*)
- CENSUS (1820): 2 male slaves 26 to 44 years old, 1 fcm under 14, 1 fcm 14 to 25, 2 fcms 45 and up, 1 fcf under 14, 1 fcf 14 to 25, 1 fcf 26 to 44, 1 fcf 45 and up – 2 engaged in agriculture, 1 in commerce, and 1 in manufacturing.
- DEED OF TRUST (September 17, 1821): To secure debts he owed to Wilkins Watson and Reuben Norvell, James Pinn took a deed of trust with Ch. Mundy and secured it with cattle, hogs, a bay mare, 4 feather beds, 6 sheep, 11 geese, 1 secretary, 1 cupboard, 1 walnut table, 1 gun, 1 loom, 1 horse cart, wood, cotton wheel, plantation utensils, carpenter's tools, kitchen furniture, 6 chairs, 1 trunk, and his crops of corn, tobacco, and wheat. (*Deed Book O, pg 723*)
- DEED (September 27, 1821): James Pinn sold John Cooper 150 acres on Porage [Partridge] Creek for $100. (*Deed Book P, pg 25*)

- DEED (August 3, 1822): John Cooper and Jensey Pinn (the wife of James Pinn) sold James London, Jr. 45 acres on Porage [Partridge] Creek, which had been purchased from Reuben Norvell, for $250. (*Deed Book P, pgs 217-218*)

PINN, JAMES

- CENSUS (1860): James Pinn (25, black), Mariah (22, black), [illegible] (6, black), Wm. J. (3, black).

PINN, JAS.

- CENSUS (1860): Jas. Pinn (70, black, born in Virginia), Eliza (30, mulatto, born in Virginia), John T. (43, black), Lavenia (33, black).

PINN, JAMES

- COMM. REV. 1861 A: age 16.

PINN, JAMES TURNER

- COURT ORDER BOOK (April 1851): The Court ordered that he be registered, but there is no Register entry in that name.
- PERSONAL PROPERTY TAX (1860): 1 male free negro 21 to 55 years old, 1 cattle worth $10, household furnishings worth $15 – aggregate value: $25.
- COMM. REV. 1861 A: no age or occupation given.

PINN, JOHN

- PERSONAL PROPERTY TAX (1850): 1 male free negro over 16 years old (1860): 1 male free negro 21 to 55, aggregate value: $0.

PINN, JOHN

- COMM. REV. 1861 A: also known as "Big John," age 40.

PINN, JOHN T.

- CENSUS (1860): John T. Pinn (35, black, carpenter), Martha (36, black).

PINN, JOHN TURNER

- COURT ORDER BOOK (February 1856): The Court ordered that he be registered.
- COMM. REV. 1861 A: age 40, farmer.

PINN, JOHN Y.

- [*NOTE: This may be the same as John T. Pinn.*]
- CENSUS (1850): John Y. Pinn (25, black, laborer, $4,000 real estate), Martha (25, black), James (6, black), Wm. (4, black), Jesse (3, black), John (2, black), Robert (1, black).

PINN, JOICY

- COMM. REV. 1861 A: Female, age 65.

PINN, JOSEPH

- CENSUS (1840): 1 fcf 24 to 36 years old, 1 male slave 36 to 55, 1 female slave 36 to 55 – 1 engaged in agriculture, 1 in manufacturing.

PINN, LIVINIA/LAVENIA

- COURT ORDER BOOK (February 1860): The Court ordered that her registration be renewed, but there is no Register entry in that name.
- COMM. REV. 1861 A: age 25.

PINN, LUCINDA

- CENSUS (1850): Lucinda Pinn (37, black), Rosey (female, 40, black), Louisa (15, black), George (11, black), Thomas (8, black), Marshal (6, black)
- COURT ORDER BOOK (April 1851): The Court ordered that she be registered, but there is no Register entry in that name.
- DEATH CERTIFICATE INDEX: Died April 27, 1880.

PINN, MADISON

- DEATH CERTIFICATE INDEX: Died October 14, 1883.

PINN, MARIA

- MARRIAGE REGISTER (1827): Maria Pinn, daughter of Turner Pinn, married Bartlett Sparrow.

PINN, MARTHA

- COMM. REV. 1861 A: age 38.
- DEATH CERTIFICATE INDEX: Died February 5, 1891.

PINN, POLLY

- MARRIAGE REGISTER (1829): Polly Pinn, daughter of Turner Pinn, married Richard Tuppence.

PINN, RAWLEY

- MILITARY SERVICE: was listed as a mulatto taxable in Buckingham county in 1774 and head of a household in Amherst (7 white people) in 1783 and in 1785 (8 mulattoes). He served in the Revolution from Amherst. (*www.free-africanamericans.com*)
- CENSUS (1790): 8 mulattoes.
- DEED (March 18, 1800): Rawley and Saray Pinn sold George and William Clarke a tract of land on Mill and Porriage [Partridge] Creeks for £100. Both Rawley and Saray wrote their names rather than making their marks. (*Deed Book I, pg 161*)
- TAX LIST (1800): 2 white males over 21, 1 horse.

PINN, ROLLA

- MARRIAGE REGISTER (1827): Rolla Pinn married Susannah Scott, daughter of Samuel Scott.

PINN, ROWLAND

- PERSONAL PROPERTY TAX (1823): 1 free mulatto, 1 horse – 12¢ tax.
- CENSUS (1830): 1 fcm under 10 years old, 1 fcm 10 to 24, 2 fcm 24 to 36, 1 fcf under 10, 1 fcf 10 to 24, 1 fcf 36 to 55.

PINN, SARAH

- DEATH CERTIFICATE INDEX: Died September 18, 1892.

PINN, TURNER

- TAX LIST (1800): 1 white male over 21.
- CENSUS (1810): 8 free coloreds.
- CENSUS (1820): 2 fcms under 14 years old, 1 fcm 26 to 44, 3 fcfs under 14, 3 fcfs 14 to 25, 1 fcf 26 to 44 – 1 engaged in agriculture.
- PERSONAL PROPERTY TAX (1821): 1 horse – 14¢ tax (1822): 2 horses – 27¢ tax (1823): 1 free negro, 2 horses – 24¢ tax (1824): 1 free mulatto, 1 horse – 12¢ tax (1825): same – 12¢ tax (1826): same – 12¢ tax (1827): same (1828): 1 free mulatto, 2 horses – 24¢ tax (1829): 1 free mulatto, 4 slaves, 2 horses - $1.80 tax (1831): 1 free mulatto, 3 slaves, 1 horse – 81¢ tax (1840): 2 horses – 16¢ tax
- CENSUS (1830): 2 fcm 10 to 24 years old, 1 fcm 36 to 55, 3 fcfs 10 to 24, 3 fcfs 24 to 36, 1 fcf 36 to 55.
- CENSUS (1840): 1 fcm under 10 years old, 1 fcm 10 to 24, 1 fcm 24 to 36, 1 fcm 55 to 100, 2 fcfs 10 to 24, 1 fcf 24 to 36, 1 fcf 36 to 55, 2 male slaves 24 to 36 – 4 engaged in navigation.
- DEED (February 1, 1842): Turner and Joicey Pinn sold David Staples 105 acres adjoining Samuel Scott on Porridge [Partridge] Creek for $450. Both Turner and Joicey made their marks. (*Deed Book Y, pgs 362-363*)
- DEED OF TRUST November 25, 1843): Turner Pinn bought 178 acres from the Campbell family for $300, to be paid in installments, and took a deed of trust with Jese Mundy. (*Deed Book Z, pg 147*)
- PERSONAL PROPERTY TAX (1850): 1 male free negro over 16 years old.
- CENSUS (1850): Turner Pinn (80, black, laborer), Joica (70, black), John (40, black), Levinia (20, black), Saml. (16, black).

PINN, Unnamed Females

- DEATH CERTIFICATE INDEX: Died December 14, 1882.
- DEATH CERTIFICATE INDEX: Died April 1884.

PINN, WM. HENRY

- COMM. REV. 1861 A: age 13.

PLEASANTS, DOUGLAS

- DEATH CERTIFICATES (1867): Died in Amherst in September of consumption at age 18, born in Amherst, informant was his former owner Geo. T. Pleasants. (*Pg 119, #55*)

POWELL, ISAAC

- CENSUS (1820): 1 fcm 14 to 25 years old, 1 fcf 14 to 25 – 1 engaged in commerce.

POWELL, WASHINGTON

- CENSUS (1840): 1 fcm 36 to 55 years old, 1 male slave under 10, 1 female slave under 10, 1 female slave 10 to 24, 1 female slave 36 to 55, 1 white male 20 to 30.

PRESTON, RICHARD

- PERSONAL PROPERTY TAX (1860): 1 male free negro 21 to 55 years old – aggregate value: $0.
- COMM. REV. 1861 A: no age given, farmer.

PRISCILLA

- COURT MINUTE BOOK (June 1817): Priscilla versus Coppedge: ". . . it is ordered & decreed that the error in the recordation [recording] of the Deed of emancipation made by the said Thomas Coppedge to the Compl[aina]nts . . . be corrected agreeable to the prayer thereof and that the said Complnts & their offspring are free persons and of right so at the day of the recordation of the deed of emancipation aforesaid Viz: on the 27th day of March 1784 but this decree is not to prejudice the rights of the creditors of the said Tho. Coppedge . . .."

REDCROSS, ELIZA

- PERSONAL PROPERTY TAX (1831): 1 free mulatto, 1 horse – 6¢ tax.

REDCROSS, ELIZA

- COURT ORDER BOOK (July 1860): The Court ordered that she be registered, but the earliest Register entry in that name is 1863.
- COMM. REV. 1861 A: age 53.

REDCROSS, JOHN

- [*NOTE: These entries represent at least 2 men by this name.*]
- HEADS OF FAMILIES (1783): 11 white persons.
- HEADS OF FAMILIES (1785): 11 white persons.
- CENSUS (1790): 11 white souls.
- COURT ORDER BOOK (May 1802): William Bryant versus John Redcross in Chancery. [*No description of the suit was given.*]

- COURT ORDER BOOK (May 1802): David S. Garland was appointed administrator of the estate of John Redcross.
- MARRIAGE REGISTER (1807): John Redcross married Susanna Thomas, alias Humbles.
- CENSUS (1810): 6 free coloreds.
- PERSONAL PROPERTY TAX (1828): 1 free mulatto, 1 horse – 12¢ tax (1829): 1 free mulatto, 1 horse – 10¢ tax.
- CENSUS (1830): 2 fcm under 10 years old, 1 fcm 10 to 24, 1 fcm 36 to 55, 1 fcf under 10, 2 fcfs 24 to 36, 1 fcf 55 to 100.
- CENSUS (1840): 1 fcm under 10 years old, 1 fcm 24 to 36, 1 fcm 55 to 100, 1 fcf 36 to 55 – 3 engaged in agriculture, 1 in navigation.
- CENSUS (1850): John Redcross (75, mulatto), Susan (60, mulatto), Paulus (23, mulatto).
- CENSUS (1860): John Redcross (80, mulatto, no occupation), Suckey (70, mulatto).
- DEATH (1861): died at home of Tarleton and Eliza Redcross Johns (*Amherst County Indians*, Edgar Whitehead)

REDCROSS, MARCELLUS

- DEATH CERTIFICATES (1859): listed among the slaves, died at age 1 year and 8 months, son of Paul Redcross. (*Pg 84, #11*)

REDCROSS, MARCELLUS

- CENSUS, DEATH (1860): 3 months old, free male mulatto, born in Virginia, died in April of croup after being sick 1 day.

REDCROSS, P.

- CENSUS, DEATH (1860): 2 months old, free mulatto female, born in Virginia, died in April of unknown disease after being sick 1 day.

REDCROSS, P.

- COURT ORDER BOOK (July 1860): The Court ordered that he be registered, but there is no Register entry in that name.

REDCROSS, PATRICK HENRY

- PERSONAL PROPERTY TAX (1840): 1 horse – 8¢ tax.

REDCROSS, PAULUS

- PERSONAL PROPERTY TAX (1860): 1 male free negro 21 to 55 years old, 1 horse worth $10, 2 cattle worth $15, household furnishings worth $20 – aggregate value: $45.
- CENSUS (1860): Paulus Redcross (22, mulatto, farming, $223 personal estate), Frances (23, mulatto, domestic), Leona (6, mulatto), Varland (3, mulatto), Wm. (3 months, mulatto), Margaret Tyree (mulatto, domestic).

- CENSUS, AGRICULTURAL (1860): total value of machinery owned: $5 – 1 horse, 1 milk cow, 1 other cattle, 1 swine, total value of livestock was $153 – 350 bushels of Indian corn, 2,300 pounds of tobacco, 10 bushels of Irish potatoes, 25 pounds of butter – value of slaughtered animals: $15.
- COMM. REV. 1861 A: age 30, farmer.

REDCROSS, Unnamed Female

- COMM. REV. 1861 A: age 30.

REDCROSS, WILLIAM

- CENSUS (1850): Wm. Redcross (45, mulatto, laborer), Jane (38, mulatto), Polly (20, mulatto), Ann (15, mulatto), John (14, mulatto), Jane (10, mulatto), Sally (7, mulatto), Mary (5, mulatto), Edmund (2, mulatto), Frances (1, mulatto).

REED, JIMMY

- DEATH CERTIFICATES (1864): Died in Amherst in August of "Hooping Cough" at age 4 months, born in Amherst, son of Jim and Amanda Reed. (*Pg 109, #15*)

RICHESON, CATHERINE

- DEATH CERTIFICATES (1864): Died in Amherst in June of a fever at age 20, no parents or informant listed. (*Pg 109, #23*)

RICHESON, PAUL

- DEATH CERTIFICATES (1864): Died in Amherst in May of a fever at age 9. (*Pg 109, #25*)

RICHESON, POMPEY

- DEATH CERTIFICATES (1864): Died in Amherst in February of pneumonia at age 18. (*Pg 109, #26*)

RICHESON, ROBERT

- DEATH CERTIFICATES (1864): Died in Amherst in June of a fever at age 8. (*Pg 109, #24*)

RITCHEY/RICHEY, SOLOMAN

- LAND BOOK, 1787-1844: 170 acres on both sides of Pedlar River. Ritchey's warrant was dated 1803, and the land was surveyed in 1815).
- PLAT BOOK NUMBER 2, 1803-1930: A total of 150 acres on Staton's Creek was surveyed for Ritchey in 1817, as well as 116 acres on both sides of Pedlar River.
- PLAT BOOK NUMBER 2, 1803-1930: 100 acres on both sides of the middle fork of Pedlar River were surveyed for Ritchey in 1821.
- PERSONAL PROPERTY TAX (1823): 1 free negro, 1 horse – 12¢ tax (1824): same (1825): same (1826): same (1828):

1 free negro, 2 horses – 24¢ tax (1829): 1 free negro, 1 horse – 10¢ tax.

ROBERTSON, EDMOND

- CENSUS (1830): 2 fcm under 10 years old, 1 fcm 24 to 36, 1 fcf under 10, 2 fcfs 10 to 24.

ROSS, JEFFERSON

- CENSUS (1850): Jefferson Ross (40, mulatto, farmer), Martha (18, mulatto), Wiatt (1, mulatto)

RUCKER, BENJAMIN

- CENSUS (1850): Benjamin Rucker (75, black, no occupation).

RUTHERFORD, BOOKER

- DEATH CERTIFICATES (1864): Died in Amherst in September of diphtheria at age 10, possibly born in Albemarle County, no parents listed, informant was his former owner T. Rutherford. (*Pg 109, #17*)

RUTHERFORD, HENRY

- DEATH CERTIFICATES (1864): See Booker. Age 8 months. (*Pg 109, #19*)

RUTHERFORD, JEFF

- DEATH CERTIFICATES (1864): See Booker. Age 3. (*Pg 109, #20*)

RUTHERFORD, MARY

- DEATH CERTIFICATES (1864): See Booker. Age 5. (*Pg 109, #22*)

RUTHERFORD, PAUL

- DEATH CERTIFICATES (1864): See Booker. Age 14. (*Pg 109, #21*)

RUTHERFORD, SILAS

- DEATH CERTIFICATES (1864): See Booker. Age 9. (*Pg 109, #18*)

SCOTT, ALEXANDER

- CENSUS (1830): 1 fcm 10 to 24 years old, 1 fcm 55 to 100, 1 fcf 10 to 24, 1 fcf 55 to 100.
- CENSUS (1850): Alexander Scott (95, mulatto) and Amanda Taylor (18, mulatto) were listed in the household of W. Staton (white, farmer).

SCOTT, BENJAMIN

- CENSUS (1820): 2 fcms 14 to 25 years old, 1 fcm 26 to 44, 1 fcf 14 to 25, 1 fcf 26 to 44, 1 fcf 45 and up.

SCOTT, CHS.

- CENSUS (1820): 2 fcms 45 years or older, 1 fcf under 14, 1 fcf 14 to 25, 1 fcf 45 or older – 1 engaged in commerce.

SCOTT, DELAWARE

- COURT ORDER BOOK (April 1851): The Court ordered that he be registered.

SCOTT, JANE

- DEATH CERTIFICATES (1864): Died in Amherst on December 24 of "Apoplexy" at age 25, no parents listed, informant was her former owner S. B. Scott. (*Pg 109, #28*)

SCOTT, JOHN

- CENSUS (1820): 3 fcms 26 to 44 years old, 1 fcm 45 and older, 2 fcfs 14 to 25, 1 fcf 26 to 44 – 1 engaged in commerce.

SCOTT, JOHN

- CENSUS (1820): 1 fcm 26 to 44 years old, 1 fcm 45 or older, 1 fcf under 14, 1 fcf 14 to 25, 2 fcfs 26 to 44, 1 fcf 45 or older – 1 all other persons except Indian not taxed – 2 engaged in commerce.

SCOTT, JOHN C.

- PERSONAL PROPERTY TAX (1822): 1 free mulatto, 1 horse – 14¢ tax.

SCOTT, LOUVENIA

- DEATH CERTIFICATES (1864): Died in Amherst in September of old age at 90, no parents listed, informant was her former owner W. W. Scott. (*Pg 109, #30*)

SCOTT, MADISON

- COURT ORDER BOOK (March 1851): The Court refused to renew his registration because of evidence that he was not a resident of Amherst County.

SCOTT, MARY JANE

- COMM. REV. 1861 A: age 35.

SCOTT, MILES

- DEATH CERTIFICATES (1864): Died in Amherst in April of old age at 80, no parents listed, informant was his former owner W. B. Scott. (*Pg 109, #29*)

SCOTT, NANCY

- CENSUS (1810): 4 free coloreds.

SCOTT, PLEASANT

- CENSUS (1850): Pleasant Scott (30, black, boatman), Sally (26, black), James (6, black).

- COURT ORDER BOOK (March 1851): The court ordered that his registration be renewed, but there is no Register entry in that name.

SCOTT, SAMUEL

- [*NOTE: There was also a white Samuel Scott living in Amherst County at the same time, and some of the following entries may be his.*]
- DEED (August 11, 1810): James and Jane Dillard sold Samuel Scott 100 acres on Porage [Partridge] Creek for $100. (*Deed Book L, pg 404*)
- DEED (June 15, 1815): Samuel and Judah Scott sold Reuben Carver 100 acres on Porage [Partridge] Creek for $400. (*Deed Book M, pg 662*)
- DEED (December 6, 1816): John and Liza London sold Samuel Scott 110 acres on Porage [Partridge] Creek for $300. (*Deed Book N, pgs 297-298*)
- CENSUS (1820): 2 fcms under 14 years old, 1 fcm 26 to 44, 6 fcfs under 14, 1 fcf 26 to 44 – 1 engaged in agriculture.
- DEED OF TRUST (January 1, 1821): Samuel and Judah Scott were indebted to Alexander Jewell for $500 and took a deed of trust with John and James Dillard. (*Deed Book O, pgs 587-588*)
- PERSONAL PROPERTY TAX (1822): 1 free mulatto, 1 horse – 14¢ tax (1824): 1 free mulatto, 1 horse – 12¢ tax (1825): same (1826): same (1829): 1 free mulatto, 1 horse – 10¢ tax (1831): 1 free mulatto, 1 horse – 6¢ tax (1840): 1 slave, 2 horses – 46¢ tax.
- CENSUS (1830): 3 fcm under 10 years old, 1 fcm 10 to 24, 1 fcm 36 to 55, 3 fcfs 10 to 24, 4 fcfs 24 to 36, 1 fcf 36 to 55.
- DEED (December 23, 1839): Reuben and Nancy Carver sold Samuel Scott 100 acres on Porage [Partridge] Creek for $400. (*Deed Book X, pg 271*)
- CENSUS (1840): 5 fcm 10 to 24 years old, 1 fcm 24 to 36, 1 fcm 55 to 100, 2 fcfs 10 to 24, 1 fcf 24 to 36, 1 fcf 36 to 55, 1 male slave 55 to 100 – 2 engaged in agriculture, 2 in manufacturing, 1 in navigation.
- DEED (January 29, 1843): Samuel and Judah Scott sold Charles Mundy 116 acres on Porage [Partridge] Creek for $227.27. (*Deed Book Z, pg 49*)
- DEED (December 18, 1852): David Irwin sold Samuel Scott 10 acres near New Glasgow [now Clifford] for $200. (*Deed Book BB, pg 433*)
- DEED (July 21, 1852): Francis and Sarah Sutton sold Samuel Scott 8 to 15 acres on the northeast side of the road from New

Glasgow [Clifford] to Temperance for $115. (*Deed Book DD, pg 430*)

- DEED (July 1, 1854): Charles Perrow, commissioner, sold Samuel Scott a 3-acre spring lot at David S. Garland's [in Clifford] for $65.23. (*Deed Book CC, pgs 310-311*)

SCOTT, SAMUEL B.

- [*See note for Samuel Scott.*]
- DEED (January 6, 1852): Thomas Kirkpatrick, court appointed commissioner, sold Samuel B. Scott, Jr., "a free mulatto man," 64 acres on Juniper Creek known as Mays' old mansion house tract. Samuel Scott, father of the grantee, had purchased it for $144 and gave it to his son. (*Deed Book BB, pgs 379-380*)
- DEED (April 8, 1854): Roy B. Scott sold Samuel B. Scott 204 ¼ acres on Harris Creek for $4,000. (*Deed Book CC, pg 279*)
- DEED (December 5, 1855): Wm. And Anne Hix sold Samuel B. Scott 135 acres on Harris Creek for $1,493.25. (*Deed Book DD, pgs 83-85*)
- CENSUS, AGRICULTURAL (1860): 200 improved acres, 140 unimproved acres, total value of land owned was $7,000 – total value of machinery: $130 – 6 horses, 1 ass, 3 milk cows, 4 working oxen, 2 other cattle, 7 sheep, 34 swine, total value of livestock was $991 – 225 bushels of wheat, 750 bushels of Indian corn, 200 bushels of oats, 4,000 pounds of tobacco, 20 pounds of wool, 3 bushels of beans, 30 bushels of Irish potatoes, 20 bushels of sweet potatoes, 400 pounds of butter – value of slaughtered animals: $320.

SCOTT, WILLIAM

- COURT ORDER BOOK (April 1860): The Court ordered that he be registered.
- PERSONAL PROPERTY TAX (1860): 1 male free negro 21 to 55 years old, household furnishings worth $10 – aggregate value: $10.
- CENSUS (1860): Wm. Scott (30, mulatto), Mary (30, mulatto), Nancy (11, mulatto), Betsey (10, mulatto), Joe (7, mulatto), Wm. (6, mulatto), Edward (5, mulatto), Mariah (3, mulatto), Susan (1, mulatto).
- COMM. REV. 1861 A: age 39, farmer.

SELDON, GEO.

- COURT ORDER BOOK (April 1860): The Court ordered that he be registered, but there is no entry in that name.

SHEFFIELD, JOHN

- PERSONAL PROPERTY TAX (1850): 1 male free negro over 16 years old.

SHELTON, BENJAMIN

- PERSONAL PROPERTY TAX (1828): 1 free mulatto, 1 horse – 12¢ tax.

SHELTON, SAML.

- DEATH CERTIFICATES (1864): Died in Amherst in March of heart disease at age 55, no parents listed, informant was his former owner R. Shelton. (*Pg 109, #31*)

SHEPHERD, JAMES

- PERSONAL PROPERTY TAX (1840): 1 free mulatto, 4 slaves, 5 horses - $1.60 tax.

SHEPHERD, JOHN

- CENSUS (1860): John Shepherd (23, mulatto, farming), Sarah Johns (17, mulatto, domestic), Dedda Johns.

SHEPHERD, JULIA

- DEATH CERTIFICATES (1864): Died in Amherst in September of "Hooping Cough" at age 8, no parents listed, informant was her former owner Elasnu [?] Shepherd. (*Pg 109, #33*)

SINGLETON, GEORGE

- PERSONAL PROPERTY TAX (1860): 1 male free negro 21 to 55 years old – aggregate value: $0.

SLAUGHTER, ANN

- COURT ORDER BOOK (April 1860): "The Court orders that Sandy Slaughter Aged 17 years & William Slaughter aged 19 years, free persons of colour, and children of Ann Slaughter, be bound out to Richd. D. Shackleford by one of the Overseers of the Poor, deputating that said Shackleford shall pay $40 a year for each of said free negroes & one third of which is to be paid to their mother and the balance to be paid to them."

SMITH, ELISHA

- COMM. REV. 1861 B: Male, age 25, mechanic.

SMITH, JULIA

- COURT ORDER BOOK (April 1851): The Court ordered that her registration be renewed, but there is no Register entry in that name.

SMITH, MILLER

- COURT ORDER BOOK (April 1851): The Court ordered that his registration be renewed, but there is no Register entry in that name.

SMITH, NATHAN

- DEATH CERTIFICATES (1864): Died in Amherst in July of spasms at age 9 months, no parents listed, informant was his former owner Mary F. Smith. (*Pg 109, #34*)

SMITH, S[C]IPIO

- COURT ORDER BOOK (June 1856): The Court ordered that his registration be renewed, but the earliest entry in that name is 1856. [*NOTE: It is possible he previously registered in another county.*]
- COURT ORDER BOOK (September 1864): The Court ordered that his registration be renewed.
- COMM. REV. 1861 B: age 64, mechanic.

SMITH, SEATON

- CENSUS (1860): Seaton Smith (female, 70, black), Harry Smith (70, black).

SMITH, WM. H.

- DEATH CERTIFICATES (1864): Died in Amherst in March of heart disease at age 53, son of Joel F. and S. Smith. (*Pg 109, #32*)

SNEAD [SNEED], BETSEY ANN

- [*NOTE: There may be more than one Betsey Snead represented here.*]
- CENSUS (1840): 1 fcf 24 to 36 years old – 1 engaged in agriculture.
- COURT ORDER BOOK (March 1851): The Court ordered that her registration be renewed.
- COURT ORDER BOOK (June 1860): The Court ordered that she be registered.

SNUFFER, OWEN

- MARRIAGE REGISTER (1834): Owen Snuffer married Cleopatria A. Terry, daughter of Thomas R. Terry.

SORRELL, MARY

- COMM. REV. 1861 A: age 22.
- COMM. REV. 1861 B: age 23.

SOUTHARD, ANGELINE

- COMM. REV. 1861 A and B: age 30.

SOUTHARD, BE[R]LINDA

- COMM. REV. 1861 A: age 37.
- COMM. REV. 1861 B: age 38.

SOUTHARD, PHOEBE/PHOEBY

- COMM. REV. 1861 A: age 17.
- COMM. REV. 1861 B: age 18.

SOUTHARD[S], ROBERT

- PERSONAL PROPERTY TAX (1850): 1 male free negro over 16 years old, 1 horse etc. – 10¢ tax.
- PERSONAL PROPERTY TAX (1860): 1 male free negro 21 to 55 years old, household furnishings worth $25 – aggregate value: $25.
- COMM. REV. 1861 A: age 40, farmer.
- COMM. REV. 1861 B: age 50.

SOUTHARD, SALLY

- COMM. REV. 1861 A: age 40.
- COMM. REV. 1861 B: age 45.

SOUTHARD[S], WILLIAM

- PERSONAL PROPERTY TAX (1826): 1 free mulatto, 2 horses - 24¢ tax (1827): same (1828): 1 free mulatto, 1 horse - 12¢ tax (1829): same - 10¢ tax (1831): same – 6¢ tax (1840): same – 8¢ tax.
- CENSUS (1830): 1 fcm 10 to 24 years old, 1 fcm 24 to 36, 5 fcfs under 10, 1 fcf 24 to 36.
- PERSONAL PROPERTY TAX (1850): 1 male free negro over 16 years old, 1 horse etc. - 10¢ tax.
- CENSUS (1850): Wm. Southards (55, mulatto), Sally (36, mulatto), Parthena (16, mulatto), Wm. (19, mulatto), Eldridge (12, mulatto), Preston (10, mulatto), 4 more children whose names are not listed.
- COURT ORDER BOOK (March 1851): "The application of Wm. Southard for [a] certificate is continued." [*NOTE: His name does not appear in the Register.*]

SPARROW, BARTLETT[E]

- MARRIAGE REGISTER (1827): Bartlett Sparrow married Maria Pinn, daughter of Turner Pinn.
- CENSUS (1830): 1 fcm under 10 years old, 1 fcm 24 to 36, 1 fcf under 10, 1 fcf 24 to 36.
- CENSUS (1840): 2 fcms under 10 years old, 1 fcm 10 to 24, 1 fcm 36 to 55, 2 fcfs under 10, 1 fcf 10 to 24, 1 fcf 24 to 36 – 2 engaged in agriculture.
- PERSONAL PROPERTY TAX (1850): 2 male free negroes over 16 years old, 1 horse etc. - 10¢ tax.
- CENSUS (1850): Bartlett Sparrow (50, black), Mariah (45, black), Mary (22, black), James (20, black, laborer), Simpson (18, black, laborer), Turner (15, black), Cyrus (15, black), Joiasy (12, black), John (6, black), Levenia (1, black).

- COURT ORDER BOOK (March 1851): The Court ordered that his registration be renewed, but the earliest Register entry in that name is 1851. [*NOTE: It is possible he had registered previously in another county.*]
- PERSONAL PROPERTY TAX (1860): 1 male free negro over 55 years old, 1 horse worth $25, cattle worth $35, household furnishings worth $35 – aggregate value: $95.
- CENSUS (1860): Bartlett Sparrow (60, black, cooper, $700 personal estate), Martha (54, black), Joysa A. (18, black), Jno. T. (15, black), Lavenia (11, black).

SPARROW, BARTLETT

- COMM. REV. 1861 A: age 39, farmer.

SPARROW, JAMES

- COURT ORDER BOOK (March 1851): The Court ordered that his registration be renewed, but the earliest Register entry in that name is 1851. [*NOTE: It is possible he had registered previously in another county.*]
- CENSUS (1860): James Sparrow (32, black), Lucinda (25, black), Wm. (2, black), [Infant] Sparrow (1 month, black).

SPARROW, JAMES HENRY

- COURT ORDER BOOK (February 1860): The Court ordered that his registration be renewed, but the earliest Register entry in that name is 1860. [*NOTE: It is possible he had registered previously in another county.*]
- PERSONAL PROPERTY TAX (1860): 1 male free negro 21 to 55 years old, 1 horse worth $75, 1 cattle worth $10 – aggregate value: $85.

SPARROW, JOHN S.

- COMM. REV. 1861 A: age 15, farmer.

SPARROW, SAMPSON

- COURT ORDER BOOK (February 1860): The Court ordered that his registration be renewed, but there is no Register entry in that name.

SPARROW, SIMPSON

- COURT ORDER BOOK (March 1851): The Court ordered that his registration be renewed, but the earliest Register entry in that name is 1851. [*NOTE: It is possible he had registered previously in another county.*]
- PERSONAL PROPERTY TAX (1860): 1 male free negro 21 to 55 years old – aggregate value: $0.
- COMM. REV. 1861 A: no age given farmer.

SPARROW, TURNER

- COURT ORDER BOOK (March 1851): The Court ordered that his registration be renewed, but the earliest Register entry in that name is 1851. [*NOTE: It is possible he had registered previously in another county.*]
- PERSONAL PROPERTY TAX (1860): 1 male free negro 21 to 55 years old, 1 cattle worth $10 – aggregate value: $10.
- COMM. REV. 1861 A: age 30, miller.

SPARROW, WM.

- CENSUS (1850): Wm. Sparrow (45, mulatto, wood chopper), Hannah (40, mulatto), Jane (31, mulatto), Sally (23, mulatto), Amos (18, mulatto), Benjamin (13, mulatto), Abram (12, mulatto), James (10, mulatto), Albert (9, mulatto), Frances (8, mulatto), Mary (6, mulatto), Susan Pinn (15, black).

SPOONER [?], GEORGE W.

- PERSONAL PROPERTY TAX (1850): 1 male free negro over 16 years old.

STEWART, ELIZABETH

- COMM. REV. 1861 A: age 25.

STEWART, SAWNEY

- COURT ORDER BOOK (June 1856): The Court ordered that his registration be renewed, but the earliest Register entry in that name is 1856. [*NOTE: It is possible he had previously registered in another county.*]
- PERSONAL PROPERTY TAX (1860): 1 male free negro 21 to 55 years old, household furnishings worth $20 – aggregate value: $20.
- COMM. REV. 1861 A: age 40, mechanic.

SUTHERS, R.

- CENSUS (1860): R. Suthers (40, mulatto, farmer), Sally (39, mulatto), Frances (19, mulatto), B. (10, mulatto), N. M. (6, mulatto), and Saml. (70, black, blacksmith) were listed in the household of L. Suthers (white).

TAYLOR, ALEX/ALEXANDER EVANS

- PERSONAL PROPERTY TAX (1860): 1 male free negro 21 to 55 years old – aggregate value: $0.
- COMM. REV. 1861 A: no age given, blacksmith.
- COMM. REV. 1861 B: age 40.

TAYLOR, ISABELLA

- CENSUS (1850): Isabella Taylor (58, mulatto) and 4 unnamed children (all white) were listed in the house hold of Richeson Taylor (white).

TAYLOR, RICHARD

- CENSUS (1840): 2 fcms under 10 years old, 1 fcm 10 to 24, 1 fcm 24 to 36, 1 fcf under 10, 1 fcf 24 to 36 – 2 engaged in agriculture.
- CENSUS (1850): Richard Taylor (32, mulatto, farmer), Mary (34, mulatto), Sarah (10, mulatto), Isabella (8, mulatto), Richeson (6, mulatto), Mary J. (5, mulatto), Victory (2, mulatto), Nancy (3, mulatto).

TERRY, AD[D]ISON

- PERSONAL PROPERTY TAX (1860): 1 male free negro 21 to 55 years old, 1 horse worth $5, 1 cattle worth $15, household furnishings worth $20 – aggregate value: $40.
- COMM. REV. 1861 A: age 26, farmer.

TERRY, ALBERT

- CENSUS (1830): 1 fcm under 10 years old, 1 fcm 24 to 36, 1 fcf under 10, 1 fcm 10 to 24.
- PERSONAL PROPERTY TAX (1831): 1 free mulatto, 1 horse - 6¢ tax. (1840): 1 horse - 8¢ tax.
- CENSUS (1840): 1 fcm under 10 years old, 1 fcm 10 to 24, 1 fcm 24 to 36, 3 fcfs under 10, 1 fcf 10 to 24, 1 fcf 24 to 36, 1 fcf 55 to 100 – 4 engaged in agriculture.
- PERSONAL PROPERTY TAX (1850): 1 male free negro over 16 years old, 3 horses etc. - 30¢ tax.
- CENSUS (1850): Albert Terry (45, mulatto, farmer), Elsed (36, mulatto), Emily (32, mulatto), Adison (21, mulatto, laborer), Nicholas (18, mulatto, laborer), 6 more children (all unnamed).
- COURT ORDER BOOK (March 1851): "The application of Albert Terry for [a] certificate is continued."
- PERSONAL PROPERTY TAX (1860): 1 male free negro 21 to 55 years old, 1 horse worth $5, 2 cattle worth $35, household furnishings worth $50, 2 sheep/hogs worth $10 – aggregate value: $100.
- COMM. REV. 1861 A and B: age 50, farmer.

TERRY, ALFRED

- CENSUS (1830): 1 fcm under 10 years old, 1 fcm 10 to 24, 1 fcf under 10, 1 fcf 10 to 24.

TERRY, DIC[E]Y DIANNA

- PERSONAL PROPERTY TAX (1828): 1 free mulatto, 1 horse - 12¢ tax (1829): same - 10¢ tax.

TERRY, E.

- CENSUS (1860): E. Terry (28, mulatto, domestic), A. Terry (30, mulatto, farmer), A. Terry (2, mulatto), and W. Terry (45, mulatto, laborer) were listed in the household of J. E. Powell (stonemason).

TERRY, ELIJAH

- COMM. REV. 1861 A: age 17, farmer.

TERRY, ELIZABETH

- COMM. REV. 1861 A: age 23.

TERRY, ESTEL[L]

- COMM. REV. 1861 A and B: Female, age 50.

TERRY, G. D.

- CENSUS, DEATH (1860): 3 months old, free mulatto male, born in Virginia, died in February of croup after being sick 7 days.

TERRY, HENRY

- CENSUS (1850): Henry Terry (30, mulatto, farmer).

TERRY, JAMES A.

- COMM. REV. 1861 B: age 19.

TERRY, JANE

- CENSUS (1850): Jane Terry (30, mulatto), Elizabeth (4, mulatto), John (7, mulatto).

TERRY, JULIA [A.]

- COMM. REV. 1861 A: age 20.
- COMM. REV. 1861 B: age 22.

TERRY, MARSHALL

- COMM. REV. 1861 B: Male, age 17.

TERRY, NICOLA

- DEATH CERTIFICATES (1858): Male, died of dysentery at age of 11 months, born in Amherst, son of Addison E. Terry. (*Pg 1, #14*)

TERRY, REUBEN

- CENSUS (1860): Reuben Terry (24, mulatto), L. (26, mulatto), Zach (5, mulatto), T. (2 months, mulatto).

TERRY, SOPHRONIA/SYPHRONIA

- COMM. REV. 1861 A: Female, age 22.
- COMM. REV. 1861 B: age 24.

TERRY, WILL

- CENSUS (1810): 7 free coloreds.

- CENSUS (1820): 1 fcm under 14 years old, 1 fcm 45 or more, 3 fcfs under 14, 1 fcf 14 to 25, 1 fcf 26 to 44, 1 fcf 45 or more – 2 engaged in agriculture.
- PERSONAL PROPERTY TAX (1821): 2 horses - 27¢ (1822): same (1823): same - 24¢ tax (1824): 1 free mulatto, 2 horses - 24¢ tax (1825): 3 horses - 36¢ tax (1826): 1 free mulatto, 2 horses - 24¢ tax (1827): same.

TINSLEY, ASHBY

- DEATH CERTIFICATES (1865): Died in Amherst in March of unknown causes at age 1, son of Geo. and Caroline Tinsley. (*Pg 114, #16*)

TINSLEY, MARY

- DEATH CERTIFICATES (1864): Died in Amherst in July of croup at age of 4 months, born in Amherst, daughter of B. and P. Tinsley. (*Pg 110, #14*)

TINSLEY, SIMUEL [?]

- DEATH CERTIFICATES (1864): Female, died in Amherst in June of a cold at age of 2 months, born in Amherst, no parents listed. (*Pg 110, #15*)

TOBIAS

- LAND BOOK, 1787-1844 (March 11, 1796): Tobias, "a Free Black man," was issued 210 acres on the south branches of Hatt Creek; issue was later withdrawn.
- LAND BOOK, 1878-1844: Under the same warrant, he was issued 47 acres in 1798.
- LAND BOOK, 1787-1844: Under the same warrant, he was issued 163 acres in 1799.
- COURT ORDER BOOK (1801-1802): Tobias, a free negro, versus Alexander McAlexander In Chancery: "On the motion of the Complainant [Tobias] by his Attorney . . . The Commonwealth's Writ of Injunction is granted him to stay all further proceedings on a Judgment and execution recovered against him in this Court by the Dft [Defendant] in the bill mentioned till the further order of this Court concerning the same on his giving bond with sufficient security in the penalty of £20 whereupon the said Tobias together with John Campbell (Waggoner) his security[,] entered into and acknowledged
- COURT ORDER BOOK (1801-1802): Same case: "On the motion of the Plaintiff [Tobias] by his attorney[,] leave is granted him to amend his bill upon the payment of costs."

TOM

- Tom (14, mulatto) is listed in the household of Matilda Thompson (white).

TUPPENCE/TWOPENCE, RICHARD

- CENSUS (1830): 2 fcms under 10 years old, 1 fcm 24 to 36, 1 fcf 24 to 36.
- CENSUS (1840): 1 fcm under 10 years old, 3 fcms 10 to 24, 1 fcm 36 to 55, 1 fcf under 10, 1 fcf 24 to 36 – 1 engaged in agriculture, 1 in navigation.

TURNER, ISENA [?]

- DEATH CERTIFICATES (1864): Died in Amherst in January of dropsy at age 22, born in Amherst, no parents or informant listed. (*Pg 110, #11*)

TURNER, Unnamed Males

- DEATH CERTIFICATES (1864): Died in Amherst of unknown causes at age 57, born in Amherst, no parents listed, informant was his former owner I. S. Turner. (*Pg 110, #19*)
- DEATH CERTIFICATES (1864): Died in Amherst of a fever at age of 19, born in Amherst, no parents listed, informant was his former owner I. S. Turner. (*Pg 110, #10*)

TYLER, ELIZABETH

- COMM. REV. 1861 B: age 17.

TYLER, HENRY

- COMM. REV. 1861 A: age 19.
- COMM. REV. 1861 B: age 19, shoemaker.

TYLER, JAMES

- COMM. REV. 1861 A: age 15.
- COMM. REV. 1861 B: age 14.

TYLER, JOHN

- CENSUS, AGRICULTURAL (1850): 105 improved acres, 10 unimproved acres, total value of land owned was $420 – total value of machinery: $20 – 2 horses, 3 milk cows, 2 working oxen, 3 other cattle, 20 swine, total value of livestock was $150 – 30 bushels of wheat, 250 bushels of Indian corn, 200 bushels of oats, 30 bushels of Irish potatoes, 100 pounds of butter, 1 ton of hay, 4 pounds of flax – total value of orchard products: $20.

TYLER, JOHN, Jr.

- COMM. REV. 1861 B: age 26, shoemaker.

TYLER, JOHN N. [?] V. [?]

- COMM. REV. 1861 B: age 16.

TYLER, LOUVINA

- COMM. REV. 1861 B: Female, age 44.

TYLER, NANCY

- CENSUS, DEATH (1860): 22 years old, free mulatto female, born in Virginia, died in July of a fever after being sick 14 days, occupation: spinning and weaving.

TYLER, PHILLIP

- COMM. REV. 1861 B: age 75.

TYLER, SUSAN L.

- COMM. REV. 1861 B: age 78.

TYLER, TABITHA

- COMM. REV. 1861 A: age 45.
- COMM. REV. 1861 B: age 54.

TYLER, WESLEY

- COMM. REV. 1861 B: age 20, shoemaker.

TYLER, WILLIAM

- COURT ORDER BOOK (March 1851): The Court ordered that his registration be renewed.
- PERSONAL PROPERTY TAX (1860): 1 male free negro 21 to 55 years old, 1 horse worth $25, 2 cattle worth $40, household furnishings worth $15, sheep/hogs worth $10

TYLER, WM.

- CENSUS (1860): Listed in the household of Nancy Simpson (white) were: Wm. T. Simpson (35, white, shoemaker), Wm. Tyler (49, mulatto, shoemaker, $150 personal estate), Tabitha Tyler (50, mulatto), Wm. A. Tyler (20, mulatto, jobing), Henry Tyler (18, mulatto, laborer), Elizabeth Tyler (17, mulatto, domestic), Jas. Tyler (14, mulatto), P. A. Tyler (5, mulatto).
- COMM. REV. 1861 A: age 50, shoemaker.
- COMM. REV. 1861 B: age 46, shoemaker.

TYLER, WM., Jr.

- COMM. REV. 1861 A: age 20.

TYREE, CHARLES

- CENSUS (1840): 1 fcm under 10 years old, 1 fcm 24 to 36, 1 fcf 10 to 24 – 1 engaged in agriculture.
- CENSUS (1850): Charles Tyree (36, mulatto), Harriet (28, mulatto), Lewallen (10, mulatto), Margaret (9, mulatto), Betsey (6, mulatto), Wm. (4, mulatto), Robert (2, mulatto), Charles (1, mulatto).
- PERSONAL PROPERTY TAX (1860): 1 male free negro 21 to 55 years old – aggregate value: $0.
- CENSUS (1860): Chas. Tyree (46, mulatto, chairmaker).
- COMM. REV. 1861 A and B: age 50, farmer.

TYREE, ELIZ[ABETH]

- CENSUS (1860): Eliz. Tyree (17, mulatto, domestic) was listed in the household of Richard Carter (white, farmer).
- COMM. REV. 1861 A: age 21.
- COMM. REV. 1861 B: age 22.

TYREE, GEO.

- DEATH CERTIFICATES (1859): Listed among the slaves but designated as free. Died in March of croup at age 5, son of Reuben and S. Tyree, informant was his father who was a "Free Negro." (*Pg 85, #35*)

TYREE, HARRIETT

- COMM. REV. 1861 A: age 48.
- COMM. REV. 1861 B: age 56.

TYREE, JOE

- COMM. REV. 1861 A: no age given, farmer.

TYREE, JOEL E.

- DEATH CERTIFICATES (1858): Died of dysentery at age of 4 months, son of Reuben I. Tyree. (*Pg 1, #15*)

TYREE, LEWIS

- COMM. REV. 1861 A: age 17.
- COMM. REV. 1861 B: age 18.

TYREE, MARGARET

- COMM. REV. 1861 A: age 19.
- COMM. REV. 1861 B: age 20.

TYREE, NANCY

- DEATH CERTIFICATES (1859): Listed among the slaves but designated as free. Died July 5 of typhoid fever at age 22, daughter of Wm. Tyler. (*Pg 85, #40*)

TYREE, PALMYRA

- DEATH CERTIFICATES (1857): Male, died December 30 of St. Anthony's Fire; place of death, age, and parents are blank. (*Pg 66, #11*)

TYREE, REUBEN

- PERSONAL PROPERTY TAX (1860): 1 male free negro 21 to 55 years old, 1 horse worth $100, 1 cattle worth $30, household furnishings worth $25 – aggregate value: $155.
- COMM. REV. 1861 A and B: age 30, farmer.

TYREE, SUVANIA [SAUVANY?]

- COMM. REV. 1861 A: Female, age 23.
- COMM. REV. 1861 B: Female, age 25.

TYREE, WM.

- COMM. REV. 1861 A: age 35, farmer.

TYRY, HARRIET

- CENSUS (1860): Harriet Tyry (38, mulatto, domestic), Wm. H. (15, mulatto), R. (10, mulatto), Jas. (11, mulatto), Frances (9, mulatto), M. (7, mulatto), Jo. (6, mulatto), Jo. (3, mulatto), S. (2 months, mulatto).

TYRY, THOMAS

- CENSUS (1860): Thomas Tyry (30, mulatto), J. (30, mulatto), Nancy (60, mulatto), Jas. W. (2, mulatto).

TYRY, WILLIAM

- PERSONAL PROPERTY TAX (1860): 1 male free negro 21 to 55 years old – aggregate value: $0.

UMBLES, EZEKIEL

- CENSUS (1830): 2 fcms under 10 years old, 1 fcm 36 to 55, 1 fcf under 10, 1 fcf 24 to 36.
- CENSUS (1840): 1 fcm under 10 years old, 3 fcms 10 to 24, 1 fcm 36 to 55, 1 fcf under 10, 1 fcf 10 to 24 – 3 engaged in agriculture, 2 in manufacturing.

VALENTINE, ISHAM

- WILLIAM CABELL'S COMMONPLACE BOOK (March 9, 1780): "Sent by Isham Valentine a free Negro, 1 pr. [pair] Silver mounted Pistols and Bullet Moulds [molds] to [my son] Colo. Sam. J. Cabell [with his troops in Charleston, South Carolina]. Also all his Clothes, etc., Consisting of one Blue Broad Cloth Coat, one white ditto Vest & Pr. Breeches with Silver oval buttons, 1 pr. mosquito Curtains Seven shirts 5 of which [are] Ruffled at the Hands [cuffs], 1 pr. Sheets, 2 Towels . . .."
- According to www.freeafricanamericans.com, Valentine was living in Dinwiddie County when he applied for a pension for his military service.

WALKER, HARRIETT

- DEATH CERTIFICATES (1864): Died in Amherst in September of suffocation at age of 1 month [Sudden Infant Death Syndrome?], born in Amherst, daughter of Clem and Harriett Walker, informant was her former owner S. B. Walker. (*Pg 110, #33*)

WALKER, JOHN

- DEATH CERTIFICATES (1865): Died in Amherst in September of suffocation [Sudden Infant Death Syndrome?] at the age of 1 month, son of Clem and Harriet Walker, informant was his former master I. B. Walker. (*Pg 114, #36*)

WARE, JNO. A.

- DEATH CERTIFICATES (1858): Died August 12 of dysentery at age of 1 year and 4 months, son of Jno. M. and S. Ware. (*Pg 1, #13*)

WARE, MARGARET

- DEATH CERTIFICATES (1857): Died February 6 of "Cholic" at age of 68, born in Amherst, daughter of John McDaniel, wife of Jno. Ware, informant was her son [unnamed]. (*Pg 67, #35*)

WARWICK, JAMES

- PERSONAL PROPERTY TAX (1860): 1 male free negro 21 to 55 years old – aggregate value: $0.
- COMM. REV. 1861 A: age (probably 40).
- COMM. REV. 1861 B: age 35, mechanic.

WASHINGTON

- MANUMISSION: Will of Thomas Higginbotham (recorded February 12, 1834): ". . . It is my wish and desire that all my Negroes be set free, viz: Nancy my cook woman, Maria and her two sons Tom Carey and John Waller Caleb and their increase. Washington, Charles, Dandridge, William, Daniel Spencer, Polley, Isaac, Carter, Ann and her children [and] their increase. Charlotte & her children and [their] increase. Kitty and her Children and [their] increase. Jean and her children and [their] increase. Betsey and her children and [their] increase. China and her children and [their] increase provided they are willing to leave the state, if not they may chose any of my Brothers or Sisters they are willing to serve. 15th. It is my wish and desire that should I dispose of any of the special legacies it is to be made up to them out of my estate . . .." (*Will Book 9, pg 47*)
- LEGISLATIVE PETITION (December 8, 1836): To the Speaker and Members of the Senate and House of Delegates of the General Assembly of Virginia: The Petition of Washington a free man of color respectfully and humbly sheweth that he was born a slave within this Commonwealth and raised by Doctor James Powell now of the County of Amherst, that he will be forty four years of age on the 26th day of July 1837: That some eight or nine years ago the said Doctor Powell sold him to a certain Thomas Higginbotham of the said county of Amherst who he faithfully served as a slave untill [sic] some time in the month of February 1835, when the said Higginbotham departed this life testate, a copy of whose last will and testament hath

been duly recorded in the Circuit Superior Court of Law and Chancery for the County of Amherst . . . a copy of which said will is . . . part of this humble Petition . . . the said Thomas Higginbotham did by virtue of the same, kindly and humanely make provision for the emancipation of all the slaves which he might own at the date of his death (your Petitioner being one named and so provided for thereby) but the said Higginbotham[,] well knowing that it was contrary to the laws of this commonwealth then and now in force for slaves so manumitted, to remain in the state more than twelve months after their manumission shall take effect and not knowing whether the Legislature would permit them in whole or in part so to remain, and not knowing but that the slaves or some of them, might prefer to remain with his relations or some one of them, rather than to leave the state and in many cases their nearest and dearest relations . . . they were given the right to choose a master or mistress from amongst the brothers and sisters of the said decedent. That shortly after the death of the said Thomas . . . the . . . Executor feeling difficulties about the construction of the said will, filed his will [illegible], asking the counsel and instruction of the Court . . . upon the points following, to wit (and perhaps others) 1st. Did the persons of color therein mentioned . . .take their freedom unconditionally . . . upon the death of the testator and if so which of them[.] 2nd. If they are not to take title to freedom unconditionally [,] did they have a conditional title thereto, depending upon their election to leave the common-wealth. 3rd. If so entitled as last aforesaid, upon their electing aforesaid, how and in what manner should that election be made known to the Court so as to be obligatory upon the persons concerned. 4th. In case of the said persons electing to accept their freedom and to leave the state, did the will authorize the Executor to defray the expenses of their transportation out of other portions of the Estate in his hand. Your Petitioner states that he is informed that the said Court entertained the said cause which is now before it and that although no response has been as yet given to the first inquiry, and perhaps for the reason that none was necessary, it has by interloculatory order decided that all the slaves of the decedent took upon his death the right to freedom conditioned upon their electing to leave the commonwealth . . . [that the will did not authorize estate money be applied to their transportation] and your Petitioner & others situated like him are now and have ever since been hired out to raise the said fund . . . That he [the petitioner] understands that the Court . . . also appointed the Rev. Charles H. Page to correspond with the Executive Governments of the neighboring non slave holding states, as well as with the manager of agents of the African Colonization Society . . . about the admission of free persons of color within their limits, with these and to see what aid the Society could or would afford toward transporting them to their colony [in Liberia], and he has been informed that the information from the states is discouraging, most of them having proper laws and regulations, which although not prohibitory, yet in effect by requiring security for good behavior and that they [the freed slaves] will not become chargeable upon the parish or poor roll of the county, is to the stranger and pennyless [sic] colored man, equal to prohibition to a residence amongst them . . . Your Petitioner states that about 22 years ago he married Nice a woman of color now the property of Mrs. Margaret Coleman and that by his said wife he hath had thirteen children, eight of whom are still alive the younger of which is about two years of age and five have died, and being now liable to a separation from them, he comes before your house to humbly ask that in this case you will release the rule denying to free persons of color the right to reside within the state—That he asks it in part because he has ever been honest, faithful and true to his Master and Mistress, humble and obedient to all his superiors, because he loves his wife and children, and loves the country where he was born and raised, in sight of the bigg [sic] mountains, and away from the Sea—That he wishes not to go to Liberia amongst strangers a good country for the youthful, who can learn new things, manners and pursuits, and form new connections in life, but to him that time is passed, he is too old to learn new things, manners, or habits and he desires to form no new connections in this life—He begs to be permitted to re-main where he can be with his beloved wife and children—She it is believed will bear no more children, and he [is] at an age that promises not many more years—He will he hopes be enabled to procure testimonials of his good conduct, and Petitioners uniting with him in the prayer of this his Petition . . . and as is duly bound he will ever pray.

- AFFIDAVIT signed by James Powell, with an attached list of 81 names supporting the petition. "I raised the petitioner Washington and know him to be an honest obedient Slave, humble submissive in his deportment much attached to his wife and children, and should be much gratified for him to remain with his family."

- DECISION of the Legislature (December 19, 1836): "Reasonable."

WAUGH, MARY

- DEATH CERTIFICATES (1865): Died in Amherst in April of a cold at the age of 1, born in Amherst, daughter of John and Matilda Waugh. (*Pg 114, #32*)

WAUGH, ROBERT

- DEATH CERTIFICATES (1864): Died in Amherst in October of unknown causes at age of 1, born in Amherst, no parents listed. (*Pg 110, #22*)

WEAVER, JAMES

- COMM. REV. 1861 B: age 35.

WHITE, ANDRU

- DEATH CERTIFICATES (1864): Died in Amherst in December of measles at age of 25, no parents or informant listed. (*Pg 110, #37*)

WHITE, HENRY

- DEATH CERTIFICATES (1864): Died in Amherst in July of typhoid fever at age of 22, no parents or informant listed. (*Pg 110, #40*)

WHITE, LUVENIA

- DEATH CERTIFICATES (1864): Died in Amherst in January of jaundice at age of 20, no parents or informant listed. (*Pg 110, #35*)

WHITE, SUSAN

- DEATH CERTIFICATES (1864): Died in Amherst in July of dysentery at age of 3 months, no parents or informant listed. (*Pg 110, #39*)

WHITE, TOM

- DEATH CERTIFICATES (1864): Died in Amherst in July of unknown causes at age of 4 months, no parents or informant listed. (*Pg 110, #38*)

WHITESIDES, BENJAMIN

- TAX LIST (1800): 1 white male over 21, 1 horse.
- CENSUS (1810): 4 free coloreds.
- PERSONAL PROPERTY TAX (1823): 1 free negro, 2 horses - 24¢ tax (1824): same (1826): 1 free negro, 1 horse - 12¢ tax (1827): same (1828): same.
- CENSUS (1830): 1 fcm under 10 years old, 1 fcm 24 to 36, 1 fcm 55 to 100, 1 fcf 10 to 24, 1 fcf 24 to 36, 1 fcf 55 to 100.

WILLIAMS, ISABELLA [ISBELL]

- PERSONAL PROPERTY TAX (1827): 1 free mulatto, 1 horse - 12¢ tax (1828): same (1840): 2 horses - 16¢ tax.
- CENSUS (1840): 1 fcm 10 to 24 years old, 1 fcm 36 to 55, 1 fcf under 10, 1 fcf 36 to 55 – 2 engaged in agriculture.

WILLIAMS, RICHARD

- PERSONAL PROPERTY TAX (1850): 1 male free negro over 16 years old.

WILSHER, OBADIAH

- DEATH CERTIFICATES (1864): Died in Amherst in February of rheumatism at age of 70, born in Amherst, no parents or informant listed. (*Pg 110, #32*)

WINGFIELD, Unnamed Male

- DEATH CERTIFICATES (1864): Died in Amherst in November of spasms at the age of 21 days, born in Amherst, son of Adaline Wingfield, informant was his former owner N. A. Wingfield. (*Pg 110, #21*)

WINTERS, BETSEY

- COMM. REV. 1861 A and B: age 16.

WINTERS, EDWARD

- CENSUS (1840): 1 fcm 10 to 24 years old, 2 fcfs 10 to 24, 1 fcf 55 to 100 – 2 engaged in agriculture, 1 in manufacturing and trade.

WINTERS, GEORGE

- DEATH CERTIFICATES (1866): Died in Amherst in February of consumption at age 60, a farmer, born in Nelson County, son of Wm. and Nancy Winters. (*Pg 117, #121*)

WINTERS, GEORGE W.

- CENSUS (1840): 1 fcm 24 to 36 years old, 2 fcfs under 10, 1 fcf 24 to 36 – 1 engaged in agriculture, 1 in manufacturing and trade.
- PERSONAL PROPERTY TAX (1850): 1 male free negro over 16 years old.
- CENSUS (1850): George Winters (44, black), Nancy (29, black), Lucy (14, black), Martha (3, black), Wm. (9, black), John (6, black), Betsey (6, black), Mary (6, black).
- PERSONAL PROPERTY TAX (1860): 1 male free negro 21 to 55 years old, cattle worth $30, household furnishings worth $20 – aggregate value: $50.
- COMM. REV. 1861 A: age 53, farmer.
- COMM. REV. 1861 B: age 54, farmer.

WINTERS, JOHN

- COMM. REV. 1861 A: age 16.
- COMM. REV. 1861 B: age 17.

WINTERS, LUCY

- COMM. REV. 1861 A and B: age 21.

WINTERS, MARY

- COMM. REV. 1861 A and B: age 14.

WINTERS, NANCY

- COMM. REV. 1861 A and B: age 45.

WINTERS, NANCY

- DEATH CERTIFICATES (1871): Died in Temperance Township in Amherst County in May of consumption at age 16, born in Amherst, unmarried, daughter of Geo. and Nancy Winters, informant was her brother John Winters. (*Pg 3 index, #43*)

WINTERS, WM.

- COMM. REV. 1861 A and B: age 19.

WISE, ARTHUR

- COMM. REV. 1861 B: age 12.

WISE, FRANCES

- COMM. REV. 1861 A: Female, age 45.
- COMM. REV. 1861 B: age 30.

WISE, MARTHA

- COMM. REV. 1861 B: age 28.

WISE, REUBEN H.

- PERSONAL PROPERTY (1850): 1 male free negro over 16 years old.
- PERSONAL PROPERTY (1860): 1 male free negro 21 to 55 years old, cattle worth $25, household furnishings worth $25 – aggregate value: $0.
- COMM. REV. 1861 A: age 35, farmer.
- COMM. REV. 1861 B: age 34, farmer.

WOODROOF, JULIANNA

- DEATH CERTIFICATES (1864): Died in Amherst in June of typhoid fever at the age of 30, born in Amherst, informant was her former owner A. M. Woodroof. (*Pg 110, #31*)

WOODRUFF, WYATT

- According to the files of the Amherst County Historical Museum, Wyatt Woodruff, a freed slave, operated a blacksmith shop at the corner of Route 130 and Salt Creek Road (Virginia 650).

- An undated clipping from the *Amherst New-Era Progress* regarding a reunion of Woodruff's descendants notes that he was born a slave circa 1832 and took his master's last name. He was later sold to Nathan Rucker of Elon, who freed him. Woodruff apprenticed himself to blacksmith Thomas Townley and, in 1870, was the only black business owner listed on the Amherst County census.

WRIGHT, MARY

- DEATH CERTIFICATES (1864): Died in Amherst in July of "Hooping Cough" at age of 5, born in Amherst, daughter of Jane Wright. (*Pg 110, #44*)

APPENDICES

Table A: Amherst County Free & Slave Populations, 1810-1860: Numerical and (Percentage of Total Population)

YEAR	FREE WHITE	SLAVE	FREE COLORED
1810	5,143 (49%)	5,207 (49%)	198 (2%)
1820	4,610 (44%)	5,567 (53%)	246 (2%)
1830	5,883 (49%)	5,925 (49%)	260 (2%)
1840	6,426 (51%)	5,777 (46%)	373 (3%)
1850	6,353 (50%)	5,953 (47%)	393 (3%)
1860	7,167 (51%)	6,278 (45%)	297 (2%)

Table B: Percentage of Black Population Growth, 1810-1860: Amherst County (in regular type) compared to *Virginia* (*italics*)

YEAR	FREE COLORED	%	SLAVE	%
1810	198	0	5,207	0
	30,570	*0*	*392,516*	*0*
1820	246	+20%	5,567	+6%
	36,883	*+17%*	*425,148*	*+8%*
1830	260	+ 5%	5,927	+6%
	47,348	*+22%*	*469,757*	*+9%*
1840	373	+30%	5,777	-3%
	49,842	*+ 5%*	*448,987*	*-5%*
1850	393	+ 5%	5,953	+3%
	54,333	*+ 8%*	*472,528*	*+5%*
1860	297	-32%	6,278	+5%
	58,042	*+ 6%*	*490,865*	*+4%*

Table C: Free Coloreds as a Percentage of the Black Population

YEAR	AMHERST COUNTY	VIRGINIA
1810	4%	7%
1820	4%	8%
1830	4%	9%
1840	6%	10%
1850	6%	10%
1860	5%	11%

Table D: Free Colored Household Size: Amherst County

YEAR	NO. OF HSEHLDS.	LARGEST HSEHLD.	SMALLEST HSEHLD.	AVERAGE HSEHLD
1810	28	13	1	5.5
1820	34	12	1	6.8
1830	46	13	1	5.0
1840	50	13	1	6.1
1850	61	15	1	6.0
1860	53	16	1	4.9

Table E: Female Heads of Households: Amherst County

YEAR	NUMBER OF FEMALE HEADS OF FAMILIES	TOTAL FREE COLORED HOUSEHOLDS
1810	5	28
1820	1	34
1830	9	46
1840	8	50
1850	11	61
1860	12	53

Table F: Free Coloreds Living in White Households: Amherst Co

YEAR	TOTAL COLORED POPULATION	NUMBER OF FC's IN WHITE HOUSEHOLDS	(%)
1810	198	45	(23%)
1820	246	41	(17%)
1830	260	20	(8%)
1840	373	64	(17%)
1850	393	28	(7%)
1860	297	49	(16%)

Table G: Households with Free Coloreds in Amherst County. (Name of White Household Head, Number of Free Coloreds Living There, *Number of Slaves Owned*)

1810: Isaiah Alley, 1, *4* – Henry Ballinger 1, *5* – John P. Burks 1, *5* – Micajah Camden 1, *10*–Anselem Clarkson 1, *5*–John C. Cobbs 1, *0* – Miles Cooksey 1, *8* – Nathaniel Davis 1, *3* – Daniel Dumviss 1, *0* – Fleming Duncan 1, *5* – John Ellis 2, *26* – Anderson Evans 1, *1* – Thomas V. Goodrich 1, *1* – Charles Higginbotham 1, *1* – Joseph Higginbotham 12, *25* – Ambrose Lucas 1, *13* – John McDaniel 6, *26* – Samuel Sale 1,*1* – George W. Taylor 1, *4* – Godfrey Tolar 1, *52* – William Tungate 3, *0* – Benjamin Watts 1, *7* – Arthur White 2, *3*.
1820: Charles Barrett 8, *17* – David Clarkson 3, *0* – Arthur B. Davies 1, *5* – John Dillard 1, *13* – John Harden 1, *2* – Thomas Lane 1, *15* – George P. Luck 2, *14* – Roderick McCulloch 1, *15* – Cornelius Sale 2, *11* – Lindsey Sandidge 1, *5* – Joel F. Smith 4, *4* – James F. Taliaferro 3, *8* – Richeson Taylor 3, *0* – Thomas Waugh 8, *8* – Thomas Wiatt 2, *10*.
1830: Jho. Anderson 1, *5* – Scott Burks 1, *0* – Thomas Coppedge, Sr., 1, *1* – Lucy Dodd 1, *2* – Sarah Duncan 1, *8* – Richard S. Ellis 1, *61* – Richard Eubank 1, *2* – Hezekiah Fulcher 1, *0* – Alexander Jewell 1, *0* – Joseph Milstead 7, *0* – William Reddon 1, *0* – Philip Thurmond 1, *1* – William Thurmond 1, *13* – Robert Tinsley 1, *3*.

1840: Thomas Barr 1, *7* – Joseph O. Bryant 1, *0* – Samuel Burks 7, *13* – Lucretia Carter 2, *0* – Peter Cashwell 3, *19* – William Coffey 1, *0* – Elizabeth Davies 1, *14* – William Dillard 1, *43* – Daniel Driskill 1, *46* – Richard S. Ellis 1, *29* – Alfred Flipped 5, *24* – David S. Garland 8, *40* – James P. Garland 1, *21* – Lewis Harrison 1, *14* – Leroy Hicks 1, *0* – Absalom Higginbotham 3, *16* – Rufus A. Higginbotham 1, *3* – Edmund W. Hill 3, *4* – David Johns 5, *0* – Mary Jones 1, *10* – Judith Martin 1, *0* – Livinia Mays 3, *0* – Willis Mays 1, *23* – Benjamin Norvell 1, *25* – Nathan D. Rucker 1, *10* – Thomas L. Taylor 3, *0* – Peter P. Thornton 1, *13* – Roderick Waugh 1, *26* – Thomas P. Waugh 3, *4* – Pitt Woodruff 1, *6*.

Table H. Summary of Personal Property Taxes, Amherst County Free Coloreds

YEAR	NO. OF TAX-PAYERS	TOTAL TAXES PAID	HIGHEST TAX PAID	LOWEST TAX PAID	AVG. TAX
1821	16	$3.16	$0.54	$0.14	$0.20
1822	18	4.11	.67	.14	.23
1823	24	5.49	.71	.12	.23
1824	23	3.36	.24	.12	.15
1825	20	3.60	.48	.12	.18
1826	19	3.12	.36	.12	.16
1827	20	2.88	.24	.12	.14
1828	19	3.35	.71	.12	.18
1829	26	4.70	1.80	.08	.18
1831	21	2.50	.81	.06	.12
1840	17	3.68	1.60	.08	.22
1850	42	1.90	.30	.10	.05

Table I: Place of Birth: Amherst County Free Coloreds

PLACE OF BIRTH	NUMBER F.C.s BORN THERE	% OF AMHERST F.C.s
Amherst County	98	59%
Nelson County	16	10%
State of Virginia*	15	9%
Fluvanna County	10	6%
Goochland County	7	4%
Buckingham County	5	3%
Appomattox County	3	2%
Bedford County	3	2%
Campbell County	3	2%
City of Richmond	2	1%
Albemarle County	1	1%
Augusta County	1	1%
Chesterfield County	1	1%
Hanover County	1	1%
King & Queen County	1	1%

* Specific birthplace not otherwise known.

Table J: Dates of Birth, Amherst County Free Coloreds

YEARS	NUMBER BORN	% OF AMHERST FCs
18th century – 1800	158	17%
1801 – 1810	66	7%
1811 – 1820	96	10%
1821 – 1830	121	13%
1831 – 1840	209	22%
1841 – 1850	185	20%
1860	104	11%

Table K: Frequency of Registration

YEAR	TOTAL REGISTRATIONS	REGISTERING 1st TIME	REGISTERING 2nd TIME	REGISTER'G 2nd+ TIME
1822	3	3		
1823	2	2		
1825	3	3		
1826	1	1		
1827	3	3		
1828	20	13	7	
1829	1	1		
1830	3			
1831	9	6	2	1
1832	15	10	5	
1833	1	1		
1834	2	2		
1835	4	4		
1836	3	2		1
1837	5	5		
1838	2	2		
1839	2	2		
1840	1	1		
1841	6	6		
1842	4	4		
1843	29	29		
1844	21	18	3	
1845	20	19	1	
1846	3	1		2
1847	8	5	3	
1849	1		1	
1850	13	9	1	3
1851	40	16	17	7
1852	5	2	1	2
1853	4	1	3	
1854	6	3	2	1
1855	3	1	1	1
1856	23	8	2	13
1857	9	5		4
1858	2	2		
1859	2	1		1
1860	77	62	1	15
1861	9	8		1
1862	1			1
1863	12	10		2
1864	8	4		4

Table L: Color Classifications and Frequency: Amherst County Register of Free Blacks

COLOR DESIGNATION	NUMBER OF PERSONS SO CLASSIFIED
Bright mulatto	110
Dark	68
Brown	45
Bright	35
Dark mulatto	26
Mulatto	21
Black	18
Dark brown	18
Light	14
Bright brown	5
Very dark	4
Light mulatto	3
Chocolate brown	2
Light brown	2
Brown mulatto	1
Dark black	1
Nearly white	1
Very black	1
Very mulatto	1
Yellow	1

Table M: Virginia Counties with the Largest Free Black Populations

1790		**1800**		**1810**	
Accomack	721	Accomack	1,541	Accomack	1,860
Henrico	580	Nansemond	910	Nansemond	1,269
Dinwiddie	561	Southampton	839	Richmond*	1,189
Southampton	559	Northampton	654	Southampton	1,109
Nansemond	480	Richmond*	607	Petersburg	1,089

1820		**1830**		**1840**	
Accomack	2,100	Accomack	2,544	Henrico	2,939
Nansemond	1,393	Petersburg	2,032	Accomack	2,848
Southampton	1,306	Richmond*	1,956	Dinwiddie	2,764
Richmond*	1,235	Southampton	1,745	Norfolk	2,390
Petersburg	1,165	Nansemond	1,698	Southampton	1,799

1850		**1860**	
Henrico	3,637	Dinwiddie	3,746
Dinwiddie	3,296	Henrico	3,590
Accomack	3,295	Accomack	3,418
Norfolk	2,307	Norfolk	2,803
Nansemond	2,144	Nansemond	2,480

* Refers to the city, not the county

ENDNOTES: Chapter 1

[1] The French and Spanish escapees formed settlements of their own or took shelter with resident Indian tribes. Melungeons—mixed Indian, Negro, and European peoples—are documented in the Appalachians as early as 1600.

2 The Virginia arrivals were among 350 Africans captured by Portuguese in a mountainous area of northern Angola and were en route to slavery in Spanish Mexico when their vessel was seized by two ships, the *White Lion* and the *Treasurer*. The latter also sailed to Virginia but appears to have unloaded (or lost to escape) only a few women. For more information, see *Love and Hate in Jamestown* (2003) by David A. Price.

Cassandra Newby-Alexander of Norfolk State University writes in "An African Perspective" in *Virginia Secrets* (page 7) that the Angolan captives were probably not the first blacks brought to the colony as "a March 1619 census listed 32 people of color in the service of Virginia planters." Another census, taken after the Indian Massacre of 1622, showed 19 of the 20 original Angolans still alive, plus another four blacks.

The next colony to receive shipments of Negroes was New Netherlands [modern New York State] when the Dutch West India Company brought 11 males to New Amsterdam [New York City] in 1626.

[3] At least two of the blacks who arrived in the 1620s were free by mid-century; one became a substantial land-and-slave owner himself, and others formed small farming communities around the Tidewater. Historian Ira Berlin estimates that as many as a fifth became free. [Ira Berlin, *Many Thousands Gone: The First Two Centuries of Slavery in North America* (Cambridge, Massachusetts: Belknap Press of Harvard University Press, 1998), 95]

Anthony Johnson, the land and slave owner noted above was probably one of the original 20 Angolans who arrived in 1619. In 1654, his black servant John Casar demanded that he be released from his indenture, since he had served more than his time. The Court initially agreed but later reversed itself and declared him Johnson's slave for life.

[4] John Rolfe is credited with being the first Englishman in Virginia to cultivate tobacco on a large scale, planting his first crop in 1612. He experimented with the native plant used by the Indians but eventually discarded it because of its strong, bitter taste and poor growth habits. Rolfe imported tobacco seeds (probably illegally) from Spanish possessions in South America and the West Indies, blending the different varieties until he developed "Sweet-Scented" tobacco. (From "Tobacco: Gold in the Piedmont," by Sherrie S. McLeRoy. *Lynch's Ferry*, May-June 1976, page 23)

---

6 Massachusetts, for example, developed the "Body of Liberties" in 1641, which applied to both Negro and Indian slaves. It "outlawed bond slavery except when taken in just wars, when strangers sold themselves to us, or when sold to us." As author Oscar Reiss wrote, "This was the height of hypocrisy, however, because these expeditions were precisely the means whereby slaves were obtained." [Oscar Reiss, *Blacks in Colonial America* (Jefferson, North Carolina: McFarland & Company, Inc. 1997), 10-11]

7 Benjamin Brawley, *A Social History of the American Negro* (Project Gutenberg EBook, 2004).

8 Virginia was not alone during this period in attempting to constrain its burgeoning black population. When England took control of New Netherlands [the colony of New York] in 1663, for example, it encouraged the importation of slaves because of its own financial interests in the Royal African Company. By the end of the 17th century, New York was one of the most important slave ports in the colonies, the city had the largest population of urban blacks, and slave labor had become essential. To control them, the colony passed its first slave laws in 1665, decreeing that Christians could be enslaved only by selling themselves or being captured in war. Fourteen years later, they relaxed that policy as it applied to Indians: New York Indians could not be made slaves, but those natives made slave in other colonies could be brought into New York. In 1706, that law would be amended again to allow only Negroes as slaves.

Massachusetts also enslaved captured Indians (though the natives did not "endure the yoke" well) and imported black slaves. It had a relatively small number of blacks, but the laws of the Puritan colony were influenced by emigrants from Barbados, with a heritage of much stricter controls. Slave children could be sold, whites could not trade with blacks, and both slave and free blacks had curfews. Echoing the Virginia law, Massachusetts also prohibited miscegenation for the "Better Preventing a Spurious Mixt Issue." (Reiss, op. cit., 65-67)

Connecticut also allowed slavery. Though it provided more legal rights for them, it also had laws more restrictive than those in Massachusetts. Already, free blacks were required to carry their free papers with them at all times.

The extreme northeastern colonies had fewer slaves. The exception was Rhode Island, which was becoming a major player in the slave trade by the end of the 16th century. As in New York, the large plantations surrounding the major cities required enormous numbers of slaves. Rhode Island followed the trend of other colonies with large black populations and very strictly controlled both the slaves and their importation.

Pennsylvania, as Oscar Reiss observed in *Blacks in Colonial America*, preferred slaves to white servants "because they worked for life." Even Quakers were slaveholders in this period. By the end of the century, blacks had been legally defined as separate from other servants.

South Carolina formally recognized slavery in 1672, and soon sanctioned an odd form of it in which the master owned the slave's services but not his person. Georgia, fearful of being unable to attract white workers who could not compete with slave labor, actually prohibited the institution for many years and was the last colony to formally recognize it, in 1750.

9 In 1710, for example, a Surry County slave named Will was freed for alerting authorities to a planned slave uprising.

10 Department of Commerce, Bureau of the Census, *Negro Population, 1790-1915* (Washington, D.C., 1918), 54fn.

11 Berlin, op. cit., 123.

12 Ira Berlin estimates that more than 15,000 African slaves were carried beyond the Fall Line between 1720 and 1776. (The Fall Line marks the transition from the Virginia Tidewater to the Piedmont and runs roughly north-south through Richmond.) (op.cit., page 122)

13 Jeffrey R. Kerr-Ritchie, *Freedpeople in the Tobacco South: Virginia, 1860-1900* (Chapel Hill, University of North Carolina Press, 1999), 18.

14 Reiss, op. cit., 145-146.

15 Among the Fairfax Resolves was this clause: "Resolved . . . that during our present difficulties & distress, no slave ought to be imported into any British Colonies on this Continent; & we take this opportunity to declare our most earnest wishes to see an entire stop forever to such a wicked, cruel, & unnatural trade." (Reiss, op. cit., 170)

16 Ibid., page 172.

17 Much has been made of the fact that Jefferson personally owned slaves and freed very few, even in his will. The answer is debt. Jefferson owed enormous sums—more than $100,000 at the time of his death—for his own and family expenses, some dating back decades. His situation worsened when the Panic of 1819 closed Virginia's banks. Desperate to save *Monticello*, he tried to raise money through a lottery, but it failed. He was also driven to provide for his daughter Martha Randolph, whose husband was an abusive spendthrift. *Monticello's* overseer, Edmund Bacon, later recalled that Jefferson wished to free his slaves, but the estate could not afford the loss of that much capital. In the end, the house

and most of the slaves were sold to satisfy those debts after Jefferson's death in 1826.

As he grew older, Jefferson had changed his opinion regarding the mental ability of blacks, admitting that it had been based on observations made only in Virginia. From believing that they were a lower species of humanity than whites, he concluded their seeming inferiority was due to their "degraded condition" as slaves.

18 This act is said to have been inspired by the horror that many felt on learning that some owners had re-enslaved men who had substituted for them in Revolutionary War service. (Berlin, op. cit., 278)

19 Other than by will, slaves could be freed by deed, just the same as if the owner were transferring a piece of land.

Virginia's capital was moved to Williamsburg in 1699 and then to Richmond in 1779, reflecting the westward movement of the residents.

20 Hopkins' will stipulated that, with few exceptions, the male slaves would be freed when they turned 44 and the females at 40. It also exempted the cook, "Old Judy," from being required to go with the other slaves to the courthouse to be listed for the estate inventory, since she "doth at present far exceed either of those ages." Hopkins wanted her to continue as cook "with sufficient assistants . . . so long as she may be able to" and be paid at least $6 a year. The executors were allowed to delay or suspend the emancipations if circumstances arose which they felt would "render it dangerous either to my own Family, or to the Country at large." This was not to apply to his "head-waterman Jacob," however, unless the man had committed a crime, "which I trust will never be, being long satisfied from abundance of experience of his Integrity." (Deed Book 4, 86-109)

John Lynch (1740-1820) gave the land for and was the namesake of the City of Lynchburg (adjoining Amherst County on the south), chartered in 1786 where his ferry crossed the James River. His brother, Col. Charles Lynch (1736-1796), forsook the family's Quaker faith to join the military. He is said to be the source of the phrase "lynch law" for his zealous prosecution of area Tories, who were tied to a tree in the yard of his home and whipped.

21 Berlin, op. cit., 286.

22 Prosser and his followers planned to kidnap Governor Monroe and establish a black state in Virginia. Like many runaways before them, they planned to flee west, into the mountains, if their uprising failed. As Oscar Reiss wrote in *Blacks in Colonial America* (206-207): "The results of this uprising, like the others, were strict antiblack laws and more intense patrol activity, and it is said that this uprising was one of the factors in the formation of the American Colonization Society."

[23] Philip J. Schwarz, "Emancipators, Protectors, and Anomalies: Free Black Slaveowners in Virginia," *Virginia Magazine of History and Biography* 95, no. 3, July 1987: 331.

[24] According to "Dred Scott case: the Supreme Court decision," found at www.hectv.org/documents, Attorney General William Wirt "decided that the words 'citizens of the United States' were used in the Acts of Congress in the same sense as in the Constitution, and that free persons of color were not citizens, within the meaning of the Constitution and laws." A later Attorney General agreed with the U. S. Secretary of State when he refused to issue passports to free coloreds because they were not citizens.

[25] Indeed, by 1860, it would be nearly 60,000.

[26] Henry Noble Sherwood, Ph.D., "The Formation of the American Colonization Society," *Journal of Negro History* 2, no. 3 (1917): online edition from University of North Carolina at Chapel Hill: 8.

[27] Ibid., 10.

[28] J. P. Guild, *Black Laws of Virginia: A Summary of the Legislative Acts of Virginia concerning Negroes from Earliest Times to the Present* (Richmond, Virginia: Whittet & Shepperson, 1936), 99.

[29] Mercer (1778-1858) was a lawyer, Virginia delegate, and U.S. Congressman who devoted several decades to the Liberia Colony project. In 1841 he became interested in starting his own colony as an empresario in the Republic of Texas. He received a contract from Pres. Sam Houston in 1844 for a colony there, but it was involved in such controversy that he finally sold his interest in 1856.

[30] Sherwood, op. cit., 8.

[31] Clarke (1810-1888), a prolific author and editor, founded the Church of Disciples (Unitarian) in Boston and formulated its "Five Points of Unitarianism." As well as abolition, Clarke supported women's rights. After retiring from Boston pulpits, he moved to West Newton, Mass., where his neighbors included Nathaniel Hawthorne, whom he both married and buried, and Harriet Beecher Stowe. It was Clarke who urged another friend, Julia Ward Howe, to write more uplifting lyrics to the song *John Brown's Body*: the result was the *Battle Hymn of the Republic*.

[32] Rev. James Freeman Clarke, *Present Condition of the Free Colored People of the United States* (New York: American Anti-Slavery Society, 1859), 3-5.

[33] Leon Litwack, "The Federal Government and the Free Negro," in *Free Blacks in America, 1800-1860*, ed. John H. Bracey, Jr., August Meier, and Elliott Rudwick (Belmont, California: Wadsworth Publishing), 149.

[34] The four largest free black populations—in Maryland, New York, Pennsylvania, and Virginia—grew at or near 110% every decade from 1840 to 1860. (1840: 209,811. 1850: 231,751. 1860: 247,938.)

[35] Christopher M. Curtis, "Can These be the Sons of Their Fathers? The Defense of Slavery in Virginia, 1831-1832" (Masters thesis, Virginia Polytechnic Institute and State University, 1997), 2-6. Posted online at www.scholar.lib.vt.edu/theses.

Thomas R. Dew, *Review of the Debate in the Virginia Legislature of 1831 and 1832* (Richmond, Virginia, 1832). Posted online at www.digitalhistory.uh.edu.

The debate was spurred in part by (1) divisions between coastal and Piedmont Virginia with the Trans-Alleghany section that would later split off as West Virginia and (2) the enormous growth of anti-slavery societies in the South during the 1820s, with the result that there were more such societies in the Upper South than in the North.

[36] Wilma A. Dunaway, "Put in Master's Pocket: Cotton Expansion and Interstate Slave Trading in the Mountain South," in *Appalachians and Race: The Mountain South from Slavery to Segregation*, ed. by John C. Inscoe (Lexington: University Press of Kentucky, 2001), 121.

[37] Slaves were usually allowed to keep a portion of the wages they earned; many were thus able to buy their freedom, or that of a family member. Iron furnaces were one industry that hired many slaves throughout Piedmont Virginia, usually through markets held at the end of the year; one of these took place in Amherst County.

[38] Clarke, op. cit., 16.

[39] These "top five" counties are all in: the Eastern Shore, Virginia's end of the Delmarva Peninsula; Southside, along or near the North Carolina border; and the Richmond-Petersburg corridor.

[40] Freeman, op. cit., 7.

[41] Ira Berlin, *Slaves Without Masters: The Free Negro in the Ante-bellum South* (New York: Pantheon Books, 1974), 374-376.

[42] The authors could find no record of manumissions for this period in the county deed books.

[43] Other localities also lodged complaints. For a brief discussion, see *Black Confederates and Afro-Yankees in Civil War Virginia* ,203-204.

[44] Amherst County Court Order Book, 1864-1868: July Court 1864, 9-10.

ENDNOTES: Chapter 2

[45] Sir William Talbot, *The Discoveries of John Lederer, in Three Several Marches from Virginia to the West of Carolina, and Other Parts of the Continent* (originally published 1672, republished 1891), 19.

[46] Samuel R. Cook, "Monacans and Mountaineers: A Comparative Study of Colonialism and Dependency in Southern Appalachia" (Ph.D. dissertation, University of Arizona, 1997), 61-63.

Karenne Wood and Diane Shields, *The Monacan Indians: Our Story* (Madison Heights, Va.: Monacan Indian Nation, n.d.) 1-6.

[47] Thomas Jefferson, *Notes on the State of Virginia* (Chapel Hill: University of North Carolina Press, reprinted 1955).

[48] According to the map accompanying a May 2007 *National Geographic* article on Jamestown, this physical devastation began with Hernando de Soto in 1539: "Communities that never met a European were wiped out as epidemics spread along trade routes." ("A World Transformed" map supplement, May 2007)

[49] Melanie Dorothea Haimes-Bartolf, *Policies and Attitudes: Public Education and the Monacan Indian Community in Amherst County, Virginia, from 1908 to 1965* (Ph.D. dissertation, Virginia Commonwealth University, 2004), 8.

Susan Myra Kingsbury, *The Records of the Virginia Company of London* (Washington: Government Printing Office, 1906), 3 and 30. [This expedition did not visit Monahassanaugh.]

[50] Cook, *Monacans and Mountaineers,* 65.

[51] He likely visited Monahassanaugh in Nelson County.

[52] Wood and Shields, *Our Story*, 14-15.

[53] Sometime between 1710 and 1720, a Scottish trader named Hughes built a home and trading post just off an Indian trail that connected the "Great Trading Road" and the "Warrior's Road." Located on Otter Creek, it is near the Otter Creek Campground on the Blue Ridge Parkway. Hughes is considered the first permanent resident of modern Amherst County. He was married to Nicketti, whom tradition says was the daughter of Opechananough, chief of the Pamunkeys and brother of Powhatan.

Only two other men are known to have explored as far west as Amherst prior to 1734. Allen Tye came south from the Shenandoah Valley and discovered a river which he named for himself. The Tye River lies in modern Nelson County and is best known for Crabtree Falls, a series of falls—the highest in Virginia—which empty into it. Allen Tye is thought to have continued moving west and become a pioneer of Kentucky.

John Findlay is believed to have explored up the James River until he reached Nelson County; Findlay Mountain, between U.S. Highway 29 and the James, is named for him. This may be the same John Findlay who met Daniel Boone while both served in the French and Indian War and who, in 1769, guided Boone into Tennessee.

[54] Modern U. S. Highway 29 closely follows the "Great Trading Road." Another road which parallels the James west through the county—Virginia Route 130—crossed the mountains to connect with the "Warrior's Road" (U. S. Highway 11) that ran north-south through the Valley of Virginia. Houck (*Indian Island in Amherst County*, 38) lists an alternate route that left the Great Trading Road at Colleen, looped west to Lowesville, southwest to near Forks of Buffalo, then south to join County Road 635 west of Agricola; this placed it between Tobacco Row and the Blue Ridge.

Highway 130 passes through the southern gap in the Tobacco Row Mountains east of Agricola; Potato Hill is to the south and High Peak to the north. The gap itself is shown on an 1859 map of Virginia as Indian Grave Gap, one of the few such place names in Amherst County.

[55] Dr. William Cabell reported settlers killed by Indians in 1743 at Balcony Falls on the James River where Amherst, Bedford, and Rockbridge Counties come together.

[56] Evans' map also shows one village on White Rock Hill in Lynchburg (south end of old downtown) and another across the river in Amherst County, probably the camp near Horse Ford mentioned earlier.

From this point on in the narrative, the authors will refer to the Amherst Indians as Monacans for simplicity's sake, though the reader should bear in mind that, specifically, the people being discussed could have been Saponi, Tutelo, or one of the other allied tribes.

[57] Dr. Cabell's wife Elizabeth was the great-granddaughter of Trader Hughes and Nicketti (see footnote 53), and that connection helped protect their family from serious attacks.

[58] Catherine Hawes Coleman Seaman, *Tuckahoes and Cohees: The Settlers and Cultures of Amherst and Nelson Counties 1607-1807* (Sweet Briar, Virginia: Sweet Briar College Printing Press, 1992), 96.

[59] Eastern tribes had received grants of land in earlier treaties, but, as noted on page 29, the Sioux do not appear to have ever received theirs.

[60] William may have been Robert Johns, Sr.'s brother; Thomas was most likely Robert's oldest son.

[61] Lenora Higginbotham, *Amherst County, Virginia In the Revolution: Including Extracts from the "Lost Order Book," 1773-1782* Lynchburg, Virginia: J. P. Bell Company, 1951), 9-24, 142.

[62] Edgar Whitehead, "Amherst County Indians," *Richmond (Va.) Times*, April 19, 1896, page 8.

[63] Cook, *Monacans and Mountaineers*, 93.

A modern monument at the Bear Mountain cemetery lists the Monacan ancestral names: Johns, Branham, Hicks, Lawless, Beverly,

Adcock, Redcross, Knuckles/Duff, Clark, Roberts/Nuckles, Willis, Hamilton, and Terry.

64 The Johns family is of Welsh descent and immigrated to America in the early 17th century. After initially settling in Maryland, the family moved in several directions, including Virginia.

Sorting out the Amherst Johns family is very difficult because of the common custom of repeating names in every generation.

65 Mary Gresham Johns was born circa 1726 in Spottsylvania County, in the historic territory of the Manahoac tribe. She appears on 1783 "Heads of Household" list for Amherst County with seven whites and 5 blacks living there, and her son Robert, Jr. is shown with a household of three whites. (Mary is also in the 1785 list.) These descriptions reflect the changing attitudes and uncertainty regarding the legal status of Virginia's Indians as well as local accommodation of people well known to county officials.

66 Quoted in Houck, *Indian Island in Amherst County*, 63.

67 William Evans' brother Benjamin is listed on the 1783 Heads of Households with 6 white residents, but in 1785 they are mulattoes.

68 Sadly, many Virginia Indians such as those in Amherst County may have chosen during this time to deny their heritage and list themselves as colored or black in order to escape being uprooted from their homes.

69 The sale was reported by Edgar Whitehead in his 1896 article on *Amherst County Indians*.

70 *Spring Hill* was adjacent to *Union Hill*, the home of Landon's father Dr. William Cabell.

71 This settlement no longer exists and should not be confused with another Oronoco on U. S. Highway 60 atop Brown Mountain.

72 Pedlar River lies to the east, Enchanted Creek to the north, and Browns Creek to the south. Mountain tops are Rice to the north, Bluff to the west, and Big Piney to the south.

73 The first Beverly record in Amherst County is 1792, when Francis Beverly married Mary Williams, a spinster, with the consent of her mother Nancy. Is she Isabella's sister? Isabella named her daughter, who appears in the Amherst Register, Nancey. She may also be Sarah Ann Taylor Beverly's mother; descendants have linked Isabella to Sarah Ann's father, Richeson Taylor, and Isabella lived with Sarah Ann and Fred in later years.

74 C. H. C. Seaman and Bertha F. Wailes, "The Issues of AB County: Elements of Cohesion and Dissolution," paper given at Sweet Briar College (Virginia) August 1972, pages 3-4.

---

75 Many of the county's remote villages did not get paved roads or electricity until the 1950s because of the rugged terrain. And in 1951, there were still eleven one-room schools.

76 William Harlan Gilbert, Jr., "Surviving Indian Groups of the Eastern United States," *Annual Report of the Board of Regents of the Smithsonian Institution*, June 30, 1948.

77 Whitehead, "Amherst County Indians."

78 Ibid.

79 The county built a small log school for the Indians around 1868 on the banks of Falling Rock Creek; also used as a church, today it is one of the oldest surviving buildings in the Settlement and is on both the Virginia and National Registers of Historic Places. The school was staffed only intermittently for decades and poorly attended because of the difficulty of transportation and the agricultural schedule. Going just through 7th grade, it was the only school Indians would attend until the county's public schools were integrated in the mid-1960s. Today it houses the Monacan Nation's museum.

80 Wood and Shields, *Our Story*, 23-25.

81 Houck, *Indian Island in Amherst County*, 61-67 and 81-83.

82 Bertha Pfister Wailes, "Backward Virginians: A Further Study of the Win Tribe" (Master's thesis, University of Virginia, 1928), 11-12.

83 Eugenics (the term was first used in 1883) was a product of the great scientific revolution of the late 19th century, when science seemed the new god that could cure all ills. It literally means "well born," and the movement first concentrated on positive aspects of breeding. The explosive growth of the lower classes, however, brought out its negative aspects; even Teddy Roosevelt became a proponent, fearing that the diminution of the higher classes would mean "race suicide." Both the founder and first director of the Eugenics Record Office were members of the American Breeders Association (today the American Genetics Association); they used "the agricultural model of breeding the strongest and most capable members of a species while making certain that the weakest members do not reproduce." Pedigrees were used to "show the power of heredity," and field workers collected thousands of them to "scientifically" quantify the data. (Information from University of Virginia Health System website article on "Eugenics.")

84 Appalled readers should bear in mind that the hot topic in recent years, after successful animal tests, has been the question of whether to clone human beings.

85 Today its records are maintained by the Cold Spring Harbor Laboratory, a large genetic research firm in Long Island, which has

placed a number of ERO documents online to help those studying this period.

86 "Brochure Advertising *Mongrel Virginians*," 1926. In collection of University of Albany, SUNY. Online:www.eugenicsarchives.org.

87 Plecker was born in Augusta County, Virginia mere days before the start of the Civil War in 1861. After graduating from medical school in 1885, he practiced in several areas before settling in Hampton. Plecker was named public health officer there in 1902 and became known for his innovations in the maternity field and for his meticulous records. So he was a natural choice for registrar when the state Bureau of Vital Statistics was formed in 1912. He died in 1947, a year after he retired from the Bureau.

88 Adolf Hitler is said to have modeled Germany's sterilization law of 1933 on Virginia's. And Dr. Plecker himself boasted of his Virginia records that "Hitler's genealogical study of the Jews is not more complete."

89 Some of these photographs can be viewed online at www.eugenicsarchive.org; select "Estabrook" as the subject and click on "Field Notes."

90 Wailes, "Backward Virginians," 57.

91 Wailes also reported that tuberculosis was rampant in the group, but no sanitarium would take Indians [thesis written 1928]. Only in recent decades had many "come down" out of the mountains to take jobs vacated by Negroes, who had their own farms or more lucrative jobs. The few poor roads, made worse by inclement weather, kept many from the mission school. Their poor posture resulted from carrying heavy loads of wood and water on their backs. Few owned land; most were sharecroppers, tenant farmers, or orchard workers.

92 The other large populations reported that year were 233 in King William County and 159 in the City of Norfolk.

93 The notice did concede graciously that the physician, midwife, or minister completing such certificates could put a question mark for race when he believed the person(s) involved were colored but he did not wish to state that fact in the local record. It also applied to Negroes, Malays, Mongolians, West Indians, East Indians, Mexicans, Filipinos, "or any other non-white mixture" trying to get away with a white designation.

94 Peter Hardin, "Documentary Genocide: Families' Surnames on Racial Hit List," *Richmond (Virginia) Times-Dispatch*, March 5, 2000.

Russell E. Booker, Jr. headed the Bureau of Vital Statistics from 1982 to 1995.

95 Ibid.

---

96 Letter found on website of Virginia Bureau of Vital Statistics.

97 Branham was also listed in Bedford County; Clark, Hartless, Hicks, Southerds [et al], Terry, and Johns in Rockbridge County; and Beverly in Roanoke and Washington Counties.

98 Tribes were required to prove that they had been in continuous existence since at least 1900, a task made considerably more difficult by Dr. Plecker's eliminating all trace of them in official records.

In the late 1990s, Virginia's tribes also began seeking federal recognition from the United States Congress.

99 Virginia's other tribes are the Eastern Chickahominy, Nansemond, Pamunkey, Mattaponi, Upper Mataponi, Rappahannock, and Chickahominy.

100 Natural Bridge is a natural stone arch 215' high, 90' long, and 150' at its widest point. The ancestral Monacans called it the bridge of God. George Washington surveyed it and carved his initials in one wall (still visible), and Thomas Jefferson bought it in 1774 from King George III for 20 shillings. It is now open to visitors.

101 The Virginia Council on Indians is the result of a sub-committee formed in 1982 to study the relationship between the state and its native residents. Each recognized tribe has a representative on the Council.

102 *Buffalo Ridge Cherokee: The Colors and Culture of a Virginia Indian Community* was published by BRC Books of Madison Heights in 1995. Heritage Books published the revision—*Buffalo Ridge Cherokee: A Remnant of a Great Nation Divided*—in 1995.

103 Anita L. Wills, "Excerpt from Buffalo Ridge Cherokees," www.aagsnc.org.

104 Anita L. Wills, "225 Years after Yorktown and We're still Not Honoring the Virginia Black Soldiers who Fought There?" History News Network (www.hnn.org), October 10, 2005.

105 Wood and Shields, *Our Story*, 20.

106 The Virginia State Library is now named The Library of Virginia and has been moved from its Victorian building on Broad Street to a new facility close by.

107 The Library of Virginia has many Registers or similar documents in its collection from the cities of Lynchburg* and Petersburg, and the counties of Accomack, Alleghany, Amelia, Arlington, Augusta, Bath, Bedford, Brunswick*, Campbell, Charles City, Charlotte, Chesterfield, Dinwiddie, Essex, Fauquier*, Fluvanna, Giles, Goochland, Greensville, Halifax, Henrico, King George, Lancaster*, Loudoun*, Lunenburg, Mecklenburg*, Northampton*, Northumberland, Orange, Princess Anne [now the City of Virginia Beach], Rappahannock, Roanoke, Rockbridge, Southampton, Westmoreland, and York. [* indicates it has been published]

These county registers have also been published: Fairfax, Pittsylvania, Rockingham, and Surry.

108 Melvin Patrick Ely has compared enforcement of the registration law to modern policemen who "issued traffic tickets for failing to wear a seatbelt only if they first stopped a driver for some other reason." In *Israel on the Appomattox: A Southern Experiment in Black Freedom from the 1790s through the Civil War* (New York, Alfred A. Knopf, 2004), 252.

109 It is possible, of course, that Beverly first registered prior to 1822 and that his entry is in the missing volume. That still leaves a gap of at least 28 years between registrations.

110 "Petition of Leanty, Mary her daughter, and Henry her son." Filed January 25, 1837; Petition number A1023. In manuscript collection of the Library of Virginia, Richmond.

111 Will of John Warwick, probated March 20, 1848. Amherst County Will Book No. 11, page 577.

112 Davies' 16 slaves (one born after he wrote his will) were valued at more than $9,000 in his inventory. (Amherst County Will Book 13, 51 and 236)

113 Amherst County Will Book 16, 137-140. The estate inventory on page 179 lists 44 slaves, some of whom Day had bequeathed to specific persons.

114 Guild, *Black Laws of Virginia*, 108-109.

115 Ibid., 102 and 105.

116 Legislative petition of Lucy Watts, filed December 8, 1834. In the manuscript collection of the Library of Virginia.

117 Legislative petition of William Howard, filed November 14, 1809. In the manuscript collection of the Library of Virginia.

ENDNOTES: Chapter 4

118 Statistic tables for this chapter are in the Appendix. As in previous chapters, the term free colored or free person of color refers to both Negroes and Indians, as those with "mixed" blood.

119 This imbalance may have been even more pronounced in cities. Lynchburg's free black population of 1860, for example, was 44% male and 56% female.

120 During the Revolutionary War, Negro boatmen were essential pilots on the James River between Buckingham and Amherst, transporting commissary supplies. On a statewide level, these men were most often found in counties and towns along the James and Appomattox Rivers, main transportation arteries for carrying Piedmont tobacco to Richmond markets.

121 Inventory of James Foster dated April 12, 1861. Amherst County Will Book No. 16, page 75.

122 Elijah Fletcher, who later owned the plantation which is now Sweet Briar College, wrote a friend in 1813: "We have some free Negroes here, and it is a general remark that the slaves who have good masters are in a better situation." (Martha von Briesen, *Letters of Elijah Fletcher* (Charlottesville: University of Virginia Press, 1965), 77-78.

123 Luther Porter Jackson, *Free Negro Labor and Property Holding in Virginia, 1830-1860* (New York: D. Appleton-Century Company, 1942), 215.

124 It is possible that this is not an increase at all but rather reflects more diligent recordkeeping in the wake of Nat Turner's Rebellion.

125 Death records from 1854, 1857 to 1860, and 1864 to 1865 were studied; the intervening years are missing for Amherst County.

ENDNOTES: Chapter 5

126 Causes of death as recorded in the records (alphabetical): apoplexy, "A Complaint," B. fever, bronchitis, cancer, cold, colic, consumption, croup, diphtheria, dropsy, dysentery, enteritis, fever, flux, heart disease, influenza, jaundice, measles, old age, pneumonia, rheumatism, St. Anthony's Fire, scarlet fever, scrofula, spasms, suffocation, typhoid fever, "unborn," unknown causes, whooping cough, worms.

127 Farm Lands in Amherst County:

Year	Total # Farms	Cash Value	Unimproved Acres	Improved Acres
1850	not given	$1,833,563	116,486	110,150
1860	666	2,874,596	132,949	111,969

"Free Afro-Virginians were a nascent black middle class under siege, but several acquired property before and during the war. Approximately 169 free blacks owned 145,976 acres in the counties of Amelia, Amherst, Isle of Wight, Nansemond, Prince William, and Surry, averaging 870 acres each." (Erwin L. Jordan, Jr., *Black Confederates and Afro-Yankees in Civil War Virginia* (Charlottesville: University of Virginia Press, 1995), 209.

128 Luther Porter Jackson, *Free Negro Labor and Property*, 109-111 and 136.

129 Ibid., 128.

130 Amherst County Deed Book E, 111-112.

131 Amherst County Deed Book CC, 254.

132 Amherst County Deed Book DD, 334-341.

133 Amherst County Will Book 16, 196.

ENDNOTES: Chapter 6

134 Lee Marmon, unpublished history of Amherst County, 1976, 34-39.

135 For more information on "The Highland Prisoners," see *From the Barren Hills of Caledonia: The Journey of the Oxford* by Sherrie S. McLeRoy. (*Virginia Cavalcade*, Spring 1989.)

136 A 1985 survey of the county's graveyards indicates that more than half a dozen slave cemeteries still exist in Amherst. Among them are Old Keys Church near Shipman, Sweet Briar College, and the Pettyjohn cemetery on Route 685.

137 1860 Slaveholders:

# Slaves held	In Amherst Co.	In Virginia
1	116	11,085
2	77	5,989
3	63	4,474
4	51	3,807
5	36	3,233
6	49	2,824
7	32	2,393
8	26	1,984
9	21	1,788
10 to 14	80	5,686
15 to 19	59	3,088
20 to 29	39	3,017
30 to 39	20	1,291
40 to 49	7	609
50 to 69	3	503
70 to 99	5	243
100 to 199	1	105
200 to 299	0	8

138 Ely, *Israel on the Appomattox*, 128-129.

BIBLIOGRAPHY

BOOKS AND OTHER PUBLISHED SOURCES

Amherst County Museum & Historical Society. *Gravestone Inscriptions in Amherst County, Virginia.* Revised edition, 1999.

Berlin, Ira. *Slaves without Masters: The Free Negro in the Antebellum South.* New York: Pantheon Books, 1974.

________. *Many Thousands Gone: The First Two Centuries of Slavery in North America.* Cambridge, Massachusetts: Belknap Press of Harvard University Press, 1998.

Bogger, Tommy L. *Free Blacks in Norfolk, Virginia, 1790-1860: The Darker Side of Freedom.* Charlottesville, Virginia: University Press of Virginia, 1997.

Boxley, Mary Frances, compiler. *Graveyard Inscriptions in Amherst County, Virginia.* Amherst, Virginia, 1985.

Bracey, Susan L. *Life by the Roaring Roanoke: A History of Mecklenburg County, Virginia.* Mecklenburg County, Virginia: Mecklenburg County Bicentennial Committee, 1977.

Bradford, S. Sydney. "The Negro Ironworker in Ante Bellum Virginia." *Journal of Southern History*, Vol. XXV, May 1959.

Brown, Alexander. *The Cabells and Their Kin.* Richmond, Virginia: Garrett & Massie, Inc., second edition, 1939.

Clarke, James F. *Present Condition of the Free Colored People of the United States.* New York, 1859.

Cohen, David W. and Greene, Jack P., editors. *Neither Slave nor Free: The Freedmen of African Descent in the Slave Societies of the New World.* Baltimore: Johns Hopkins University Press, 1972.

Cook, Samuel R., Johns, John L., and Wood, Karenne. "The Monacan Nation Powwow: Symbol of Indigenous Survival and Resistance in the Tobacco Row Mountains. In *Powwow.* Edited by Clyde Ellis, Luke Eric Lassiter, and Gary H. Dunham. Lincoln: University of Nebraska Press, 2005.

Delaney, Ted and Rhodes, Phillip Wayne. *Free Blacks of Lynchburg, Virginia, 1805-1865.* Lynchburg, Virginia: Warwick House Publishing, 2001.

Department of Commerce, Bureau of the Census. *Negro Population, 1790-1915.* Washington: Government Printing Office, 1918.

Dew, Thomas Roderick. *Review of the Debate on the Abolition of Slavery in the Virginia Legislature of 1831 and 1832.* Richmond, Virginia: T. W. White, 1832.

Dunaway, Wilma A. *The First American Frontier: Transition to Capitalism in Southern Appalachia, 1700-1860.* Chapel Hill: University of North Carolina Press, 1996.

_______. "Put in Master's Pocket: Cotton Expansion and Interstate Slave Trading in the Mountain South." *Appalachians and Race: The Mountain South from Slavery to Segregation*, ed. John C. Inscoe. Lexington: University Press of Kentucky, 2001.

Ely, Melvin Patrick. *Israel on the Appomattox: A Southern Experiment in Black Freedom from the 1790s through the Civil War*. New York: Alfred A. Knopf, 2004.

Fall, Ralph E. *The Diary of Robert Rose: A View of Virginia by a Scottish Colonial Parson, 1746-1751*. Verona, Virginia: McClure Press, 1977.

Gilbert, William Harlan, Jr. "Surviving Indian Groups of the Eastern United States." *Annual Report of the Board of Regents of the Smithsonian*, June 30, 1948.

Guild, J. P. *Black Laws of Virginia: A Summary of the Legislative Acts of Virginia concerning Negroes from Earliest Times to the Present*. Richmond, Virginia: Whittet & Shepperson, 1936.

Hantman, Jeffrey L. "Monacan Archaeology and History. *Lynch's Ferry: A Journal of Local History*. Spring/Summer 1992.

Hardesty's Historical and Geographical Encyclopedia: Special Virginia Edition. New York: H. H. Hardesty and Company, 1884.

Harris, Leslie M. *In the Shadow of Slavery: African Americans in New York City, 1626-1863*. Chicago: University of Chicago Press, 2003.

Hening, William Walter (editor). *The Statutes at Large: being a Collection of all the Laws of Virginia from the First Session of the Legislature, in the Year 1619*. New York: R. & W. & G. Bartow, 1823.

Horton, James Oliver. *Free People of Color: Inside the African American Community*. Washington, D.C.: Smithsonian Institution Press, 1993.

Houck, Peter W., M.D. *Indian Island in Amherst County*. Lynchburg, Virginia: Progress Printing Co., Inc., 1984.

Inscoe, John C., editor. *Appalachians and Race: The Mountain South from Slavery to Segregation*. Lexington: University Press of Kentucky, 2001.

Jackson, Luther Porter. *Free Negro Labor and Property Holding in Virginia, 1830-1860*. New York: D. Appleton-Century Company, 1942.

Jefferson, Thomas. *Notes on the State of Virginia*. Chapel Hill: University of North Carolina Press, reprinted 1955.

Johnston, James Hugo. *Race Relations in Virginia & Miscegenation in the South, 1776-1860*. Amherst, Massachusetts: The University of Massachusetts Press, 1970.

Jordan, Ervin L., Jr. *Black Confederates and Afro-Yankees in Civil War Virginia*. Charlottesville, Virginia: University Press of Virginia, 1995.

Kerr-Ritchie, Jeffrey R. *Freedpeople in the Tobacco South: Virginia, 1860-1900*. Chapel Hill: University of North Carolina Press, 1999.

Kingsbury, Susan Myra. *The Records of the Virginia Company of London*. Washington: Government printing Office, 1906. In Rountree Collection of Library of Virginia.

Litwack, Leon F. "The Federal Government and the Free Negro." In *Free Blacks in America, 1800-1860*. ed. John H. Bracey, Jr., August Meier, and Elliott Rudwick. Belmont, California: Wadsworth Publishing.

Mann, Charles C. "America, Found & Lost." *National Geographic* 211, No. 8 (May 2007): 32-55.

McIlwaine, H. R. *Minutes of the Council and General Court of Colonial Virginia, 1622-32, 1670-76, with Notes and Excerpts from Original Council and General Court Records, into 1683, Now Lost.* Richmond, Virginia: Colonial Press, Everett Waddy Co., 1924.

McLeRoy, Sherrie and William. *Passages: A History of Amherst County.* Lynchburg, Virginia: Peddler Press, 1977.

_______. *Strangers in Their Midst: The Free Black Population of Amherst County, Virginia.* Bowie, Maryland: Heritage Books, Inc., 1993.

Morgan, Edmund S. *American Slavery, American Freedom: The Ordeal of Colonial Virginia.* New York: W. W. Norton and Company, Inc., 1975.

Mullin, Gerald W. *Flight and Rebellion: Slave Resistance in Eighteenth Century Virginia.* New York: Oxford University Press, 1972.

Munford, Beverly B. *Virginia's Attitude Toward Slavery and Secession.* New York: Longmans, Green and Co., 1909.

Newby-Alexander, Cassandra. "An African Perspective." *Virginia Secrets: America's 400th Anniversary: Jamestown 2007.* Roanoke, Va.: Leisure Publishing Company, 2005.

Phillips, U. B. *American Negro Slavery: A Survey of the Supply, Employment, and Control of Negro Labor as Determined by the Plantation Regime.* New York: D. Appleton-Century Company, Inc., 1940.

Price, David A. *Love and Hate in Jamestown: John Smith, Pocahontas and the Heart of a New Nation.* London: Faber and Faber Limited, 2003.

Reiss, Oscar. *Blacks in Colonial America.* Jefferson, North Carolina: McFarland & Company, Inc., 1997.

Russell, John Henderson. *The Free Negro in Virginia, 1619-1865.* New York: Negro University Press, 1969.

________. "Colored Freeman as Slave Owners in Virginia." *Journal of Negro History*, Volume 1, June 1916.

Schwarz, Philip J. "Emancipators, Protectors, and Anomalies: Free Black Slaveowners in Virginia." *Virginia Magazine of History and Biography*, Vol. 95, No. 3, July 1987.

Seaman, Catherine Hawes Coleman. *Tuckahoes and Cohees: The Settlers and Cultures of Amherst and Nelson Counties, 1607-1807.* Sweet Briar, Virginia: Sweet Briar College Printing Press, 1992.

Smith, J. David. "Legal Racism and Documentary Genocide: Dr. Plecker's Assault on the Monacan Indians." *Lynch's Ferry: A Journal of Local History*, Spring/Summer 1992.

Stampp, Kenneth M. *The Peculiar Institution: Slavery in the Ante-Bellum South.* New York: Random House, 1956.

Sweeny, Lenora Higginbotham. *Amherst County, Virginia in the Revolution: Including Extracts from the "Lost Order Book" 1773-1782.* Lynchburg, Virginia: J. P. Bell Company, 1951.

Sweig, Donald, ed. *Registration of Free Negroes Commencing September Court 1822, Book No. 2 and Register of Free Blacks 1835 Book 3.* Fairfax, Virginia: History Section, Office of Comprehensive Planning, 1977.

Talbot, Sir William. *The Discoveries of John Lederer, in Three Several Marches from Virginia to the West of Carolina, and Other Parts of the Continent.* Originally published in London, 1672. Republished in Charleston, South Carolina, 1891.

Von Briesen, Martha. *Letters of Elijah Fletcher.* Charlottesville: University of Virginia Press, 1965.

Wood, Karenne and Shields, Diane. *The Monacan Indians: Our Story.* Madison Heights, Va.: Office of Historical Research, Monacan Nation, 1999.

Woodson, C(arter) G. *Free Negro Heads of Families in the United States in1830: Together with a Brief Treatment of the Free Negro.* Washington: The Association for the Study of Negro Life and History, Inc., 1925.

_______. "The Negroes of Cincinnati Prior to the Civil War." *Free Blacks in America, 1800-1860*, edited by John H. Bracey, Jr., August Meier, and Elliott Rudwick. Belmont, California: Wadsworth Publishing Company, Inc.

Writers Program of the Works Progress Administration in the State of Virginia. *The Negro in Virginia.* New York: Hastings House, 1940.

MANUSCRIPT AND GOVERNMENT SOURCES

Amherst County Court Clerk's Office (Amherst, Virginia): Deed Books, Will Books, Marriage Registers, Land Plat Books, Minute Books, Court Order Books.

Bolton, Herbert Eugene. "The Free Negro in the South before the Civil War." Thesis, University of Pennsylvania, 1899.

Census of the United States: Amherst County, Virginia: Population, Death, and Agricultural Schedules for 1783, 1785, 1790, 1810, 1820, 1830, 1840, 1850, and 1860.

Cook, Samuel R. "Monacans and Mountaineers: A Comparative Study of Colonialism and Dependency in Southern Appalachia." Ph.D. dissertation, University of Arizona, 1997.

Crews, W. C. "Sally Taylor's Tavern." Works Progress Administration of Virginia Historical Inventory, 1936.

Haimes-Bartolf, Melanie Dorothea. "Policies and Attitudes: Public Education and the Monacan Indian Community in Amherst County, Virginia, from 1908 to 1965." Ph.D. dissertation, Virginia Commonwealth University, 2004.

Library of Virginia (Richmond, Virginia): Records re Amherst County: Personal Property Tax Books, Land Grants, Legislative Petitions, Death Certificates (Death Records Indexing Project of the Virginia Genealogical Society), Rountree Collection of Virginia Indian Documents, and Amherst County Register of Free Blacks, 1822-1864.

Marmon, Lee. Unpublished history of Amherst County, Virginia.

Rountree, Helen C. "Rountree Collection of Virginia Indian Documents." Library of Virginia, 2005.

Seaman, C. H. C. and Wailes, Bertha F. "The Issues of AB County: Elements of Cohesion and Dissolution." Paper given at Sweet Briar College (Virginia), August 1972. In Rountree Collection of Library of Virginia.

Virginia Historical Society (Richmond, Virginia): Dr. William Cabell's Commonplace Book.

Waibel, Paul B. "Slavery in Lynchburg." Unpublished research paper, University of Virginia Branch, Lynchburg, Virginia, 1965.

Wailes, Bertha Pfister. "Backward Virginians: A Further Study of the Win Tribe." Master's thesis: University of Virginia, 1928. In Rountree Collection of Library of Virginia.

NEWSPAPERS

Lynchburg Daily Virginian.

Hardin, Peter. "Documentary Genocide: Families' Surnames on Racial Hit List." *Richmond (Virginia) Times-Dispatch*, March 5, 2000.

Whitehead, Edgar. "Amherst County Indians." *The Richmond (Virginia) Times*, April 19, 1896.

INTERNET SOURCES

Brawley, Benjamin. *A Social History of the American Negro: Being a History of the Negro Problem in the United States; Including a History and Study of the Republic of Liberia.* Originally published 1921. Released by Project Gutenberg EBook, 2004.

Cold Spring Harbor Laboratory. Long Island, New York. http://www.eugenicsarchives.org.

Curtis, Christopher M. "'Can These be the Sons of their Fathers?' Slavery in Virginia, 1831-1832." Masters thesis, Virginia Polytechnic Institute and State University, 1997: http://www.scholar.lib.vt.edu/theses.

Dew, Thomas R. *Review of the Debate in the Virginia Legislature of 1831 and 1832.* Originally published Richmond, Virginia, 1832. Posted online at http://www.digitalhistory.uh.edu

"Documenting the American South." University of North Carolina at Chapel Hill: http://docsouth.unc.edu.

Geostat Center: Collections: Historical Census Browser. University of Virginia Library. http://www.fisher.lib.virginia.edu/collections/stats/histcensus.

Heinegg, Paul. http://www.freeafricanamericans.com: "Virginia Slaves Freed after 1782: Amherst County," "Personal Property Tax List, 1782-1822: Amherst County," and "Service in the Revolutionary War: Amherst County."

"Laws on Slavery." http://www.virtualjamestown.org.

National Park Service, "African Americans at Jamestown," http://www.nps.gov/colo/Jthanout/AFRICANS.html.

"Research Aid for Death Certificates & Mortality Schedules." http://www.rootsweb.com.

Sherwood, Henry Noble, Ph.D. "The Formation of the American Colonization Society." *Journal of Negro History*, Vol. 2, No. 3, July 1917.

Electronic edition courtesy of University of North Carolina at Chapel Hill, "Documenting the American South" (see above).
Wills, Anita L. "225 Years after Yorktown and We're still Not Honoring the Virginia Black Soldiers who Fought There?" October 10, 2005. History News Network. http://hnn.org.

INDEX

CPSIA information can be obtained at www.ICGtesting.com
Printed in the USA
BVOW04s0813050314

346741BV00003B/5/P

9 780788 443732